RACE, CRIMINAL JUSTICE, AND MIGRATION CONTROL

Race, Criminal Justice, and Migration Control

Enforcing the Boundaries of Belonging

Edited by

MARY BOSWORTH, ALPA PARMAR,
YOLANDA VÁZQUEZ

UNIVERSITY PRESS

UNIVERSITY PRESS

Great Clarendon Street, Oxford, OX2 6DP,
United Kingdom

Oxford University Press is a department of the University of Oxford.
It furthers the University's objective of excellence in research, scholarship,
and education by publishing worldwide. Oxford is a registered trade mark of
Oxford University Press in the UK and in certain other countries

Published in the United States of America by Oxford University Press
198 Madison Avenue, New York, NY 10016, United States of America

British Library Cataloguing in Publication Data
Data available

Library of Congress Control Number: 2017947316

ISBN 978–0–19–881488–7

Printed and bound by
CPI Group (UK) Ltd, Croydon, CR0 4YY

MB: For Anthony with whom I've become a migrant.

AP: For my parents Nalini and Dinesh, and my grandparents, and the routes they chose.

YV: For my grandparents, Ausencio and Evangelina León, and my mother, Raquel, who showed me that all work and every human being should be equally respected and valued.

Acknowledgements

This collection of essays has its roots in a two-day event at the Centre for Criminology at the University of Oxford, in September 2016, during which most of the contributors came and spent time together sharing their ideas. We would like to thank everyone from that event and, of course, all the contributors to this volume. It has been a great pleasure to get to know everyone in this book and to work together as editors. The event was funded by Mary's European Research Council Grant number 313356, which has generously supported Mary's research and the work of Border Criminologies more generally over the last five years. We would also like to thank Kate West who helped organize the workshop, Gabrielle Watson who helped us polish the essays by providing crucial and careful copy-editing assistance, and Emma Burtt who helped compile the index.

Mary, Alpa, and Yolanda
Oxford and Cincinnati, OH

Foreword

In 2014 I wrote a review essay of two collections on 'Crimmigration' in *Sociology of Race and Ethnicity*[1] in which I identified some troubling gaps between the sociology of race and the emerging body of literature in criminology and law on migration control. In this collection, Mary Bosworth, Alpa Parmar and Yolanda Vázquez have produced a book in which 'race' is centred in the analysis of immigration and criminal justice. This idea passed through a conference phase in Oxford in September 2016. I participated in this by invitation, and got a feel for the range and type of interventions colleagues working in Criminology, Sociology, and Law (plus some who are not housed within universities) and across the world, were bringing to the table. I thank them for tying me intellectually to a key phase in the book's conception, and thus binding me to the project of highlighting the profound, multiple and complex articulations of 'race', crime, law, and borders arising in the first decades of the twenty-first century.

For a while, critical race scholars have been arguing that the sociology of migration has avoided engagement with 'race', and that this is part of a broader epistemological struggle about power and representations.[2] With the coining of the concept of 'crimmigration' (Stumpf 2006), a new space was opened up, with critical criminologists investigating the overlap of immigration and criminal justice from a number of perspectives. Indeed, as Katja Franko Aas (2013: 23) neatly summarizes: 'The project of creating an ordered society through penological intervention has thus become increasingly intertwined with the control of the border and the project of creating a bordered society'.

In this scholarship the focus is rightly on the State, but also on the people problematized as immigrants, and their experiences crossing borders. And borders produce both 'race' (and therefore racism), and criminals. As a sociologist working on the ideas and practices of racisms for a quarter of a century, and with a taste for historical contexts, I have been frustrated by scholarly work on migration which makes 'race' invisible when it seems so visible from where I am standing. I have written elsewhere about how negotiating the UK's immigration rules has been an intensely personal and painful experience (Garner 2014), but my story is a minor one, way, way down the end of the spectrum at the other extreme of which bodies wash up on Mediterranean beaches, or lie undiscovered in deserts. These stories are definitely about economics; state policies; individual agency; networks, and so on. My argument is that these

---

[1] The two books are: K. F. Aas and M. Bosworth (eds) (2013), *The Borders of Punishment: Migration, Citizenship, and Social Exclusion*. Oxford: Oxford University Press; and M. J. Guia, M. van der Woude, and J. van der Leun (eds) (2013), *Social Control and Justice: crimmigration in the age of fear*. Utrecht: Eleven International Publishing. The article, 'Crimmigration: When Criminology (Nearly) Met the Sociology of Race and Ethnicity' appears in *Sociology of Race and Ethnicity* 1(1): 198–203.

[2] The most up-to-date set of these critiques, with all the relevant historical references can be found in the same edition of *Sociology of Race and Ethnicity*, under the section heading 'Race, Ethnicity, and Immigration'.

topics are cut transversally by 'race': in other words, whatever else immigration's tango with the criminal justice system is about, it is also, irrevocably, about racism.

Racism is a set of ideas; practices with measurable outcomes, and, above all, it is a power relationship. Whatever else racism is, and there is a certain amount of latitude in defining it, the question of power lies at its heart. We need to be aware of the history of 'race' and what functions this concept has performed and continues to perform. In this view, 'race' has never been only to do with physical differences, but also culture. So when you read 'race' in this short foreword, I am referring to the ways in which over centuries, bodies and culture have been amalgamated and interpreted to produce 'races', which are placed in hierarchical relationships to one another.

The concept of 'race' always denotes an uneven playing field. Even the fallacious idea that all races are equal but different (fallacious because it revolves around 'race' being a departure point) is relatively recent. One of the functions of 'race' is to establish and entrench the notion of this kind of difference and group membership to a point where 'race' goes without saying. It is merely a feature of the social and natural worlds, and alternative readings are thus unnatural. This point might seem simple and obvious but it is a key element for understanding how immigration regulations divide the world's population into nationalities and 'races', and subsequently triage those seeking entry to the nation. The early immigration acts, in the USA, Canada, Australia, and the UK, focussed on controlling the movement of particular groups and/ or the protection of populations from perceived cultural infection. Immigration rules became a racialized prophylactic.

While there is now generally more to contemporary immigration rules than race alone, it is indisputable that border controls began with race overtly in mind, and have only recently become more complicated. But there is a limit to how complicated it can really be, when the patterns of outcomes are so stark. This book is, therefore, fuelled by the recognition that like discourse on national identity, discourse on immigration is not often about rational civic standards, but about emotions that do not have to make sense, or be logical, or relate to empirical facts and figures (Ioanide 2015). The discourse about national identity is scarcely linked to what official documents say, and neither is discourse about immigration. People are plucked from other statuses (citizen, tourist, student) and propelled into the immigration discussion: but this plucking is not random.

As increasing numbers of laws apply to immigrants, and prospective employers of immigrants, new crimes appear and implicate a wider range of agents. Some university admissions staff are now de facto immigration agents. Not only are the laws now different but the punishments are as well: civil offences metamorphose into criminal ones. Lines between crime and punishment get shifted so that immigration status influences the punishment. When we stand back and look at the patterns emerging from these activities, it seems clear that both immigration and criminal justice regimes are crossing over, and that the principal casualties of this overlap are people of colour. Standing back further, we identify that conditions surrounding mobility are far more dangerous for brown bodies. If this is the case, we need to ask in whose interest is it that studies of immigration and crime do not deploy concepts of racialization and racism as a matter of course? This book is an impressive starting point in interrogating this.

Once there are immigration rules and laws there are consequently ways to break the rules and laws and thus to produce criminal acts. These offences are primarily to do with overstaying visas; undocumented entry and access to resources; and technical matters arising from non-compliance with sets of conditions attached to various visas. The work in his book deals with how these offences are policed and punished, in an era when governments are increasingly eroding the historic distinction between (civil) immigration law and criminal law (Stumpf 2006), with various agencies (including employers, local authorities, and universities) involved in identifying infractions, making criminals and punishing them. Borders, this body of work makes clear, produce criminals and racialize people. These processes result in what Ben Bowling (2013: 292) calls 'border harms'. One of those harms is racialization.

So, borders make immigrants; borders make criminals; and borders make 'race'. Yes. To be clear, racialization does not only produce 'black' people, 'Asians', 'Latinx', Muslims, Poles, with particular meanings attached to those labels in particular places and particular times. In the same process, it also produces 'white' people.

If 'race' and criminals are produced through borders, it is also in the occasional 'mismatch' of person to category that the usual functioning is most clear (where the types of people who are not really criminals become so due to border-crossing regulations). Already in popular discourse on immigration in the UK and the USA (Garner 2015; Lacayo 2017) people of colour—regardless of their actual status—are identified as the subject matter. So many white people have the idea that non-white people might be immigrants and or criminals in their minds. The UK Home Office has a reputation for the draconian application of immigration rules, and sometimes they affect the families of white British people, or failing that honorary white UK people such as Americans: wealthy and or professional status Americans (Hill 2017a; 2017c; Russell 2017; BBC News 2017). When these people are affected, it is deemed newsworthy in a way that stories of people of colour falling foul of the same types of regulations are not. Similarly, the lack of clarity surrounding Brexit spurred the creation of a campaign, The 3 million, to highlight the cases of EU nationals resident in the UK.[3] These former are the archetypal 'good immigrants', who contribute, and pay taxes and do not end up in detention centres. The same newsworthiness may attach to people of colour with white spouses, such as the Singaporean Irene Clennell (Hill 2017b) who was prohibited from returning to her husband of 27 years for several months.

Yet for thousands of non-EU nationals in the UK for example, unsuccessful (but non-refundable) visa applications; detention; deportation; and undocumented existence have become the common lot. Their stories are seldom reported sympathetically, or from their standpoints. As we know from other areas of scholarship, the construction of racialized groups is also about what is omitted from representations. Simply put, currently crossing borders for people of colour is not like crossing them as a white person, particularly if your passport is not 'powerful'.[4] Moreover, as Guild

---

[3] https://www.the3million.org.uk/

[4] Henley & Partners have produced the fascinating 'Visa Restriction Index' since 2007. This index ranks nations in order of how frequently their nationals require visas to cross the borders of other countries. The lower the score, the more powerful the passport. The 2017 index can be found here: http://visaindex.com/#.

and Bigo (2009) point out, in a number of developing-world countries, the border is actually at the consulate in their country rather than the physical space of a land crossing, airport, or seaport terminal.

Standpoint is thus significant. If your repeated experience of crossing borders is of a freedom of movement formality, this might lead to you a particular set of research priorities, whereas if your experience is of anxiety, exasperation, and occasional humiliation, the salience of borders to movement will resonate differently. In the social sciences, like many other areas within academia, what we learn, what we research, what knowledge is and should consist of are contested. They are, to an extent, the reflection of the dominant ideas and the dominant groups at a given moment. It is my hope that this book reflects the given moment when the scales in terms of research into borders and crime began to tip toward one in which the importance of 'race' begins an ineluctable journey from the margins to the mainstream.

Steve Garner

REFERENCES

Aas, K. F. (2013) 'The ordered and the bordered society: Migration control, citizenship, and the northern penal state'. In K.F. Aas and M. Bosworth (eds). *The Borders of Punishment: Migration, Citizenship, and Social Exclusion*, Oxford: Oxford University Press, 21–39.

BBC News (2017), 'US couple who ran Inverness guesthouse cannot stay in Britain', 19 October. http://www.bbc.co.uk/news/uk-scotland-highlands-islands-41682841

Bigo, D. and Guild, E. (2009), 'Mapping the Limits of Freedom', film in 7 parts: https://www.youtube.com/watch?v=Fq3_cipzEmI

Bowling, B. (2013), 'Epilogue. The Borders of Punishment: Towards a Criminology of Mobility', in K. F. Aas and M. Bosworth (eds), *The Borders of Punishment: Migration, Citizenship, and Social Exclusion*. Oxford: Oxford University Press, 291–306.

Garner. S. (2014), 'Am I the Small Axe or the Big Tree?' In G. Yancy (ed) *White Self-criticality beyond Anti-racism: How does it feel to be a white problem?* Lanham, MD: Lexington Books, 189–210.

Garner, S. (2015), *A Moral Economy of Whiteness: four frames of racialising discourse*. London: Routledge.

Hill, A. (2017a), 'US physician assistant may be forced to quit UK because of visa nightmare', *Guardian*, 4 August: https://www.theguardian.com/uk-news/2017/aug/04/us-surgeon-may-be-forced-to-quit-uk-because-of-visa-nightmare

Hill, A (2017b), 'Irene Clennell finally granted visa to live in Britain', Guardian, 25 August: https://www.theguardian.com/uk-news/2017/aug/25/irene-clennell-deported-british-woman-finally-granted-uk-visa

Hill, A. (2017c), 'Family split across Atlantic accuse Home Office of inhumanity', Guardian, 19 October: https://www.theguardian.com/uk-news/2017/oct/19/family-split-across-atlantic-accuse-home-office-of-inhumanity

Ioanide, P. (2015), *The Emotional Politics of Racism: How feelings trump facts in an era of color-blindness*. Stanford, CA: Stanford University Press.

Lacayo, C. (2017), 'Perpetual Inferiority: Whites' Racial Ideology toward Latinos', *Sociology of Race and Ethnicity* 3(4): 566–79.

O'Carroll, L. (2016a), 'Dutch woman with two British children told to leave UK after 24 years', Guardian, 28 December: https://www.theguardian.com/politics/2016/dec/28/dutch-woman-with-two-british-children-told-to-leave-uk-after-24-years

O'Carroll, L. (2016b), 'German neuroscientist also told to leave UK after residency rejection', Guardian, 29 December: https://www.theguardian.com/uk-news/2016/dec/29/german-neuroscientist-told-to-leave-uk-residency-application-rejected-monique-hawkins

Russell, G. (2016), 'Deportation for Christmas: Home Office condemned for action against US couple in the Highlands', *The Nation*, 20 December: http://www.thenational.scot/news/14976245.Deportation_for_Christmas__Home_Office_condemned_for_action_against_US_couple_in_the_Highlands/

Stumpf, J. (2006), 'The Crimmigration Crisis: Immigrants, Crime, and Sovereign Power', *American University Law Review* 56(2): 367–419.

Contents

IV. RACE, DETENTION, AND DEPORTATION

List of Abbreviations

ACLU	American Civil Liberties Union
ACRO	Criminal Records Office (UK)
BAME	black, Asian, and minority ethnic
CBP	Customs and Border Patrol (US)
CCU	Home Office Command and Control Unit (UK)
CPS	Child Protective Services (US)
DACA	Deferred Action for Childhood Arrivals
DAPA	Deferred Action for Parents of Americans
DCM	detainee custody manager
DCO	detainee custody officer
DHS	Department of Homeland Security (US)
ECHR	European Convention on Human Rights
EU	European Union
FRONTEX	European Border and Coast Guard Agency
HMIP	Her Majesty's Inspectorate of Prisons
ICE	Immigration and Customs Enforcement (US); Immigration Compliance and Enforcement (UK)
ICIBI	Independent Chief Inspector of Borders and Immigration
IE	Immigration Enforcement
IRC	Immigration Removal Centre
IRCA	Immigration Reform and Control Act 1986 (US)
NGO	non-governmental organization
SMT	Senior Management Team
STHF	Short Term Holding Facility
UNHCR	United Nations High Commissioner for Refugees

List of Contributors

Ana Aliverti is Associate Professor at the School of Law, University of Warwick, Research Associate at the Centre for Criminology, Oxford, and a member of the Border Criminologies Research Group. Ana's research sits at the intersection of criminal law, criminal justice, and border regimes. Her book, *Crimes of Mobility* (Routledge, 2013), was co-awarded the British Society of Criminology Best Book Prize for 2014.

Hindpal Singh Bhui is an Inspection Team Leader at HM Inspectorate of Prisons. He manages inspections of all forms of custody and heads inspection of the immigration detention estate in the UK. He has trained prison monitors in a number of other countries and currently chairs the inspectorate's policy forums on prisoner resettlement and immigration detention. He has led thematic reviews on foreign prisoners, immigration detention, and the experiences of Muslim prisoners. His PhD research was on issues of legitimacy and coherence in the detention of foreign nationals. He was formerly a probation officer and a prison-based foreign national specialist. He was also a criminal justice lecturer and edited the *Probation Journal* for ten years. He has published a number of articles and chapters on prisons, probation, foreign prisoners, and immigration detention.

Susan Bibler Coutin holds a PhD in anthropology from Stanford University and is Professor of Criminology, Law and Society and Anthropology at the University of California, Irvine. Her research has examined legal and political advocacy by and on behalf of immigrants to the United States. With Sameer Ashar, Jennifer Chacón, and Stephen Lee, she is currently conducting NSF-funded research regarding how brokering organizations help immigrants navigate the legal uncertainty surrounding executive relief.

Louise Boon-Kuo is a lecturer at the University of Sydney Law School. Louise previously worked as a solicitor and coordinator in community legal centres, specializing in refugee and criminal law. She has taught at the University of Technology, Sydney and Sydney University, as well as providing continuing legal education for lawyers and migration agents. Louise's research focuses on the intersection between criminal justice and migration law, particularly the transnational character of migration policing. Her most recent research examines the migration policing of undocumented migrants in Australia. Louise is currently working on the project Blacklists and the (de)criminalization of conflict resolution in partnership with the Transnational Institute (the Netherlands) and the International State Crime Initiative (UK). The project examines the impacts of terrorist proscription on the resolution of armed conflicts, in particular those in Somalia, Turkey, and Israel/Palestine.

Mary Bosworth is Professor of Criminology and Fellow of St Cross College at the University of Oxford and, concurrently, Professor of Criminology at Monash University, Australia. She is Director of the Centre for Criminology and Director of Border Criminologies, an interdisciplinary research group focusing on the intersections between criminal justice and border control. She conducts research into the ways in which prisons and immigration detention centres uphold notions of race, gender, and citizenship and how those who are confined negotiate their daily lives. Her research is international and comparative and has included work conducted in Paris, Britain, the USA, and Australia.

Ben Bowling is Professor of Criminology & Criminal Justice and Action Executive Dean of the Dickson Poon School of Law, King's College London. His books include *Violent Racism*

(OUP, 1999), *Racism, Crime and Justice* (with Coretta Phillips, Longman, 2004), *Policing the Caribbean* (OUP, 2010), *Global Policing* (with James Sheptycki, Sage, 2012), *Stop & Search: Police Power in Global Context* (with Leanne Weber, Routledge, 2012), and the four-volume *Global Policing and Transnational Law Enforcement* (with James Sheptycki, Sage, 2015). He has been an adviser to the UK Parliament, Foreign and Commonwealth Office, Equality and Human Rights Commission, the European Commission, Interpol, and the United Nations. Ben is a founding member of StopWatch, a charity that works to inform the public about the use of stop and search and to promote fair, effective, and accountable policing.

Eddie Bruce-Jones is Senior Lecturer in Law at Birkbeck College School of Law, University of London, where he teaches and researches on human rights, European law, race, sexuality, and migration. His forthcoming book *Race in the Shadow of Law* (Routledge/GlassHouse) explores racism, activism, and the law in Germany. He serves on the Editorial Board of the *Journal of Asylum, Immigration and Nationality Law*, the Board of Trustees of the UK Lesbian and Gay Immigration Group, and the Board of Directors of the Institute of Race Relations. He is a member of the New York Bar.

Jennifer M. Chacón is Professor of Law and Senior Associate Dean for Administration at the University of California, Irvine, School of Law. She is a leading expert on the intersection of criminal and immigration law and law enforcement. Professor Chacón is the author of a forthcoming textbook on immigration law and has written more than fifty law review articles, book chapters, expert commentaries, and shorter articles and essays on immigration, criminal law, constitutional law, and citizenship issues. Professor Chacón was the Convenor of the Immigration Policy Advisory Committee to then-Senator Barack Obama during his 2008 presidential campaign and an outside adviser to the Immigration Transition Team of President-Elect Barack Obama from November 2008 to January 2009. She is currently a fellow and board member of the American Bar Foundation (ABF).

Steve Garner is Professor of Critical Race Studies and Head of the Department of Criminology and Sociology at Birmingham City University, UK. He has published widely on whiteness, as well as racism and its intersection with class and nation in a variety of geographical contexts, such as England, Ireland, the USA, and Guyana. He is the author of *A Moral Economy of Whiteness* (2015); *Whiteness: an introduction* (Routledge, 2007); *Racisms* (Sage, 2nd edition, 2017); and *Racism in the Irish Experience* (2004) as well as numerous book chapters, and articles in such journals as 'Ethnic and Racial Studies', 'Ethnicities', and 'Sociology', among other journals. He is currently working on skin lightening practices and discourses.

Tanya Golash-Boza is Associate Professor of Sociology at the University of California, Merced. Tanya is the author of five books, the latest of which is *Deported: Immigrant Policing, Disposable Labor and Global Capitalism* (New York University Press, 2015). She has published over a dozen articles in peer-reviewed journals on deportations, racial identity, critical race theory, and human rights, and has written on contemporary issues for *Al Jazeera*, *The Boston Review, The Nation, Counterpunch, The Houston Chronicle, Racialicious, The Chronicle of Higher Education*, and *Dissident Voice*. Her innovative scholarship was awarded the Distinguished Early Career Award from the Racial and Ethnic Minorities Studies Section of the American Sociological Association in 2010. In 2013, she was awarded the UC Merced Senate Faculty Award for Distinguished Scholarly Public Service.

Lirio Gutiérrez Rivera is Assistant Professor at the School for Urban and Regional Studies at the National University of Colombia Medellin Campus. Her research focuses on violence, marginality, gangs, and migrant social mobility (the case of Palestinian entrepreneurs) in Latin America, particularly in Honduras. Her recent study looked at the impact of crime-control policies on the prison system in Honduras. Currently, she is looking at women's organizations in Medellin, Colombia and their attempt to influence urban planning and spatial policies to create a safer city.

Mark Johnson is Reader in Anthropology at Goldsmiths, University of London. He has conducted research funded by the Arts and Humanities Research Council and the British Academy about Filipino migrant experiences of living and working in Saudi Arabia and Hong Kong. Recent publications focused in particular on surveillance include his 2015 article 'Surveillance, Pastoral Power and Embodied Infrastructures of Care among Migrant Filipinos in the Kingdom of Saudi Arabia', *Surveillance & Society* 13(2): 250–64 and (forthcoming, with Maggy Lee and Mike McCahill) 'Beyond the All Seeing Eye: Filipino Migrant Domestic Workers' Contestation of Care and Control in Hong Kong', *Ethnos: Journal of Social Anthropology*.

Emma Kaufman is a lecturer in Law and Bigelow Teaching Fellow at the University of Chicago Law School. Her scholarship focuses on the relationship between criminal and immigration law. Emma received her undergraduate degree from Columbia, her JD from Yale Law School, and her doctorate from the University of Oxford, where she was a Marshall Scholar. Her doctoral dissertation drew on a year of ethnographic research in men's prisons to examine the treatment of non-citizens in the British criminal justice system. In 2015, her book *Punish and Expel: Border Control, Nationalism, and the New Purpose of the Prison* was published by Oxford University Press. Emma's recent projects examine the rise of prisons classified by citizenship status, the use of interstate prison compacts, and the origins of prisoner repatriation treaties.

Maggy Lee is Professor of Sociology at the University of Hong Kong. Maggy's research is in the areas of criminology, borders and mobility, lifestyle migration, transnational professionals, and human trafficking. Maggy was previously a criminal justice researcher at the Institute for the Study of Drug Dependence and lecturer in sociology at Birkbeck College, University of London, and lecturer in sociology at the University of Essex.

Michael McCahill is a senior lecturer in Criminology in the School of Education and Social Sciences at the University of Hull. His main research interests include the social impact of 'new surveillance' technologies and media representations of crime and surveillance. He has published widely on the topic of surveillance and social control. His books include *The Surveillance Web* (2002, Willan), *Surveillance and Crime* (2011, Sage, with Roy Coleman), and *Surveillance, Capital and Resistance* (2014, Routledge, with Rachel L. Finn).

Sanja Milivojević is a senior lecturer at La Trobe University, Melbourne, Australia. Her research interests are trafficking in people, borders, and mobility; security technologies, surveillance, crime, and sexting; gender and victimization; and international criminal justice and human rights. Sanja has worked as a researcher on various projects with the Institute for Criminological and Sociological Research in Belgrade and the Victimology Society of Serbia. She is a recipient of national and international grants including a Criminology Research Council grant for a project on young people and sexting (with Professors Murray Lee and Thomas Crofts, as well as Drs Alyce McGovern and Michael Salter). Sanja is a NSW representative at the Australian and New Zealand Society of Criminology's Committee of Management and editorial board member for journals Temida (Serbia) and The Human

Rights Defender (Australia). She has been a visiting scholar at Belgrade University's Faculty for Special Education and the University of Zagreb Law School (2013) and a Public Interest Law Fellow at Columbia University's Law School (2001–2002). Sanja has participated in over thirty international and domestic conferences and has published in English and Serbian. Her latest book (with Crofts, Lee, and McGovern) *Sexting and Young People* is published by Palgrave (2015).

Alpa Parmar is Departmental Lecturer in Criminology and an Associate Director of the Border Criminologies research group at the University of Oxford. Alpa's scholarship focuses on the intersection of race, gender, criminalization and citizenship. Her current research project is on policing migration and understanding its racialized impacts. Alpa conducts empirical research on race and crime and has published on policing minority ethnic groups and perceptions of crime amongst British Asian communities. More recently, she has written about how criminology attends to race and intersectionality.

Gabriella E. Sanchez is a fellow at the Migration Policy Institute at the European Migration Institute. Her research documents the organizational dynamics present in criminalized markets along migrant trails, her work focusing on the facilitation of irregular migration. She is the author of *Human Smuggling and Border Crossings* (2015, Routledge).

Yolanda Vázquez is Associate Professor at the University of Cincinnati College of Law, where she teaches in the areas of migration and crime. Her research focuses on the impact on law and society by the expanding relationship between immigration law and the criminal justice system. Her current scholarship explores the role that race and racism play in the racial disparities that have occurred by the merger between these two systems, specifically why Latinos in the United States are disproportionately impacted as well as the long term consequences to Latinos as a social group residing in the US. In addition to her articles and other writings, she is currently completing a book on crime, migration, and racial subordination in the US with Routledge.

Sophie Westenra graduated at the top of her year on the LLB at King's College London and is now studying for the BCL at Oxford on a full scholarship. This is Sophie's third publication in the fields of criminology and immigration, where her interests centre around the increasing criminalization of the immigration process. Prior works appear in *The Routledge Companion to Criminological Theory and Concepts and Theoretical Criminology*.

Race, Criminal Justice, and Migration Control

Enforcing the Boundaries of Belonging

Mary Bosworth, Alpa Parmar, and Yolanda Vázquez

We are living through a period of mass mobility in which certain forms of migration and asylum are increasingly restricted by law. On the one hand, the forces of global capitalism, working in tandem with nation states, permit privileged classes to move freely in the name of economic efficiency and growth. On the other, the growing numbers of people who are forced to move in search of work, safety, and other opportunities face legal barriers to their arrival and settlement. These two underlying forces in immigration policy, towards inclusion and exclusion, are highly racialized. They are also influenced by socioeconomic status and gender.

Most people on the move are from the Global South. In 2015 the United Nations estimated that over 244 million migrants lived outside their country of birth (United Nations 2016). That same year, the United Nations Refugee agency UNHCR reported that globally one in every 122 people was either a refugee, internally displaced, or seeking asylum. Most of those in these groups hail from poor countries and, since 2005, women have surpassed men in Europe and North America (UNHCR 2015).

Though rarely explicitly acknowledged, concerns about race and ethnicity animate many of the state and popular responses to the growing number of migrants and refugees seeking entry. The ongoing 'refugee crisis' in Europe offers a clear example of how fears over ethnic and religious integration trump international law and humanitarian concerns, under conditions of economic insecurity. Following the arrival of significant numbers of Syrians fleeing conflict in their homeland, European Union (EU) member states have expended considerable energy closing their borders. Notwithstanding some important initial exceptions in Germany, Austria, and Sweden, many EU member states have been reluctant to offer them sanctuary. Despite considerable evidence of the economic boon migrants and refugees bring with them, fears about integration have triumphed in an era where a number of European countries are grappling with the alienation of second-generation migrant communities (Boe 2016). Thus, even though they were carried out by a group of predominantly French and Belgian citizens, the 2016 Paris and Brussels attacks led to calls for increased border control across Europe. In this way, and in other less dramatic examples too, religious and ethnic differences of resident populations and those seeking to arrive are cast as inherently dangerous, at odds not only with national identity but also with our collective security.

In the United States, mass arrivals from the Global South have been met with similar hostility while long-term resident irregular populations have been stigmatized by an association with crime and deviance. Legislative attempts by the Obama administration to open pathways for certain, 'deserving' long-term resident irregular migrants through such policies as the 'Deferred Action for Childhood Arrivals' as well as 'Deferred Action for Parents of Americans'[1] have amplified concerns about the dangers posed by irregular migrants and those newly arrived. As a result, meaningful immigration reform has been stymied. As in Europe, campaigns against the entry of both Central Americans and Syrians fleeing violence have sprung up, stoked by fears of criminal and terrorist motives. Compounding matters, racist tropes about Mexicans as criminals were reanimated during the divisive 2016 US presidential campaign. Since taking up the presidency in 2017, Donald Trump has maintained his xenophobic stance, ushering in a series of executive orders that not only banned refugee claimants from majority Muslim countries (Executive Office of the President 2017a; 2017b) but also poured money into internal and external border control, focusing on the southern border (Exec. Order No. 13767, 82 FR 8793, Jan 25, 2017). In response, immigration arrests are on the rise (Sacchetti 2017).

While border control is, legally, an administrative matter, as scholars in the field of border criminology have made clear, criminal justice plays an important role in many of the mechanisms for managing migration. Jurisdictions such as the UK, Australia, and the United States have created a host of new criminal offences for immigration violations (Aliverti 2013; Stumpf 2006). Criminal law enforcement agents have likewise acquired additional roles and responsibilities in determining the nationality of criminal suspects and enforcing immigration law within the border and beyond (Aliverti 2015; Chácon 2010; Weber 2012). Immigration-related prosecutions in the criminal justice system currently outnumber all other federal criminal prosecutions in the United States, including drugs and weapons prosecutions. US Immigration and Customs Enforcement is now the largest investigative arm of the US Department of Homeland Security (Chácon 2012; Eagly 2013). In Europe, national and transnational police forces intercept irregular migrants at the border and within national territory (Aas and Gundhus 2015; Mutsaers et al. 2015; Parmar 2014) at increasingly higher rates than ever before. In Australia, migrants are vigorously prosecuted for attempting to enter its borders.

The use of such punitive measures has subjected increasing numbers of foreign nationals, with various immigration statuses, to detention and incarceration. Across the globe, new facilities have been built and old ones restructured. Prisons have set

---

[1] Known by the acronyms DACA and DAPA, respectively. DACA, which was founded in 2012, allows some undocumented people who arrived as children to receive a renewable two-year period of 'deferred action' from deportation, during which they may continue in education or the military and engage in paid work. DAPA, introduced to expand the provisions of DACA and to allow some parents of lawful permanent residents or US citizens differed action was enjoined by the case of *U.S. v. Texas*, by twenty-eight states that opposed the provision. At the time of writing, questions remain over the continuation of DACA and the fate of DAPA and *U.S. v. Texas* under the Trump administration.

up novel processes of admission to identify foreigners and sometimes host immigration officers to facilitate their deportation (Kaufman 2015). Foreign populations now represent on average 20 per cent of prison inmates, reaching extraordinary highs in countries such as Switzerland (71.4 per cent), Luxembourg (68.8 per cent), Cyprus (58.9 per cent), Greece (57.1 per cent), Belgium (44.2 per cent), and the United States (25 per cent).[2] New carceral spaces have sprung up in a national web of immigration detention centres designed to facilitate identification and expulsion (Bosworth 2014). These sites of administrative detention appear both in country and offshore, extending their powers to deport (Bosworth 2011; Flynn 2014; Hasselberg 2016; Wong 2015).

Historically, constructions of threat and law and order responses to such threats have formed along race lines (Ngai 2004; Ong Hing 2004). Stereotypical notions of suspicion, criminality, and inferiority are assigned to migrants, reinforcing common-sense justifications of racial differences that are already deeply embedded within cultural value systems (Kobayashi 1990). Racial profiling, fears about national security and processes of 'othering' convene within concerns about mobility.

Given the enduring racialized disproportionality within the immigration and criminal justice systems, it seems inevitable that such matters would become further entrenched in the growing use of the criminal justice system in migration control. Yet, so far, border criminologists and crimmigration law scholars have rarely placed such matters at the centre of their analysis. Although some have highlighted the relationship between race, gender, migration, and crime (Brotherton and Kretsedemas 2008; Vázquez 2015), for the most part, the ways that the intersection between migration, border control, and criminal justice create a dynamic system of racial and ethnic disparities remains under-explored theoretically and empirically. As a result, and despite the obvious racialized outcome of these policies and processes, their effects on migrants remain obscured in academic debate (Garner 2015), while the diversity of 'migrants' themselves is overlooked (although see: Bucerius and Tonry 2014; Erel et al. 2016; Kibria et al. 2013; Shantz 2010).

Since Bell's (1992) call to 'get real' about race and the persistence of racism in America, the field of critical race theory has generated new insights about crime, law, and deviance and the sociology of education (Romero 2008). This approach offers an important lens for understanding the coalescence between criminal justice and migration, and the racialized practices they uphold, by placing race at the centre of analysis. Research beyond the United States has been reticent to adopt this frame, however, and despite calls by criminologists for a clearer examination of the reconfiguration of race and crime and how racialization has changed its form (Phillips and Webster 2013), much criminology has avoided direct discussion of race. Instead, it continues to be treated merely as one variable among others, mentioned only in passing (Parmar 2017a; Phillips and Bowling 2003). Studies of the intersection between criminal justice and migration control have also neglected the chance to incorporate intersectional perspectives which privilege analyses of race, thereby obscuring how key concepts such as 'migrant' are racially coded (Parmar 2017b; Potter 2015).

---

[2] Source: http://www.prisonstudies.org/world-prison-brief-datahttp://www.bop.gov/about/statistics/statistics_inmate_citizenship.jsp

By generating a conversation between critical race, criminology, migration, and legal scholars with the explicit aim of foregrounding race and ethnicity, this book starts to respond to this lacuna in the literature. Drawing on a range of perspectives and disciplinary backgrounds, the chapters are united by a focus on the relationship between migration control and the social construction of race and racism. With contributions from transnational and inter-disciplinary scholars, multi-level reflections that are conceptual, theoretical, and empirical, this collection of essays seeks to reorient the burgeoning field of literature on migration control in criminology and criminal law around issues of race.

Organized into four sections with a separate foreword and epilogue, the chapters draw on a range of legal and empirical research from around the world. Broadly speaking, they follow the chronology of border control, starting at the border, before moving to the police, courts and the law, and then prison, detention, and deportation. In so doing, they reveal different points at which race comes into focus and disappears from view. While, for the most part, the accounts portray a worrying reliance on xenophobic ideas about otherness, together the chapters also reveal the precariousness of and discontinuities in racialization and the ways in which race is reanimated at certain moments and in novel ways. Above all they demonstrate the social, moral, and individual costs of organizing the world in this way.

Part I, 'Race, Borders, and Social Control', demonstrates the fluidity of the border under conditions of mass mobility. Traditionally defined as a geographical dividing line, where migrants attempt to enter or are expelled, these days, the border is wide-ranging and often invisible. It remains ever present in the lives of particular migrants, long after it is crossed. By expanding the circumstances in which migrants are expected to demonstrate their admissibility in daily life to spaces within the receiving nation as well as en route, the border relies on and creates race, gender, and class markers as proof of belonging.

In the first chapter, Maggy Lee, Mark Johnson, and Michael McCahill illuminate the wide-ranging impact of border control in their research on Filipino migrant domestic workers in Saudi Arabia and Hong Kong. Drawing on policy documents and interviews with Filipino migrant domestic workers, this chapter describes wide-ranging methods and modalities of surveillance that continue even after authorized entry into the receiving country. Such strategies, which commence before they leave the Philippines, maintains the women's racialized identity as the 'ideal global care labour[er]' (Guevarra 2014: 131) and keep them 'in their place' in the receiving countries.

In Chapter 2, Gabriella Sanchez expands on the discussion of the racialized nature of border enforcement policies and rhetoric by focusing on the more familiar criminological figure of the 'smuggler'. While border control policies and the rhetoric surrounding smuggling cast these individuals as inherently criminal, young and foreign men from the Global South, Sanchez points out that the reality is more complex. Smugglers include men as well as women of all ages, origins and legal statuses. Their actions are often driven by goals other than deviance or financial profit, as they seek to acquire and mobilize protection, care, and social capital.

In Chapter 3, Lirio Gutiérrez Rivera examines how the historical relationship between the United States and Honduras continues to impact the way in which Honduran women and their children are forced to flee their community and are negatively categorized in US migration and crime policies. Through an examination of documents and reports on internal displacement, migration, and violence against women alongside interviews with Honduran women and US asylum attorneys, this chapter traces the links between historical notions of race, gender, and class with contemporary politics. In so doing, it reveals the racial and gendered nature of the barriers facing undocumented Honduran women and children seeking refuge in the United States.

Having set out the wide-ranging nature and impact of the border, we turn in Part II to policing. In this section, we see the ways in which states around the world have created new forms of governance by drawing on formal and informal practices of policing in their management of foreign nationals. The chapters illuminate how migration control and perceptions of immigration status support already racialized and gendered police practices as well as new ways in which the processes theoretically and empirically intersect.

Ben Bowling and Sophie Westenra introduce this section in Chapter 4 by setting out an account of how racism shapes immigration policing in the UK. The police cast some as inherently suspect based on their physical appearance and assumptions about their nationality or ethnicity. Through its reliance on racist logics, the multi-level nature of policing migration and its intersections in the territory, at the border and beyond the border, reinforces a system of 'global apartheid'.

In Chapter 5, Sanja Milivojević describes how migrants are policed in the Western Balkans. Focusing on an under-researched area in the Global South, and by drawing on elite interviews and analysis of local media, Milivojević highlights how border policing reinforces and shapes concepts of belonging and danger by race and class. In this way, the chapter suggests, borders remain present within the everyday lives of migrants based on their race, gender, and class, regardless of their location.

In Chapter 6, Louise Boon-Kuo critically assesses the policing of migration in Australia by examining two contrasting dynamics in the policing and regulation of street-based migration. By focusing on how border practices intersect with racialized hierarchies in the policing of migrant illegality within Australia, this chapter reveals tensions between the legal categories of citizenship and the broader production of race. On the one hand, Boon-Kuo suggests, critical race theory illuminates the racialization of migrant illegality. For example, differential legal regimes and safeguards for arrest/detention predicated on non-citizenship function to exclude and marginalize. On the other hand, police apprehension of 'illegal' migrants is often bound up with broader racialized policing projects that decentre the significance of legal status. This finding echoes criminological studies that point to the role of the police in constituting multiple modalities of differentiated 'citizenship'. Thinking through these practices, this chapter raises questions about how race is both formed and obscured through the low-visibility policing of migration.

In Chapter 7, which ends Part II, Alpa Parmar draws on empirical research conducted in British police custody suites to illuminate how notions of belonging are racialized through interactions with the police. The chapter shows how, and with what consequences, criminalization, migration, race, gender, and socio-economic status intersect when the police are asked to respond to migration and fears about migrants. The empirical detail in the chapter demonstrates how policing can be used as a tool by which to govern and question the presence of minority ethnic groups in the UK and how national origin becomes a proxy for race. The argument underscores how racial hierarchies, empire, and nationhood are reconstituted through police practice—both symbolically and physically.

Part III moves from policing to explore how the law and courts construct and reinforce racial hierarchies and societal notions of race and racism within the area of migration and crime. Specifically, these chapters bring together critical perspectives about the legislative and legal practices that directly or indirectly racialize migrant groups whilst aiming to protect or process them through the criminal justice system.

Ana Aliverti begins the discussion in Chapter 8 by focusing on the ways in which court staff in the Birmingham criminal courts use the concept of 'culture' to account for crimes among foreign national defendants. Drawing also on a selection of Court of Appeal decisions, she identifies a hardening of gender and racial stereotypes about non-Western subjects. The use of 'cultural' stereotypes and the underlying racial biases used by the courts and often deployed by court actors reinforces racialized ideals of citizenship and has damaging consequences both inside and outside the courtroom.

In Chapter 9, Yolanda Vázquez examines how the enactment and implementation of migration and crime laws and policies in the United States have shaped and been shaped by race and racism. Specifically, she discusses the racialization of the 'criminal alien' as Latino and the way in which this category has shaped contemporary notions of race and racial identity. She argues that the historical construction of Latinos as inferior and temporary labourers continues to influence the way in which migration and crime policies are created in a post-racial society. At the same time, these policies reinforce the nation-state's understanding of race and racism, racial ideology, and the position that Latinos hold within American society. Through the category of the 'criminal alien', societal attitudes and beliefs are formed that view Latinos as dangerous to the nation, national identity, and its citizens, legitimizing increasingly harsh migration and criminal laws, policies, and practices that disproportionately impact Latinos and reinforce their racial inequality.

In Chapter 10, Jennifer Chacón and Susan Bibler Coutin illuminate how court decisions pertaining to immigration allow for consideration of race in the policing of migrants in the United States. The resulting doctrinal exceptionalism sanctions race-based practices that impact individuals regardless of citizenship (Chacón 2010). Chacón and Bibler Coutin in this chapter examine how law and legal doctrine influence practice, exploring some of the ways Latino racial identity is produced on the ground in the United States through the enforcement of immigration law. By examining how Latino racial identity in the United States is understood by and produced through court decisions and responses to it, this chapter illuminates the way in which Latino identity and undocumented status in the United States operates not only to the detriment of Latinos, but also to render invisible unauthorized migrants belonging to other white, black, and Asian racial groups and sub-groups. This also serves to generate false oppositional narratives about Asian immigrant groups as legal and economically desirable (in moderation), and Latino immigrant groups as 'illegal' and economically undesirable.

In Chapter 11, the final contribution to this part, Eddie Bruce-Jones offers an alternative view of the racialized nature of the law, by turning his attention to refugee law and how it is taught. According to Bruce-Jones, a crisis model frames our notions of the violence experienced by refugees, which entrenches the belief that their legal claims reflect an exceptional and generally individualized form of violence that is bound by political borders. He highlights recent social imaginings of the refugee in Europe, and in particular in the UK, as both a racialized criminal subject and a racialized subject in need of humanitarian intervention—a dual characterization which serves both to legitimize state logics of security and further stabilize state-building discourses of human rights. This chapter argues for an expanded definition and understanding of refugees, recognizing the historically situated violence, particularly against people coming from the Global South to Europe and North America.

Finally, in Part IV of the book, the chapters turn to the final sites of border control: the prison, the immigration detention centre, and deportation. Drawing on a range of empirical research and conceptual frames, the chapters illuminate the ways in which race and racism are created and reinforced in policy documents and in the everyday lived experiences of migrants and detention staff.

Hindpal Singh Bhui begins this section, in Chapter 12, by arguing that narratives about security, extremism, and migration undermine positive engagement between prison staff and Muslim prisoners in England and Wales. This narrative, which he links to historical factors of British colonialism and the current climate of anti-migrant feeling, alienates prisoners from staff, with potentially dire effects. Calling for greater research on foreign and Muslim prisoners, Bhui looks for ways out of the current deadlock that characterizes a number of penal institutions.

In Chapter 13, Mary Bosworth also pays attention to the relations between those who are incarcerated and the staff who lock them up. Her chapter, which draws on fieldwork in two British Immigration Removal Centres (IRCs), shows how staff rely on ideas of race and nationality to make sense of detainees, their own job, and the institutions in which they work. Designed as places to expel unwanted foreign citizens, IRCs are highly racialized institutions as nearly all resident within them are minority ethnic. By focusing on staff accounts, who themselves are ethnically diverse, rather than detainees, this chapter seeks to widen our understanding of the ways in which these institutions of confinement maintain, reinforce and maybe sometimes disrupt ideas of race and belonging in British society.

Tanya Golash-Boza ends this section in Chapter 14 with an explanation of how and why immigration law enforcement targets black and Latino men in the United States. Drawing on interviews conducted with deportees in the Dominican Republic, Jamaica, and Guatemala and data from the Office of Immigration Statistics, on-the-ground practices of policing with immigration law enforcement cooperation explain the gendered and racialized patterns of deportation. Police officers are more likely to be active in communities where blacks and Latinos live. They are also more likely to stop and arrest black and Latino men due to both implicit and explicit racial bias. Together, these factors contribute to higher rates of deportation and detention for black and Latino men.

By placing race at the heart of our analysis, this collection of essays offers a fresh and urgently needed perspective on border control, moving forward the debate and understanding of such matters in criminology and criminal law across the globe. Given that the vast majority of those subject to internal and external border controls are minority ethnic people from the Global South, such work is long overdue as it is integral to our understanding of current migration and crime policies. The chapters in this volume show how explicit discussion about the race and the racializing role of migration control can be important for transforming the way we think about migration matters.

Individually each of the chapters show how racialization occurs, is perpetuated, and reimagined in different institutional, geographical, and conceptual spaces when criminal justice and migration systems cross. As a whole, the book demonstrates how these constituent crimmigration spaces connect and speak to each other through race and because of race. The *language* of race also lubricates the cogs of the system and their smooth functioning to (re)produce racial hierarchies. As a number of the chapters underscore, the law frames both criminal justice and migration systems, and thus acts as a key site where the 'colour line of race' (Du Bois 1996) is enforced. The law, potentially, is also a place where resistance could be effectively harnessed.

It is hard to be optimistic about our ability to challenge the harsh responses to mass mobility identified in this collection. Yet, as Leanne Weber (2015: 164) has trenchantly observed, 'This is the time to move beyond critique and towards a positive project of rebordering the world for a globalized age.' This book offers a few glimpses of what could be done in the classroom, in the field, and in the community. As migration control increasingly intersects with the field of criminal justice, criminologists and legal scholars are particularly well placed to challenge its racialized and exclusionary logic. To do so effectively, we not only need evidence of what is going on, but also a commitment to think otherwise. As the authors in this collection demonstrate so powerfully, contemporary migration control policies do more than affect those whom they target, they divide and diminish us all.

REFERENCES

Aas, K. and Gundhus, H. (2015), 'Policing Humanitarian Borderlands: Frontex, Human Rights and the Precariousness of Life', *Journal of Criminology* 55(1): 1–18.

Aliverti, A. (2013), *Crimes of Mobility: Criminal Law and the Regulation of Immigration.* Abingdon: Routledge.

Aliverti, A. (2015), 'Enlisting the Public in the Policing of Immigration', *British Journal of Criminology* 55(2): 215–30.

Bell, D. (1992), *Faces at the Bottom of the Well: The Permanence of Racism.* New York: Basic Books.

Boe, C. S. (2016), 'From *Banlieue* Youth to Undocumented Migration: Illegalized Foreign-Nationals in Penal Institutions and Public Spaces', *Criminology & Criminal Justice* 16(3): 319–36.

Bosworth, M. (2011), 'Deporting Foreign National Prisoners in England and Wales', *Citizenship Studies* 15(5): 583–95.

Bosworth, M. (2014), *Inside Immigration Detention*. Oxford: Oxford University Press.

Brotherton, D. and Kretsedemas, P. (2008), *Keeping out the Other: A Critical Introduction to Immigration Enforcement Today*. New York: Columbia University Press.

Bucerius, S. and Tonry, M. (eds) (2014), *The Oxford Handbook of Ethnicity, Crime and Immigration*. Oxford: Oxford University Press.

Chacón, J. (2010), 'A Diversion of Attention? Immigration Courts and the Adjudication of Fourth and Fifth Amendment Rights', *Duke Law Journal* 59(8): 1564–1633.

Chacón, J. (2012), 'Overcriminalizing Immigration', *Journal of Criminal Law & Criminology* 102(3): 613–62.

Du Bois, W. E. B. (1996, first published 1903), *The Souls of Black Folk*. London: Penguin Classics.

Eagly, I. (2013), 'Criminal Justice for Noncitizens: An Analysis of Variation in Local Enforcement', *New York University Law Review* 88: 1126.

Erel, U., Murji, K., and Nahaboo, Z. (2016), 'Understanding the Contemporary Race–Migration Nexus', *Ethnic and Racial Studies* 39(8): 1339–60.

Executive Office of the President (2017a), Protecting the Nation From Foreign Terrorist Entry Into the United States, E.O. 13780 of Mar 6, 2017, 82 FR 13209.

Executive Office of the President (2017b), Border Security and Immigration Enforcement Improvements, E.O. 13767 of Jan 25, 2017, 82 FR 8793.

Flynn, M. (2014), 'There and Back Again: On the Diffusion of Immigration Detention', *Journal on Migration and Human Security* 2(3): 165–97.

Garner, S. (2015), 'When Criminology (Nearly) Met the Sociology of Race and Ethnicity', *Sociology of Race and Ethnicity* 1(1): 198–203.

Guevarra, A. R. (2014), 'Supermaids: The Racial Branding of Global Filipino Care Labour', in B. Anderson and I. Shutes (eds), *Migration and Care Labour—Theory, Policy and Politics*. Basingstoke: Palgrave Macmillan, 130–50.

Hasselberg, I. (2016), *Enduring Uncertainty: Deportation, Punishment and Everyday Life*. Oxford: Berghahn.

Kaufman, E. (2015), *Punish and Expel: Border Control, Nationalism, and the New Purpose of the Prison*. Oxford: Oxford University Press.

Kibria, N., Bowman, C., and O'Leary, M. (2013), *Race and Immigration*. London: Wiley.

Kobayashi, A. (1990), 'Racism and the Law in Canada: A Geographical Perspective', *Urban Geography* 11(5): 447–73.

Mutsaers, P., Simpson, J., and Karpiak, K. (2015), 'The Anthropology of Police as Public Anthropology', *American Anthropologist* 117(4): 786–9.

Ngai, M. (2004), *Impossible Subjects: Illegal Aliens and the Making of Modern America*. Princeton, NJ: Princeton University Press.

Ong Hing, B. (2004), *Defining America Through Immigration Policy*. Philadelphia, PA: Temple University Press.

Parmar, A. (2014), 'Ethnicities, Racism, and Crime in England and Wales', in S. Bucerius and M. Tonry (eds), *Oxford Handbook of Ethnicity, Crime, and Immigration*. Oxford: Oxford University Press, 321–59.

Parmar, A. (2017a), 'Race, Ethnicity and Criminal Justice: Refocussing the Criminological Gaze', in M. Bosworth, C. Hoyle, and L. Zedner (eds), *The Changing Contours of Criminal Justice*. Oxford: Oxford University Press, 55–69.

Parmar, A. (2017b), 'Intersectionality, British Criminology and Race: Are We There Yet?', *Theoretical Criminology* 21(1): 35–45.

Phillips, C. and Bowling, B. (2003), 'Racism, Ethnicity and Criminology: Developing Minority Perspectives', *British Journal of Criminology* 43(2): 269–90.

Phillips, C. and Webster, C. (eds) (2013), *New Directions in Race, Ethnicity and Crime*. London: Routledge.

Potter, H. (2015), *Intersectionality and Criminology: Disrupting and Revolutionizing Studies of Crime*. Abingdon: Routledge.

Romero, M. (2008), 'Crossing the Immigration and Race Border: A Critical Race Theory Approach to Immigration Studies', *Contemporary Justice Review* 11(1): 23–37.

Sacchetti, M. (2017), 'Immigration Arrests Soar under Trump: Sharpest Spike Seen for Non Criminals', *Washington Post*, May 17, 2017. Available at: https://www.washingtonpost.com/local/immigration-arrests-up-during-trump/2017/05/17/74399a04-3b12-11e7-9e48-c4f199710b69_story.html?utm_term=.e99e9f8c0172

Shantz, J. (ed.) (2010), *Racism and Borders: Representation, Repression and Resistance*. New York: Algora Publishing.

Stumpf, J. (2006), 'The Crimmigraton Crisis: Immigrants, Crime, and Sovereign Power', *American University Law Review* 56(2): 367–419.

United Nations (2016), *International Migration Report 2015: Highlights*. Available at: http://www.un.org/en/development/desa/population/migration/publications/migrationreport/docs/MigrationReport2015_Highlights.pdf

UNHCR (2015), *Global Trends. Forced Displacement in 2015*. Geneva: UNHCR. Available at: http://www.unhcr.org/uk/statistics/unhcrstats/576408cd7/unhcr-global-trends-2015.html.

Vázquez, Y. (2015), 'Constructing Crimmigration: Latino Subordination in a "Post-Racial" World', *Ohio State Law Journal* 76(3): 599–657.

Weber, L. (2012), 'Policing a World in Motion', in J. McCulloch and S. Pickering (eds), *Borders and Crime: Pre-crime, Mobility and Serious Harm in an Age of Globalization*. London: Palgrave/Macmillan, 35–53.

Weber, L. (2015), 'Prospects for Peace at the Border', in L. Weber (ed.), *Rethinking Border Control for a Globalizing World. A Preferred Future*. Abingdon: Routledge, 153–65.

Wong, T. (2015), *Rights, Deportation, and Detention in the Age of Immigration Control*. Stanford, CA: Stanford University Press.

I

RACE, BORDERS, AND SOCIAL CONTROL

1

Race, Gender, and Surveillance of Migrant Domestic Workers in Asia

Maggy Lee, Mark Johnson, and Michael McCahill

INTRODUCTION

Migrant care work and the control of migrant care workers are highly charged topics in policy and politics. There has been much debate about the 'maid trade' (Constable 2007); the commodification of care and the transnational movement of labour in the 'global economy of care' (Parreñas 2005); and the inequalities of gender, race/ethnicity, class, and immigrant status that migrant care labour embodies (Anderson and Shutes 2014). Migration controls and enforcement within countries of origin and at destination sites are typically presented by governments as a means of protecting both migrant labour and local workers from illegitimate competition.

Yet migration control is not simply about keeping people out; it is also concerned with producing, sorting, and admitting 'desirable' temporary workers based on particular forms of differential inclusion and ideologies of race, gender, and nation. Differential inclusion might broadly be understood as the process by which 'regulatory regimes [including surveillance] produce differentiation and stratification of migrants' statuses and subjectivities' (Andrijasevic and Anderson 2009: 363). As a result, 'technologies of control', surveillance, and 'enforcement rituals' have been developed not simply to banish but to monitor and keep migrants 'in their place' (De Genova 2013; Pickering and Weber 2006). The temporary workers are expected to return 'home' when their labour is no longer wanted.

This chapter goes beyond the study of state-centred law-and-order control of 'immigrants' in the Global North to examine how different sorts of racialization and gendering are reflected and reproduced in the surveillance of migrant domestic workers from the Philippines to Hong Kong and Saudi Arabia. The Philippines is one of the biggest labour-exporting countries in the world.[1] As of December 2013, the number of overseas Filipinos was estimated to be over 10.2 million (out of a

---

[1] Successive administrations have benefited from the overseas workers' cash remittances to the country, which in 2014 amounted to around US$27 billion or approximately 8.5 per cent of the country's GDP. See http://www.bsp.gov.ph/publications/tables/2016_07/news-07152016a1.htm (last accessed 17 July 2017).

Race, Gender, and Surveillance of Migrant Domestic Workers in Asia. Maggy Lee, Mark Johnson, and Mike McCahill. © Maggy Lee, Mark Johnson, and Mike McCahill, 2018. Published 2018 by Oxford University Press.

total population of some 90 million in the Philippines). Forty-one per cent of these emigrants were 'temporary migrants' primarily working as documented contract labourers in Asia.[2] The Philippine state plays a critical role in producing and exporting women as the 'ideal global care labour' (Guevarra 2014: 131).

These women, who are concentrated in household service work, cleaning, and caregiving, are deeply embedded as subordinate labour groups in the global division of domestic labour where race and gender intersect in migration control practices beyond the actual geographic border and the criminal justice system. Domestic migrant workers are routinely subjected to an extensive and highly diffuse process of surveillance and 'social sorting' (Lyon 2005). In their country of origin, migrants have to 'consent' to multiple forms of surveillance as a condition of mobility; in their countries of destination, they are subjected not only to threats of being criminalized, imprisoned, and deported as irregular migrants but also to more mundane forms of monitoring and racialized othering (Human Rights Watch 2006; Strobl 2009).

This chapter draws on primary sources including policy documents, official and NGO reports, ethnographic interviews with Filipino migrant domestic workers in Saudi Arabia (2007–2009) and ongoing research in Hong Kong (from 2014), and a variety of secondary literature.[3] In drawing these diverse sources of evidence together, we ask: what are the processes of racialization and gendering that mark and marginalize Filipino migrant domestic workers in the Asian context? How does surveillance by state and non-state agencies and employers operate to monitor and keep Filipina migrant women 'in their place' in countries of origin and destination? And, ultimately, what can a transnational study of the surveillance of migrant domestic workers tell us about the nature of migration control?

RACE, GENDER, AND SURVEILLANCE

Surveillance, defined as the 'collection and analysis of information about populations in order to govern their activities' (Haggerty and Ericson 2006: 3), has been a central feature of the state monopoly on the 'legitimate means of movement' (Torpey 2000). The state uses 'technologies of control' to differentiate between 'legitimate' and 'illegitimate' mobilities, to restrict migrants' access to public space, to redraw moral boundaries, and to defend the body politic from the foreign Other (McDowell and Wonders 2010: 55).

Surveillance practices designed to control migrant labour have always been highly racialized, legitimating a particular social order based on claims about cultural and biological differences, notions of 'desirable' labour and labour requirements. In his account of the surveillance regimes directed at Turkish migrants in Germany, for

    [2] For the Philippine government's 'stock estimates' of overseas Filipinos, see http://cfo.gov.ph/downloads/statistics/stock-estimates.html (last accessed 17 July 2017).
    [3] Fieldwork in Hong Kong by Lee, Johnson, and McCahill working with project RA Lenlen Mesina was funded by the British Academy [SG151983] and research in Saudi Arabia by Johnson and the late Alicia Pingol was funded by the AHRC [AH/E508790/1/APPID:123592].

instance, Cagatay (2011: 798) found that during the 1960s 'migrant workers were evaluated primarily in terms of their potential with respect to manual labour'. As a result, there was considerable emphasis on medical examinations to ensure that migrants were 'fit' for manual labour.

There is a long history of racialized medicalization of migrant labour. For example, Molina (2011: 1025) found that Mexicans were regarded as 'unclean' and 'ignorant of basic hygiene habits' by the American authorities and were forced to undergo 'intrusive, humiliating, and harmful baths and physical examinations' at the US–Mexico border in the early twentieth century. 'Race, rather than symptoms, became shorthand for disease carriers ... Thus public health policies helped to secure the US–Mexico border and to mark Mexicans as outsiders even before the advent of more focused gatekeeping institutions, such as the border patrol' (Molina 2011: 1025–7). Notions of the 'quality' of migrant labour are not neutral, however. Livingston (2005: 137–40) thus argued that compulsory physical fitness examinations imposed on South African native miners by the Europeans in the 1930s and 1940s represented a form of 'biomedical gaze'; it 'objectified' African male bodies and was based upon medical, colonial, missionary, and industrial definitions of 'able-bodied' men, which emphasized 'youthful vigour' and 'extra weight' rather than 'wisdom and experience of age'.

As Livingston's work suggests, the racialization of migrants is further shaped by assumptions about gender and sexuality. Migrant women's bodies in particular are regarded as boundary markers and subject to gender-specific sexual controls, in part because of their 'reproductive capacity to produce alien or mixed offspring' (Lan 2008: 854).[4] Gendered surveillance regimes often involve extensive internal and external medical examination. This included intrusive gynaecological examinations of women migrating as would-be fiancées from the Indian subcontinent in the 1970s by British immigration officials, in the highly discriminatory practice known as 'virginity testing'. As Smith and Marmo (2011: 148–9) argued, the 'testing' of virginity was used as a form of 'moral scrutiny through ascertaining physical integrity'. The practice was directed at women of particular 'race', nationality as well as marital status, age, and class, under a restrictive British immigration control regime heavily focused on keeping out 'undesirable' non-white migrants.

The situations we describe in Asia are similar to but distinct from those discussed above. While surveillance practices are directed at and involve the production and social sorting of different sorts of gendered bodies, they are not primarily organized around distinctions based on skin colour. Rather, they create hierarchies of foreign Others that go beyond a black/white dichotomy. Writing in the context of Taiwan, Lan (2006: 16) argued that racialization of foreign maids is a 'multi-layered process of stratified otherization' that collapses cultural differences into fixed, essentialized characteristics of racialized bodies marked and measured in terms of comportment and conduct. For example, Filipina women are often

---

[4] For a discussion of the social and legal implications of migrant children in Hong Kong, see Constable (2014).

imagined as 'the Westernized other' and difficult to manage; Indonesian women from rural villages with Muslim conventions are seen as 'the traditional other' and 'naturally "suited to hard work and no days off"' (Lan 2006: 77). Overall, migrant women are to be sorted and scrutinized as suitably 'defeminized and disciplined servants' according to 'racial narratives' that essentialize differences among migrant groups (Lan 2006: 244).

RACIALIZATION AND CONTROL OF MIGRANT DOMESTIC LABOUR IN ASIA

In Asia, as elsewhere, migrant women are the primary suppliers of paid domestic service. These women, who bear the adverse impact of the triple 'feminizations of work, poverty and migration', within the context of the 'increasing informalization, casualization and precarity of work' in the global market (Spitzer and Piper 2014: 1011), are essentialized and exported as contract labourers to perform intimate home-based care work. In the Philippines, a range of state agencies and non-state for-profit institutions form a migration industry to co-produce a dominant discourse about 'ideal global care labour' (Guevarra 2014: 131; Rodriguez and Schwenken 2013). As Guevarra (2014: 144–5) has argued in the context of 'racial branding' of Filipina 'supermaids', a multitude of institutional actors seek to inscribe putatively 'natural qualities' of care and work ethic on Filipina women and raise the '"quality" of Filipino workers with respect to their global South counterparts'. Filipina women are seen as docile, caring, hardworking, and naturally suited to be maids. Through the production and marketing of these women as model domestic workers, institutional actors including the government, licensed labour recruitment and placement agencies, and pre-departure training institutions seek to profit from the international trade of domestic workers. In the process, Filipina women are subject to diffuse forms of monitoring by state and non-state agencies in both countries of origin and destination.

Pre-departure processes of surveillance

In the Philippines, migrant domestic workers are subject to a highly elaborate and formalized system of pre-departure monitoring premised on file-based data collection and embodied surveillance. They must go to great lengths and bear significant financial costs to produce a wide range of documents and files before they are able to travel. Participants in our study described being forced to produce numerous dossiers from different agencies prior to departure, including authenticated birth certificate and marriage certificate; passport; work visa; voters' registration card; National Bureau of Investigation clearance; local police clearance; local government (*barangay*) clearance; baptismal certificate; medical certificate from an accredited clinic; school credentials/diplomas from high school or college; attendance certificate from the pre-departure orientation seminar; overseas employment certificate; overseas workers' welfare association identity card. These data are extracted from different bodies and administrative networks, including labour recruitment agencies, pre-departure training professionals, medical practitioners, the church, the police, and other government agencies.

Although file-based surveillance practices apply to everyone in the Philippines and make up the digital persona that facilitates seamless movement for some social groups, these interventions are directed specifically at migrant workers who have to produce a vast range of documents in negotiating the embodied encounters of surveillance. As research participants in Hong Kong told us in the focus group discussion:

So many questions, questions about me, about my job, about my family. The recruitment agency wants to see everything, birth certificate, marriage contract, diploma, resident certificate, you have to put everything together ... Only people who want to work abroad need to get National Bureau Investigation clearance or local police clearance. If your name is recorded with a 'hit' [with the same name as someone who has a criminal record], they will give you another schedule so they can check your name. The transportation and the time is lost already when that happens, and I have to go back again for clearance.

Before they are allowed to leave, Filipino migrant workers are subject to compulsory medical examinations and screening for a number of diseases and conditions, including hepatitis, tuberculosis, and HIV. The state's facilitation of mandatory HIV testing for migrant workers is particularly controversial as it contravenes national laws protecting workers against HIV-based discrimination and mandatory HIV testing in the Philippines (ILO 2009: 37–40). Rather than protecting the migrants' health, critics point out, these kinds of pre-departure medical examinations identify, mark, and read their bodies as suspicious and potential 'disease carriers'. Such practices capture not only the diffuse nature of migratory control but also the new logics of 'policing at a distance', as the locus of control is dispersed 'upstream' to identify and immobilize 'risky' populations at source (Lee 2013). Migrant workers are thus caught up in an increasingly complex process of file-based and embodied surveillance.

Participants in our study were often unclear about the exact nature or procedures of the medical examinations they were required to undergo. They complained that the accredited clinics were only interested in making money, especially when clinics insisted on carrying out 'unnecessary' tests or sold products to them (for example, expensive glasses when there was nothing wrong with their eyesight). Women travelled long distances to accredited clinics for their physical examinations where they were examined in a cursory or assembly line fashion, as prospective migrant workers in one research study reported:

They call for you to prepare. Then you enter a cubicle [to undress]. For us, for example, there were 12 of us ... The doctor checks us one by one but we're all standing next to each other. It's really embarrassing ... [W]e once complained to the doctor, 'Why did you group us with these kids when we're already 40?' They got angry, 'Then don't work abroad!'

(Action for Health Initiatives 2006: 17)

Migrant workers deemed 'medically unfit' are refused their work permit and visa to leave the Philippines. Pregnant migrant workers fall into this category. Indeed, women have to submit to a pre-departure pregnancy test and to mandatory preg-nancy tests on a regular basis in some countries of destination.[5] As one participant in Hong Kong told us,

If the clinics say you are unfit, or there is something wrong, you have to do the test again, you have to pay again ... You can go to another clinic, sometimes the results could be differ-ent ... I had a medical, X-ray, physical, dental, all that. Then coming to Manila, because it was three months and the medical expired, so another medical. Then coming to Hong Kong I had another medical. So how many times? Three times! Medical! ... Once the clinic said to me, 'you're pregnant'. I'm not! I know they're wrong. But the recruitment agency called my employer anyway.

The physical surveillance of migrant women blurs the distinction between immigra-tion and labour control. An extended chain of data collection processes and bodily interventions that regulates the flow of migrant domestic labourers helps produce discourses about model domestic labour. Migrant women who 'run around' on their own are thought to have transgressed normative boundaries of female propriety and racialized boundaries of space and belonging. Such views are evident in pre-depart-ure orientation seminars that preach family values and abstinence from sex and preg-nancy tests in the Philippines through to the scrutiny of migrant women's everyday movements in the countries of destination. As Paul (2015) suggests, Filipina women are in fact more likely than men to encounter resistance to their independent migra-tion. They are able to secure familial support by casting migration as *fulfilment* rather than transgression of gendered roles as devoted wife, dutiful daughters, and caring mother. Her conclusion is that, while 'women migrants break [some] gender barriers when it comes to their independent labor migration, they do so by "doing," rather than "undoing," gender' (2015: 1). In other words, women must performatively produce the normatively good Filipina migrant, just as they must volunteer their personal information and submit themselves to physical inspection as a condition of their mobility away from home and out of their country.

Surveillance in countries of destination

Hong Kong is heavily dependent on migrant labour within the home. On average, one in eight local households employs a migrant domestic worker (Yip 2014). In 2016 there were over 335,000 documented female migrant workers employed as full-time domestic workers. Approximately 53 per cent of them come from the Philippines, slightly less than half from Indonesia, and much smaller numbers from Thailand, Sri Lanka, Nepal, and India because of the various restrictions (Hong Kong Census and Statistics Department 2016: figure 4.48).[6] Although most of our research participants who were able to produce the required documents reported

[5] In some labour importing countries such as Malaysia and Singapore (and Taiwan until 2003), female migrant workers' sexuality is policed through mandatory pregnancy tests during contract and are repatriated if they are found to be pregnant (Garces-Mascarenas 2008; Lan 2006).
[6] There are complex socio-political and economic factors behind the specific patterns of the 'maid trade' (Constable 2007).

relatively trouble-free experiences of border crossings at the point of entry into Hong Kong, their narratives reveal how race acts as a marker to facilitate or hinder cross-border mobilities. A number of them described how they were routinely singled out by immigration officials and told to line up at a separate queue—or in a 'discrimination line' implicitly reserved for foreign maids, as one of our research participants called it—for sustained questioning and thorough inspection of documents at the airport.

These experiences are not unique to migrant domestic workers in Hong Kong. There are estimated to be more than 7.4 million female migrant domestic workers in the Middle East (Oishi 2005: 5, cited in Pande 2014: 27) and more than 1.5 million migrant domestic workers in Saudi Arabia (Human Rights Watch 2008). They come from a range of countries in Asia and Africa and are stratified within and across a gendered and racialized economy of care. Racialization is made and marked in a number of ways. For example, white British or Irish nurses may work alongside nurses from India or the Philippines, but the latter commonly report that their wages are considerably less than that of their white counterparts. While the former may live in separate and largely segregated gated housing compounds alongside other white expatriates, the latter are more likely to be forced by cost or contract to live in housing provided by local hospitals. These racialized forms of differential inclusions are mirrored in domestic work, an occupation overwhelmingly associated with women from Asia and Africa. Though the latter may be explained in terms of economic difference that makes domestic work in more affluent countries a viable economic strategy for women from poorer countries, those differences tend to be naturalized in terms of race and gender. Moreover, the differential wages among higher-paid professional carers are mirrored in wage differentials paid to women from different places so that Filipinos are normally paid more than Indonesians and other 'Asian' workers while women from African countries are reportedly paid the least, a practice common throughout the region (Human Rights Watch 2008: 73; de Regt 2008). The naturalization of difference is also evident in what Elyas (n.d.: 7) refers to as 'moral panics' that characterize both academic and popular media reporting about foreign domestic workers from Asia and Africa in that country. They are described as a 'necessary' evil (Omari 2003) and perceived to be responsible for promoting lazy and indolent behaviour, threatening religious beliefs and practices, including allegations of 'magic and sorcery' (Al-Khamees 2009), and of sexual immorality (Khudhairi 2003, cited in Elyas n.d.: 7).

The legal framework

Migrant domestic workers are kept in their place through restrictive immigration laws and policies in the countries of destination. In Hong Kong there are strict conditions of stay and rules that reinforce their outsider status. Examples include their exclusion from the ability to apply for permanent residence after seven years of continuous employment, the 'live-in' requirement, and the 'tied-visa scheme' that restricts domestic workers' ability to change employers within their two-year renewable contract as well as the 'two-week rule', which dictates that domestic workers have to leave Hong Kong within two weeks upon termination of their contract. Together, such matters 'trap workers who are in an abusive or exploitative situation, including cases tantamount to forced labour' (Justice Centre Hong Kong 2016: 66). They also render workers vulnerable to sanctions if they fall foul of immigration rules (or respond through 'visa run').[7] Since 2003, migrant domestic workers have been required to 'live in' with their employers often in extremely cramped conditions, including in a shared room with a child or an elderly person or in the kitchen (Justice Centre Hong Kong 2016: 64). Those who 'live out' (even with their employers' approval) are subject to periodic crackdowns, arrests, and heavy penalties, including imprisonment and deportation (Lee 2015).[8] The 'spectacle of enforcement' such as immigration raids and mass deportation aim not so much at netting illegalized immigrants but at creating a climate of fear and disciplining migrants through (the threat of) heightened enforcement directed at their bodies and movements (De Genova 2013).

In Saudi Arabia, a system of state-sponsored bonded labour underpins the racialized process of discrimination (Frantz 2013). The primary features of that system are the absence of employment rights, a visa sponsorship process that confers enormous powers on employers, who are deemed legally to be the workers' guardians and responsible both for migrant workers' conditions of stay in that country, restrictions on mobility including routine and unsanctioned confiscation of employees' passports, and other forms of confinement, such as restrictions on the use of mobile phones. This doubly 'privatized' but, in reality, state-produced and -sanctioned relation between sponsor/employer and migrant/employee consolidates the former's power and control over the latter. Saudi authorities rarely, if ever, intervene to protect migrant domestic workers' interests either as foreign residents or employees.[9]

Face-to-face surveillance and confinement

Participants in our Hong Kong study talked about having to observe a curfew during their day off (typically early evening), not being allowed to wear make-up or 'revealing' clothes, and being discouraged by employers from going out with other migrant domestic workers because they were regarded as a 'bad influence on them'. Although migrant domestic workers are not required to undergo mandatory pregnancy tests in Hong Kong, employers are known to ask domestic workers to be retested upon

---

[7] According to government figures, a total of 962 migrant domestic workers were arrested in 2015 for suspected immigration offences, mainly 'overstaying' and 'unlawful employment' (Boase Cohen and Collins Chambers 2016).

[8] For a discussion of the consequences of the 'live-in' rule from the migrants' perspective, see http://hkhelperscampaign.com/en/faq/.

[9] The state benefits politically and economically from a system of structural violence (Gardner 2010; see also Mahdavi 2011: 95–7) that grants its citizens unregulated power over domestic labour with practically assured impunity and at minimal cost to the state itself. It is not only the case that migrant workers are denied permanent residency and citizenship rights, but also that the system of migrant visa sponsorship makes the employer a proxy for the state.

arrival.[10] Others terminate the contract of workers who become pregnant even though this is illegal under local anti-discrimination legislation. Employers do not just monitor their domestic employees labour in their home but are also entrusted with forms of surveillance on behalf of the state (for example, over conditions of stay). Yet, the Hong Kong government rarely intervenes to ensure that employers abide by the few legal requirements that they are meant to observe in respect of their domestic employees (Constable 2007). Seen in this light, the employers arguably become 'an extension of state power, and the practices of sex and labor control over foreign maids in private households thus become capillary effects of immigration control' (Lan 2008: 856).

In Saudi Arabia where more continuous physical interaction characterizes employee and employer relations and where they have little recourse to legal redress in the case of abusive employers, many domestic workers run away from their employers and become irregular 'freelance' workers (Johnson and Wilcke 2015).[11] According to one report, an estimated '86,000 housemaids ran away in a year' in Saudi Arabia (Estimo 2015). However, the risk and gamble of such actions is high since 'absconding' from sponsors is criminalized. Workers may be detained and/or deported if caught by the authorities or, sometimes considered just as bad, they may end up in the 'house of care' for 'runaway' domestic workers managed by the Philippine Embassy in Riyadh. As Sonmez et al. (2011) write:

Workers who try to escape from their abusive employers are considered absconders. Both running away from the sponsor's home and hiding or protecting runaway domestic workers are illegal and punishable by law. Government officials have even labelled runaway maids as threats to national security. Police are dispatched to search for runaway workers while the local newspapers publish photographs of absconders. When found, workers are imprisoned and then deported. The women are treated as criminals and some have reported being physically or sexually abused while in the custody of police or other authorities.

For those trapped in such circumstances, as Lan (2007) observed in her study of undocumented migrant domestic workers in Taiwan, the trade-off is sometimes perceived to be between 'legal servitude' and a form of 'free illegality'. In Saudi Arabia, however, migrant domestic workers may 'freelance' if they can obtain the help and assistance of other migrant compatriots, especially those who are in middle-class positions and occupations in the country who are able to offer both safe passage and a secure home, though often in exchange for domestic labour in their homes (Johnson 2010). Social networks extending across class lines involve forms of informal surveillance of more precarious migrants by more privileged migrants and include careful watching and face-to-face encounters, as well as monitoring contacts made through mobile phones and social media. Those forms of surveillance between migrants are pertinent not only because they are a consequence of selective forms of

---

[10] For a discussion of the practice and impact of health testing on migrants, see St John's Cathedral HIV Education Centre (2008).

[11] Some migrant domestic workers contest their working conditions in other ways, for example, through moral claims that appeal to religious sensibilities of their employers (Elyas and Johnson 2014; but see Vlieger 2011).

'non-surveillance' (Hintjens 2013) by the state but because they too may become sites for the rearticulation of gendered ideologies and practices, thereby reaffirming persistent racial stereotypes about impoverished, vulnerable, and/or unruly Filipina domestic workers (Johnson 2015).

Surveillance in the public space

The surveillance and regulation of migrant domestic workers' movements also take place in a more mundane manner. As McDowell and Wonders (2010) argue, technologies of control directed at migrants restrict their access to public space, exclude them from social services, and generate feelings of being 'out of place' and 'suspect'. In Hong Kong, migrant domestic workers reported being stopped or 'moved on' by the police and monitored by private security guards who 'do the rounds checking the activities of Filipinas' during their day off, especially when their movements appeared to challenge the authorities' conceptions of space, what should typically occur in an area, and who belongs.[12] Two testimonies from our focus group vividly illustrate the policing of space and its impact on individuals:

I bring all my paperwork with me, even when I go on holiday. I bring everything with me all the time, my passport, my employment contract, visa, everything ... I store all the papers in my handbag, when it's my day off on Sunday. I always have them, everywhere I go.

Once I was riding a bicycle. A police officer followed me, and I was afraid. Why did he follow me? He stopped me and said, 'Show me your identity card. Do you live here?' I said, 'No, I'm just visiting my friend. It's my day off.' So he asked, 'Why are you cycling on the bus lane? Where is your place of employment? I will go and check.' I gave him my address. I don't know if he checked or not. I didn't go back to cycle again.

In Saudi Arabia, state-sanctioned and state-enforced conventions not only sustain racialized wage differentials among workers but are also premised on gender regimes that ascribe to men power and authority over the household—for example, through control of the movement and travel of domestic workers and their wives and children. This is not the product of unchanging cultural norms and social practices. Rather, the legitimacy of the ruling elite depends in part on its being seen to moderate and guard against the corrupting influence of foreign cultures, including that embodied by migrant domestic workers, by publically affirming the privacy of the home and the 'protection' of the modesty of women within it (Al-Rasheed 2007: 128–9; Doumato 2000). Migrant domestic workers venturing outside the home may also find themselves monitored by the 'religious police', rather than regular police, who enforce religious norms and monitor interactions between women and men (Johnson 2015: 256).

---

[12] In Hong Kong, tens of thousands of migrant domestic workers congregate in Statue Square and other areas of Central District every weekend sitting on makeshift rugs or cardboard on public footpaths and parks. Constable (2007: 4–7) described the public and local business reactions against migrant domestic workers' weekend 'invasion'. During a particularly contentious public debate in 1992, various proposals were made to remove off-duty migrant domestic workers to alternative gathering places, including underground car parks.

Surveillance in the private space

Finally, migrant domestic workers are subject to diffuse forms of surveillance mobilized to organize and monitor their everyday behaviour and being in the home. In Hong Kong, live-in domestic workers are routinely subject to surveillance camera ('nanny cams') by employers in the home (Johnson et al., forthcoming).[13] Digital technologies intensify household employers' continuous and unpredictable forms of watching at a distance. As one research participant recorded in her smartphone diary in our study:

> The surveillance camera is on the top of the cabinet, the whole room can be viewed through the monitor ... My employer can see it from his cell phone and the mother can see it from her ipad in the room ... I will sleep at the foot of my ward's bed, they can see me the whole night. There is always camera shooting and I am the only character.

The routine and continuous use of surveillance cameras by employers reinforces the 'home' as a site where social relations based on racialized difference and power between the employer and migrant workers are negotiated and enacted on an everyday basis. As domestic workers are often uncertain about the number, location, reach, and destination of the images recorded, as well as who might be watching and when, they generally regard digital surveillance in the home as particularly invasive. Research participants in Hong Kong talked about employers calling to ask them about an event or an action they observed at a distance. Alternatively, on return from work, an employer might ask or challenge them about a prior event or action that indicated they had either been watching at the time or had subsequently reviewed the day's events, which had been recorded. In this way, this practice of control seems to operate through the continuous ambiguity of never knowing when one is being watched, by whom and exactly what one might be called to account for.

Digital surveillance enables their employers not just to monitor them at a distance but also to interrupt, direct, and interfere in their work. Employers normally justify the use of such strategies on the grounds of protecting the elderly or children. In practice, the impact of overt and covert surveillance demonstrates what can be regarded as 'gendered ironies of care and control' (Johnson et al., forthcoming). Domestic workers in our study reported that they did not necessarily become more conscientious about what they were doing, but rather more self-conscious about what it *looked like* they were doing on camera. For example, one of the participants recounted how she had been playing and dancing with her new employer's young daughter when she received a call from the employer asking her why she was shaking her daughter and telling her to move the camera so she could see her.

In Saudi Arabia, the use of surveillance cameras in the home to monitor domestic workers has not yet been widely reported (Human Rights Watch 2008; Johnson and Wilcke 2015). One reason may be simply that in comparison to the other more

---

[13] The Office of the Privacy Commissioner of Hong Kong (2015) has issued 'notes' on employers' use of surveillance cameras in the home, but these remain guidelines and the practice is not legally regulated or proscribed.

visible forms of monitoring and control (including confiscation of passports and restrictions on movement and on the use of mobile phones), the use of digital cameras may go unnoticed or unremarked. It may be also that they are unnecessary since there are often other adult family members present in the home to do the work of watching and monitoring that, in Hong Kong, is done by surveillance camera. That is likely to change as Saudi women increasingly enter the workforce enabled by increasing educational attainment and their domestic labour.

CONCLUSION

As Bowling and Westenra (this volume) argue, migration control perpetuates 'a highly racialized and gendered immigration enforcement system beyond the border internally and externally', especially in the form of 'pre-entry controls', 'border protection', 'in-country enforcement' and 'diffuse local surveillance'. This chapter demonstrates that, at least in the Asian context, migration control and surveillance characterized by the control of disembodied data and disciplinary techniques directed at migrant bodies go far beyond the criminal justice system before and beyond territorial borders. Migrant domestic workers are not just subjected to some of the most intrusive bodily inspections but also pay in time and resource to produce the largely file-based documents required to enable them to even get near an international border. The nature of migration control is racialized, classed, and gendered insofar as the requirements demanded are contingent on the nature of the contract and the work to be taken up, perceptions about the differential risks posed by women, and the ethnic and national characteristics ascribed and inscribed by the demands of both employers and governments in sending and receiving countries. Those processes also produce retrospectively a bureaucratically documented and naturalized account of a racially stereotyped, gendered subject originating in and growing out of their place of origin.

Through our transnational analysis of female migrants in two different locales, we have argued that migrant domestic workers in both Hong Kong and Saudi Arabia are at the sharp end of surveillance based on gendered and racialized notions of domestic labour. The governments of both place little or no restrictions on the forms of monitoring that domestic workers may be subject to, particularly in the home. At the same time, they effectively withdraw from even minimal forms of monitoring to ensure that employers abide by the few legal requirements that they are meant to observe in respect of their domestic employees. Those selective forms of non-surveillance underpin material forms of gender and racial discrimination and enable forms of labour coercion.

The mechanisms through which gender and racial distinctions are created and sustained are multiple, and they produce differential forms of i(m)mobilities. In their country of origin, women's mobilities are conditioned by their willingness to produce a documented identity as proper women and good Filipino migrant workers in processes that involve not only the state but also non-state surveillance agents. Migration is thus contingent on forms of social sorting at source that performatively produce gender normative subjects that conform to notions of defeminized and disciplined servants. In the countries of destination, there are a range of processes that racially assign and seek to keep different sorts of migrant women in their place as foreign residents and disposable workers. Most of these processes of monitoring and control are undertaken by non-state agents and employers on a daily basis. However, they are all enabled by an immigration system and conditions of stay that differentiate between various sorts of racially marked foreign residents. Ultimately, differential inclusion is underpinned by a criminal justice system that can bear down heavily on migrants through the threat of criminalization and deportation. Any resistance in the form of living out or freelancing not only renders migrants 'irregular', but also invites additional forms of moral opprobrium and racialized othering.

REFERENCES

Action for Health Initiatives, Inc. (2006), *Health at Stake: Access to Health of Overseas Filipino Workers*. Available at: http://www.achieve.org.ph/Philippine%20SoH%20Report.pdf

Al-Khamees, M. A. (2009), *The Impact of Servants of the Family and Society*. Riyadh: Dar Al-Watan.

Al-Rasheed, M. (2007), *Contesting the Saudi State: Islamic Voices from a New Generation*. Cambridge: Cambridge University Press.

Anderson, B. and Shutes, I. (2014), *Migration and Care Labour: Theory, Policy and Politics*. Basingstoke: Palgrave MacMillan.

Andrijasevic, R. and Anderson, B. (2009), 'Conflicts of Mobility: Migration, Labour and Political Subjectivities', *Subjectivity* 29: 363–6.

Boase Cohen and Collins Chambers (2016), 'Government Protection of Foreign Helpers "Simply Inadequate"', 11 February. Available at: http://www.boasecohencollins.com/en/news/208-government-protection-of-foreign-helpers-simply-inadequate

Cagatay, T. (2011), 'Surveillance of Immigrants from Turkey in Germany: From the Disciplinary Society to the Society of Control', *International Sociology* 26(6): 789–814.

Constable, N. (2007), *Maid to Order in Hong Kong—Stories of Migrant Workers*. Ithaca, NY: Cornell University Press.

Constable, N. (2014), *Born Out of Place*. Berkeley, CA: University of California Press.

De Genova, N. (2013), 'Spectacles of Migrant "Illegality": The Scene of Exclusion, the Obscene of Inclusion', *Ethnic and Racial Studies* 36(7): 1180–98.

De Regt, M. (2008), 'High in the Hierarchy, Rich in Diversity: Asian Domestic Workers, their Networks, and Employers' Preferences in Yemen', *Critical Asian Studies* 40(4): 587–608.

Doumato, E. (2000), *Getting God's Ear: Women, Islam and Healing in Saudi Arabia and the Gulf*. New York: Columbia University Press.

Elyas, N. (undated), 'Changing Women's Roles: Filipina Migrant Domestic Workers and their Female Employers in Saudi Arabia'. Madinah: Taibah University. Unpublished manuscript.

Elyas, N. and Johnson, M. (2014), 'Caring for the Future in the Kingdom of Saudi Arabia: Saudi and Filipino Women Making Homes in a World of Movement', in M. de Regt and B. Fernandez, *Migrant Domestic Workers in the Middle East: The Home and the World*. Basingstoke: Palgrave Macmillan, 141–64.

Estimo, R. C. (2015), 'Why 86,000 Housemaids Ran Away in a Year!' *Arab News*, 22 October. Available at: http://www.arabnews.com/featured/news/824001

Frantz, E. (2013), 'Jordan's Unfree Workforce: State-Sponsored Bonded Labour in the Arab Region', *The Journal of Development Studies* 49(8): 1072–87.

Garces-Mascarenas, B. (2008), 'Old and New Labour Migration to Malaysia: From Colonial Times to the Present', in M. Schrover, J. Van Der Leun, L. Lucassen, and C. Quispel (eds), *Illegal Migration and Gender in a Global and Historical Perspective*. Amsterdam: Amsterdam University Press, 105–26.

Gardner, A. (2010), 'Engulfed: Indian Guest Workers, Bahrain Citizens and the Structural Violence of the *Kafala* System', in N. De Genova and N. Peutz (eds), *The Deportation Regime: Sovereignty, Space and Freedom of Movement*. Durham, NC: Duke University Press, 196–223.

Guevarra, A. R. (2014), 'Supermaids: The Racial Branding of Global Filipino Care Labour', in B. Anderson and I. Shutes (eds), *Migration and Care Labour—Theory, Policy and Politics*. Basingstoke: Palgrave Macmillan, 130–50.

Haggerty, K. and Ericson, R. (eds) (2006), *The New Politics of Surveillance and Visibility*. Toronto: University of Toronto Press.

Hintjens, H. M. (2013), 'Screening In or Out? Selective Non-surveillance of Unwanted Humanity in EU Cities', *Surveillance and Society* 11(1/2): 87–105.

Hong Kong Census and Statistics Department (2016), *Women and Men in Hong Kong—Key Statistics (2016 edition)*. Hong Kong: Hong Kong Census and Statistics Department.

Human Rights Watch (2006), *Swept Under the Rug: Abuses against Domestic Workers Around the World*. New York: Human Rights Watch.

Human Rights Watch (2008), *'As If I Am Not Human': Abuses Against Asian Domestic Workers in Saudi Arabia*. New York: Human Rights Watch.

Johnson, M. (2010), 'Diasporic Dreams, Middle-Class Moralities and Migrant Domestic Workers among Muslim Filipinos in Saudi Arabia', *The Asia Pacific Journal of Anthropology* 11(3–4): 428–48.

Johnson, M. (2015), 'Surveillance, Pastoral Power and Embodied Infrastructures of Care among Migrant Filipinos in the Kingdom of Saudi Arabia', *Surveillance and Society* 13(2): 250–64.

Johnson, M., Lee, M., and McCahill, M. (forthcoming), 'Beyond the "All seeing Eye": Filipino Migrant Domestic Workers' Contestation of Care and Control in Hong Kong', *Care and Control in Asian Migrations. Ethnos: Journal of Social Anthropology*.

Johnson, M. and Wilcke, C. (2015), 'Caged in and Breaking Loose: Intimate Labour, the State and Migrant Domestic Workers in Saudi Arabia and other Arab Countries', in S. Friedman and P. Mahdavi (eds), *Migrant Encounters: Intimate Labor, The State and Mobility across Asia*. Philadelphia, PA: University of Pennsylvania Press, 135–59.

Justice Centre Hong Kong (2016), *Coming Clean: The Prevalence of Forced Labour and Human Trafficking for the Purpose of Forced Labour amongst Migrant Domestic Workers in Hong Kong*.

Khudhairi, S. I. (2003), *Social Problems of Household Labour*. Riyadh: Faculty of Arts Research Center, King Saud University.

Lan, P.-C. (2006), *Global Cinderellas: Migrant Domestics and Newly Rich Employers in Taiwan*. London: Duke University Press.

Lan, P.-C. (2007), 'Legal Servitude and Free Illegality: Migrant "Guest" Workers in Taiwan', in R. S. Parreñas and L. C. D. Siu (eds), *Asian Diasporas: New Formations, New Conceptions*. Stanford, CA: Stanford University Press, 253–77.

Lan, P.-C. (2008), 'Migrant Women's Bodies as Boundary Markers: Reproductive Crisis and Sexual Control in the Ethnic Frontiers of Taiwan', *Signs: Journal of Women in Culture and Society* 33(4): 833–61.

Lee, D. (2015), 'Hong Kong Domestic Helpers Arrested in Crackdown on "Live-out" Maids', *South China Morning Post*, 29 January. Available at: http://www.scmp.com/news/hong-kong/article/1694810/4-hong-kong-domestic-helpers-arrested-crackdown-live-out-maids

Lee, M. (2013), 'Human Trafficking and Border Control in the Global South', in K. F. Aas and M. Bosworth (eds), *The Borders of Punishment: Migration, Citizenship, and Social Exclusion*. Oxford: Oxford University Press, 128–45.

Livingston, J. (2005), *Debility and the Moral Imagination in Botswana*. Bloomington, IN: Indiana University Press.

Lyon, D. (2005), 'The Border is Everywhere: ID Cards, Surveillance and the Other', in E. Zureik and M. B. Salter (eds), *Global Surveillance and Policing: Borders, Security, Identity*. Cullompton: Willan, 66–82.

Mahdahvi, P. (2011), *Gridlock: Labor, Migration, and Human Trafficking in Dubai*. Stanford, CA: Stanford University Press.

McDowell, M. G. and Wonders, N. A. (2010), 'Keeping Migrants in their Place: Technologies of Control and Racialized Public Space in Arizona', *Social Justice* 36(2): 54–72.

Molina, N. (2011), 'Borders, Laborers, and Racialized Medicalization: Mexican Immigration and US Public Health Practices in the 20th Century', *American Journal of Public Health* 101(6): 1024–31.

Office of the Privacy Commissioner for Hong Kong (2015), *Monitoring and Personal Data Privacy at Work: Points to Note for Employers of Domestic Workers*. Hong Kong: PCPD.

Oishi, N. (2005), *Women in Motion: Globalisation, State Policies and Labor Migration in Asia*. Stanford, CA: Stanford University Press.

Omari, S. M. (2003), *Saudi Women and Maids*. Riyadh: Al-Yaom newspaper.

Pande, A. (2014), 'Forging Intimate and Work Ties: Migrant Domestic Workers Resist in Lebanon', in B. Fernandez and M. de Regt (eds), *Migrant Domestic Workers in the Middle East: The Home and the World*. New York: Palgrave Macmillan, 27–49.

Parreñas, R. S. (2005), *Children of Global Migration: Transnational Families And Gendered Woes*. Stanford, CA: Stanford University Press.

Paul, A. (2015), 'Negotiating Migration, Performing Gender', *Social Forces* 94(1): 271–93.

Pickering, S. and Weber, L. (eds) (2006), *Borders, Mobility and Technologies of Control*. Dordrecht: Springer.

Rodriguez, R. and Schwenken, H. (2013), 'Becoming a Migrant at Home: Subjectivation Processes in Migrant-Sending Countries Prior to Departure', *Population, Space and Place* 19: 375–88.

Smith, E. and Marmo, M. (2011), 'Uncovering the "Virginity Testing" Controversy in the National Archives: The Intersectionality of Discrimination in British Immigration History', *Gender & History* 23: 147–65.

Sonmez, S., Apostopoulos, Y., Tran, D., and Rentrope, S. (2011), 'Human Rights and Health Disparities for Migrant Workers in the UEA', *Health and Human Rights Journal* 13(2): 17–35. Available at: https://www.hhrjournal.org/2013/08/human-rights-and-health-disparities-for-migrant-workers-in-the-uae/

Spitzer, D. L. and Piper, N. (2014), 'Retrenched and Returned: Filipino Migrant Workers During Times of Crisis', *Sociology* 48(5): 1007–23.

St John's Cathedral HIV Education Centre (2008), 'State of Health of Migrants 2007—Mandatory testing'. Available at: http://www.sjhivctr.com/research/2007/HIVreport08eng.pdf

Strobl, S. (2009), 'Policing Housemaids: The Criminalization of Domestic Workers in Bahrain', *British Journal of Criminology* 49(2): 165–83.

Torpey, J. (2000), *The Invention of the Passport: Surveillance, Citizenship and the State*. Cambridge: Cambridge University Press.

Vlieger, A. (2011), 'Sharia on Domestic Workers: Legal Pluralism and Strategic Maneuvering in Saudi Arabia and the Emirates', *Journal of Islamic Law and Culture* 12(2): 166–82.

Yip, P. (2014), 'Hong Kong Must Address the Social Costs of Hiring Domestic Helpers', *South China Morning Post*, 3 February. Available at: http://www.scmp.com/comment/insight-opinion/article/1419267/hong-kong-must-address-social-costs-hiring-domestic-helpers

2

Portrait of a Human Smuggler

Race, Class, and Gender among Facilitators of Irregular Migration on the US–Mexico Border

Gabriella E. Sanchez

The 25 January 2016 online edition of *Al Jazeera Magazine* includes a special report entitled 'Portrait of a Human Smuggler' (Holman 2016). It features the face of an adult man hiding in the shadows. His eyes are barely visible, but his dark skin, prominent cheekbones, and thick lips are not hard to notice. A fast-changing legend next to the face reads: 'I am a guide. I work with one of the cartels. My work is to bring people from Honduras into the U.S.' These short sentences foreshadow the actual article, which is prefaced by an even more sinister tagline: 'for the cartel and the smuggler, there is an immovable bottom line: the migrants are merchandise, to be profited from one way or the other'.

The hypervisibility of contemporary migration flows has generated significant interest in human smugglers, and reports of their activities are ubiquitous. Smugglers, as the facilitators of irregular migration, are most often characterized as young and violent men from the Global South who are responsible for the tragic journeys of migrants around the world. Media and law enforcement reports blame them for a long list of tragedies, ranging from the deaths of migrants drowning in rough seas (Kirchgaesnner 2016) and the suffocation of women and children riding in the back of lorries, trains, and containers (Johnston 2015; Dunai 2016) to cases of sexual abuse and exploitation (Darby and Price 2016) and the abandonment of people in transit in desolate, dangerous, and inaccessible regions (Hooper et al. 2015; Price 2017). Researchers have also written extensively about the disregard of smugglers for the lives of migrants, in the process building a vast corpus of empirical research focused on the documentation of migrant victimization where the smuggler stands as the leading perpetrator. Graphic testimonies of migrant kidnapping (Casillas 2017; Dimmitt 2013; Slack 2015), extortion (Isacson et al. 2014; Vogt 2013), forced labour (Brennan 2014; Izcara Palacios and Yamamoto 2017), sexual assault, trafficking, and torture (Donnelly and Hagan 2014) provide evidence of the vulnerability of migrants in transit and the risks they face in the context of their journeys. Movies, documentaries, and popular literature have also rushed to document the most dramatic, graphic experiences of migrants at the hands of smugglers, whose actions are almost single-handedly framed as inhumane.

Clandestine migration and its facilitation *are* dangerous. The testimonies of many migrants and their families documented in policy briefs and scholarly publications attest clearly and poignantly to these facts. Irregular migrant journeys often involve travelling while relying on dangerous mechanisms, under extreme environmental conditions and across vast distances (Mainwaring and Brigden 2016). Many migrants become the target of criminals, and while attempting to escape from them sustain serious physical injuries (Ochoa O'Leary 2012). Thousands die or go missing during their transits (Martínez et al. 2014) and women are more likely to die than men during their journeys (Pickering and Cochrane 2013).

While many of these tragedies are indeed the result of the negligence or abuse of migration facilitators or smugglers, there are at least two important facts to consider. First, smuggling practices do not occur in a vacuum: their emergence and growth go hand in hand with the escalation of migration restrictions. Smuggling reflects the demand for channels for mobility amid the rapid decrease of safe and legal routes and highlights the increasing restrictions imposed on specific migrant flows.

Second, despite their frequent appearance in media exposés, best-selling books, and movies, and in academic, government, and law enforcement reports, smugglers and their dynamics have hardly been the subject of empirical inquiry (Achilli 2015; Sanchez 2015). Their experiences and identities, unless framed from a state-centred or criminological perspective, have remained absent from most policy, academic, and media conversations. This absence has allowed for largely gendered, often racist and classist representations of smugglers that remain unexamined and unquestioned. This chapter seeks to address this gap.

Relying on ethnographic data collected among smuggling facilitators and their clients on the US–Mexico border, this contribution counters the often uncritical messages concerning the facilitation of clandestine migration and its actors. Smuggling facilitation is far from based on exploitation or profit alone. Participant observation conducted among twelve women charged with human smuggling offences and twenty-five women who travelled with smuggling facilitators in the US Southwest states of Arizona and Utah reveals a high level of cooperation, solidarity, and trust, essential to the survival of both migrants and those behind their journeys, who are often migrants themselves. Furthermore, while mainstream narratives of irregular migration tend to represent smuggling facilitators as young and foreign men from the Global South who become rich at the expense of the poor and weak, those who facilitate irregular border crossings include men as well as women of all ages, often migrants themselves living also in precarious conditions and who share the same ethnicity of those who travel with them. In short, smuggling far from constitutes solely a criminal, immoral system of clandestine transportation led by men of colour profiting from the misery of those in transit. Instead, it stands as a system of strategies developed from below by the marginalized in an effort to acquire and mobilize protection, care, and social capital in and for the spaces where migrants, smugglers, and their communities converge.

RACIALIZING THE SMUGGLER

Historically, migration flows have been characterized as invasions, especially when they involve the journeys of gendered and racialized Others (de Haas 2008; Pastore et al. 2006). In North America, current representations of migration flows have mostly focused on depictions of migrants riding atop cargo trains, traversing deserts on foot, or looking exhausted and unkempt as they are detained by immigration authorities against the background of what is construed to be the US–Mexico border. These representations have also included images and narratives of the United States Border Patrol agents as overwhelmed by the arrivals of unaccompanied migrant women and children from Central America seeking asylum, alongside extensive coverage on the criminal and inhumane acts of human smugglers.

Characterizations of smugglers as Mexican males involved with criminal organizations vested in the facilitation of the flows of 'illegal aliens' are part of the US 'gendered construction of immigrant danger' (Golash-Boza and Hondagneu-Sotelo 2013). Current migration flows into the United States have been blamed on smugglers by the media and politicians alike, and claims that smuggling organizations have developed efficient mechanisms to market their services across entire sections of the continent have been voiced at length.[1]

In the context of US national security discourses, smugglers have been historically and systematically racialized as Mexican. US narratives of 'coyotes'—the colloquial term for smugglers in the United States and Latin America—depict them as violent and criminal Mexican men who prey on 'illegal aliens', a proxy for Mexican migrants (Chavez 2013). Journalistic reports of smugglers who abandon migrants in the desert (Lordsburg 2016) or who lie to their clients in order to secure their business and fail to deliver on their promises depict them as Mexican (Saul 2016). Coyotes are also described as possessing an almost animalistic sexual prowess (Darby and Price 2016), a characterization that echoes that of Latinos as unable to control their sexual drive or as sexually promiscuous (Asencio 2010).

In recent years, coyotes have become habitually portrayed as operating in connection with other illicit enterprises, namely Mexican drug traffickers (another role prominently racialized in geopolitical risk narratives). An onslaught of reports suggests Mexican drug-trafficking organizations haven taken over the migrant smuggling market (Slack 2015), racializing smugglers as Mexican by proxy.

Among the pantheon of characterizations of young males of colour as national security threats, migrant smugglers generate particular concern. Not only are they able to overcome border restrictions and enforcement, but scholars have claimed they are increasingly becoming constituted as members of dangerous criminal networks of transnational reach, or as possessing impressive levels of organizational sophistication and technological prowess (Andreas 2000). Smugglers are also dangerous for what they *could* do. Some researchers have argued migrant smugglers are

---

[1] For examples of the coverage see Kahn (2016); Palencia and Menchu (2016); and Solis (2016).

involved in the trafficking of women and children for the sex trade (Europol-Interpol 2016), in the smuggling of nuclear material (Zaitseva and Steinhäusler 2014), and even in the intentional—or even worse, unintentional—smuggling of terrorists into the United States (Bensman 2016). Their earnings are routinely claimed to exceed those of other criminal markets such as drug or weapons trafficking (Naim 2005), their resources and connections allowing them to evade or corrupt law enforcement at will, leaving behind a trail of suffering and death.

While the role of smugglers must not be minimized, the often sensational-ist nature of the rhetoric of tragedy, death, violence, and transnational crime that dominates the narratives of irregular migration ultimately mask the fact that clan-destine migrations and their facilitation are a response to the lack of channels for legal entry and transit for so many yet specific migrant Others. Furthermore, amid the panic caused by the gendered, racialized, and often racist narratives of smuggling and those behind their facilitation, its complex and multifaceted dynamics as one of many paths into irregular migration have hardly been the subject of academic inquiry.

FINDING THE SMUGGLERS

Despite the abundance of references to smugglers in media, law enforcement, pol-icy, and academic circles, there is a shortage of empirical data on their activities. The alleged inaccessibility of smuggling has led many to focus solely on the law enforce-ment aspects of the practice, such as the identification of smuggling networks and their alleged members, their techniques, routes, and costs (Europol-Interpol 2016). While descriptions of the operations of smuggling groups abound in these reports, the vast majority are based on the most extreme, graphic, and stereotypical exam-ples of smuggling cases, typically those involving failed journeys, significant loss of life, or extraordinary instances of violence or neglect (Koser 2008; Zhang 2008). Accounts also exclude the less sinister forms of irregular migration facilitation, such as smuggling carried out among and on behalf of friends and family members that lack criminal intentions or profit expectations (Abel 2012). Also overlooked are visa overstays and the many instances when migrants rely solely on the individual, col-lective, and/or aggregated knowledge acquired over generations to move on to their desired destination (Sanchez and Natividad 2017).

The study of smuggling as a practice must involve the deployment of methodolo-gies that identify the ways in which people 'consent, resist and reshape the social rela-tions of power within a complex matrix of domination and subordination' (Fonow and Cook 2005). Through this lens, smuggling can be approached not only as a crime against the state and its borders, but also as a romanticized exercise of resistance and agency on the part of migrants. Constraints to mobility and responses to challenge them are hardly experienced in isolation: they are instead collective acts imposed and challenged by people through mechanisms that are dependent on collabor-ation and trust (Alpes 2017). Ethnographic interactions among migrants and smug-gling facilitators operating in the US–Mexico migration corridor reveal smuggling is constituted as a communal and collective strategy rather than as an individual mobility project (Sanchez 2015). It is a task facilitated by migrants for migrants (Achilli 2015). This finding alone expands the discursive field that narrowly portrays it as a crime carried out by clandestine transnational criminal networks, avoiding the reinscription of simplistic notions that reduce it to the domain of male, criminal, and foreign Others.

This chapter is based on two independent studies on border-crossing facilitation. It primarily focuses on the experiences of women as migrants as well as smuggling facilitators. In both cases I recruited participants relying on my personal contacts in Mexican migrant communities across the US Southwest where for the last eight years I have conducted research on the facilitation of smuggling and irregular migration. All interviews were conducted in Spanish. The first round of fieldwork was conducted in the city of Phoenix, Arizona between June 2009 and December 2010. It involved twelve interviews with Mexican migrant women who had direct involvement in the facilitation of smuggling along the US–Mexico border. Data were collected through face-to-face interviews and supplemented with information found in court records involving the respondents' convictions for migrant smuggling. Access to interviewees was secured through personal contacts in the local migrant community in Phoenix, Arizona, where I had previously conducted social services work among Mexican migrant women, and by soliciting the collaboration of former clients, friends, and their relatives. I did not identify women as 'smugglers' or 'coyotes'. Drawing from Mary Romero's methodological approaches on Chicana domestic workers (Romero 1992), I was aware of the stigma connected with the facilitation of border crossing as well as of the vulnerability of its facilitators in the context of immigration enforcement controls, and therefore I reached out to my networks, making clear I was interested in researching the experiences involving the border crossings of Mexican women and their implications to the safety of themselves and their families. On one occasion, I was asked by one respondent if that was actually a topic worthy of being studied, who then urged me to look for a more interesting theme.

The second project involved twenty-five open-ended interviews conducted between March 2014 and December 2015 with Mexican and Central American migrant women who successfully crossed the US–Mexico border with the assistance of a smuggling facilitator. During April to May 2014 and December 2015 I resided in Salt Lake City, Utah, a city of 190,000 inhabitants, at the home of my main contact, a member of the Mexican immigrant community known for her work assisting migrants in securing goods and services upon their arrival to the city. This relationship was central to my gaining access to a large group of Latino migrant women, and allowed me to know and interact with the respondents and their families on a more personal level.

In both projects, I openly disclosed my work as a researcher, and conducted participant observation alongside interviews. I spent time with respondents, their friends, and family members at churches, libraries, schools, stores, and waterparks; on weekend outings to the mountains, at casinos, and at their places of employment; I met with their employers, neighbours, and co-workers, most of whom were aware of the nature of my respondents' border-crossing experiences. The data collected from these additional sources ratified the statements of my respondents and further increased the validity of their responses.

WOMEN AND SMUGGLING

The women interviewed did not fall within a specific category nor fit a unique profile. If at all, they shared what Achilli (2015) refers to as a 'protracted condition of illegality'. They lacked state-sanctioned immigration status. All of them had entered the United States with the assistance of a smuggling facilitator and remained undocumented.

Among all women, the decision to migrate had been their own, for motives ranging from domestic violence to family reunification goals to the personal desire to get an education or to travel. They specifically sought the assistance of a smuggling facilitator as a way to improve their chances of a successful and safe crossing. All women had opted to travel with a smuggler after having been denied a US visa. Smugglers were not hard to find: their own friends or relatives had at some point travelled with one, or they had friends and families who were themselves involved in the facilitation of transits.

Blanca's[2] testimony is reflective of the immediacy of smuggling ties among migrants. She travelled from Mexico with her cousin, who was known in her community in central Mexico for guiding groups to the US–Mexico border. Blanca's husband, Moreno, was already in Salt Lake City and wanted to be reunited with his wife:

My husband was already here and wanted me with him so I came. I just told my dad and told him that I was going to leave. My dad thought it was going to be very dangerous … [But] I traveled with my husband's cousin. He was the one who used to guide [people] from the village. He came to the house and met with my dad and told him: I'll take care of your daughter, I'll help her. What I mean is that I am taking responsibility for her [journey], he said. And that way my dad was less worried. And that was how I came. But my husband's cousin *was not a smuggler*: he was a migrant too; he just worked putting together groups for the other guy, the one who waited for us at the border.

Blanca travelled with a relative who performed a specific task in smuggling. Her cousin was connected to a group who facilitated border crossings. These ties gave Blanca the confidence to engage in a journey that, while precarious, was marked by the protection her cousin would provide. She also felt protected by the promise that her relative had made to her father. She was, however, prompt to emphasize that her relative was not a smuggler per se, but rather a member of her own community, who would bring clients to another guide who would in turn lead the group to their destination. While the tasks he performed would have been defined as those of a smuggler, Blanca did not consider her relative as such.

---

[2] All names have been changed to protect the identity of respondents.

Women's experiences as migrants also give them an opportunity to learn the tasks involved in the facilitation of border crossings. The often dramatic incidents that are experienced in smuggling may also lead them to feel inclined to assist others in transit, including the facilitators themselves. Marilu, for example, had travelled with a smuggler who treated her well but who was arrested in the process of transporting her group. In response, Marilu volunteered to stay at the safe house for a few days assisting the facilitator's wife with her tasks:

We had been walking for several days but the smuggler treated us well. It just took a very long time to get to where we would get picked up. When we got to the meeting point, we had to jump into a car; the coyote drove the women first, *he wanted us to be safe* [my emphasis]. We got to a vacant lot in Phoenix and the coyote said, my wife is waiting for you ... his wife was nice. I was the only woman in that group so she asked if I could please prepare food for the rest and I did. Then [the facilitator's wife] got a call that her husband had gotten caught [by Border Patrol]. I did not feel at risk so I told the lady I could stay there and help her. I cooked and cleaned for the groups, I just watched and learned. A few days later a driver came that was finally going my way so I left, and the lady was very grateful that I had helped her. I learned a lot being there.

The narratives of smuggling often emphasize the victimization and violence migrants face at the hands of smugglers, and fail to identify the kinds of interaction that take place between migrants and smugglers. In the case of Marilu, she believed the wife of the facilitator who guided her would need help in the absence of her husband and opted to support her in solidarity. Marilu was never forced to stay at the safe house, even though she had to remain there until a driver who could transport her to Salt Lake City arrived.

Many of the women shared similar stories of supporting male and female smuggling facilitators during their transits. Angelica, for example, described a tense moment in the experience of a migrant she travelled with:

Before we started walking the guide told me to get a pack of lozenges, that they were going to come in handy when we walked through the desert. He said, put them under your tongue with the wrapper and all, that way you won't get thirsty and your mouth won't get dry. And I did. But that day we had walked for too long. We ran out of water, of everything and there was a guy there who was ... he was about to pass out. And all I had left was the wrapping of my last lozenge. Right as he was going to collapse, we ran toward him and I put the wrapper under this tongue. It was as if he had come back to life. The coyote freaked out, he and his helpers came and we cared for the guy, we gave him water, and he recovered.

Caring for migrants in transit while simultaneously facing the extreme conditions of the trail constitutes a challenge for both smugglers and migrants. Together they are often faced with the decision of having to leave injured or hurt migrants behind. The decision is not easy, as multiple respondents disclosed, having witnessed people they had walked with for days being too weak or hurt to continue the journey or even die ('You just want to stay, but how? You have walked all that way too and don't want to get caught,' said Angelica, who disclosed that eventually the group decided to leave the young man and his companion by a road where they would be picked up by Border Patrol). While smugglers and migrants often come together to rescue or support those in extreme distress, at other times they also make the decision to leave those they travel with behind with the hope that rescue arrives for them.

On occasions, women are known to protect and provide care even against their facilitation partners' wishes. Mrs Quintas, at sixty-two years of age, entered the smuggling facilitation market by occasionally hosting migrants in transit. Court records attested to her concern for the people she housed. On one occasion, she went as far as demanding that coyotes hiding from the police left her apartment as she believed they were scaring the two young migrants staying in her home. In court records, one of the two men staying with her one night testified:

She was a very nice lady. The coyotes took us to her place after they found out police had found the safe house. The coyotes walked right into her apartment saying they would need to spend the night there along with my friend and I. And so, Mrs Quintas got angry and she told them: 'you are only scaring these kids. They can stay but not you.' Once the coyotes were gone, Mrs Quintas fed us and then set up blankets in the kitchen so that we could spend the night. She fed us breakfast before someone else stopped by to pick us up.

WOMEN, SMUGGLING, AND PRECARITY

Among the women charged with smuggling, their introduction to facilitation involved performing smuggling-related tasks in response to requests for help from friends or relatives. Respondents expressed that at times they feel obliged to accept, especially if their relatives were male or elderly, or if they had come to their help at a time of need. Leonor, for example, was arrested and convicted for what a prosecutor argued was her participation in a complex migrant smuggling ring. Leonor had been living with her elderly aunt and uncle, who had welcomed her, her husband, and their child into their apartment at a time when they could not afford rent on their own. A few days after moving into her relatives' apartment, Leonor realized they were cooking and delivering food and water to a house where migrants stayed. 'They were old, and sometimes they were not able to carry the food to the back of the car on their own so I helped them with that. That was my way of paying back.' Leonor was arrested when during surveillance she was identified as the woman placing a water case on the boot of her uncle's car.

While assisting friends and family members constitutes a frequent entry point for women into smuggling, financial motivations also rank high in women's decisions to participate and/or join smuggling groups. Most women were employed full time, yet had been looking for an opportunity to make additional income. Women expressed a desire for independence and found in smuggling a mechanism to support themselves. Among the women in the Arizona group one owned a food truck, another had a house cleaning service, and several were self-employed as nannies, maids, or office cleaners, which often allowed them to set their own schedule. The opportunity to connect with smuggling facilitators and business opportunities came through the connections the women made in their primary jobs (those providing their most significant or consistent form of income). Elizabeth owned a food truck, but had a second job at weekends in a beauty salon.

It was here where she first met two brothers who often spoke about their work coordinating border crossings:

I met them at the salon. They were clients. I approached them myself, I told them I could get them people I knew through the salon, and that was how I started to work with them.

Elizabeth's statement also highlights a common trait among facilitators: their entrepreneurial nature. As Zhang noted in his work among Chinese migrant smugglers, having worked independently for most of their lives or having to depend on informal markets, facilitators tend to have a history of being resourceful and on the lookout for business opportunities (Zhang 2007). Elizabeth worked as a coordinator, also putting migrants in contact with her two partners.

As previously noted, a common trope in the mainstream narratives of smuggling is the notion that smuggling profits are substantial. In fact, smuggling is often described as one of the most profitable of illicit markets, behind drug trafficking and the sex trade (Europol-Interpol 2016). While the earnings cited in the literature are impressive, the realities of the smuggling economy at the micro level challenge that notion. The very fact that women remain employed despite and during their participation in the facilitation of smuggling services reveals the limitations of smuggling-related income.

Among all women, smuggling-related income was supplemental only— while welcome, it could not be entirely relied on. This is because contrary to the perception that smuggling services are in high demand, they are rather unpredictable in nature. Facilitators are not guaranteed a specific income or compensation for their services. There is in fact no way for a facilitator to know in advance or with precision the number of crossings he or she will be asked to help with over a specific period or the kind of support migrants in transit will need. Factors as dissimilar as weather and the intensity or frequency of surveillance also play a role in the availability of work for smuggling facilitators (Andreas 2000). These variables often translate as reduced smuggling-related opportunities and, consequentially, bring limited, inconsistent earnings. Mayra, a woman convicted for using her bank account to receive smuggling fees, questioned about the extent and destination of her profits, stated: 'I used the money to make my car payment—I have a small Ford. I also use the money to pay for gas and for my other monthly bills.'

Mayra's bank account records verified her claims. Her smuggling-related earnings had not exceeded a couple of hundred dollars per month at the peak of her participation in facilitation. Her main source of income came from her work at a local catering business. Her total monthly earnings never exceeded US$600.

The unreliability of smuggling leads most smuggling facilitators to hold jobs in more stable and predictable markets. This is specially the case for women, who hold full-or part-time jobs in the service and hospitality industries aware that smuggling earnings alone will not cover their expenses.

Along these lines the gender pay gap is also an important factor to consider in how smuggling impacts women's experiences in the market. The majority of the tasks women perform in smuggling are feminized. They cook, clean, or take care of children; receive and process smuggling fees; and broker contacts between migrants and facilitators. These tasks, while fundamental in the success of clandestine journeys, yield significantly less compensation than that received by men: women make about 50 per cent less than men, who are most often among those driving vehicles along highways, acting as guides or lookouts across vast distances; transporting groups out of state; and serving as security or enforcement staff at safe houses. Women's tasks in smuggling are often perceived as menial or peripheral, while those performed by men are construed as more dangerous and physically challenging and therefore as more valuable or important (Sanchez 2016).

Given the disparity, many women opt at times to be paid in-kind, exchanging smuggling services for goods or services in times of need. Women are also more likely to use their earnings to cover household expenses such as rent, food, the payment of basic utilities, and school supplies and uniforms for their children. Smuggling earnings are immediately recirculated into the local economies of border and migrant communities, used to cover basic everyday needs. In other words, the earnings facilitators receive are far from destined to enrich large transnational criminal organizations as law enforcement and policy narratives claim (Europol-Interpol 2016). Instead, they remain among working-class, low-income communities along the migrant trail.

ANALYSIS AND CONCLUSION

The journeys of irregular migrants have captured the attention of migration scholars. Yet the most visible of irregular migration's actors alongside the migrant, the smuggler, has remained a stigmatized, feared, and often despised character, almost invariably characterized as violent, criminal, and foreign. Perhaps unwittingly, this has led to an exaggerated focus on experiences of victimization in migration scholarship, a subsequent silencing of perspectives of smuggling facilitators, and a lack of engagement with critical approaches towards the facilitation of migration.

Literature depicting the graphic and raw nature of clandestine migratory transits has given rise to a specific body of work that while important at identifying abuse patterns has often been at risk of fetishizing migrants and their experiences, in the process reinscribing notions of irregular migration as inherently abject, criminal, and savage. Relying on problematic tropes of violence and victimization as analytical cornerstones, despite regular calls for the need to change narratives, as scholars we often forget that there is more to consider than the stories, the tragedies, the victims, the violence, and the vilification of migration spaces. The so-called migration 'crisis' in Europe and the plight of Latin American unaccompanied minors to the United States, along with the many other high-profile examples of human mobility of late, seem to have only refuelled the collective demand for controlled/closed borders (de Haas 2008). This call has been critically answered through scholarly engagements with borders as spaces of despair, death, and decay where migrant and refugee bodies become irreparably damaged through the deployment of immigration laws and enforcement practices and the inhumane actions of depraved human smugglers. Yet again, our interventions as scholars have hardly (1) engaged in criticism of our own colonial gaze when it comes to the treatment of migration or (2) been effective at expressing alternative imaginaries and views of borders that can lead to conceiving, articulating, and then mobilizing change (Weber 2015).

Showcasing the racialization of smuggling, and describing the roles of women in smuggling, constitutes an attempt to draw attention to how the narrow emphasis of smuggling as a crime has led not just to the reification of notions of migrants as victims, but to that of those behind their journeys as criminals. By outlining basic elements of smuggling dynamics and the experiences of its actors I do not seek to romanticize smugglers or their communities nor to mask the often violent intentions of some smuggling organizations and their manifestations. However, I do challenge the blanket label given to smugglers as transnationally organized or as set up in sophisticated networks of international reach. To monolithically and consistently designate migrant smuggling as networks glamorizes activities that are far from sophisticated and, as Koser (2008) states, the actions of smugglers who are indeed predatory. Notions of smugglers' prowess, riches, leadership, and hierarchical organization have been consistently mobilized despite little or no evidence. The emphasis on narratives of organized crime and national security threats have instead hidden the profoundly private and often intimate dynamics of smuggling and its actors—both migrants and smugglers alike—which has in turn allowed the practice to be perceived as under the domain of transnational criminals of poor repute.

While the dramatic experiences of migrants are effective at capturing the public's attention momentarily—and in generating an almost preternatural sense of condemnation against smugglers' actions—they are also fast forgotten amid other stories of global suffering. Furthermore, the frequency and the visibility of these tragedies seem to have a minimal impact, if any, on migration policy or practice. In fact, mainstream narratives of smuggling have systematically exonerated the state from its role in the creation of regimes of vulnerability, which in turn rely on the mobilization of migration enforcement practices that target the most unprotected of migrants—those deemed ineligible to secure documents that would otherwise grant them access to safe transit and who often work as smugglers themselves.

As migration restrictions have expanded globally, it is common for many to suggest that the demand for smuggling services has also expanded or to explain the materialization of human smuggling in places where it had not been seen before as a sign of the growing power of criminalized smuggling networks. There are less conspiratorial reasons for smuggling's emergence.

As smuggling increasingly becomes articulated as unprecedented, academics must challenge the ahistorical engagements that often render invisible the community-initiated and -centred forms of protection from those who throughout history have been rendered undesirable or unwanted. Smuggling is only one of the multiple mechanisms and efforts that, in response to colonial and imperialistic practice, have been devised by the people to counteract restrictions to migration. As such, overcoming surveillance and control should not merely be depicted as a task pertaining to the realm of powerful networks of transnational criminals. At the centre of our analysis should be not just those we portray as smugglers, but rather as Crouch and Missbach state, those who are arrested for smuggling (Crouch and Missbach

2013)—or as this paper has identified, the ways in which the marginalized become further criminalized.

The experience of migration—with its tragedy, its joys, its uncertainty, and hope—constitutes an essential element of migrants' individual, private, and intimate histories. Conceiving clandestine journeys solely as criminal is to rewrite the history of migrants by force, and in a way dispossessing them from something that truly and solely belongs to them.

REFERENCES

Abel, R. M. (2012), 'Who's Bringing the Children? Expanding the Family Exemption for Child Smuggling Offenses', *Michigan Law Review First Impressions* 110: 52–62.

Achilli, L. (2015), *The Smuggler: Hero or Felon?* Florence: European University Institute.

Alpes, M. J. (2017), 'Why Aspiring Migrants Trust Migration Brokers: The Moral Economy of Departure in Anglophone Cameroon', *Africa* 87(2): 304–21.

Andreas, P. (2000), *Border Games*. Ithaca, NY: Cornell University Press.

Asencio, M. (2010), *Latina/o Sexualities: Probing Powers, Passions, Practices, and Policies*. New Brunswick, NJ: Rutgers University Press.

Bensman, T. (May 2016), 'The Ultra-Marathoners of Human Smuggling: How to Combat the Dark Networks that Can Move Terrorists over American Land Borders', *Homeland Security Affairs* 12, Essay 2 (May). Available at: https://www.hsaj.org/articles/10568

Brennan, D. (2014), *Life Interrupted: Trafficking into Forced Labor in the United States*. Durham, NC: Duke University Press.

Casillas, R. (2017), 'Visible and Invisible: Undocumented Migrants in Transit through Mexico', in S. Bender and W. Arrocha (eds), *Compassionate Migration and Regional Policy in the Americas*. London: Palgrave Macmillan, 143–58.

Chavez, L. (2013), *The Latino Threat: Constructing Immigrants, Citizens, and the Nation*. Stanford, CA: Stanford University Press.

Crouch, M. and Missbach, A. (2013), *Trials of People Smugglers in Indonesia: 2007–2012*. Centre for Indonesian Law, Islam and Society. Melbourne: Melbourne Law School, University of Melbourne.

Darby, B. and Price, B. (2016), 'Rape Trees, Death Migrants and the Consequences of an Open Border', *Breitbart*, 25 April. Available at: http://www.breitbart.com/texas/2016/04/25/rape-trees-dead-migrants-consequences-open-border/2016

De Haas, H. (2008), 'The Myth of Invasion: The Inconvenient Realities of African Migration to Europe', *Third World Quarterly* 29(7): 1305–22.

Dimmitt, A. L. (2013), 'Mexico's Missed Opportunities to Protect Irregular Women Transmigrants: Applying a Gender Lens to Migration Law Reform', *Pacific Rim Law & Policy Journal* 22: 713–49.

Donnelly, R. and Hagan, J. M. (2014), 'The Dangerous Journey: Migrant Smuggling from Mexico and Central America, Asia, and the Caribbean', in L. A. Lorentzen (ed.), *Hidden Lives and Human Rights in the United States: Understanding the Controversies and Tragedies of Undocumented Immigration*. Santa Barbara, CA: Praeger, 71–106.

Dunai, M. (2016), 'Police Recount Journey of 71 Migrants who Died in Austria as Investigation Ends', *Reuters*, 12 October. Available at: http://www.reuters.com/article/us-europe-migrants-austria-bodies-idUSKCN12C1V9

Europol-Interpol (2016), Executive Summary, *Migrant Smuggling Networks: Joint Europol-Interpol Report*. Brussels: Europol-Interpol. Available from: https://www.europol.

europa.eu/sites/default/files/documents/ep-ip_report_executive_summary.pdf+&cd=2&hl=en&ct=clnk&gl=us

Fonow, M. M. and Cook, J. A. (2005), 'Feminist Methodology: New Applications in the Academy and Public Policy', *Signs: Journal of Women in Culture and Society* 30(4): 2211–36.

Golash-Boza, T. and Hondagneau-Sotelo, P. (2013), 'Latino Immigrant Men and the Deportation Crisis: A Gendered Racial Removal Program', *Latino Studies* 11(3): 271–92.

Holman, J. (2016), 'Portrait of a People Smuggler', *Al Jazeera Magazine*, 25 January. Available at: http://www.aljazeera.com/indepth/features/2015/12/portrait-people-smuggler-151231125324569.html

Hooper, J., Kingsley, P., and Quinn, B. (2015), 'Smugglers Abandon Migrant Ship off Italy in New Tactic to Force Rescue', *The Guardian*, 2 January. Available at: https://www.the-guardian.com/world/2015/jan/02/smugglers-abandon-migrant-ship-italy-ezadeen

Isacson, A., Meyer, M., and Morales, G. (2014), *Mexico's Other Border: Security, Migration, and the Humanitarian Crisis at the Line with Central America*. Washington DC: Washington Office on Latin America. Available at: http://www.wola.org/files/mxgt/report

Izcara Palacios, S. P. and Yamamoto, Y. (2017), 'Trafficking in US Agriculture', *Antipode*. doi: 10.1111/anti.12330.

Johnston, C. (2015), 'Migrants Suffocated in Overcrowded Hold of Boat, Say Reports', *The Guardian*, 16 August. Available at: https://www.theguardian.com/world/2015/aug/15/migrants-suffocated-in-overcrowded-hold-of-boat-reports-say

Kahn, C. (2016), 'Surge of Central American Migrants to US could Rival 2014 Wave', National Public Radio, 1 June. Available at: http://www.npr.org/2016/06/01/480335693/surge-of-central-american-migrants-to-u-s-could-rival-2014-wave

Kirchgaesnner, S. (2016), 'People Smuggler Behind 700 Deaths at Sea is Convicted in Italy', *The Guardian*, 13 December. Available at: https://www.theguardian.com/world/2016/dec/13/people-smuggler-behind-700-deaths-at-sea-is-convicted-in-italy

Koser, K. (2008), 'Why Migrant Smuggling Pays', *International Migration* 46(2): 3–26.

Lordsburg, N. M. (2016), 'Border Patrol Agents Rescue Undocumented Migrants Abandoned in Desert', KVIA, 23 December. Available at: http://www.kvia.com/news/new-mexico/border-patrol-agents-rescue-undocumented-migrants-abandoned-in-desert/229017040

Mainwaring, D. and Brigden, N. (2016), 'Beyond the Border: Clandestine Migration Journeys', *Geopolitics* 21(2): 243–62.

Martínez, D. E., Reineke, R. C., Rubio-Goldsmith, R., and Parks, B. O. (2014), 'Structural Violence and Migrant Deaths in Southern Arizona: Data from the Pima County Office of the Medical Examiner, 1990–2013', *Journal on Migration and Human Security* 2(4): 257–86.

Naim, M. (2005), *Illicit: How Smugglers, Traffickers and Copycats are Hijacking the Global Economy*. New York: Random House.

Ochoa O'Leary, A. (2012), 'Of Coyotes, Crossings, and Cooperation: Social Capital and Women's Migration at the Margins of the State', in T. Matejosky and D. Wood (eds), *Political Economy, Neoliberalism, and the Prehistoric Economies of Latin America*. Bingley, UK: Emerald Group, 133–60.

Palencia, G. and Menchu, S. (2016), 'Central Americans Surge North, Hoping to Reach U.S. before Trump Inauguration', *Reuters*, 24 November. Available at: http://www.reuters.com/article/us-usa-trump-immigration-centralamerica-idUSKBN13J2A7

Pastore, F., Monzini, M., and Sciortino, G. (2006), 'Schengen's Soft Underbelly? Irregular Migration and Human Smuggling across Land and Sea Borders to Italy', *International Migration* 44(4): 95–119.

Pickering, S. and Cochrane, B. (2013), 'Irregular Border-crossing Deaths and Gender: Where, How and Why Women Die Crossing Borders', *Theoretical Criminology* 17(1): 27–48.

Price, B. (2017), 'Human Smugglers Abandon 4-Year-Old Girl in Desert', *Breitbart*, 5 March. Available at: http://www.breitbart.com/texas/2017/03/15/human-smugglers-abandon-4-year-old-girl-desert/

Romero, M. (1992), *Maid in the USA*. New York: Routledge.

Sanchez, G. (2015), *Human Smuggling and Border Crossings*. London: Routledge.

Sanchez, G. (2016), 'Women's Participation in the Facilitation of Human Smuggling: The Case of the US Southwest', *Geopolitics* 21(2): 387–406.

Sanchez, G. and Natividad, N. (2017), 'Reframing Migrant Smuggling as a Form of Knowledge: A View from the US-Mexico Border', in C. Guznay and N. Witjes (eds), *Border Politics: Defining Spaces of Governance and Forms of Transgressions*. Switzerland: Springer International Publishing, 67–84.

Saul, J. (2016), 'Border Mayhem: Murder, Extortion and Trafficking by a Devil', *Newsweek Online*, 16 September. Available at: http://www.newsweek.com/smuggler-coyote-migrants-deaths-violence-hostage-cocaine-499851

Slack, J. (2015), 'Captive Bodies: Migrant Kidnapping and Deportation in Mexico', *Area* 48(3): 271–7.

Solis, D. (2016), 'Immigrant Flow of Families and Children at Border Matches Crisis of a Few Years Ago and Can Get Significantly Worse', *Dallas News*, 17 October. Available at: https://www.dallasnews.com/news/immigration/2016/10/17/central-american-migrant-flow-rises-level-2014-surge

Vogt, W. A. (2013), 'Crossing Mexico: Structural Violence and the Commodification of Undocumented Central American Migrants', *American Ethnologist* 40(4): 764–80.

Weber, L. (ed.) (2015), *Rethinking Border Control for a Globalizing World: A Preferred Future*. Vol. 55. Abingdon and New York: Routledge.

Zaitseva, L. and Steinhäusler, F. (2014), *Nuclear Trafficking Issues in the Black Sea Region*. Non-Proliferation Papers no. 39. Geneva: Non-Proliferation Consortium.

Zhang, S. (2007), *Smuggling and Trafficking in Human Beings: All Roads Lead to America*. Westport, CT: Praeger and Oxford: Harcourt Education.

3

Gender, Race, and the Cycle of Violence of Female Asylum Seekers from Honduras

Lirio Gutiérrez Rivera

INTRODUCTION

Located in Central America, Honduras is one of the poorest, most unequal, and violent countries in the world. In 2014, the Human Development Index report from the United Nations Development Programme ranked it at 131, on a 188-point scale on which Niger ranked lowest (United Nations Development Programme 2016). The social, political, and economic conditions of Honduras are harsh: there has been political instability and increasing violence since the coup d'état in 2009. The homicide rate is 59 per 100,000 (Gagne 2016). Non-state armed actors, including *maras*,[1] gangs, and other organized crime groups, control residents and local economies in many low-income urban neighbourhoods. Around 70 per cent of Hondurans live in poverty, more than two-fifths (42.6 per cent) of whom live in extreme poverty (United Nations Development Programme, undated).

Poverty, inequality, and, increasingly since the turn of the century, gender-based violence and crime has forced many Hondurans to migrate internally and externally in search of safety. According to the Global Report on Internal Displacement, gender-based and criminal violence and gangs internally displaced 174,000 women, children, and men in Honduras in 2015 (Internal Displacement Monitoring Centre 2016). In one year (2014–15), the number of internally displaced persons in Honduras increased six times. Today they account for around 2.5 per cent of the total population.

The number of people fleeing Honduras and the Central American region is shocking. Even though there are no official records of the total sum on the move, asylum requests by men, women, and children have increased exponentially in receiving

[1] Gang presence is not new in Central America; their presence in the cities dates from the mid-twentieth century. However, gangs proliferated in Central America in the late 1980s. *Maras* evolved from some of the local street gangs into more sophisticated organizations with transnational roots because of the migration/deportation of some of its members from the United States (Cruz 2010; Rodgers et al. 2009). Today there are two *maras*: the Mara Salvatrucha and the 18th Street Gang (La Dieciocho).

countries. In just one year, in 2015, for example, Costa Rica registered a 176 per cent increase in asylum claims, in Mexico there was a 164 per cent increase, and in the United States asylum claims rose by 250 per cent (Sturm 2016). More than half of those fleeing violence and gangs, whether displaced internally in Honduras or abroad, are women and their children, or unaccompanied minors (United Nations Refugee Agency 2015). There are no signs that these internal and/or external movements will stop as violence, inequality, and poverty persist.

The difficult conditions that characterize the lives of many Hondurans in their home country and abroad intersect with race, gender, and class differences that have roots in colonialism and US foreign policy in the Central American region. Colonialism and US influence have created racial categories as well as political, economic, and social structures that legitimize unequal power relations that subordinate and oppress certain sectors of society in the home and receiving countries. Women and children from disadvantaged socio-economic backgrounds, distinguished by 'ethnoracial markers' such as skin tone and colour, are placed at the bottom of the scale of social stratification, where they have restricted access to resources, and their subordination, exploitation, discrimination, and exclusion is normalized (Bailey et al. 2016; Massey 2009).

This chapter explores how race, gender, and class intersect in the forced migration of Honduran women. Scholarship on Central American migration is not new (Blanchard et al. 2011; Golash-Boza 2015; Menjívar 2013; Zilberg 2011). Yet, although scholars have taken into account the role that gender plays in migration (Kron 2007, 2016; Menjívar and Abrego 2012; Menjívar and Salcido 2002; Morales Hernández 2014), the effect of race and racism in the mobility, subordination, and oppression of these women has rarely been examined. Further compounding matters, surprisingly little attention has been paid to the historical relationship between the United States and Central America or the ways in which migration and crime policies have disproportionately and negatively impacted Central American women and their children.

This chapter argues that Honduran women are caught in a cycle of violence linked to global migration, crime policies, and the historical relationship between the United States and Central America. It further suggests that these factors produce and are themselves a direct consequence of gender and racial inequalities. To develop this argument, I draw upon the declarations of thirty-five women aged between eighteen and sixty seeking asylum in the United States from 2014 to 2016 that I gathered in a research project on gender and urban violence, as well as a series of reports on gender-based violence and internal displacement and the emerging secondary literature in this area of border criminology.

In the following section I discuss the impact of gender-based violence on Honduran women in Honduras and abroad, its connection to the unequal relations between the United States and Central America, and contemporary migration and crime policies. This section also explores the intersections of gender-based violence with race and class. The next section is based on the declarations of Honduran women seeking asylum in the United States. It discusses the reasons behind this cycle of violence as well as the subordination and oppression of Honduran women. The chapter concludes that racial and gender inequalities are linked to global and historical processes that legitimize violence and oppression towards Honduran women in their home country and abroad.

OVERVIEW OF THE CYCLE OF VIOLENCE SUFFERED BY HONDURAN WOMEN

Honduras is a difficult and dangerous place for women, especially for those from the lower socio-economic classes whose lives are characterized by restricted access to labour markets, health, and education. Inequality in Honduras is both gendered and racialized. Women experiencing inequality and poverty generally have a dark skin tone, or their physical characteristics signal their indigeneity or African descent (Bailey et al. 2014). Racial categories and skin tone in Latin America are highly correlated with social privilege or discrimination; people with lighter skin tones generally enjoy more privileges than those with darker skin colour. In addition to being at the bottom of the social hierarchy, those with darker skin are excluded, exploited, and experience a wide range of discrimination (Bailey et al. 2016; Hunter 2007; Massey 2009).

The structural inequality of racialized Honduran women connects to Latin America's history, as the discrimination and exclusion of certain groups based on racial categories and skin tone colour (also known as colourism) have their roots in European colonialism (Hunter 2007; Mignolo 2005; Quijano 2000; Wade 2010). In his now classic article 'Coloniality of Power, Eurocentrism, and Latin America', Quijano (2000) maintains that historical racial categories that were set during the colonial period contributed to the current model of global power. Quijano refers to this global structure of power, control, and hegemony as the 'coloniality of power'. The colonial period classified the world population around an idea of 'race' that assumed and naturalized a structure of biological difference in which some 'races' were considered inherently inferior or superior in relation to others.

Poverty and inequality also contribute to structural (Galtung 1969) and racial violence towards and against women (Cross 2013). According to figures from 2013, one woman in Honduras is killed every 13.8 hours and on average 18 complaints about violence against women are filed every day (Centro de Derechos de Mujeres et al. 2014). Women are raped, tortured, abused physically and psychologically, and killed. Most perpetrators are men. They are usually known to the female victim and include her partner, spouse, family member, friend, or a gang member. Honduras has one of the highest rates of femicide in Latin America[2] and femicide rates are linked

---

[2] According to the Economic Commission of Latin America and the Caribbean, Honduras has the highest femicide at 13.3 per 100,000 women, followed by El Salvador (5.7 per 100,000 women), and Dominican Republic (3.6. per 100,000 women) (Gender Equality Observatory, Economic Commission for Latin America and the Caribbean 2016). Yet, according to UN Women, Honduras has the third-highest homicide rate after El Salvador and Guatemala.

to the country's homicide rate, which is also high.[3] Globally, Honduras is ranked seventh for rates of female homicides (United Nations Refugee Agency 2015).[4]

The impact of US–Honduran policies on women in Honduras

Poorer, racialized women in Honduras are not only considered inferior because of the colour of their skin, but are also subject to machismo attitudes that normalize the use of violence against women in their home and on the street. Around 20,000 complaints of domestic violence have been filed each year at the Public Prosecutor's Office since 2010 (Immigration and Refugee Board of Canada 2013). Compounding matters, women from socio-economic disadvantaged backgrounds tend to reside in low-income or poor urban neighbourhoods that are generally controlled by gangs and *maras*. In order to secure the survival of their gang and to establish themselves as an 'authority' in the neighbourhoods, gang members dominate residents through extortion, threats, and the forced recruitment of children and adolescents. Female residents with male children may be affected if they try to prevent their recruitment. In some cases, women are coerced to be 'girlfriends' of gang members or are forced to have sex with the members of the whole gang (Levenson 2013; United Nations Refugee Agency 2015).

It is important to acknowledge the historical roots of the different forms of violence that Honduran women experience in the US relationship with Central America and their ties to current migration and crime policies. Since the nineteenth century, US foreign policy towards Central America has been unilateral, aggressive, and interventionist (Loveman 2016; Schulz and Sundloff Schulz 1994). Initially it focused on limiting European influence, enabling US territorial expansion and encouraging American commerce (Loveman 2016). The nascent Central American democracies at this time viewed relations with the United States as an opportunity to enter the world market. They also saw US investment as a form of development. However, weak state formation processes and political instability, as well as different views on foreign policy, placed Central America in a subordinate position, from which the region has never fully recovered.

US foreign policy has, for many years, dominated and influenced Central American politics with the purpose of protecting US economic, political, and security interests, often at the expense of such matters locally. Honduras has been no exception. From campaigns to overthrow Leftist leaders across the region that date to the 1950s, to the more recent and well-known war on drugs, US policy has left an indelible imprint on local communities. The Honduran government's crime control policies, known as *Mano Dura*, offers a good example of this effect. In addition to a range of anti-drug and security policies like Plan Mérida, and the Central American Regional Security Initiative, these policies, targeting drug-trafficking crime and

---

[3] In 2015, the homicide rate was 44.9 per 100,000, the third-highest homicide rate on the planet (Manjoo 2015; Observatorio de Muertes Violentas de Mujeres y Femicidios 2015).

[4] The highest femicides rates are in Latin America followed by Eastern Europe and Russia. The United States and Europe have the lowest femicide rates (Small Arms Survey 2012).

violence, were established in return for US funding and assistance (Arrarás and Bello-Pardo 2015).

These policies, which reflect the asymmetrical relationship between the United States and Central America, have structurally reinforced the racialization and construction of Central Americans as poor and inferior (Kramer 2016), further strengthened by the criminalization of immigration law (Stumpf 2006) and the legal and racial violence that has targeted 'Latinos' and 'Hispanics' of Mexican and/or Central American origin (Vázquez 2015). Such matters, Bibler Coutin (2000; 2011) demonstrates, make it difficult for Central American migrants to claim political asylum even when, as I shall argue below, they provide significant evidence of systematic violence.

Violence as a push factor of internal and external migration

Violence is a key reason why women migrate internally and externally (Cantor 2014; United Nations Refugee Agency 2015). In 2015, out of a national population of 8,075,000, Honduras registered 174,000 internally displaced persons (Comisión Interinstitucional para la Protección de Personas Desplazadas por la Violencia 2015). This figure is six times higher than the previous year (Internal Displacement Monitoring Centre 2016). Approximately 51 per cent of those forced to relocate within Honduras are women (Norwegian Refugee Council and Internal Displacement Monitor Centre 2015).

Initially, female victims of violence attempt to find a safer and less violent neighbourhood in Honduras. However, due to their financial dependency and other constraints, women are often unable to afford housing in 'safer' and affluent neighbourhoods, and end up moving to a different neighbourhood controlled by the same or another gang or criminal group. When women do not succeed in relocating to another region or area of Honduras, or when it becomes clear that they will not receive protection from the state, they may attempt to leave the country. To do so, they usually travel (without documents) through Guatemala and Mexico with or without a 'coyote' (a human trafficker; see Sanchez, this volume). Once they cross the US border, they either surrender to border officers and risk time in a detention centre, or they settle in a city. Some later apply for asylum.

On their voyage, Honduran migrants are confronted by racialized and gendered immigration regimes that, as Golash-Boza (2015) points out, are designed to restrict movement northwards of persons who are black or brown (e.g. Haitians, Muslims, Central Americans, Mexicans) (see also Chacón and Bibler Coutin, this volume). Mexico is particularly dangerous for Central American migrants, especially women (Human Rights Watch 2016; Shetty 2014). Even though, on paper, its national law offers protection to persons who are at risk if returned to their country of origin, Mexican immigration officials often fail to recognize Central American migrants as refugees. In 2015, only 1 per cent of Central Americans apprehended by Mexican immigration officials were recognized as refugees or received formal protection (García Bochenek 2015). Reports from organizations such as the UN Human Rights Commission (UNHCR), suggest that Honduran (and Central American) women take extra precautions when crossing Mexico.

As Gabriela Rodriguez, the UN Human Rights Commissioner's special rapporteur on migrants, stated, 'Mexico is one of the countries where illegal immigrants are highly vulnerable to human rights violations and become victims of degrading sexual exploitation and slavery-like practices...' (Grayson 2002).

Upon arrival in the United States, female asylum seekers and undocumented migrants remain vulnerable. In addition to a restrictive legal regime, they face differential treatment and unequal access to social, cultural, and economic resources because they are racialized as 'Hispanic' or 'Latina'. Such racialization places these women once again at the bottom of the socio-economic hierarchy, where they become an 'exploitable and excludable' group (Massey 2009). Such matters are further amplified by the growing reliance on criminal law to control and regulate migrants (Aliverti 2012; Menjívar 2016; Provine and Doty 2011; Stumpf 2009; Vázquez, this volume).

At the time of writing, the US (and Mexican) governments continue to refuse to acknowledge that Salvadorians, Guatemalans, and Hondurans fleeing gender-based violence are refugees. This legal standpoint has made it difficult for Honduran women to qualify for asylum. Central Americans have been perceived and racialized as poor economic migrants and, under current migration law, are criminalized for being undocumented. For many judges and prosecutors, Honduran women escaping gender-based violence do not qualify for political asylum. Rather, they have broken the law by illegally entering the country; thus, they should be deported. However, judges have been divided since 2014, when the Board of Immigration Appeals ruled in favour of the asylum claim of a woman from Guatemala who was fleeing domestic violence. Under the claim that she was a member of a 'particular social group', that is, she was persecuted under the grounds of particularity such as 'race, religion, nationality in a particular social group, or political opinion', she qualified for asylum (Matter of A-R-C-G, *Harvard Law Review* 2015).

Attorneys defending Honduran women's asylum claims used the 'particular social group' argument in their cases. However, as most of those I interviewed indicated, this legal defence was not easy to demonstrate because of the negative perceptions of Hondurans (and Central Americans in general). Such perceptions, attorneys suggested, lead some judges to associate banal matters, such as type of dress, fingernails, and haircut with a connection to the gangs or *maras*. 'We are dealing with a particularly difficult judge', one attorney explained, 'who assumes that my client's son is part of a dangerous gang just because his nails are long. I tried to explain that he is not a gang member'. Often, the prosecution questioned the 'particular social group' argument, by arguing that Central America was neither a war zone, nor was it going through a humanitarian crisis. Such attitudes limited the defence's claim that gender-based violence towards women was a systematic problem in Honduras.

UNPACKING THE CYCLE OF GENDER-BASED VIOLENCE AGAINST HONDURAN WOMEN

Gender-based violence in the country of origin

The declarations I gathered from thirty-five Honduran women seeking asylum in the United States from 2014 to 2016 revealed that they all had experienced a similar pattern of violence in the home country and abroad. Women who fled their home had endured physical, psychological, and sexual abuse from a family member or their partner or spouse. At home, this abuse was generally carried out by their male parent (their biological father and/or stepfather) and, to a lesser degree, a female parent (their biological mother or stepmother) during childhood or adolescence. Women described being beaten, raped, and demeaned in their home. As 'Nicole'[5] reports, beatings and sexual assault from her father were accepted by her mother while growing up:

My father was an alcoholic who frequently beat my mother. In his drunken rages, my father hit me and worse, sexually abused me. When I told my mother about the abuse, she told me to keep quiet, and did nothing to stop his abuse.

The different forms of gender-based abuse and violence the women described illuminate the 'patriarchal structural violence' (Brock-Utne, cited in Mazurana and McKay 2001) inherent in Honduran society and suggest that oppression and the legitimation of male domination over women has been normalized and accepted in families and the wider society. This form of violence, the women's accounts make clear, sustains preference towards males and unequal allocation of food, health, and education (Mazurana and McKay 2001). Take, for instance, education. All the women seeking asylum whose testimonies I obtained had not finished either primary or secondary education. Parents had not sent them to school because they believed their daughter should do the domestic work at home (cleaning, cooking, caring for other family members) or were unable to go to school because they were too poor.

Pregnancy was another reason why women dropped out of school. In addition to their low level of education, nearly all of those in my sample had become pregnant at an early age (between thirteen and sixteen years old). They were unable to continue their schooling because their parents had encouraged or forced them to live with the father of the child to fulfil the gender roles expected of females as a mother and wife.

Poverty limited all of the women's options to become financially and emotionally independent. Many sought to mitigate their financial difficulties by living with their boyfriend. As 'Teresa' and 'Angela' made clear, the women often hoped their partner would offer a form of emotional protection and financial security:

At first being with [with my boyfriend] promised to be an escape from abuse I suffered at home. When [my boyfriend] asked me to move in together I hoped that he would protect me from my father's abuse. ('Teresa')

I met [my boyfriend] in the summer ... [he] was about fifty years old at the time. I believe that [my boyfriend] and his family had a lot of money and property. ('Angela')

Protection and safety, however, were often short lived. Soon after moving in, all the women in the sample experienced abuse and violence from their partner. In their declarations, they reported that intimate male partners grossly mistreated them for a range of circumstances. Issues they mentioned included violence upon becoming pregnant, violence when they searched for a job, violence when they met a friend,

---

[5] Not her real name, all participants have been given pseudonyms.

violence for failing to be at home, or simply violence because of jealousy. The following quote from 'Sara' is typical:

[My boyfriend] and I were arguing when he began violently punching and kicking me. He threw me down the stairs and rapidly punched me in the stomach over and over again until I bled . . . and lost consciousness. ('Sara')

Similarly, 'Sofia', who lived in the capital, Tegucigalpa, described how her jealous boyfriend beat her because she ran into a male friend:

The first time [my boyfriend] beat me was when my sister-in-law and I went to pick up some of my clothes from my mother's house. I ran into one of my old friends on our walk, and we talked for a while. After my sister-in-law told [my boyfriend] about my encounter with my male friend, he flew into a jealous rage. He hit me and threw me out on the street to sleep outside that night. ('Sofia')

'Carolina's partner 'punished' her by denying her sustenance: 'The threats grew worse, and [my boyfriend] continued to deprive me of food as a way to abuse and control me, she reported. The partner of 'Teresa' hired a hitman:

I am confident that [my boyfriend] hired the man on the motorcycle to kill me. Only three or four days before I was shot, he told me that he would rather see me 'buried' or underground than with another man. ('Teresa')

In all cases, the women reported that their partners sought to oppress and subordinate them. As Lomot (2013: 24) notes, 'domestic violence keeps women out of the economy through fear'. In turn, their financial dependence on their partners makes it difficult for women to leave. When the women in this group did finally depart, typically they either first returned to their parents or went to a relative's house. Here they were often exposed yet again to violence and abuse. Many were urged to go back to their partner. Such treatment was evidently considered 'normal':

While I was hopeful that [my boyfriend] would not abuse me, I was accustomed to abuse at home, and thought that some degree of violence was acceptable in a relationship. My mother used to tell me that it was natural for my husband to beat me from time to time. Most of Honduran society believes this too. ('Gladys')

The Honduran women in my sample were not only unsafe in their homes, but they also experienced gender-based violence in their neighbourhoods. Most could only afford to live in low-income areas that were dominated by gangs and/or *maras*. Whereas gangs (or *pandillas*) are more local, 'home-grown' gangs, *maras* are gangs with transnational roots because of the migratory patterns of their members (Rodgers et al. 2009). Both gangs and *maras* use different forms of violence to control resources and residents.

Some women pointed out that when their partners joined the gang, they became more violent in the house not only because gang members encouraged the use of violence towards women, but also because of alcohol and drug consumption and the use of firearms:

After [my boyfriend] began associating with these gang members, the brutality and frequency of his beating escalated. He became even more reckless than he was before. He assaulted me with knives and guns. Once, he attacked me with a knife and left a scar on my arm. ('Carolina')

Others were victimized because their partner was a member of a 'security' group. Because of failed police reforms and democratization processes which, in turn, have led to the proliferation of 'self-help security' groups in low-income urban neigh-bourhoods (Willis 2015), public security has become decentralized in Honduras as it has in many other countries in Latin America. In Honduras, some residents of very violent neighbourhoods have established their own 'security' groups in the absence of state protection, with the purpose of protecting residents from the *maras* and gangs. Both gangs and *maras* perceive these 'security' groups as a challenge to their authority and attack them as well as their families, including the women.

Simply being a member of a certain family may also be a reason for persecution by gang members. For example, when a male relative (i.e. a brother or a nephew) refuses to comply with threats from a gang, gang members may threaten and torment the whole family. Female relatives are bullied, stalked, beaten, and raped. Threats and violence from gang members displace women and their family. Initially, they move to another house or neighbourhood. As 'Vanessa' describes, they moved constantly hoping they could go back to their house:

We bought a new cell phone number. We began to move from house to house, not staying for more than a day or two. After about nine days we had exhausted the places we could stay and everyone returned to the house, hoping the danger had passed. ('Vanessa')

While women sought protection from the state when the threats and violence con-tinued, they rarely received it. Instead, all of the women reported that the police discouraged them from filing a report. These state officials too, it seemed, perceived the women as subordinates:

I went to the police and asked for a protective order that would prevent [my boyfriend] from coming to my home. The police told me that these types of threat and violence are common within domestic relationships and there was nothing they could do ... The officers told me it was normal for a man to force his woman to have sex. Then one of the officers gave me the complaint back and told me that as [my boyfriend's] woman I just had to put up with it.' ('Nicole')

The lack of protection for female victims of violence, their lives of poverty, and persistent violence, abuse, and threats from a partner or gang member are part of a common cycle of gender-based violence that Honduran women experience and that leads to their internal and external migration. This cycle of gender-based vio-lence not only reinscribes racial and gender categories established in the colonial period that have kept women from the lower classes subordinated, oppressed, and at the bottom of Honduran society, but, more recently has become a push factor for Honduran women to migrate abroad. 'After two months of [harassment from] (my partner)', 'Ana' reported,

I decided my son and I needed to leave Honduras. I didn't think we could hide from him forever in Honduras. The Mara Salvatrucha are everywhere. I left in May 2014 with my son. We arrived at the US border later that month.

On November 9, 2014, I gave birth to my second son in New York. Since he was born, Alfredo has found out through posts by mutual acquaintances on social media that I am in the United States and that I gave birth to his child here. I did not give my son (his father's) last name because I did not want him to have the last name of a gang member who had [threatened me and] treated me so badly.

I now work in a Mexican restaurant to support myself and my two sons. I am very happy that Alfredo is not involved in my son's life. I don't want him to be raised by a gang member and I don't want him to ever be forced to join a gang. (Ana)

While some, like 'Ana', manage to escape, as the next section will demonstrate, in their attempts to flee gender-based violence in their home country many women endure new forms of gender-based violence and racism upon arrival in the United States.

Gender-based violence abroad and qualifying for asylum

Upon arriving in the United States, Honduran women seeking asylum encounter new forms of racial and legal violence in the 'complex manner in which law exerts its influence and control' (Menjívar and Abrego 2012: 1383). As undocumented migrants, they are controlled and regulated by immigration law that has 'gradually intertwined with criminal law' (Menjívar and Abrego 2012: 38), casting them as unwanted and suspect racial 'others'. 'Sharon' offers an example:

While my asylum case was pending, I was in (New Jersey) when a police officer pulled me over and informed me that there was a problem with my licence plate. I had borrowed the car from my uncle that morning because my ride to work had cancelled last minute and I had no other way to make the long commute to work.

When I was pulled over, the ID I produced listed my name as X, I sometimes use (that) name which is my mother's maiden name because I never had a good relationship with my father and still have painful memories of his abuse. The officer believed I was trying to misrepresent my identity even though that was never my intent. I was arrested and charged on four offences. My public defender explained the circumstances of what happened and that I had used the car without reason to believe it was stolen … I was placed later on probation. I completed all my community service. ('Sharon')

As Carbado (2005) explains, 'racial naturalization' is a method of categorization that determines inclusion and exclusion. As criminal law and immigration law intersect, asylum seekers from Latin America like 'Sharon' are placed at the bottom of the US socio-economic hierarchy, where they are exploited and excluded (Massey 2009). This was the experience of all the Honduran women from the sample. Many struggled to find work and like 'Luz', those who succeeded were concentrated in precarious and poorly remunerated fields: 'When I arrived in the US,' she recalled, 'I first found a job picking fruit, and then worked as a housekeeper.' Others remained dependent on a family member or were unable to work altogether because they were in a detention centre with their children.

As Menjívar (2011) observes, illegal status places migrants at the bottom of society with limited access to resources and rights in transit countries (i.e. Mexico) and the receiving country. Thus, undocumented status intersects with race and with class, as

Honduran women have limited access to education, housing, employment (that is, only in unqualified jobs). As Vázquez (2015) points out, race plays a role in criminalizing, controlling, and subordinating certain migrants, particularly those with ethno-racial markers and/or brown, black, or dark skin colour. The construction of Honduran and Central American migrants as 'criminal aliens' is part of the larger structure of crimmigration that involves their racialization, incarceration, detention, and removal (Vázquez 2015). It also undermines their demands for sanctuary.

The use of criminal law to control immigrants, and the comments made at hearings support the negative and racialized perceptions of Hondurans (and Central Americans) as 'free riders', 'criminals', and 'dangerous' people, which are prevalent in both official discourses and media representations. As studies have pointed out, immigration law and enforcement have become a site for racial formation and differential treatment of certain groups considered inferior (Bosworth et al. 2008; Massey 2009; Provine and Doty 2011). Thus, Honduran asylum seekers are more likely to be discriminated against at immigration hearings because of their skin colour or colourism (see *People v. Bridgeforth*).

CONCLUSIONS

For female asylum seekers from Honduras, neither their country of origin nor the receiving country (including the United States) are safe places. As I have shown in this chapter, women are caught in a cycle of violence that inspires their internal and external migration. Even though scholars have observed the feminization of migration, this chapter highlights that the feminization of migration in Honduras (as well as El Salvador and Guatemala) is linked to violence. The violence experienced by Honduran woman is also connected to migration and crime policies and the US–Central American relationship, which criminalizes, subjugates, and oppresses Honduran women on the basis of their race, gender, and class.

Such racial and gender categories are rooted in colonialism. In the United States and Honduras, these categories are based on different colonial histories, yet both established ethno-racial differences and skin colour to classify the population and to determine which racial groups had more social and economic entitlement than others (Bailey et al. 2016). In her discussion of the work of Maria Lugones (2008) on colonialism, race, and gender, Kerner points out that, aside from establishing racial categories to classify, subordinate, and exploit certain groups, colonialism also introduced a Western gender system which oppressed females:

The second and dark side of the modern/colonial gender system is, by contrast, constituted by the suppression of alternative ways of organizing sex, gender and sexuality that flourished in various world regions before European colonization. What was put in their place by colonization were racist modes of dehumanization and exploitation of colonized females. (Kerner 2013: 14)

This 'coloniality of gender' (Lugones 2008) in tandem with the racially based system of power and classification takes its shape through migration law, official discourses, public policies, and daily practices in which Honduran women are not entitled to avenues for social mobility and are perceived as unworthy and inferior in their home country and abroad because they are racialized as Hispanic, Latina, or Central American. Within the global context of crime, migration, and justice (Bosworth et al. 2008), racial categories such as Hispanic, Latina, Afro, black (Negro), indigenous (*indígena* and the derogatory term indio), as well as other markers of difference such as skin colour, continue to be a powerful source of disenfranchisement and violence experienced by Honduran women in their home country as well as abroad.

REFERENCES

Aliverti, A. (2012), 'Making People Criminal: The Role of the Criminal Law in Immigration Enforcement', *Theoretical Criminology* 16(4): 417–34.

Arrarás A. and Bello-Pardo, E. D. (2015), 'General Trends of Prisons in the Americas', in J. D. Rosen and M. W. Brienen (eds), *Prisons in the Americas in the Twenty-First Century: A Human Dumping Ground*. Lanham, MD: Lexington Press, 1–14.

Bailey, S. R., Fialho, F. M., and Penner, A. M. (2016), 'Interrogating Race: Color, Racial Categories, and Class Across the Americas', *American Behavioral Scientist* 60(4): 538–55.

Bailey S. R., Saperstein A., and Penner A. M. (2014), 'Race, Color and Income Inequality across the Americas', *Demographic Research* 31(24): 735–56.

Bibler Coutin, S. (2000), *Legalizing Moves: Salvadoran Immigrants' Struggle for the U.S. Residency*. Ann Arbor, MI: University of Michigan Press.

Bibler Coutin, S. (2011), 'Falling Outside: Excavating the History of Central American Asylum Seekers', *Law and Social Inquiry* 36(3): 569–96.

Blanchard, S., Hamilton, E. R., Rodríguez, N., and Yoshioka, H. (2011), 'Shifting Trends in Central American Migration: A Demographic Examination of Increasing Honduras–U.S. Immigration and Deportation', *The Latin Americanist* 55(4): 61–84.

Bosworth, M., Bowling, B., and Lee, M. (2008), 'Globalization, Ethnicity and Racism: An Introduction', *Theoretical Criminology* 12(3): 263–73.

Cantor, D. J. (2014), 'The New Wave of Forced Displacement Caused by Organized Crime in Central America and Mexico', *Refugee Survey Quarterly* 33(3): 34–68.

Carbado, D. (2005), 'Racial Naturalization', *American Quarterly* 57(3): 633–58.

Centro de Derechos de Mujeres, Red Nacional de Defensoras de Derechos Humanos de Honduras, Foro de Mujeres por la Vida, JASS-Honduras, Centro de Estudios de la Mujer (2014), *Situación de las violencias contra las mujeres en Honduras*. Available at: http://protectioninternational.org/wp-content/uploads/2014/07/Informe-Violencia-Mujeres-Honduras-RelatoraONU-Junio2014final.pdf

Comisión Interinstitucional para la Protección de Personas Desplazadas por la Violencia (2015), 'Caracterización del desplazamiento interno en Honduras'. Available at: http://www.jips.org/system/cms/attachments/1048/original_Informe_caracterizacion_desplazamiento.pdf

Cross, K. (2013), *The Gendered Effects of Structural Violence*. Proceedings of the 2013 American Political Science Association Annual Meeting, 1–32.

Cruz, J. M. (2010), 'Central American *Maras*: From Youth Street Gangs to Transnational Protection Rackets', *Global Crime* 11(6): 379–98.

Gagne, D. (2016), *2016 Homicide Round-up*, 16 January. Insight Crime.

Galtung, J. (1969), 'Violence, Peace, and Peace Research', *Journal of Peace Research* 6(3): 167–91.

García Bochenek, M. (2015), 'How Immigration Detention and Procedural Shortcomings Undermine Children's Right to Seek Asylum', *Birkbeck Law Review* 3(2): 258–77.

Gender Equality Observatory for Latin America and the Caribbean (2016*), Femicide Latin America and the Caribbean, 2014*. Economic Commission for Latin America and the Caribbean (ECLAC). Available at: http://oig.cepal.org/en

Golash-Boza, T. M. (2015), *Deported. Immigrant Policing, Disposable Labor, and Global Capitalism*. New York and London: New York University Press.

Grayson G. W. (2002), 'Mexico's Forgotten Southern Border: Does Mexico Practice at Home what it Preaches Abroad?' *Backgrounder*, Center for Immigration Studies, 1–11. Available at: http://cis.org/MexicoSouthernBorder-Policy

Human Rights Watch 2016, *Closed Doors: Mexico's Failure to Protect Central American Refugee and Migrant Children*. Available at: https://www.hrw.org/report/2016/03/31/closed-doors/mexicos-failure-protect-central-american-refugee-and-migrant-children#page

Hunter, M. (2007), 'The Persistent Problem of Colorism: Skin Tone, Status, and Inequality', *Sociology Compass* 1(1): 237–54.

Immigration and Refugee Board of Canada (2013), 'Honduras: Domestic Violence, Including Legislation and Protection Available to Victims (2010–November 2013)'. Available at: http://www.refworld.org/docid/52ce9dd14.html

Internal Displacement Monitoring Centre (2016), *People Internally Displaced as a Result of Conflict and Violence*. Available at: http://www.internal-displacement.org/global-report2016/#ongrid

Kerner, I. (2013), 'Differences of Inequality: Tracing the Socioeconomic, the Cultural and the Political in Latin America Postcolonial Theory', desiguALdades.net, Working Paper Series 60: 1–27. Berlin. Available at: http://www.desigualdades.net/Resources/Working_Paper/60-WP-Kerner-Online.pdf?1386253816

Kramer, P. A. (2016), 'Shades of Sovereignty: Racialized Power, the United States and the World', in F. Costigliola and J. M. Hogan (eds), *Explaining the History of American Foreign Relations*.Cambridge: Cambridge University Press, 245–70.

Kron, S. (2007), 'Coyotes, norteños transeúntes y viudas blancas: Transmigración, género y ciudadanía en la frontera guatemalteco-mexicana', Conference paper presented at Taller internacional, Derecho, ciudadanía y género en América Latina, Free University Berlin.

Kron, S. (2016), '"No nacimos de la nada": Border Struggles and Maternal Politics in Mexico', *Citizenship Studies* 20(5): 579–94.

Levenson, D. T. (2013), *Adios Niño. The Gangs of Guatemala City and the Politics of Death*. Durham, NC and London: Duke University Press.

Lomot, R. (2013), 'Gender Discrimination: A Problem Stunting Honduras' Entire Economy', *Global Majority E-Journal* 4(1): 15–26.

Loveman, B. (2016), 'U.S. Foreign Policy toward Latin America in the 19th Century', in *Oxford Research Encyclopedia of Latin American History*, 1–31.

Lugones, M. (2008), 'Colonialidad y género', *Tabula Rasa* 9: 73–101.

Manjoo, R. (2015), *United Nations Report of the Special Rapporteur on Violence Against Women, its Causes and Consequences*. United Nations, 31 March.

Massey, D. S. (2009), 'Racial Formation in Theory and Practice: The Case of Mexicans in the United States', *Race and Social Problems* 1(1): 12–26.

'Matter of A-R-C-G' (2015), *Harvard Law Review*, 128: 2090–7. Available at: https://harvardlawreview.org/2015/05/matter-of-a-r-c-g/

Mazurana, D. and McKay, S. (2001), 'Women, Girls, and Structural Violence: A Global Analysis', in D. J. Christie, R. V. Wagner, and D. A. Winter (eds), *Peace, Conflict, and Violence: Peace Psychology for the 21st Century*. Englewood Cliffs, NJ: Prentice-Hall.

Menjívar, C. (2011), 'The Power of the Law: Central Americans' Legality and Everyday Life in Phoenix, Arizona', *Latino Studies* 9(4): 377–95.

Menjívar, C. (2013), 'Central American Immigrant Workers and Legal Violence in Phoenix, Arizona', *Latino Studies* 11(2): 228–52.

Menjívar, C. (2016), 'Immigrant Criminalization in Law and the Media: Effects on Latino Immigrant Workers' Identities in Arizona', *American Behavioral Scientist* 60(5–6): 597–616.

Menjívar, C. and Abrego, L. (2012), 'Legal Violence: Immigration Law and the Lives of Central American Immigrants', *American Journal of Sociology* 117(5): 1380–421.

Menjívar, C. and Salcido, O. (2002), 'Immigrant Women and Domestic Violence: Common Experiences in Different Countries', *Gender and Society* 16(6): 898–920.

Mignolo, W. (2005), *The Idea of Latin America*. Oxford: Blackwell Publishing.

Morales Hernández, S. (2014), 'Central American Migrants in Transit through Mexico; Women and Gender Violence; Challenges for the Mexican State', *Procedia—Social and Behavioral Sciences* 161: 263–8.

Norwegian Refugee Council and Internal Displacement Monitoring Centre (2015), *Global Overview 2015: People Internally Displaced by Conflict and Violence*. Available at: http:// www.internal-displacement.org/assets/library/Media/201505-Global-Overview-2015/ 20150506-global-overview-2015-en.pdf

Observatorio de Muertes Violentas de Mujeres y Femicidios (2015), *Resultados del análisis enero–diciembre 2015*, Observatorio de la Violencia, Instituto Universitario en Democracia, Paz y Seguridad, Universidad Nacional Autónoma de Honduras, 11: 1–12. Available at: http://www.iudpas.org/pdf/Boletines/Genero/MMEd11EneDic2015.pdf

Provine, D. M. and Doty R. L. (2011), 'The Criminalization of Immigrants as a Racial Project', *Journal of Contemporary Criminal Justice* 27(3): 261–77.

Quijano, A. (2000), 'Coloniality of Power, Eurocentrism, and Latin America', *Nepantla: Views from the South* 1(3): 533–80.

Rodgers, D., Muggah, R., and Stevenson, C. (2009), 'Gangs of Central America: Causes, Costs and Interventions', Small Arms Survey Working Paper 23, Graduate Institute of International and Development Studies, Geneva, Switzerland.

Schulz, D. E. and Sundloff Schulz, D. (1994), *The United States, Honduras, and the Crisis in Central America*. Boulder, CO: Westview Press.

Shetty, S. (2014), 'Most Dangerous Journey: What Central American Migrants Face when They Try to Cross the Border', *Human Rights Now* Blog, 20 February. Available at: http:// blog.amnestyusa.org/americas/most-dangerous-journey-what-central-american- migrants-face-when-they-try-to-cross-the-border/

Small Arms Survey (2012), *Femicide: A Global Problem*, Research Note 14: 1–4. Available at: http://www.smallarmssurvey.org/about-us/highlights/highlight-rn14.html

Stumpf, J. (2006), 'The Crimmigration Crisis: Immigrants, Crime, and Sovereign Power', *American University Law Review* 56(2): 367–419.

Stumpf, J. (2009), 'Fitting Punishment', *Washington and Lee Law Review* 66: 1683–741.

Sturm, N. (2016), 'UNHCR Calls for Urgent Action as Central America Asylum Claims Soar'. 5 April. Available at: http://www.unhcr.org/news/latest/2016/4/5703ab396/ unhcr-calls-urgent-action-central-america-asylum-claims-soar.html

United Nations Development Programme, Honduras (undated), *Reducción de la pobreza*. Available at: http://www.hn.undp.org/content/honduras/es/home/ourwork/povertyreduction/overview.html

United Nations Development Programme (2016), *Human Development Reports: Human Development Indicators, Honduras*. Available at: http://hdr.undp.org/en/countries/profiles/HND/

United Nations Refugee Agency (2015), *Women on the Run: First-Hand Accounts of Refugees Fleeing El Salvador, Guatemala, Honduras, and Mexico*. Available at: http://www.unhcr.org/publications/operations/5630f24c6/women-run.html

Vázquez, Y. (2015), 'Constructing Crimmigration: Latino Subordination in a "Post-Racial" World', *Ohio State Law Journal* 76(3): 599–657.

Wade, P. (2010), *Race and Ethnicity in Latin America*. London and New York: Pluto Press.

Willis, G. D. (2015), *The Killing Consensus: Police, Organized Crime, and the Regulation of Life and Death in Urban Brazil*. Berkeley, CA: University of California Press.

Zilberg, E. (2011), *Space of Detention: The Making of a Transnational Gang Crisis between Los Angeles and San Salvador*. Durham, NC and London: Duke University Press.

Case law

ABC v. Thornburgh, 760 F. Supp (N.D. Cal. 1991).

People v. Bridgeforth, New York Court of Appeals, 2016.

II

RACE, POLICING,
AND SECURITY

4

Racism, Immigration, and Policing

Ben Bowling and Sophie Westenra

INTRODUCTION

Immigration policing is a vexed political and social issue in many parts of the world. In January 2017, following presidential candidate Donald Trump's pledge to deport 11 million undocumented migrants, the US Homeland Security Secretary recommended the deployment of troops to support police and immigration officers in the detection, apprehension, detention, and removal of illegal immigrants. Across Europe, policing the flows of the hundreds of thousands of refugees arriving from North Africa and the Middle East has preoccupied policymakers for the last several years. And in the UK, the focus of this chapter, immigration control was one of the key issues that influenced the June 2016 vote to leave the European Union. In each case, the starting point for official debates is that illegal immigration is a growing problem that requires new and more vigorous defensive, surveillant, coercive, and punitive interventions. This approach is most eye-catching when migrants clash with border police as they breach the fences erected to keep them out. However, control measures also include new laws, special courts, detention centres, and the deployment of military and police forces. All efforts focus on excluding and removing the problem of the unwanted immigrant.

This chapter focuses on immigration policing as one element of an emerging 'crimmigration control system' (Bowling and Westenra forthcoming; Stumpf 2006). We define policing broadly as law enforcement, investigation, order maintenance, surveillance of suspect populations, and information sharing (Reiner 2010) as they appear in relation to immigration. This form of police work focuses on surveillance of the movement of people across borders and within domestic space, detection of those who arrive unlawfully or overstay visa conditions, and feeds into punishment and deportation. It also includes measures to control migrants' access to work, housing, healthcare, and transport. These practices are carried out by an assemblage of police and immigration officers, aided by members of the public, the private sector, and community agencies who are drawn in to policing processes.

The goal of this chapter is to explore the ways in which racism shapes immigration policing. We use the concept of racism to examine the *discourse* that defines phenotypic difference between people as a criterion for inclusion and exclusion and

Racism, Immigration, and Policing. Ben Bowling and Sophie Westenra. © Ben Bowling and Sophie Westenra, 2018. Published 2018 by Oxford University Press.

the actual *practices* of exclusion based on visible difference. We examine the persistence of difference in defining immigration as a problem in public policy, how ethnic and racial differences contribute to the formation of suspicion and shape enforcement practices. Examining the role of domestic police, immigration officers, and emerging global policing practices, we conclude that ideas about race and ethnicity contribute to law, police culture, and enforcement practices at various 'sites of enforcement' (Weber and Bowling 2004). We argue that migration policing *within* the border, *at* the border, and *beyond* borders tends to invoke racial and ethnic characteristics in ways that create 'suspect communities'. This, we suggest, leads to restrictions on the enjoyment of fundamental rights and freedoms consistent with Richmond's (1994) claim that a system of global *apartheid* is being created.

IMMIGRATION POLICING: SITES OF ENFORCEMENT

Mass migration of human populations is an enduring feature of human history and of contemporary life in a globally connected world. Millions of people cross borders every day for work or leisure; others are on the move fleeing poverty, famine, and war, or in search of a better life. Migration is a key facet of global neoliberal thinking, an imperative to ensure that labour is free to move to where goods are manufactured and where services are required. It provides a crucial economic engine not only through migrant labour but also the estimated $600 billion that is returned in the form of remittances to migrants' families overseas. While the global economy requires migration to be unrestricted, however, new forms of surveillance, coercion, and control have emerged.

In a globally mobile world, the border has moved from the physical edges of nation states to become more variegated and diffuse (see Milivojević in this volume). Airports, often in the geographical heartland of a country, for example, are key locations for the entry and exit of passengers through border control. Moreover, new technologies allowing people on the move to be tracked before they leave their destination and after they have arrived disperse the border. As a result, we can say that there has been a proliferation of 'sites of enforcement' at which immigration law is enforced and through which migrant communities are regulated (Weber and Bowling 2004). Figure 1 illustrates the multisite immigration policing system.

Immigration policing is a multi-level and highly complex system. Its central plank is the border check that is carried out by the UK Border Force, but also includes internal controls operated by Immigration Enforcement and various branches of national, metropolitan, shire, and city police services. Internal immigration law enforcement has become transversal, crossing boundaries between internal and external, public and private organizations and reaching into many aspects of social life (Bowling 2013: 297; Pickering and Weber 2013). Police-like powers of search, seizure, and arrest have been granted to Border Force and Immigration Enforcement officials, which allow them to operate as a fully functioning independent police force (Macdonald and Toal 2010). As coercive powers 'migrate' from the criminal justice system into agencies that were previously regarded as administrative, the

TRANSNATIONAL SURVEILLANCE AND ENFORCEMENT

Carriers' liability	Harmonization of asylum policy	European Border and Coastguard Agency	Interpol travel documents database	Five Eyes' Initiative

PRE-ENTRY CONTROLS

Immigration liaison officers (posted overseas)	Extraterritorial borders control	Consulting shared databases	Watch lists/ No fly lists	Pre-entry clearance
	Border posts	Border patrols	Fences	Military

BORDER PROTECTION

Border Force	Border Force Intelligence Directorate	National Border Targeting Centre	National Crime Agency	Special Branch

IN-COUNTRY ENFORCEMENT

Immigration Compliance and Enforcement (ICE)	Enforcement by domestic police forces	Immigration checks on crime victims and witnesses	Multi-agency enforcement teams (Nexus)	Special Branch
Employer sanctions	Public 'tip off' hotlines	Landlord vetting of tenants' 'right to rent'	University student surveillance	Entitlement cards
Health service checks	Private security	Field intelligence officers	Government departments/ MP surgeries	Driving while 'illegal' policing

DIFFUSE LOCAL SURVEILLANCE

Fig. 1 Migration policing: sites of enforcement, developed from Weber and Bowling (2004)

responsibility to police the border stretches. These days, within the border, employers, landlords, and healthcare providers are required by law to check the immigration status of applicants, tenants, and patients. Beyond the border, airlines are enlisted as private immigration enforcers, subject to fines under the Immigration (Carriers' Liability) Act 1987 for allowing passengers to board flights to Britain with inadequate documentation. The 'sites of enforcement' framework set out in Figure 1 guides our understanding of the dynamics of these developments in immigration policing. Our discussion now turns to the intersection between race and the various spheres of domestic enforcement and surveillance, border control, and extraterritorial policing.

RACE, RACISM, AND MIGRATION

The starting point for understanding racism is the belief in 'race' as a valid way of categorizing human beings into immutable, unchanging, inherently different populations identified by biological characteristics (Kleg 1993). According to Kleg, the idea of race is associated with visible differences in skin and eye colour, hair texture, body shape, and other physical features that are taken as indicators of differences in geographical origin. It is well established that differences between so-called races are literally only skin deep: genetic differences within racially defined populations are as great as those between such populations. The fact that race, as a means of differentiating populations, has no scientific basis does not diminish its impact or consequences (Montagu 1943). It takes on a 'common sense meaning' in which characteristics and significance are attributed to imagined biological differentiation. This view is closely related to the belief that specific racial groups exhibit negative social or cultural characteristics that will pollute others if they are allowed to mix with those outside their group. The ideology of racism rests on the belief that 'certain groups are innately, biologically, socially, morally superior to other groups based on what is attributed to be their racial composition.' (Kleg 1993: 95). Notions of racial purity and exclusivity can be found in extremist discourses as well as popular understandings of racial difference (ibid.). Following from this, the implicit or explicit assumption is that specific geographical areas—continents, countries, or parts of those countries—'belong to' or should be designated to one or other particular group (Richmond 1994). The idea of racial territorialism and exclusivity are an important feature of both political and popular discussions of migration, appearing either explicitly or implicitly in racially coded language (Smith 1989).

The construction of the racial or ethnic other has changed over time. Historically, a range of groups seen as 'others' included Jews, gypsies, and Irish travellers (Weber and Bowling 2008). At times, the attribution of otherness has focused on all those not seen as members of the 'British race' including 'white' ethnic minorities such as Southern and Eastern Europeans, a phenomenon referred to as xeno-racism by Fekete (2001). The racialization of practice and ideology and its pseudo-scientific basis developed through the nineteenth and early twentieth centuries (Bolt 1971; Reeves 1983: 176). This approach fitted with the historical context, justifying the growth of the Empire and the establishment of colonies (see Bruce-Jones, this volume). However, it was in the second half of the twentieth century, when black people from the Empire and New Commonwealth came to live and bring up their children in Britain, that a new ideology was ushered in. Asynchronic ideological deracialization (Reeves 1983: 178) is a process that explains the discrepancy between 'the social observer['s] informed assessment of a situation as "racial", and the account offered by the social actors, in which no mention is made of racial processes'. This state of affairs may be further confirmed in 'the experience of racial minority groups who feel that their lives are circumscribed by unjust racial practices of which whites appear callously oblivious' (Reeves 1983: 178).

Racism can take an extreme version that can be found in the history of formal racial state formations and in both historical and contemporary explicitly racist political parties or movements. These tend to prohibit (either culturally or by law) sexual contact between races, restrict rights to employment, social contact, and settlement. This thinking lies behind policies that seek to separate residential settlement, places of work, transport, entertainment, and sexual relations that can be found in various forms of segregation, ghettoization, apartheid, and the 'colour bar' (Richmond 1994; Smith 1989). It also underpins less extreme practices of restrictions on the numbers of migrants who are perceived to be racially different and policies directed at removing them. Smith (1989) argues that the ideology of 'race', pervading political discourse and 'common-sense' racism, is the medium through which iniquitous social and economic arrangements secure popular legitimacy. De facto racial exclusion is, therefore, a politically constructed policy outcome. For Smith, institutional racism is a pervasive process sustained across many different social institutions whose policies produce a mutually reinforcing pattern of racial inequality. Organizations develop conventions that distinguish 'the deserving from the undeserving and the reputable from the debased' that invoke attributes of race or ethnicity, explicitly or implicitly, as criteria for inclusion and exclusion in dispensing scarce resources (Smith 1989: 102).

Richmond (1994) argues that both the *practices* of Western migration control systems and the *ideological justifications* articulated to defend these measures are strikingly similar to those of the South African apartheid system now discredited and prohibited under international law. These include the explicitly racist variants (to be found in the literature and websites of extreme right-wing groups and political parties) that refer to the preservation of the 'white race' from racially or culturally inferior people and also the more moderate discourses referring to the maintenance of Britain's ethnic and national identity, Christian religion, and the English language. Like apartheid, Western migration policies are also justified as a means to preserve state security and to defend communities against threats to law and order. The requirement to regulate population movement is also coupled with the desire to maintain economic advantage, and to control immigrants' access to employment, housing, education, and healthcare. Policies of separation, containment, and exclusion and their justifications, which were argued forcefully in South Africa until the demise of the apartheid regime, are now being promulgated across the Global North and are being emulated in the more powerful emerging economies (Richmond 1994).

RACE, IMMIGRATION, AND POLICING IN THE UK

In the wake of recent political events such as the 2016 UK referendum vote to leave the European Union, the 'migration crisis', and presidential campaigns abroad, it is clear that the kinds of racial thinking referred to in the previous section are present, in various forms, in debates about migration. Indeed, from the earliest records, public discussion about immigration has been infused with concern about 'race' (Fryer

1984; Gordon 1983; 1985). Extreme right-wing politicians point to the problems that minorities are believed to bring with them (such as crime, disorder, and ethnic conflict), while popular racism is mobilized around such issues as the depression of wages; pressures on housing, schools, and public services; and fears of cultural change. However, not all would accept that immigration policing is racist. Rather, immigration policing is presented as a necessary response to the 'illegal migrant', 'bogus asylum seeker', or 'foreign national criminal' based on 'intelligence-led' assessments of 'risk'. This is what Reeves (1983: 189) terms 'sanitary coding'. As a key component of the emerging adiaphorized crimmigration control system (Bowling and Westenra forthcoming), this is the perfect narrative. Such rationalization of differential treatment of human beings conceals racism but it does not force it out of existence (Aliverti 2015: 127).

The development of the UK immigration control system in the 1960s and 70s— the Commonwealth Immigrants Acts of 1962 and 1968, and the Immigration Act 1971—institutionalized racism. No use is made of overt racial categories: the 1962 Act purported only to control immigration from the Commonwealth through the use of employment vouchers; the 1968 Act to control citizens of the UK and colonies who had 'no substantial connection with Britain'; and the 1971 Act to grant individuals with a family relationship—i.e. a father or grandfather born in the UK—a special position in law (Reeves 1983: 209). Yet the informed social observer would note the substitution of racial categories for superficially non-racial ones that coincided with other features of black and Asian migrants at the time, i.e. the fact that many of the so-called 'coloured immigrants' were unable to obtain jobs from abroad, or that their father or grandfather would not have been born in Britain. The 1971 introduction of the concept of patriality 'injected a clear as opposed to a discrete racial distinction into official immigration policy' (Holmes 1988: 309). Indeed, these Acts are widely taken as beginning the process of institutionalizing racism in the British state (Gordon 1983: 12). The application of state coercion to black migrants on entry, as well as in policing those already in the country, was thus legitimized, albeit concealed in non-racial terms. Moreover, the implementation of these obliquely racialized laws generated further racialized practice. Because it is impossible to tell a 'legal' from an 'illegal' immigrant, or an immigrant from a citizen born in Britain, these laws inevitably enshrined policing practices in which suspicion and coercion fell on all those who *appeared* to be immigrants (Gordon 1983: 17; see Parmar, this volume).

Domestic policing in the UK has been deeply shaped by its relationship to enforcing immigration law (Bowling 1998; Gordon 1983). It is notable that domestic police forces (and the Immigration Service) were exempt from anti-discrimination legislation—such as the 1965 and 1976 Race Relations Acts—despite their frequently racist behaviour and deteriorating relationship with black and minority ethnic populations, because the state required the police to enforce immigration control. In practice, the burden of immigration control—and the suspicion of being an illegal immigrant—fell on black and minority ethnic people. Research shows that racism and xenophobia in the public discourse was found in concentrated forms in police culture, with early observational work revealing deeply shocking levels of individual, cultural, and institutional racism (Bowling 1998; Smith and Gray 1985). Police tended to frame ethnic minorities as an unwelcome presence in British society, who were predisposed to crime and disorderliness and thus legitimate targets for proactive policing (ibid.). This led, in turn, to oppressive policing in the neighbourhoods where minority communities were concentrated. Routine practices such as stop and search, raids on workplaces and places of entertainment were all disproportionately targeted at minority communities (Bowling and Phillips 2007; Gordon 1983). At the same time, there is strong evidence that these same communities were not well served by the police when they experienced racist violence or were victims of crime more generally (Bowling 1998). The overall picture that emerges from the very extensive research on policing minority ethnic communities is one of 'over-policing' and 'under protection' (Bowling et al. 2008) rooted in institutional racism (Macpherson 1999).

IMMIGRATION POLICING WITHIN THE BORDER

Home Office policy defines the goal of internal immigration policing as creating a 'really hostile environment for illegal migrants'.[1] Leaving aside the racialized social construction of illegality through varying visa regimes and controls (an important aspect of the problem), the enforcement of such a policy inherently relies on racialized practice. Parmar (Chapter 7 of this volume) citing Goldberg 2015, states that '[m]igrants are hyper-visible, socially badged by a mix of non-belonging markers like language, dress, and implicitly skin color'. In the context of internal migration policing, however, only *some* migrants are hyper-visible because of the markers identified by Parmar and 'illegal' migrants are not visible at all, but are indistinguishable from 'legal' ones. At the same time, the Home Office's policy focus on 'illegal migrants' as its central concept has the effect of casting all visible minorities as suspicious persons (Cook 1996: 23).

Immigration Enforcement (IE) is the operational command responsible for local immigration enforcement via nineteen Immigration, Compliance and Enforcement (ICE) teams based across the UK (ICIBI 2015: 10). Working closely with local crime and intelligence teams, ICE teams comprise of arrest-trained Immigration Officers, with powers to interview, arrest, and detain suspected immigration offenders. These powers include criminal powers (under sections 28A to 28K of the Immigration Act 1971) and similar, more frequently used, administrative powers under Schedule 2. The primary focus for IE is illegal working, so ICE teams conduct workplace enforcement visits—also known as 'passport raids'—to locate and detain illegal workers with a view to removing them from the UK. More recently, IE has adopted an auxiliary strategy of engaging with businesses through 'educational

---

[1] In a BBC Radio 4 interview discussing the Immigration Bill, 10 October 2013, then Home Secretary Theresa May said the bill was intended to 'create a really hostile environment for illegal migrants [because] what we don't want is a situation where people think that they can come here and overstay because they're able to access everything they need'.

visits'. The fact that such language conjures a friendly public image is hardly coincidental. Enforcement visits have long been the subject of condemnation, viewed as 'witch-hunt[s] of the black community' (Gordon 1983: 37). There is a clear desire to de-racialize IE's policies by emphasizing its service to the community as a whole (see Jakubowski 1997). Similarly, the prioritization of 'employer engagement' and 'voluntary departures' represents employer collaboration and a saving of resources in internal migration policing. With the recognized goal of scaring workers into voluntary return, the difference between 'educational' and 'enforcement' visits is of little practical significance for minority ethnic communities. The Home Office has consistently denied allegations that IE engages in 'racial profiling' through the assertion that all enforcement activity is 'intelligence-led'. Whether or not IE engages in 'fishing expeditions',[2] this claim sets up a false dichotomy. The idea of 'intelligence-led' internal migration policing is a form of sanitary coding (Reeves 1983) that obscures the content and source of its 'intelligence' while ensuring that the burden of this form of immigration policing will fall disproportionately on people from minority ethnic backgrounds.

Both IE and Border Force have appointed Field Intelligence Officers (FIOs) within Operational Intelligence Units and Border Force Intelligence Teams respectively, to develop intelligence. In spite of this, there is an acknowledged lack of clarity in 'field intelligence' activity (ICIBI 2016: para 6.59). In fact, allegations from the public are heavily relied upon. An ICIBI inspection on the intelligence functions of Border Force and IE reported that there were a total of 74,617 allegations entered on the Intelligence Management System in the twelve months between August 2014 and July 2015. Of these, 49,109 came from the public via calls to the IE hotline, the online form 'Report an Immigration Crime' on the Gov.uk website, and possibly in person to officers. A further 7,540 allegations were forwarded from Crimestoppers and 17,818 allegations came from other government departments. The remaining 150 allegations came from MPs, presumably referring on information from constituents. This data suggests that 'intelligence-led' is synonymous with 'public tip-offs'. Although these figures do not convey how much use IE makes of these public tip-offs, IE staff have themselves noted that they are overly reliant on allegations received from members of the public, and do not gather enough intelligence through enforcement teams and FIOs (ICIBI 2016: para 6.11).

The ICIBI report on Illegal Working from December 2015 showed that in the overwhelming majority of cases the source of intelligence was rated as unreliable or unknown (ICIBI 2015). Of 184 cases, the information in 98 came from an 'untested source, information not known personally to source, and cannot be corroborated', rated as E4, one removed from the lowest rating on the scale, E (untested) 5 (suspected to be false). Meanwhile, in another 57 cases the source was 'not known, intelligence rating not shown or not clear in file'. On this basis, it is evident that

---

[2] Following the leak of intelligence documents from the 2014 Operation Centurion, Keith Vaz, chair of the House of Commons Home Affairs committee, publicly condemned the way raids appeared to be 'fishing expeditions' for particular national groups, rather than being 'intelligence-led'. See Corporate Watch (2016).

most of IE's intelligence comes from uncorroborated public-tip-offs, fundamentally undermining the concept of 'intelligence' in this context. Who are the individuals that give these 'tip-offs' and on what basis do they 'think someone is living or working in the UK illegally'? It seems likely that most are based on such visual markers as skin colour, language, and ethnicity. Indeed, of those 184 cases, 107 were high street restaurants or takeaways, mostly Indian, Chinese, or fried chicken (ICIBI 2015: para 4.3). Most of the people detained had entered the UK legally but had overstayed their leave to remain (ICIBI 2015: para 4.4). How do informers providing tip-offs know, or even suspect, that a person's leave has expired? The reliance on public allegations seems closer to an exercise in self-reinforcing prejudice than any kind of reputable intelligence.

The Home Office has enlisted the public in immigration enforcement, apparently unconcerned about the integrity of the 'intelligence' gathered or the impact on community relations. 'Communication techniques' are employed to promote 'voluntary departure schemes' by 'highlighting the risk of arrest'. Indeed, a key focus for ICE teams is to 'promote the visibility of enforcement operations' and 'encourage immigration offenders to leave the UK voluntarily', the latter being 'better for both the UK taxpayer and offenders themselves' (UK Visas and Immigration et al. 2013). For example, 'Go Home' vans and mobile billboards were piloted in 2013 in certain neighbourhoods, urging people to go home voluntarily or risk being arrested and deported (Jones et al. 2017). While the Home Secretary later admitted that the advertising vans were too much of a blunt instrument and would not be used again, a number of alternative communication techniques have found favour with the Home Office: adverts in newspapers and magazines, postcards in shop windows, and leaflets and posters that advertise immigration surgeries in faith and charity group buildings. These alternatives amount to a more sanitized code: deracialized, yet in strategic locations; sending a message while employing amicable concepts such as encouragement and voluntariness.

The involvement of the domestic police force in immigration matters has a controversial history. As former Deputy Assistant Commissioner of the Metropolitan Police, Lord Paddick, recalled, 'thirty years [ago] the police service made a conscious decision to back away from proactive immigration law enforcement because of the damage that it was causing to police community relations' (Lord Paddick 2016: col 1590). Despite this, the imperative of immigration policing is again being imposed on domestic police forces. The Home Office states that IE 'works closely with the police', among other agencies, 'to tackle immigration-related crime, to enforce compliance with immigration laws, to remove those unlawfully present ... and to deny the privileges of the United Kingdom to those in the country illegally' (IGC 2015: 410).

In response to a Freedom of Information request, the Metropolitan Police Service (MPS) admitted to passing on details of victims and witnesses of crime where there were concerns over their immigration status (Bloomer and Jeraj 2017). The MPS stated that '[t]he sharing of information by the MPS with the Home Office is assessed on a case by case basis so is not routinely carried out and will only occur where police have a genuine concern that an individual is in the country illegally'. This begs the question, on what basis might the police have a 'genuine concern' that an individual is here 'illegally'? Again, markers of difference seem bound to play a part. As to the harm this could cause, Lord Paddick points out that '[t]his could deter people from reporting crimes and gives carte blanche to perpetrators of hate crime who could target people that will be reluctant to report it' (Bloomer and Jeraj 2017). There are also broader concerns about police involvement in immigration in regards to its 'enormous damage to community relations and [the creation of] considerable animosity'. These are clearly legitimate concerns that the outcomes of enlisting the public in immigration policing will be racialized and will impact disproportionately on minority communities.

The Home Office has ignored similar concerns in introducing a new criminal offence of 'driving whilst unlawfully in the United Kingdom' under ss 43 and 44 of the Immigration Act 2016 (UK Visas and Immigration et al. 2013). The Act gives immigration and police officers the power to search an individual, premises, or a vehicle where the officer has reasonable grounds to believe that a person is in possession of a driving licence and unlawfully resident. The new power operates in conjunction with s. 163 of the Road Traffic Act 1988, which empowers the police to stop drivers without suspicion or a particular reason. HMIC (2015) survey data show that black and minority ethnic people are disproportionately subject to s. 163 traffic stops but are less likely to be arrested or fined, indicating that such stops are more likely to be groundless or speculative. Having stopped a vehicle, police officers unsatisfied 'as to the driver's identity, nationality and status' are expected to conduct an immigration check. Although Home Office Minister Lord Bates (2016) insisted that the police will use Immigration Act powers only *after* they have stopped a vehicle for an objective reason, s. 163 of the Road Traffic Act is insufficiently circumscribed to ensure the power will be exercised in such a manner. Since the purpose of the Act is to involve the police in immigration enforcement, to create a 'hostile environment' for illegal immigrants and to take them off the roads, Lord Bates' insistence that the immigration policing duty is only triggered once an individual has been pulled over for another reason, or indeed for no reason in particular, is unrealistic. The question is: on what grounds should the police initiate the non-standard practice of an immigration check? Again, visible differences such as 'race', ethnicity, and accent seem likely sources of suspicion. As the National Black Police Association (2015) warned during the parliamentary passage of the Immigration Act 2016, this amounts to 'an unwelcome return to the bad old days of SUS laws ... [the] stirring up of racial hatred and suspicion ... and will result in the police becoming the whipping boy for the immigration service'.

IMMIGRATION POLICING 'AT' THE BORDER

Immigration policing at the border is the domain of the Border Force, formed in 2012 as a Home Office law enforcement command. It is responsible for the enforcement of the Immigration Act 1971, immigration and customs checks at ports and airports, and responding to alerts from the National Border Targeting Centre, which are the product of passenger data and algorithmic analysis. Racism enters the picture through the Border Force's implementation of the visa system, including the requisite secondary examinations of algorithm-determined suspect individuals and officers' use of subjective judgment in the 'on-arrival visual selection' of suspect individuals for secondary examination. Border Force officials, conscientiously carrying out their duties, are tasked with enforcing a visa system that embodies Bauman's (1998: 92) dichotomy between 'tourist' and 'vagabond' on what are, in effect, the grounds of race, ethnicity, and class (Weber and Bowling 2008). Citizens from the vast majority of countries in Asia, the Middle East, and Africa are subject to strict visa requirements, while citizens of Western countries are visa-exempt for stays in the UK of up to six months. While the latter are desirable 'tourists', the former are presumed 'vagabonds', whose entry is perceived as a risk. Visa rules create ethnic differences in the experiences of border policing. Assuming that the hurdles in acquiring a visa are overcome, there are further pre-embarkation controls and visa checks on reaching the UK border. With policing resources targeted to 'risk', a concept inherently linked to the varying visa regimes (Vine 2013a: 3), the Border Force engages in a process of 'social sorting' (Lyon 2002).

Broeders and Hampshire (2013) identify a three-fold categorization: black-listing, grey-listing, and green-listing. Black-listing, based on transnational watchlists and pre-embarkation checks, seeks to ensure that over-stayers, failed asylum seekers, and terrorist suspects never reach the border. These individuals encounter immigration policing well beyond the UK border (see the following section). Green-listing expedites entry for the elite few: travellers who are 'low-risk', third-country nationals with Registered Traveller membership. They barely experience policing, passing unsupervised through e-Borders in the same manner as UK citizens. The 'Registered Traveller service' is reserved for citizens from a selection of 'visa-exempt' countries: the USA, Canada, Mexico, Australia, New Zealand, and the majority of South and Central America are included. Among the countries of Asia, only Brunei, Hong Kong, Japan, Malaysia, Singapore, South Korea, and Taiwan are eligible. Only Israel is eligible among countries in the Middle East. Not one African state is eligible.

All other travellers are grey-listed. This begins with the algorithmic risk profiling of passenger data followed by the dissemination of immigration intelligence alerts from the National Border Targeting Centre to frontline Border Force officials. In combination with 'on-arrival visual selection', this subjects grey-listed travellers to routine questioning, and increased likelihood of secondary examination and detention for interview. The latter disproportionately affects individuals from countries subject to strict visa regimes. Intelligence alerts are the product of targeting 'rules', which filter data obtained from Advanced Passenger Information and Name Records. Grounds for an alert would include links to 'problem routes', source or destination countries assessed as 'high risk' (ICIBI 2016: para 4.33), adverse immigration history, or being placed correctly or incorrectly, on a relevant watch list.

The use of 'on-arrival visual selection' of suspect individuals for secondary examination is considered by the Home Office to be a useful source of 'intelligence' harnessing officers' 'individual knowledge and experience' (Vine 2010: para 6.63).

The Director General of Border Force has asserted that 'there is . . . some very good intuition used by Border Force officers in the front line' (Vine 2013b: para 4.69). However, then Independent Chief Inspector of Borders and Immigration, John Vine, identified inadequacies in the use of such 'intelligence' (Vine 2010). Vine highlighted the risk of individual knowledge and experience being used 'unnecessarily and disproportionately due to discriminatory behaviour'. He noted that staff told him that the use of 'knowledge' and 'experience' varied with each person having 'their own approach'. He recommended that the issue be addressed more transparently to ensure that individual officers are not discriminating unlawfully and that resources are used efficiently. The obvious objection identified by Vine is that 'visual' selection tends to employ markers such as skin colour in forming suspicion and informing decision-making, with a differential impact on particular ethnic groups. The unintended consequences of relying on intuition are clear. As Lord Bingham argues in *The Business of Judging*, judges (and by extension police or immigration officers) can unwittingly discriminate when they seek to assess demeanour or truthfulness across languages and cultures. He argues that to 'rely on demeanour is in most cases to attach importance to deviations from a norm when there is in truth no norm' (Bingham 2000: 11). Officers' hunches, intuition, and the assessment of demeanour as a source of 'intelligence' opens up clear potential for ethnic stereotyping and discrimination. In this regard, it is important to note that ministerial authorizations permit direct racial discrimination by immigration officers under the Equality Act 2010. Immigration officers undertaking 'on-arrival visual selection' and 'pre-arrival database-informed selections' are permitted to exercise stricter and more intrusive controls on the sole basis of nationality or ethnicity (Clayton 2016: 214).

A study carried out by the Home Office in collaboration with Essex University illustrated how immigration officers' decision-making processes drew not only on objective facts, but also on subjective considerations, assumptions, and beliefs. The study found that the most important triggers were nationality and perceived socio-economic status (Bowling et al. 2012; Woodfield et al. 2007). It also illustrated the role of racial and ethnic markers in social sorting. It showed black passengers were seventeen times more likely to be stopped at UK airports in comparison to white passengers. The pattern of racial sorting was largely attributable to nationality, as people from certain countries were more likely to be detained because of the visa regimes applying to each country. The significance of Woodfield et al.'s study, however, is that it distinguished between ethnicity and nationality by collecting data from countries with racially mixed populations (i.e. Canada, USA, and South Africa). The study found that black Canadians were eight times as likely to be stopped, black South Africans ten times as likely and black Americans more than twice as likely by comparison with their white counterparts (Woodfield et al. 2007). Markers of nationality, race, and ethnicity are evidently crucial to the process of social sorting at the border. Immigration officers have wide discretion in deciding whom to detain for further questioning and to deny entry and it is clear that race and ethnic markers are used as a ground for stopping and detaining passengers.

IMMIGRATION POLICING 'BEYOND' THE BORDER

The ultimate goal of the Home Office is to obviate the need for immigration policing within and at the border, by preventing unwanted travellers from arriving in the first place. In the face of globalizing forces that threaten to unseat the privileged position of affluent Western states, the UK is all too aware of the limits of traditional territorial border control (ICAI 2017). The UK seeks to shape the international approach, sharing data and harmonizing policy with other Western states, while negotiating border enforcement measures with non-Western states (ICAI 2017). A post-colonial, deeply entrenched racism thus contributes to defining the 'problem' and the 'solution': who are the targets of migration policing, how is suspicion formed, and what practices of surveillance and enforcement are employed across the globe?

The UK has developed and promulgated a number of pre-entry measures to police migration beyond the border. Arguably, the most pervasive and harmful is the use of visa requirements in combination with carrier sanctions. While nationals of certain countries, including EU member states, the EEA countries and Switzerland, and the Five Country Conference member states, need no visa to enter the UK, nationals of other countries do. The 'success' of this system rests on the use of carrier sanctions. Under the Immigration (Carriers' Liability) Act 1987, air and sea carriers may be liable for a charge of £2,000 for each person they carry to the UK who is subject to immigration control and fails to produce a valid immigration document satisfactorily establishing his or her identity and nationality or a valid visa. Thus unwanted travellers, including vulnerable asylum seekers, are prevented from reaching UK soil. Indeed, aside from formal resettlement arrangements, managed by UK Visas and Immigration in cooperation with the United Nations High Commissioner for Refugees, there is no provision for a person to claim asylum while outside UK territory. Asylum claims can only be made in the UK, either at a point of entry—a seaport or an airport—or inside the UK. Asylum policy is similarly exploited through the use of juxtaposed controls. With UK immigration controls operating alongside those of France and Belgium at seaports and Eurostar train terminals, the UK Border is able to exercise full examination powers for immigration purposes, while denying any exercise of the right to asylum. This injustice is 'central to understanding the success of juxtaposed controls' (Ryan 2010: 17).

Softer methods of control are also deployed. The generation, storage, and dissemination of information is a significant form of power in post-industrial global society (Richmond 1994: 199). The UK has numerous agreements and arrangements with other states for sharing information on asylum claims. For example, each Five Country Conference partner has a bilateral memorandum of understanding (MOU) on data exchange with each partner. The UK has MOUs with Australia, Canada, New Zealand, and the United States for the purpose of identifying persons who have made immigration applications in more than one of these states. The aim is 'to establish identity, prevent fraudulent applications and obtain information about travel documents to aid removal'.

The UK also engages with numerous global migration organizations such as the International Organization for Migration and the United Nations High Commissioner for Refugees (UNHCR). Recognizing that global migration is a highly political subject, where even the definitions are contested, the UK seeks to influence over global policy and exerts a leadership role to establish its own objectives on the global stage (ICAI 2017). This being said, the UK also seems to recognize the limits of banding together with Western states. The senior legal adviser to the UNHCR has stated that even if developed countries 'were prepared to betray the very values on which their societies are based, by building new iron curtains and Berlin Walls around their common territory, the human flood would still find its ways' (Richmond 1994: 216; see also von Blumenthal 1991). UK Visas and Immigration has an overseas network of immigration liaison managers, who have no legal enforcement powers and who do not operate pre-clearance but act as document advisers to airlines. Their role is to provide information and training on UK passport and visa requirements and forgery awareness, with a view to preventing the carriage of inadequately documented passengers to the UK and to assisting airlines to comply with carrier liability legislation. While immigration liaison managers are posted with the agreement of the host country, question marks must be raised as to the negotiating power of the less powerful countries.

Beyond these established measures, the UK has recently adopted a cross-government Illegal Migration Strategy (unpublished). The objective of limiting arrivals in the UK and Europe, particularly along the eastern and central Mediterranean routes, now permeates all relevant government policies. Aid programmes, for example, have been re-written on this basis. One of the key focuses of the Libyan aid programme is to build the capacity of the Libyan Naval Coastguard to conduct search and interdiction operations, for the purpose of increasing the likelihood that refugees and other irregular migrants are intercepted in Libyan territorial waters. These individuals will then be delivered back to a system that leads to indiscriminate and indefinite detention and denies refugees their right to asylum. This is despite the fact that under the international definition of Official Development Assistance (ODA) all UK aid must have the welfare of developing countries, including assistance to refugees, as its main objective—not to mention this being a general breach of the government's own Human Rights Guidance. A number of officials recognize this incongruence or 'grey area', and suggest that ODA eligibility 'often depends on how you describe a project' (ICAI 2017).

CONCLUSION

This chapter has explored the impact of ideas about race, nation, and ethnicity on the practice of immigration policing. The evidence is indicative if not definitive. In general, immigration law and policing practices tend to invoke racial characteristics in ways that cast certain people as suspects, based on their physical appearance or what is imputed to be their national or ethnic origin. There is historical and contemporary evidence that border control and internal immigration policing falls disproportionately on communities defined by visible difference and that this has contributed to shaping the domestic street policing of minority ethnic communities. The individuals and communities who come under suspicion include people of colour, but also other minority ethnic and national groups who become the targets of enforcement action because they are seen as 'out of place' (Bowling et al. 2012). Research on the extent and nature of immigration policing beyond borders is in its infancy, but here too the general tendency points in the same direction.

The research evidence on the form and function of immigration policing suggests that it has the effect of restricting the enjoyment of fundamental rights—such as the freedom of movement—internationally and domestically. Operating at the nexus between immigration and criminal law, immigration policing targets people migrating from the Global South and has the effect of focusing border control and routine street-policing on migrants and their descendants—identified as 'visible minorities'—in the Global North. These observations on immigration policing practices in the UK are consistent with Richmond's (1994) claim that a system of 'global apartheid' is being created. Richmond suggests that the rich and powerful states of the world are working individually and collectively to protect their privileged position in the world in ways akin to the discredited South African system of racial segregation. The trend is towards a racialized world in which the haves and 'have nots' are separated, the latter excluded from opportunities and resources using a system of migration control, identity and pass laws that extend beyond boundaries to affect everyday life in such spheres as employment and housing. The racialized elements of these immigration policing policies and practices are usually denied by those in power and justified in the neutral terms of the social welfare of 'our people', safeguarding the economy, national security, and protecting scarce public services. However, this process of deracialization does nothing to reassure or protect those groups whose lives are circumscribed by racially unjust practices.

REFERENCES

Aliverti, A. (2015), 'Doing Away with Decency? Foreigners, Punishment and the Liberal State', in A. Eriksson (ed.), *Punishing the Other: The Social Production of Immorality Revisited*. London: Routledge, 124–44.

Bauman, Z. (1998), *Globalization: The Human Consequences*. Cambridge: Polity.

Bingham, T. (2000), *The Business of Judging: Selected Essays and Speeches*. Oxford: Oxford University Press.

Bloomer, N. and Jeraj, S. (2017), 'Met Police Hands Victims of Crime over to the Home Office for Immigration Enforcement', *Politics UK*, 5 April. Available at: http://www.politics.co.uk/news/2017/04/05/met-police-hands-victims-of-crime-over-to-the-home-office

Bolt, C. (1971), *Victorian Attitudes to Race*. London: Routledge.

Bowling, B. (1998), *Violent Racism. Victimization, Policing and Social Context*. Oxford: Oxford University Press.

Bowling, B. (2013), 'Epilogue. The Borders of Punishment: Towards a Criminology of Mobility', in K. F. Aas and M. Bosworth (eds), *The Borders of Punishment: Migration, Citizenship, and Social Exclusion*. Oxford: Oxford University Press, 291–306.

Bowling, B., Parmar, A., and Phillips, C. (2008), 'Policing Minority Ethnic Communities', in T. Newburn (ed.), *Handbook of Policing*. Cullompton: Willan, 611–41.

Bowling, B. and Phillips, C. (2007), 'Disproportionate and Discriminatory: Reviewing the Evidence on Stop and Search', *Modern Law Review* 70(6): 936–61.

Bowling, B., Phillips, C., and Sheptycki, J. (2012), 'Race, Political Economy and the Coercive State', in J. Peay and T. Newburn (eds), *Policing, Politics and Control*. Oxford: Hart Publishing, 43–68.

Bowling, B. and Westenra, S. (forthcoming), 'Towards a Crimmigration Control System? A Synthesis', *Theoretical Criminology*.

Broeders, D. and Hampshire, J. (2013), 'Dreaming of Seamless Borders: ICTs and the Pre-emptive Governance of Mobility in Europe', *Journal of Ethnic and Migration Studies* 39(8): 1201–18.

Clayton, G. (2016), *Textbook on Immigration and Asylum Law*. Oxford: Oxford University Press.

Cook, D. (1996), 'Racism, Immigration Policy and the Policing of Families', *Inter Alia* Spring: 23–6.

Corporate Watch (2016), *Snitches, Stings, and Leaks: How 'Immigration Enforcement' Works*. Available at: https://corporatewatch.org/news/2016/aug/30/snitches-stings-leaks-how-immigration-enforcement-works

Fekete, L. (2001), 'The Emergence of Xeno-Racism', *Race and Class* 43(2): 23–40.

Fryer, P. (1984), *Staying Power: The History of Black People in Britain*. London: Pluto Press.

Gordon, P. (1983), *White Law: Racism in the Police, Courts and Prisons*. London: Pluto Press.

Gordon, P. (1985), *Policing Immigration: Britain's Internal Controls*. London: Pluto Press.

Holmes, C. (1988), *John Bull's Island: Immigration and British Society 1871–1971*. London: Macmillan.

HMIC (2015), *Stop and Search Powers 2: Are the Police Using them Effectively and Fairly?* Available at: http://www.justiceinspectorates.gov.uk/hmic/wp-content/uploads/stop-and-search-powers-2.pdf

ICAI (2017), *Report: The UK's Aid Response to Irregular Migration in the Central Mediterranean: A Rapid Review—10 Mar 2017*. Available at: http://icai.independent.gov.uk/html-report/uks-aid-response-irregular-migration-central-mediterranean/

ICIBI (2015), *An Inspection of How the Home Office Tackles Illegal Working: October 2014: March 2015*. London: Independent Chief Inspector of Borders and Immigration.

ICIBI (2016), *An Inspection of the Intelligence Functions of Border Force and Immigration Enforcement: November 2015–May 2016*. London: Independent Chief Inspector of Borders and Immigration.

IGC (2015), *Asylum Procedures: Report on Policies and Practices in IGC Participating States*. Geneva: Inter-governmental Consultations on Migration, Asylum and Refugees.

Jakubowski, L. M. (1997), *Immigration and the Legalisation of Racism*. Halifax: Fernwood Publishing.

Jones, H., Gunaratnam, Y., Bhattacharyya, G., Davies, W., Dhaliwal, S., Forkert, K., Jackson, E., and Saltus, R. (2017). *Go Home? The Politics of Immigration Controversies*. Manchester: Manchester University Press.

Kleg, M. (1993), *Hate, Prejudice and Racism*. Albany, NY: State University of New York Press.

Lord Bates (2016), Rt Hon Lord Bates to Lord Rosser, *Immigration Bill—Lords' Report—Government Amendments*, 1 March (Parts 1–5 and the Recommendations of the House of Lords' Select Committee on Delegated Powers and Regulatory Reform).

Lord Paddick (2016), Immigration Bill 2015/16, House of Lords Committee, 3rd sitting, 1 February, *Hansard* col 1590.

Lyon, D. (ed.) (2002), *Surveillance as Social Sorting: Privacy, Risk, and Digital Discrimination.* London: Routledge.

MacDonald, I. and Toal, R. (eds) (2010), *MacDonald's Immigration Law and Practice.* London: LexisNexis.

Macpherson, W. (1999), *The Stephen Lawrence Inquiry.* Report of an Inquiry by Sir William Macpherson of Cluny. Advised by Tom Cook, The Right Reverend Dr John Sentamu and Dr Richard Stone (Cm 4262-1). London: HMSO.

Montagu, A. (1943), *Man's Most Dangerous Myth: The Fallacy of Race.* London: AltaMira Press.

National Black Police Association (2015), Press Release, 14 December. Available at: http://www.nbpa.co.uk/wp-content/uploads/2015/12/Final-NBPA-Press-statement-Immigration-Bill-14-December-2015.pdf

Pickering, S. and Weber, L. (2013), 'Policing Transversal Borders', in K. F. Aas and M. Bosworth (eds), *The Borders of Punishment: Migration, Citizenship, and Social Exclusion.* Oxford: Oxford University Press, 93–110.

Reeves, F. (1983), *British Racial Discourse: A Study of British Political Discourse about Race and Race-related Matters.* Cambridge: Cambridge University Press.

Reiner, R. (2010), *The Politics of the Police.* (4th edn). Oxford: Oxford University Press.

Richmond, A. (1994), *Global Apartheid: Refugees, Racism and the New World Order.* Oxford: Oxford University Press.

Ryan, B. (2010), 'Extraterritorial Immigration Control: What Role for Legal Guarantees?', in B. Ryan and V. Mitsilegas (eds), *Extraterritorial Immigration Control: Legal Challenges.* London: BRILL, 3–37.

Smith, D. J. and Gray, J. (1985), *Police and People in London.* London: Policy Studies Institute.

Smith, S. J. (1989), *The Politics of 'Race' and Residence.* London: Polity.

Stumpf, J. P. (2006), 'The Crimmigration Crisis: Immigrants, Crime, and Sovereign Power', *American University Law Review* 56: 367.

UK Visas and Immigration, Immigration Enforcement, and The Rt Hon Mark Harper (2013), *Written Statement to Parliament—Immigration enforcement: Operation Vaken.*

Vine, J. (2010), *Preventing and Detecting Immigration and Customs Offences: A Thematic Inspection of How the UK Border Agency Receives and Uses Intelligence: October–December 2010.*

Vine, J. (2013a), *Exporting the Border? An Inspection of e-Borders: October 2012–March 2013.*

Vine, J. (2013b), *An Inspection of Border Force Operations at Stansted Airport: May–August 2013.*

von Blumenthal, U. (1991), 'Dublin, Schengen and the Harmonization of Asylum in Europe', a paper presented at the First European Lawyers Conference, Brussels, 14–15 February.

Weber, L. and Bowling, B. (2004), 'Policing Migration: A Framework for Investigating the Regulation of Global Mobility', *Policing and Society* 14(3): 195–212.

Weber, L. and Bowling, B. (2008), 'Valiant Beggars and Global Vagabonds: Select, Eject and Immobilize', *Theoretical Criminology* 12(3): 355–75.

Woodfield, K., Spencer, L., Purdon, S., Pascale, J., Legard, R., Anie, A., Ndofor-Tah, C., Mouden, J., and Brennan, F. (2006), *Exploring the Decision Making of Immigration Officers: Home Office Online Report.* London: Home Office.

5

Race, Gender, and Border Control in the Western Balkans

*Sanja Milivojević**

INTRODUCTION

Borders are no longer simple, static lines separating nation states, if they ever were. Rather, as Basham and Vaughan-Williams (2013: 509) put it, these days, borders are 'mobile, bio-political and virtual apparatuses of control'. Whether geographical, internal, digital, terrestrial, or virtual in form, regulating borders and mobility has become 'a paradigmatic feature of the modern sovereign territorial state and state systems' (Basham and Vaughan-Williams 2013: 509). Borders are also spaces where the inclusive and exclusive nature of the global economic order is made evident (Borja and Castells 1997) as those included in transnational migration processes (businesspeople, tourists, skilled workers) are separated from the 'homo sacer' (Agamben 1998) of international migration—illegal(ized) non-citizens and asylum seekers. Border control, in short, aims to separate bona fide travellers from potential threats to state security and the identity of the nation.

In response to these developments, over the past decade or so, criminologists have begun to pay attention to how states in the Global North seek to prevent entry of people from the Global South. Their inquiry, however, has largely excluded analysis of the Western Balkans. Such oversight is curious given that this region, which includes countries of the former Yugoslavia—Croatia, Serbia, Montenegro, Bosnia and Herzegovina, FYR Macedonia, and Kosovo,[1] and Albania, is the second largest route for irregular migrants and asylum seekers in Europe after the Eastern Mediterranean route (Frontex 2016). In response to a variety of factors, including the expansion of the European Union (EU) in the Southeast, relaxed Schengen visa

* I would like to thank Mary Bosworth, Yolanda Vázquez, and Alpa Parmar for their insightful and constructive feedback; your time and academic guidance is much appreciated. I would also like to thank all the participants at the Race, Migration and Criminal Justice workshop, held in Oxford in September 2016 as their comments were invaluable in shaping this paper.
[1] Although Slovenia was a part of the Socialist Federative Republic of Yugoslavia it is not considered to be a part of the Western Balkans (European Commission 2016). When it was established in the early 2000s, the Western Balkans 'region' incorporated South-east European nation states that are non-EU members (Pond 2006). On 1 July 2013 Croatia joined the EU but it is still considered to be a part of the Western Balkans.

restrictions in the region, and wars in Syria, Afghanistan, and Iraq, the numbers of people passing through this region have soared and yet migration routes and border policing practices in these parts of the world continue to be overlooked.

There are many reasons for this academic blind spot. Much of the region has been unstable since the 1990s, making it a difficult place in which to conduct research. While foreign researchers face considerable language barriers, they also find it difficult to gain official access. Home-grown scholars, on the other hand, face other kinds of obstacles including limited funding from external donors, minimal support from the government research councils, and few, if any, opportunities for publication in the top academic journals which continue to be English-language, and Global North-dominated. For all of these reasons, there is a significant gap in our understanding of migration and mobility and border policing practices in this part of Southeast Europe.

My research addresses this gap. In this piece, specifically, I concentrate on the intersections between race and gender to make sense of the treatment and experiences of the men and women from the Middle East and Africa who have transited through this region towards Western Europe since the beginning of the European migrant crisis. As I will demonstrate, ideas of race, rooted in place and history, underpin and justify the punitive regimes and structural violence these migrants encounter. Race, in the Western Balkans as it does elsewhere, informs border management strategies. Closely associated with nationality and based on an assumed racial supremacy of the local white citizens, it is relied on in a variety of ways to sort people who wish to enter or remain. As my examples will demonstrate, race intersects with gender, as women and men are not perceived in quite the same way. Rather, within a racialized frame, they are subjected to distinct strategies of border enforcement.

This chapter is based on preliminary findings from a research project on mobility and border control in the Western Balkans, in the context of EU integration. The research was conducted from 2013 to 2015, and included semi-structured interviews (n = 47) with various government agencies and non-governmental organizations (NGOs) operating in the key transit countries in the region (Serbia, Croatia, FYR Macedonia, and Kosovo), as well as in Hungary and France.[2] The research also included over fifty hours of fieldwork observation in the centre for asylum seekers and along border crossings in Serbia. Finally, a media analysis of Serbian, Croatian, Macedonian, and Kosovar newspapers was conducted covering the period January 2013 to December 2016.[3] Drawing on this diverse collection of data, this chapter highlights the racialized and gendered hierarchies in operation in border policing

---

[2] In 2013, I conducted thirty interviews with a range of professionals from governmental agencies, non-governmental organizations, academia, and international non-governmental organizations in Serbia, Croatia, Hungary, and France. An additional seventeen interviews in FYR Macedonia and Kosovo were conducted in 2015. The research also included four in-depth interviews with women asylum seekers, two written submissions from governmental agencies in the region, and two transcripts of round tables organized in Bogovađa asylum centre in Serbia (all from 2013). Representatives of non-governmental organizations working on the topic in Hungary and France were interviewed in order to obtain a broader picture on trends and issues in migration and mobility in Europe.

[3] This timeframe captures the migrant crisis of 2014 and 2015, and a year before and a year after the largest movement of migrants in Europe since World War II (Parkinson 2015).

practices in the region, and outlines how such practices both produce and target racially different Others, irregular migrants and asylum seekers. It brings to the fore the racialized and gendered implications of border control policies, demonstrating how they limit the mobility of non-citizens transiting through the region. In the final section, the chapter examines how border control practices construct race in the Western Balkans, and calls for further engagement of border scholars, particularly from the Global South, in this area of criminological inquiry.

THE 'MIGRANT CRISIS' AND SECURITIZATION IN THE WESTERN BALKANS

After 9/11, border policing practices changed across the Global North (see Basham and Vaughan-Williams 2013; McCulloch and Pickering 2012). Attempts to counter transnational crime have been 'a vehicle for major contemporary changes in the state's coercive capacities' (McCulloch and Pickering 2012: 3). In this context, the 'war on terror' has almost seamlessly merged with the 'war on irregular migrants' (Gerard and Pickering 2013; McCulloch and True 2014), targeting a heterogeneous group of darker mobile bodies among whom terrorists and dangerous Others are thought to mingle.

Governing through migration control (Bosworth and Guild 2008) in the era of globalization has created 'the national' and 'the foreign', instead of the 'citizens of the world' (Aas 2007: 98). Two sharply divided groups of people have formed—'the vagabonds' and 'the tourists' (Bauman 1998). While prisons warehouse unwanted citizens across the Global North, those considered to be the 'human waste' of the Global South are confined in detention centres and camps at the shores of the Mediterranean, or along the recently erected barbed wire fence at the Serbian–Hungarian border.

The securitization of migration and racialized border policing practices, promoted by the Global North and enforced in the media and public discourse, have translated into repressive and racial border policing policies in the Global South. This process of border externalization, as Weber and Pickering (2011: 17) remind us, is 'a logical consequence of the hegemonic mentalities of risk that shape governance in late modernity'. Indeed, in the era of pre-crime engagement with the transnational and domestic crime 'problem' (McCulloch and Wilson 2016), it is not surprising that policies of *non-entrée* have been extended to the peripheries of Empire, such as Mexico, Southeast Europe, Northern Africa, and the island nations of the Pacific. Identifying, isolating, and immobilizing the Other occurs at the physical border and beyond, in practices that police internal borders at what Weber and Bowling (2004) call the 'sites of enforcement' (see also Weber 2013). Conceptually, borders are adhesive, sticking to and following those to whom they attach (see Bowling and Westenra, this volume). While these processes are not new (see, for example, the origins and the intent of the 2003 European Neighbourhood Policy—Cadier 2013; Milivojević 2013), they have gained traction over the last few years as the number of people on the move has continued to increase.

In 2014 and 2015, the world experienced 'the largest refugee crisis in Europe since World War II' (Wolfensohn 2016: 2). In order to reach their destination, thousands of these people, irregular migrants and asylum seekers from war-torn Syria, Afghanistan, and Iraq transited through Turkey and Greece, before moving on to the countries of the Western Balkans, mainly FYR Macedonia and Serbia. Over this period, according to Frontex (2017), the number of illegal border crossings on the Western Balkans route rose from 6,390 in 2012, to 19,950 in 2013, and a staggering 764,038 in 2014. In 2014 and 2015 alone, more than 807,000 people transited through the region, mostly from Syria, Iraq, and Afghanistan. It was estimated that women and children made up to 42 per cent of the migrant population (17 and 25 per cent respectively). During the crisis, over 485,000 people registered their intention to seek asylum in Serbia alone (Wolfensohn 2016: 9–10).

To 'stop the flood' (the Hungarian government's spokesperson Zoltán Kovács, cited in Kingsley 2015) of people moving towards Western Europe, a robust 'ring of friends' (Romano Prodi, cited in Cadier 2013) was sought near and far, in countries of origin and transit. In this search, the EU candidate states of the Western Balkans, particularly Serbia and FYR Macedonia, were set the task of effective migration management, as they are located at the very heart of the Western Balkans migratory route.

In mid-November 2015 the EU member states and the countries of the Western Balkans began 'selective admission practices allowing only Syrian, Afghan and Iraqi nationals (believed to be legitimate refugees coming from conflict affected countries) to cross into their territory' (Wolfensohn 2016: 10; see also Stojanović 2015). Such policies resulted in violent clashes of migrants and Macedonian police on the Greek–Macedonian border, and caused separation of many mixed-nationality couples and families (Wolfensohn 2016). After a short reprieve, during which the borders in the region were rendered semi-permeable, in March 2016 Slovenian Prime Minister Miro Cerar announced that the Balkan route 'for illegal migration no longer exists' (BBC 2016), and that the borders were permanently shut for illegal non-citizens.

In the following section I outline how these immobilizing strategies in this part of Europe were racialized and gendered in their operation. As Jock Young observed nearly twenty years ago, the criminal immigrant myth is deeply rooted in, and an important characteristic of, the exclusive societies of the Global North (Young 1999). Although less attention has been paid to it, the notion of the criminal immigrant also exists in the Global South (see Wickes and Sydes 2015), where it serves to justify counterterrorism and counter-trafficking border policing interventions.

FROM CRIMINALS TO TERRORISTS AND BEYOND

Prior to and during the migrant crisis, many of the countries of the Western Balkans sought to prevent in blunt, physical ways irregular migrants and asylum seekers from crossing the border, stopping their entry with fences, and pushing them back to the country where they came from. As one of my research participants noted satirically,

'I am expecting to see a comic soon that will portray two border police officers, a Macedonian and a Serbian, simply pushing migrants to each other, like a game of table tennis' (Respondent 4, NGO, Serbia). Those migrants who managed to cross borders were frequently encouraged to move on as quickly as possible. The non-engagement of law enforcement in Serbia resulted in a several-months delay in issuing temporary ID cards necessary to claim asylum (Respondent 1, NGO, Serbia), but also to finance their journey.[4] As one respondent pointed out, 'police are simply not processing them. I am not sure why. [Migrants] are simply coming and going' (Respondent 1, NGO, Serbia).

This approach to migration management, in which law enforcement and border police carried out the bare minimum of tasks requested by the EU, resulted in thousands of people successfully crossing the EU's southeast borders. In 2014 alone, some 16,500 intentions to seek asylum were registered in Serbia, while only about 400 submitted an actual application and 6 were given some form of protection (European Commission 2015a: 60). According to a representative from a Serbian NGO, turnover was quick: the average stay for asylum seekers in Serbia at this time was approximately three weeks (Respondent 19, NGO, Serbia).

The failure, or perhaps reluctance, of states to enforce border control and process asylum seekers rather than prevent their entry or move them on had many causes. One important factor underpinning this laissez-faire strategy sprang from the deeply embedded racism and nationalism of the local population and law enforcement agents (e.g. Morača 2014; for police abuse see Human Rights Watch 2015). According to the United Nations High Commissioner for Refugees, irregular migrants in Serbia have become commonly perceived as terrorists, thieves, and criminals (UNHCR Serbia 2014: 4). As more and more of these people arrived, the processes of separating citizens from foreigners, and members of the (white) nation and visibly different and precarious Others merged. Keeping the racially different, and presumed dangerous non-citizens on the territory of the nation was considered to be out of the question.

The police were not alone in holding these views. Rather, large protests against centres for asylum seekers that occurred in Slovenia, Serbia, and Croatia had significant public support and palpably demonstrated the reluctance to host and offer sanctuary to migrants. 'There was a big unrest of the local people [at the location where the asylum centre was supposed to be built in Croatia]', one NGO worker in Croatia reported. 'It was the same in Slovenia, they had to move the location of the centre seven times' (Respondent 11, NGO, Croatia). A Serbian government official agreed: 'We've got EUR 3 million from the EU to open a third asylum centre in Serbia ... And we failed. The xenophobia of Serbian people is immeasurable' (Respondent 5, government agency, Serbia).

The media, too, played an important role, portraying women and men border crossers through racialized and religious stereotypes. Such views appeared to cross all political lines. In a column dated 13 August 2015 in *Danas*, a progressive Serbian broadsheet known for its support for gay and minority rights, for example, columnist

---

[4] Western Union is a financial service predominantly used by irregular migrants in the region (Košut 2017). Temporary ID provided by local law enforcement serves as identity proof necessary to collect money.

Natalija Dević suggested that '[w]omen in hijabs walk along Knez Mihajlova street every night. Their hair is covered, their bodies wrapped in long black dresses, in accordance with their religion. They look at us disapprovingly. They look at us, citizens of Belgrade, in our own city … Will we have to apologise to them because we wear short skirts?' (Dević 2015).

For the majority of irregular migrants who were male, gendered and racialized fears of the 'crimmigrant Other' were encapsulated and assigned through use of the derogratory label #rapefugees.[5] As one respondent recollected, '[t]here was a protest against the asylum centre [and] a local woman … said: "Now, close your eyes and imagine that someone rapes your mother, daughter, sister" ' (Respondent 2, NGO, Serbia).

Visible markers of racial identity, such as skin colour and facial hair associated with Muslim men emerged as key points of concern for the locals, adding to perceptions of male migrants as likely terrorists or criminals. Such views bolstered the policy of non-engagement and justified the social exclusion of those who were seeking sanctuary. As one of my respondents made clear, they were further rationalized by the idea that these unwanted and potentially dangerous people would leave on their own, if left alone. Ultimately he argued, people in Serbia 'are afraid of the unknown. They think [male migrants] are terrorists, criminals … There are so many of them, they sleep in parks … they are exhausted, tired, they have dark skin, don't know the language. They look awful, have beards' (Respondent 1, NGO, Serbia).

A significant shift in migration management on the Western Balkans route occurred after the terrorist attacks in Paris in January and November 2015, and in Brussels in March 2016. Rather than non-engagement or *laissez faire*, the fear of terrorism now emerged as the key argument to strengthen the policy of *non-entrée* and keep migrants outside nation state borders. Tabloid and broadsheet media in Serbia, Croatia, and Macedonia repeatedly warned readers about male migrants/potential terrorists and the danger they bring to the region. Some examples[6] capture their tone. The problem, these papers made clear, lay in the difficulty of differentiating among these unknown Others:

Terrorists hiding amongst migrants: Hundreds have passed Serbia, many potentially still in the country (Serbia's *Telegraf*, 22 August 2015);

ISIS terrorists will arrive with migrants (Croatia's *Jutarnji List*, 8 July 2015);

Experts: Jihadists could easily infiltrate among migrants (Macedonia's *Independent*, 7 July 2016);

It's increasingly difficult to separate migrants from potential terrorists (Croatia's *Glas Slavonije*, 27 July 2016);

Was the killer from Brussels in Serbia? There are indicators that the jihadi bomber transited through the Balkans (Serbia's *Telegraf*, 23 March 2016).

Following the headlines in the traditional media, and uproar on social media, government officials in the region decided to toughen up their border rhetoric.

---

[5] #rapefugees is a Twitter hashtag that links refugees and sexual assault, often used by conservative politicians in Europe (see Baker 2016).
[6] All have been translated by the author.

Linking irregular migration, race, gender, and the risk of terrorism as a direct threat to national security justified a novel muscular approach to closing the geographical borders. In the words of Aleksandar Nikolić, the State Secretary in the Serbian Ministry for Internal Affairs (cited in Roknić 2015),

In this migrant crisis probably one of the most dangerous factors is the fact that among illegal migrants there are organised criminals and persons of interest for the law enforcement ... Serbia is a potential target for terrorists, but even more so, a potential training camp for terrorists, which is equally as dangerous and relevant.

In Croatia, a similar view was taken, with President Kolinda Grabar Kitanović (cited in *Jutarnji List*, 2 March 2016) asserting that 'an absolute control of the border' was a key priority for the Croatian government. While 'this doesn't mean shutting down the border,' she added, 'as that would be inhumane treatment of migrants', tough border control measures were nonetheless needed because of 'the protection of national security, and the protection of migrants themselves, as they are often targeted by terrorists themselves'.[7]

Concerns about the 'survival of the nation' that were driving the agenda took a particular hue. An amalgamation of the Muslim and the Racial Other into a Dangerous/Terrorist Other, revived after 9/11, achieved a new peak in the wake of the migrant crisis in Europe. The category of 'brown', as a generic 'Arab Middle-Eastern-Muslim', as Semati (2010: 257) reminds us, in conjunction with Islamophobia translated to a series of security discourses 'conflated and infected with right-wing agendas'. In migration and mobility management, this racialized anti-migration rhetoric inflected with terror has taken hold across much of the Global North and during the migrant crisis such rhetoric was promptly adopted in the countries of transit. After reports that forty jihadists entered Europe through the Western Balkans route (Bojadžijevski 2016), pressure from Brussels facilitated a border shutdown that left thousands stranded in refugee camps and at points of transit in Serbia and Macedonia (European Commission 2015b). In mid-March 2016, the Serbian Chief of Police indicated that police and military were regularly patrolling jointly the Serbian–Macedonian and the Serbian–Croatian border, and that about 1,300 people had been trapped in Serbia after the closure of the Western Balkans route (*B92* 2016). Such barriers, he hoped, would make '[migrants] realise they can't go any further, and that they will willingly return where they came from' (Rebić, cited in *B92* 2016).

In fact, at the time of writing, the migrant crisis is far from resolved. In the aftermath of further terrorist attacks within Europe, border controls in neighbouring EU countries have been further strengthened. Yet, the cost of housing thousands of migrants at the gates of the EU is yet to be revealed. The European future appears not to be as bright as was once promised, given the ongoing financial and membership crisis within the EU, and the ever-growing importance of protecting its external borders. Hence the stakes are raised for the ascending nation states and their future negotiations with the EU. With this in mind, I now turn to focus on the gendered and racialized aspects of border management in the Western Balkans as they pertain to women.

---

[7] All translated by the author.

STOPPING TRAFFIC(KING): WOMEN'S BODIES AT THE GATES OF FORTRESS EUROPE

While increasing numbers of women are on the move (Castels and Miller 1998), the majority of women from the Global South have no legal means to reach the Global North (Pickering 2011). The roadblocks they face are many, and growing. They include individual, social, structural, and cultural barriers, as well as those set by nation states that are deployed through conventional and 'humanitarian' crime prevention measures at geographical borders of Global North and Global South, and beyond. Such measures are often legitimized through political and popular narratives that link women migrants (especially irregular migrants and asylum seekers) with exploitation, discrimination, abuse, and violence (European Parliament 2014). While there is no doubt that women are indeed more vulnerable than their male counterparts at origin, transit, and destination (see Gerard and Pickering 2013), their perceived vulnerability has nonetheless been used as an immobilizing tool, especially in the context of human trafficking.

The threat of transnational crime, and especially human trafficking, has been used to regulate women's mobility in the Western Balkans and elsewhere since the late 1990s. Information campaigns, emotive language, visual warnings, border fortification, visa regimes, surveillance at the border and beyond, and other covert and overt strategies of border management have almost exclusively been wrapped in and justified through the narrative of preventing future victimization. These 'humanitarian' policy responses have been grounded in the notion of agency-deprived (and largely voiceless and invisible) ideal victims of trafficking (see Freedman 2010).

A range of 'protective' measures has been deployed for almost three decades now, aiming to prevent potential victimization through the law and order at the border framework. Fighting human trafficking, thus, goes hand in hand with the securitization of border control (see Lee 2011; O'Brien et al. 2013). A vast amount of literature has been written on various counter-trafficking strategies that have been used to prevent women from crossing borders (see, for example, Andrijasević 2007; Lee 2011; Milivojević and Pickering 2008; Milivojević and Segrave 2010; Nieuwenhuys and Pécoud 2013).

In April and May 2015 the EU passed a range of border control policies to tackle trafficking and smuggling (UN Security Council 2015). Such measures were justified in the following terms: '[t]he current refugee crisis has increased the risk of people ending up as victims of trafficking', the European Parliament asserted. 'Women and children fleeing violence are especially likely to become victims of traffickers and smugglers' (European Parliament 2016: 6–7). In light of these fears, the European Commission urged the Western Balkans nation states to 'significantly strengthen migration management and asylum policies, with a specific focus on identifying people in the need of protection' (European Commission 2015a: 59). As female irregular migrants and asylum seekers transiting through the region have been singled out as vulnerable and prone to victimization, especially trafficking (Galonja and Jovanović 2011; Morača 2014), they have been on the receiving end of new counter-trafficking migration management policies.

In my research, government agencies and NGOs in Serbia routinely identified women as vulnerable to exploitation in transit and destination, especially if they travelled alone or with unrelated male companions. They were considered at risk, too, if they were young, and if there was any indication that they might be engaged in the sex industry either in their country of origin, or while in transit.[8] Women from Nigeria, Somalia, Ethiopia, and Eritrea were considered to be particularly vulnerable (Morača 2014; Radio Slobodna Evropa 2016) as they often travelled alone and/or were suspected to be sex workers. As a result, local authorities and NGOs, who were responsible for identification of victims of trafficking, routinely reported these groups to the police (Milivojević 2014: 294–5).

Preventing women from travelling further was considered to be an effective trafficking prevention strategy:

We had 8 women from Somalia, with two, three children … They had no idea what asylum is. Given that they were potential victims of trafficking, they sold their property over there, their husbands were killed, we told them what asylum is and gave them the papers, even though they didn't ask for them. We explained what asylum is and they said yes (Police officer, cited in Morača 2014: 58).

The dangers of trafficking in countries of destination were disclosed to women during face-to-face meetings with NGOs and government agencies, and via education campaigns and posters targeting women migrants (Milivojević 2014: 294). The bottom line was: they might be trafficked if they continue the journey.

Women who did not engage with local NGOs were considered 'suspicious' and further contacts with their legal representatives were made to 'check if everything is OK' (Respondent 19, international non-governmental organization, Serbia). The fact that female migrants simply transited through the region, until the borders closed in March 2016, was identified as problematic, as it takes time for women to open up about their experiences of trafficking and exploitation. Regardless, activists and social workers were keen to 'demystify the destination' for them. As one NGO worker put it, such places 'might also be a place where they will become victims [of trafficking]' (Respondent 19, NGO, Serbia). For these women, as it was for Muslim men, the passage to the country of destination was blocked. Whereas the men were stopped for fear of terrorism, women were immobilized for their own 'protection'.

GOVERNING MIGRATION THROUGH CRIME AND VICTIMIZATION: RACIALIZED AND GENDERED BORDER POLICING PRACTICES IN THE GLOBAL SOUTH

As the chapters in this collection make clear, race and gender are the cornerstones of exclusionary border policing strategies around the world. In Europe, the migrant

---

[8] This is assessed on the basis of how women 'behave' or how are they dressed—Respondent 15, NGO, Croatia; see also Milivojević 2014: 293.

crisis of 2014–2015 demonstrates how narratives about dangerous terrorists have become a tool that can be effectively deployed in countries of origin and transit. The Western Balkans case study also indicates how quickly such narratives have blended with existing racist and exclusionary sentiments and policies in countries of transit.

Fitting neatly into the risk society framework, in which possible terrorist attacks are considered to be always imminent, irregular male migrants with visual markers of Otherness are increasingly seen as an inherent threat to national security. In 2016, Hungarian Prime Minister Victor Orbán took this logic to its natural insidious conclusion; irregular migrants, in his view, were nothing more than 'a poison ... [and] a public security and terror risk' (Quackenbush 2016). Women migrants, in contrast, are immobilized by victimization prevention strategies, in which their potential victimization at the hands of sex traffickers is used to justify a web of practices that stop them moving forward. The darkness of their skin seems directly proportional to their assumed vulnerability. For them, 'humanitarian' pre-crime measures legitimate restrictive migration and mobility policies in countries of transit. In this regard, the migrant crisis offers another example of a broader counter-trafficking conundrum in which restoring the order at the border dwarfs mobility and human rights (Lee 2011; Milivojević and Pickering 2013; Milivojević et al. 2017; Segrave et al. 2009).

In their border control strategies, countries of the Global South, like those of the Western Balkans, increasingly act as the last line of defence, where the unwanted are stopped before reaching the geographical border of Empire. While some of these measures are imposed in response to demands from the metropol (i.e. Brussels), other interventions are justified on global, 'humanitarian' grounds. Indeed, when it comes to the rescue of innocent victims of trafficking, no external pressure is needed as most agree that sex slaves have to be rescued, no matter the cost.

In the context of the narrative of victimization, it is important to underscore the fact that migrants are not merely passive subjects who have enforcement measures applied to them. Rather, they are active agents who keep resisting, and pursuing their migratory projects. As one employee of an NGO pointed out,

[w]hen you get [to Serbia] ... you are only one border crossing away from Europe ... They are led by the dream, maybe not a realistic one, but it's a dream ... You simply cannot keep them here against their wishes. How can you stop someone who has no alternative? You can't ... When you set your mind to it, you will do it, you will cross the border in your hundredth attempt. (Respondent 2, NGO, Serbia)

This is a critical insight to bear in mind, especially as the European Border and Coast Guard Agency (formerly Frontex) embarks on a new mandate in 2017 that includes the deployment of liaison officers in priority transit countries, including Serbia and FYR Macedonia (European Commission 2017).

CONCLUDING THOUGHTS: SOUTHERN CRIMINOLOGY AND RESEARCHING BORDERS IN THE GLOBAL SOUTH

Like the policies outlined in this chapter, knowledge in social sciences has long been transferred from the Global North to the Global South (Carrington et al. 2016;

Connell 2007). It is important to allow scholars from the metropolitan states of Western Europe and Northern America to research the periphery, by providing official access and removing the language barriers that may hinder such knowledge growth. At the same time, more needs to be done if we are to encourage participation of scholars from the Global South to conduct research in their local contexts, and to enable dissemination of their results. As Carrington et al. (2016: 2) note, the periphery has long served simply as a 'data-mine' for metropolitan theory; researchers from the Global South are given limited, if any, access to major research funds and academic journals, while publishing in languages other than English has limited, if any, impact on the academic debate. For such matters to change, we need to think about decolonizing criminology in the classroom, in the field, and in publishing (see Bruce-Jones, this volume).

Thinking about decolonizing criminology is also a starting point for unpacking the question of how race and gender are present (or not) in the methodological process of scholarship in border studies. Such an approach will help to develop a 'beyond-metropolitan' theory of the intersection of race and gender grounded in experiences from the Global South. The Global South has wider relevance than the light it sheds on the Global North. Processes of social exclusion described in this chapter need to be researched as they impact on southern bodies on the move. The Southern, as Carrington at al. (2016: 5) argue, if 'a metaphor for the other, the invisible, the subaltern, the marginal and the excluded', has to be at the forefront of border studies. As Weber and Pickering (2011: 1) warn, 'people die because of the ways in which the borders between the Global North and Global South are controlled. These deaths are often foreseeable and can occur by deliberate act or omission. As border scholars we are able to document practices of social exclusion at the border and beyond which target the Other, and we are able to challenge the reproduction of gendered and racialized narratives of social exclusion. A component of this challenge is for us to be bolder in sketching out the human face, and importantly the human price, of border politics in the twenty-first century.

As we continue to witness in national election campaigns and policies around the world, the racialized and gendered language of border control has transferred from the far right into the mainstream. Migration management in the Global North, and increasingly in the Global South, is racialized, gendered, and neo-colonial. All too often it is also a gross violation of human rights, if not state crime. In 2008 Poynting called for critical criminologists to challenge the robustness of the dangerous and racialized Other narrative. Research that focuses on the intersection of race and gender has never been more important. The periphery is an important part of this quest, as border policing strategies are increasingly deployed across the Global South. We need to research, and then communicate our findings to the field and beyond, to the public, policymakers, and our students on both sides of the North-South divide.

REFERENCES

Aas, K. F. (2007), *Globalization and Crime*. London: Sage.
Agamben, G. (1998), *Homo Sacer: Sovereign Power and Bare Life*. Stanford, CA: Stanford University Press.

Andrijasević, R. (2007), 'Beautiful Dead Bodies: Gender, Migration and Representation in Anti-Trafficking Campaigns', *Feminist Review* 86: 24–44.

B92 (2016), 'Oko 1,300 izbeglica zaglavljeno u Srbiji', 12 March. Available at: http://www.b92.net/info/vesti/index.php?yyyy=2016&mm=03&dd=12&nav_category=12&nav_id=1106848

Baker, K. (2016), 'Politician who Repeatedly Called Refugees "Rapefugees" Online Sparks Formal Complaint and Council Meeting Walkout', *Daily Mail*, 23 June. Available at: http://www.dailymail.co.uk/news/article-3656300/Politician-repeatedly-called-refugees-rapefugees-online.html

Basham, V. and Vaughan-Williams, N. (2013), 'Gender, Race and Border Security Practices: A Profane Reading of "Muscular Liberalism"', *The British Journal of Politics and International Relations* 15: 509–27.

Bauman, Z. (1998), *Globalization: The Human Consequences*. Cambridge: Polity Press.

BBC (2016), 'Migrant Crisis: Macedonia Shuts Balkans Route', 9 March. Available at: http://www.bbc.com/news/world-europe-35763101

Bojadžijevski, J. (2016), 'Migranti i strah od radikalizacije', VOA. Available at: http://www.glasamerike.net/a/evropa-migranti-kriza-radikalizacija/3221798.html

Borja, J. and Castells, M. (1997), *Local & Global: Management of Cities in the Information Age*. London: Earthscan.

Bosworth, M. and Guild, M. (2008), 'Governing Through Migration Control', *The British Journal of Criminology* 48(6): 703–19.

Castels, S. and Miller, M. (1998), *The Age of Migration: International Population Movements in the Modern World*. Basingstoke: Palgrave.

Cadier, D. (2013), 'Is the European Neighbourhood Policy a Substitute for Enlargement?' The Crisis of EU Enlargement, LSE IDEAS Report. Available at: http://www.lse.ac.uk/IDEAS/publications/reports/pdf/SR018/Cadier_D.pdf

Carrington, K., Hogg, R., and Sozzo, M. (2016), 'Southern Criminology', *British Journal of Criminology* 56(1): 1–20.

Connell, R. (2007), *Southern Theory: The Global Dynamics of Knowledge in Social Science*. Cambridge: Polity.

Dević, N. (2015), 'Foreigners in Belgrade', *Danas*, 13 August.

European Commission (2015a), 'Commission Staff Working Document: Serbia 2015 Report'. Available at: http://ec.europa.eu/enlargement/pdf/key_documents/2015/20151110_report_serbia.pdf

European Commission (2015b), 'Statement by Commissioner Avramopoulos Following the International Ministerial Conference "Tackling Jihadism Together" in Vienna'. Available at: http://europa.eu/rapid/press-release_STATEMENT-15-4641_en.htm

European Commission (2016), 'Countries and Regions: Western Balkans'. Available at: http://ec.europa.eu/trade/policy/countries-and-regions/regions/western-balkans/

European Commission (2017), 'Report from the Commission to the European Parliament, the European Council and the Council on the Operationalisation of the European Border and Coast Guard'. Available at: https://ec.europa.eu/home-affairs/sites/homeaffairs/files/what-we-do/policies/securing-eu-borders/legal-documents/docs/20170125_report_on_the_operationalization_of_the_european_border_and_coast_guard_en.pdf

European Parliament (2014), *Report on Irregular Women Migrants in the European Union*. Committee on Women's Rights and Gender Equality. Available at: http://www.europarl.europa.eu/sides/getDoc.do?pubRef=-//EP//NONSGML+REPORT+A7-2014-0001+0+DOC+PDF+V0//EN

European Parliament (2016), *The Gender Dimension of Human Trafficking*. Briefing. Available at: http://www.europarl.europa.eu/RegData/etudes/BRIE/2016/577950/EPRS_BRI(2016)577950_EN.pdf

Freedman, J. (2010), 'Protecting Women Asylum Seekers and Refugees: From International Norms to National Protection.' *International Migration* 48(1): 175–98.

Frontex (2016), 'Migratory Routes Map'. Available at: http://Frontex.europa.eu/trends-and-routes/migratory-routes-map/

Frontex (2017), 'Western Balkan route'. Available at: http://Frontex.europa.eu/trends-and-routes/western-balkan-route/

Galonja, A. and Jovanović, S. (2011), Zaštita žrtava i prevencija trgovine ljudima, Zajednički program UNHCR, UNOCD i IOM za borbu protiv trgovine ljudima u Srbiji, Beograd.

Gerard, A. and Pickering, S. (2013), 'Gender, Securitization and Transit: Refugee Women and the Journey to the EU', *Journal of Refugee Studies* 27(3): 338–59.

Human Rights Watch (2015), 'Serbia: Police Abusing Migrants, Asylum Seekers: Beaten, Extorted, Shoved Back Across the Border', 15 April. Available at https://www.hrw.org/news/2015/04/15/serbia-police-abusing-migrants-asylum-seekers

Kingsley, P. (2015), 'Migrants on Hungary's Border Fence: "This Wall, We Will Not Accept it"', *The Guardian*, 22 June. Available at: https://www.theguardian.com/world/2015/jun/22/migrants-hungary-border-fence-wall-serbia

Košut, I. (2017), 'Migranti se smravaju, ali neće u kampove', N1, 10 January. Available at: http://rs.n1info.com/a220364/Vesti/Vesti/Migranti-u-Beogradu.html

Lee, M. (2011), *Trafficking and Global Crime Control*. Los Angeles, CA, London, New Delhi: Sage.

McCulloch, J. and Pickering, S. (2012), 'Introduction', in J. McCulloch and S. Pickering (eds), *Borders and Crime: Pre-Crime, Mobility and Serious Harm in an Age of Globalization*. Basingstoke: Palgrave Macmillan, 1–14.

McCulloch, J. and True, J. (2014), 'Shifting Borders: Crime, Borders, International Relations and Criminology', in S. Pickering and J. Ham (eds), *The Routledge Handbook of Crime and International Migration*. Abingdon: Routledge, 367–81.

McCulloch, J. and Wilson, D. (2016), *Pre-Crime: Pre-emption, Precaution and the Future*. Abingdon: Routledge.

Milivojević, S. (2013), 'Borders, Technology and Immobility: "Cyber-Fortress Europe" and its Emerging Southeast Frontier', *Australian Journal of Human Rights* 19(3): 101–24.

Milivojević, S. (2014), 'Stopped in the Traffic, Not Stopping the Traffic: Gender, Asylum and Anti-trafficking Interventions in Serbia', in S. Pickering and J. Ham (eds), *The Routledge Handbook on Crime and International Migration*. Abingdon: Routledge, 287–301.

Milivojević, S. and Pickering, S. (2008), 'Football and Sex: The 2006 FIFA World Cup and Sex Trafficking', *Temida* 11(2): 21–47.

Milivojević, S. and Pickering, S. (2013), 'Trafficking in People, 20 Years on: Sex, Migration and Crime in the Global Anti-trafficking Discourse and the Rise of "Global Trafficking Complex"', *Current Issues in Criminal Justice* 25(2): 585–604.

Milivojević, S. and Segrave, M. (2010), 'Responses to Sex Trafficking: Gender, Borders and "Home"', in L. Holmes (ed.), *Trafficking and Human Rights: European and Asia-Pacific Perspectives*. Cheltenham: Edward Elgar Publishing, 37–55.

Milivojević, S., Segrave, M., and Pickering, S. (2017), 'The Limits of Migration-related Human Rights: Connecting Exploitation to Immobility', in L. Weber, E. Fishwick, and M. Marmo (eds), *The Routledge International Handbook of Criminology and Human Rights*. New York: Routledge, 291–300.

Morača, T. (2014), 'Migrantkinje i migranti u lokalnim zajednicama u Srbiji', ATINA and CZA. Available at: http://www.atina.org.rs/sites/default/files/Migranti%20i%20 migrantkinje%20u%20lokalnim%20zajednicama%20u%20Srbiji.finalno.pdf

Nieuwenhuys, C. and Pécoud, A. (2013), 'Human Trafficking, Information Campaigns, and Strategies of Migration Control', in M. Segrave (ed.), *Human Trafficking*. Farnham: Ashgate, 285–306.

O'Brien, E., Hayes, S., and Carpenter, B. (2013), *The Politics of Sex Trafficking: A Moral Geography*. New York: Palgrave Macmillan.

Parkinson, C. (2015), 'The Year Europe Buckled under the Biggest Refugee Crisis since World War II', *Vice News*, 31 December. Available at: https://news.vice.com/article/ the-year-europe-buckled-under-the-biggest-refugee-crisis-since-world-war-ii

Pickering, S. (2008), 'The New Criminals: Refugees and Asylum Seekers', in T. Anthony and C. Cunneen (eds), *Critical Criminology Companion*. Annandale, NSW: Hawkins Press, 169–79.

Pickering, S. (2011), *Women, Borders and Violence: Current Issues in Asylum, Forced Migration and Trafficking*. New York: Springer Science.

Pond, E. (2006), *Endgame in the Balkans: Regime Change, European Style*. Washington, DC: Brookings Institution Press.

Poynting, S. (2008), 'Ethnic Minority Immigrants, Crime and the State', in T. Anthony and C. Cunneen (eds), *Critical Criminology Companion*. Annandale, NSW: Hawkins Press, 118–28.

Quackenbush, C. (2016), 'Hungarian Prime Minister Says Europe's Migrant Crisis is a "Poison"', *Time*, 27 July. Available at: http://time.com/4425549/hungary-migration-poison-europe/

Radio Slobodna Evropa (2016), 'EU: Deca migranti i Nigerijske žene na meti trgovaca ljudima', 19 May. Available at: http://www.slobodnaevropa.org/a/27745509. html

Roknić, A. (2015), 'Ima bezbednosno interesantnih migranata sa borbenim iskustvom', *Danas*, 28 July. Available at: http://www.danas.rs/danasrs/drustvo/ima_bezbednosno_ interesantnih_migranata_sa_borbenim_iskustvom_.55.html?news_id=305551

Segrave, M., Milivojevic, S., and Pickering, S. (2009), *Sex Trafficking: International Context and Response*. Cullompton: Willan Publishing.

Semati, M. (2010), 'Islamophobia, Culture and Race in the Age of Empire', *Cultural Studies* 24(2): 256–75.

Stojanović, D. (2015), 'Four European Nations Shut Doors to "Economic Migrants"', *The Sydney Morning Herald*, 20 November. Available at: http://www.smh.com.au/world/four-european-nations-shut-doors-to-economic-migrants-20151119-gl3fvi.html

UN Security Council (2015), 'Tackling Migrant Trafficking Crisis Will Require Exceptional, Coordinated Response, Senior European Union Official Tells Security Council'. Available at: https://www.un.org/press/en/2015/sc11885.doc.htm

UNHCR Serbia (2014), 'Izveštaj sa istraživanja javnog mnjenja: Stav građana Srbije prema tražiocima azila'. Belgrade: UNHCR and CESID. Available at: http://www.unhcr.rs/ media/CeSIDUNHCR201014FINAL.pdf

Weber, L. (2013), *Policing Non-Citizens*. Abingdon: Routledge.

Weber, L. and Bowling, B. (2004), 'Policing Migration: A Framework for Investigating the Regulation of Global Mobility', *Policing and Society* 14: 195–212.

Weber, L. and Pickering, S. (2011), *Globalization and Borders: Death at the Global Frontier*. Basingstoke: Palgrave.

Wickes, R. and Sydes, M. (2015), 'Immigration and Crime', in S. Pickering and J. Ham (eds), *The Routledge Handbook on Crime and International Migration*. Abingdon: Routledge, 11–25.

Wolfensohn, G. (2016), *Gender Assessment of the Refugee and Migration Crisis in Serbia and FYR Macedonia*. Istanbul: UN Women, Europe and Central Asia Regional Office.

Young, J. (1999), *The Exclusive Society*. London: Sage.

6

Visible Policing Subjects
and Low Visibility Policing

Migration and Race in Australia

Louise Boon-Kuo

John[1] was apprehended as an undocumented migrant in early 2006 shortly after the 'riots' at Cronulla beach on 11 December 2005 (personal communication, 26 July 2008). Over a decade has passed, but the Cronulla riots, a racist attack on people viewed as 'Middle Eastern', followed by altercations between Caucasian and 'Middle Eastern' Australians, remain a landmark event in Australian race politics and a distinct policing operation (Cunneen 2009; Noble 2009a; Poynting 2006).

Like others from Arabic-speaking communities in the Canterbury-Bankstown area who felt they were 'unfairly targeted by police following the Cronulla incidents' (Community Relations Commission 2007), John believed he was stopped and searched because of his ethnicity. The police officer stopping John advised immigration that the stop was prompted by John 'looking lost' (Immigration file note, date anonymized). But John explains that police in a patrol car singled him out while he was walking down a quiet residential street to buy cigarettes. The police stopped him and nobody else who was on the street at the time, and asked him for his identification. They then took John's mobile phone to check for text messages, reflecting the post-Cronulla view of phones as key to 'rioting for a tech-savvy generation' (Goggin 2006: 9). John was then taken to the police station. 'After maybe two hours, three hours,' John explains 'after tell me "You're very clean, you're alright, but you have a bit of a problem for immigration." ' Nothing in John's immigration file indicates that he had been stopped due to suspicion about his immigration status. John was later taken to an immigration detention centre.

Vivian Alvarez Solon was born in the Philippines, married an Australian in 1984 and became an Australian citizen in 1986. Vivian divorced in 1993 and remained in Australia. Immigration had records of Vivian's identity: in 1992 she was issued

---

[1] This account is derived from the author's interview with John, a nominated pseudonym, in 2008, and from documents included in his immigration file. The material relating to the interview of John and the Cronulla riots partly draws on research published in Boon-Kuo (2017: 70–2).

a passport in her married name, which also showed her birth name, and in 1999 immigration initiated a database file in her married name, which also referenced her mother's maiden surname Alvarez. In 1999 Vivian was diagnosed as living with 'a paranoid psychotic illness complicated by alcohol and illicit substance misuse' and was reported as a missing person to the Queensland Police Service on two occasions (Commonwealth Ombudsman 2005: 10). On 30 March 2001, she was found by a passer-by in a park. She had been injured after a fall, and the next day was admitted as an involuntary patient to the psychiatric unit of the local hospital. On 13 July, immigration formally interviewed Vivian and, as before, she stated her correct date of birth, her mother's maiden name, and for the first time explained she was an Australian citizen. However, immigration failed to identify her citizenship. As a result, that day Vivian was taken into immigration detention on the basis that she was known or reasonably suspected of being an unlawful non-citizen. At this time, detention centre and immigration staff noted that Vivian was 'basically immobile' and would need assistance upon arrival given she has 'no family in the Philippines to assist her' (Commonwealth Ombudsman 2005: 15). Despite this warning, on 20 July 2001, Queensland Police escorted Vivian when she was removed by plane from Australia to the Philippines.

After Vivian's removal, Queensland Police Missing Persons Bureau continued their efforts to locate her. As early as July 2003 an immigration officer realized an Australian citizen had been erroneously deported. Following a television broadcast on missing persons, other officers came to the same conclusion. Yet, it was not until April 2005, after persistent efforts by Vivian's former husband, that immigration formally recognized that Vivian had been wrongfully removed and she was later found in the Philippines.

Vivian's case was headline news. Public outrage that a citizen had been removed led to an inquiry. It found that immigration officers interviewing Vivian made two crucial assumptions that influenced how immigration handled her case: that she was an unlawful non-citizen; and that she may have been a 'sex slave', a remark made without supporting evidence which was repeated in subsequent immigration file notes (Commonwealth Ombudsman 2005: 13, 15, 47). In Australia, Filipina women are 'stereotypically associated...with mail order brides and sex workers' (Soldatic and Fiske 2009: 291), which goes some way to explain how such an assumption was treated as fact.

These accounts each tell a story of being apprehended as an 'illegal' migrant in Australia. Read together, they also reveal how racialized assumptions about ethnicity inform exposure to coercive migration powers irrespective of formal legal citizenship.

The role of 'race' in animating migration policing discretion is critically important to understanding how contemporary low-visibility practices produce and facilitate racialized hierarchies. In the past, official policy made race an explicit basis for immigration control, as the White Australia Policy (which lasted from the 1880s to 1973) included measures to exclude 'non-white' people and favour 'white' migration. Today, the racialized discourse and dynamics of the Australian government's spectacular and highly visible maritime deterrence of asylum seekers has been the subject of significant scholarly study, as has the institution of immigration detention (Crock 1993; Grewcock 2009; Perera 2002). Internal migration policing is much less visible, which may explain why its racial dynamics have received less attention. At the same time it has different and significant implications because it occurs within the community and nation.

This chapter exposes street-based migration policing as a site of two important dynamics in contemporary practices of racialization. It first explores the inherent contradiction between the putatively race-neutral legal category of unlawful non-citizenship and the policing of migration legal status that occurs on the street. Drawing on John's experience of immigration 'arrest', and instances investigated in four Ombudsman reports of the detention of Australian citizens under migration powers, including Vivian Alvarez Solon, it argues that these examples, where an individual's 'race' was highly visible, should not be regarded as isolated but as inherent in the practice of policing status. The policing of immigration status, in other words, *produces* people as 'illegal' in particular ways and in so doing reveals the racialized stratification of citizenship and non-citizenship. The chapter then briefly explains a key way that migration law props up the myth of legal racial neutrality through its limited oversight over policing practices. It ends by considering the implications for migration and policing research.

THE LEGAL CONTEXT OF IMMIGRATION 'ARREST' POWERS IN AUSTRALIA

As 'officers' under the Migration Act 1958 (Cwlth) ('Migration Act'), s. 5, police and immigration officers hold various immigration powers analogous to those of the police in their criminal jurisdiction. Although presence in Australia without a visa is not a criminal offence, the administrative classification of 'unlawful non-citizen' status is grounds for 'arrest' and detention. I use the legislative term 'unlawful non-citizenship', which has the same meaning as the colloquial terms 'undocumented' or 'irregular' migrant, to emphasize that migration legal status is a conferred status.

The immigration powers to 'arrest' and detain are authorized by the same laws that established mandatory immigration detention in 1994. The law provides that 'If an officer knows or reasonably suspects that a person ... is an unlawful non-citizen, the officer *must* detain the person' (emphasis added) (Migration Act, ss 5, 14, 189). Detention in this context includes the process of restraining a person (Migration Act, s. 5; *Minister for Immigration and Multicultural and Indigenous Affairs v. VFAD* [2002] FCAFC 390 [150]). In street-based policing contexts, the detention power thus provides authority for immigration officers, and an additional justification for police, to deprive suspected unlawful non-citizens of their liberty. The detention power is critical in producing the 'deportability' (De Genova 2002) of individuals and is a key migration policing power.

IMMIGRATION, LAW, AND RACIALIZATION

Immigration laws have played an integral role in fashioning how 'race' and racial hierarchy are produced in Australia. Immigration was a key tool for territorial expansion and the attempted dissolution of Aboriginal and Torres Strait Islander societies as part of settler colonialism (Dauvergne 2016; Wolfe 2006). Each act of immigration control since then has affirmed state sovereignty and at the same time denied the sovereignty of Aboriginal and Torres Strait Islander peoples (Moreton-Robinson 2015). Historically, immigration controls have also distinguished between the 'race' of migrants by generating the meaning of 'whiteness'. The most infamous measure used for this function was the 'dictation test', legislatively enshrined between 1901 and 1958. The test excluded migrants who failed to accurately transcribe fifty words of a European language selected by the immigration officer if required (see, e.g., the Immigration Restriction Act 1901 (Cwlth), s. 3).

Today the legal category of unlawful non-citizenship applies to those present in Australia without a visa with no regard to 'race', nationality, gender, age, class, or sexuality. How, then, do individuals come to be racialized as suspected unlawful non-citizens? It is here that critical race theory offers resources to understand better the intersection between law and legal categories and racialized hierarchies. From the 1980s, critical race theorists in the United States started to conceive of their work as not only focused on the adverse impacts of law on racialized communities, but were also concerned with 'uncovering how law was a constitutive element of race itself: in other words, how law constructed race' (Crenshaw et al. 1995: xxv). That is, scholars in this tradition turned attention to the study of processes of 'racialization', by which term they meant the processes that generate ideas about race and make these meaningful signifiers for action and differentiation between groups.

In referencing 'race as a process of becoming rather than one of being, racializa-tion does the conceptual work of putting quotation marks around "race" ' (Sentas 2014: 34). Processes of racialization thus do not necessarily accord with racial self-identification. In this regard, scholars have recorded many instances of police targeting based on perceptions of racial identity not racial self-identification (see, e.g., Parmar 2011). The way that legal practices such as policing target constructed identities such as 'Middle Eastern' or 'Asian' emphasizes law's role in constituting race.

As David Goldberg argues, the abstract universalism of modern law itself makes it particularly apt for the constitution of racial, gendered, and classed subjectivities. It is law's very universality, in other words, that allows the illusion of racial neutrality (Goldberg 2002: 145–6). These insights open up the potential to understand legal categories such as 'unlawful non-citizenship' as racially inscribed (as well as shaped by gender, sexuality, and class). In the sense that modern racial constitution involves at its heart the 'the power to exclude and by extension include in racially ordered terms, to dominate through the power to categorise differentially and hierarchically, to set aside by setting apart' (Goldberg 2002: 9), immigration law is its emblematic forum. The central function of immigration law is to regulate inclusion and exclu-sion, and it is partly operationalized through the selective and racialized policing of suspected unlawful non-citizens.

Case study on migration policing and the Cronulla riots

The immediate precursor to the riots at Cronulla is generally ascribed to a conflict at Cronulla beach between a number of off-duty lifesavers and a group of 'Middle Eastern' men, which resulted in injury to the lifesavers. There was extensive and controversial media coverage (Hazzard 2006; Noble 2009b). Over 270,000 SMS messages were transmitted inciting the events that followed (Hazzard 2006). On 11 December 2005, about 5000 people, mostly white men, attended Cronulla beach ostensibly to protest against reports of perceived intimidating behaviour by persons described by the crowd as Lebanese and 'Middle Eastern' people from the western suburbs of Sydney. The racist nature of the Cronulla events was explicit on a number of levels. The gathering was replete with Australian flags, T-shirts, and placards with slogans such as 'We grew here, you flew here', 'Aussie BBQ. No falafel', and 'We're full, fuck off'. The crowd chased and assaulted a number of persons perceived to be 'Middle Eastern' (Hazzard 2006: 39–45).

The beach has long been a site for racialized and gendered notions in Australian popular culture, a key part of national identity. Thus the locale of this particular event brought another element to the claims of belonging enunciated by the racist protest. Aileen Moreton-Robinson writes 'At Cronulla, the white male body performatively repossessed the beach through anti-Arabic resentment, thus mimetically reproducing the racialized colonial violence enacted to dispossess Indigenous people' (Moreton-Robinson 2015: 43).

Following Cronulla, police geographically targeted their work in Sydney's western suburbs to manage the so-called 'reprisal attacks', including identifying those involved in originating or circulating SMS messages concerned to be a call to arms (Hazzard 2006: 54). Their racial targeting was evident from the geographical focus on areas populated by Arabic-speaking people, road blocks, and stops and searches of people of 'Middle Eastern' appearance. In this focus, their actions should also be understood as part of longer and ongoing forms of policing of those racialized as Middle Eastern that has been particularly prominent from the 1990s with the racialization of sexual violence in a series of sex offences in Sydney's suburbs (see, e.g., Collins et al. 2000; Grewal 2016). In Australia more broadly it has persisted through counterterrorism policing (Sentas 2014) in an environment in which the 'terrorist' threat has been racially produced as Arabic-speaking people within and outside the nation.

It was in the period following the Cronulla events that John, as detailed in the account that started this chapter, was apprehended as an unlawful non-citizen. John's testimony strongly suggested that police stopped him on the basis of his 'Middle Eastern' appearance as part of their post-Cronulla activities. In this respect John's experience is typical of the policing of incongruity in street settings. Police form suspicion not only in relation to gathering evidence for a specific crime, but as part of broader surveillance of people whose age, sex, 'race', activities, and behaviours are out of step with what is considered to be normal in the particular context of the place, time, and activity (Dixon et al. 1989: 186–7). An important consequence of police holding immigration powers alongside their criminal jurisdiction is that police have a broader range of reasons that may later be used to justify their street stop, amplifying the low visibility of the reasons for initial intervention. John's experience of having his immigration status checked following a non-migration-related street stop reflects findings that state police involvement in locating unlawful non-citizens primarily takes place in an 'opportunistic' manner as part of everyday police duties (Weber 2013: 62).

It appears that police often check immigration status on the basis that a person presents as 'foreign' in some way. A survey of New South Wales (NSW) Police conducted in 2008 and 2009 elicited 776 responses nominating a primary reason for contacting immigration to check an individual's immigration status. The largest response from police was 'doubt over identity' which, as Leanne Weber (2013: 73) notes, provides little explanation as to why police checked identity in the first place, as the check requires a name. Although the other reasons selected in the survey account for a smaller proportion, they provide stronger insight into why unlawful immigration status was suspected. Over half the reasons nominated in the survey imply that police instigated a check on the basis of racialized suspicion. The reasons included that the individual held foreign documents, was unable to speak English, held a foreign name, exhibited a non-Australian accent, or was of ethnic appearance (Weber 2013: 73).

The high number of residents born overseas makes it impossible to identify an individual's migration legal status from their perceived ethnicity or national origins.[2] If, as it appears, racialized suspicion often informs immigration status checks, then it is not surprising that these checks construct the suspect population beyond that of non-citizens. Between 20 February 2006 and 31 October 2007, over 10,000 queries were made to immigration for status checking, 17 per cent concerned persons confirmed as citizens, and a further 70 per cent involved checks on lawful non-citizens (Weber 2013: 40). Although this survey reported only on immigration status checks, the racialized assumptions informing such checks highlight that neither formal Australian citizenship nor lawful migration status necessarily protect individuals from exposure to migration policing.

The racialized migration policing of Australian citizens

The consequences of racialized assumptions on citizenship protections are starkly illustrated by a number of documented cases. In 2005, two high-profile incidents focused attention on the use of the immigration detention power to take people into custody. Australian permanent resident Cornelia Rau was wrongfully detained for ten months in 2004 and 2005 (Palmer 2005). Rau had migrated to Australia from Germany and had resided in Australia since the age of eighteen months, and was

---

[2] In mid-2015, 28.2 per cent of the estimated resident population were born overseas, 'residents' being those residing in Australia for twelve months or more over a sixteen-month period regardless of citizenship, nationality, or migration legal status (Australian Bureau of Statistics 2016).

not released from detention until her parents recognized her photo published in a newspaper and identified her. Australian citizen Vivian Alvarez Solon, as recounted at the start of this chapter, was detained and then wrongfully removed in 2001 from Australia to the Philippines, where she remained for about four years despite the department's repeated 'discovery' of the mistake (Commonwealth Ombudsman 2005). Both Rau and Alvarez Solon had a mental illness. These cases prompted widespread shock among the public that mistakes in migration policing practices could impact on Australian citizens and permanent residents. The subsequent referral of 247 cases of wrongful detention of individuals between 2000 and 2006 found that the institutional deficiencies in the Rau and Solon cases were not isolated. The Ombudsman found that in many of the 247 cases it reviewed, officers 'did not have an adequate basis on which to form a reasonable suspicion that the person being detained was an unlawful non-citizen' (Commonwealth and Immigration Ombudsman 2007). Moreover, the Ombudsman's investigations exposed ways in which assumptions about 'race', gender, and sexuality were deployed to undermine the principles of the legal protection of citizenship.

Twenty-six of the 220 matters referred to the Ombudsman involved Australian citizens who were subsequently released from detention because they were not unlawful (Commonwealth of Australia 2006: 131). Selected case studies of the detention of Australian citizens were included in four key Ombudsman reports. The problems that led to the wrongful detention of citizens and lawful non-citizens derived from a widespread mistaken understanding of legal responsibilities regarded as 'process' issues. These included having an inadequate basis for objective suspicion of status, failure to correctly identify a person, a culture of detaining persons 'carelessly or prematurely', and a recurring practice of detaining people who were unable to prove their status rather than evaluating available information to establish authority to detain (Commonwealth and Immigration Ombudsman 2007: 3).

In an assessment of how wrongful detention had occurred, the Ombudsman found the police and immigration officers targeted racialized citizens due to a range of factors. The Ombudsman reported that the tendency of officers to rely on information that a person was an unlawful non-citizen despite contrary evidence was particularly prominent 'in cases where a compliance officer noted that the decision to detain a person was because the person had an accent, was not of Anglo-Saxon appearance or could not be located on DIAC's [Department of Immigration and Citizenship's] systems' (Commonwealth and Immigration Ombudsman 2007: 3).

Police also tended to consider there may be an immigration issue 'when State police have apprehended someone whose identity is unclear and who does not fit the perceived ethnic profile of an Australian' (Commonwealth and Immigration Ombudsman 2006a: 12). This was observed in an investigation into cases of wrongful detention of nine persons with mental health and capacity issues, in eight of whom 'different ethnicity was apparent' (Commonwealth and Immigration Ombudsman 2006a: 2–3), and five of whom were Australian citizens. Noting that it is not possible to assess how widespread this issue is, the Ombudsman commented: 'the problem is real so far as it concerns people in poor mental health who face difficulty in communicating accurately with government officials' (Commonwealth and Immigration Ombudsman 2006a: 13).

Assumptions about an individual's ethnicity were found to hinder their correct identification. For example, acting on NSW Police referrals, immigration detained Mr T (the pseudonym utilized in the report) three times, once in 1999 and twice in 2003. His confinement, which amounted to 253 days in total, was the result of cumulative administrative deficiencies and systemic failures within immigration. Mr T was born and educated in Vietnam and is of Chinese ethnicity. He became an Australian citizen in 1989, five years after arrival. The failure to identify Mr T partly arose from the mistaken belief by police and immigration that Mr T was of Chinese not Vietnamese national origins (Commonwealth and Immigration Ombudsman 2006b: 30). At the time of his second, and the most lengthy, of his detentions, Mr T wrote his name in Chinese script and it was translated by a NSW Police officer who correctly recorded his date of birth but did not correctly transpose his name into English script (Commonwealth and Immigration Ombudsman 2006b: 30).

No single Ombudsman's report focused specifically on the issue of racialized assumptions and policing practices so it is not possible to know precisely the extent to which it informs police and immigration practices. It is possible to state that the powerful and routine discretion of the immigration detention provison is a problem which itself supports racialized policing. By requiring the detention of those reasonably suspected to be unlawful non-citizens, the detention provision resembles status offences which criminalize a person's being, not their conduct, and which have long been typified as expansive police powers to 'identify and eliminate threats' (Dubber 2005: 136).

The broad powers over unlawful non-citizens affect how officers' view the significance of their coercive actions. In a recent case, counsel for the Commonwealth government argued that the immigration detention provisions provided an 'umbrella of legality', which therefore meant the unlawfulness of an arrest of two minors for aggravated people smuggling did not make their subsequent detention unlawful (*SU v. Commonwealth of Australia; BS v. Commonwealth of Australia* [2016] NSWSC 8, [8], [29]). Although the argument was ultimately unsuccessful, the case highlights that part of the problem is the law itself. As such, immigration's implementation of the Ombudsman recommendations to include training on the awareness of cultural, language, and ethnic issues for all compliance officers, and on the use of translators and interpreters (Proust 2008: 39) may go some way to addressing issues in the identification of individuals, but does not provide a solution to the production of racial stratification of citizenship and non-citizenship by migration policing.

RACIAL STRUGGLES OVER CITIZENSHIP

Understanding policing practices of racialization as struggles over citizenship reflects the terrain of today's racial rule. In the contemporary period of democratic 'racial states', Goldberg argues, 'social exclusions in terms of race (complexly knotted with class and gender, ...) become the mark of social belonging, the measure of standing in the nation-state, the badge of social subjection and citizenship' (Goldberg

2002: 10). Goldberg traces the transition in racial rule from what he refers to as naturalist conceptions (predicated on inherent racial inferiority such as the apartheid regime in South Africa), to historicist claims of racial immaturity (that viewed the racially different as capable of progressing to self-governance), which came to predominate from the second half of the nineteenth century (Goldberg 2002: 74–97). A characteristic of contemporary racial rule through law is that law is not merely an instrument of racial interest designed to legitimate primary mechanisms of direct violence on the body as it was under 'naturalist' regimes that treated specified races as inferior. Rather, in contemporary democratic states, 'racial rule comes to assume the rule of law' (Goldberg 2002: 141) and 'is caught always in the struggle between subjection and citizenship' (Goldberg 2002: 105).

In this account of the contemporary state, it is not surprising that access to the entitlements of legal citizenship such as freedom to move within the country may be undermined by racialized policing practices. The legal designation of citizenship does not guarantee entitlements, nor does the legal designation of unlawful non-citizenship uniformly effect complete social exclusion. Rather, the experience of citizenship and non-citizenship is the product of constant negotiation and struggle over entitlements and political subjectivities in which policing plays an important role. The tension between racialized regimes and legal citizenship is captured in Mae Ngai's (2004: 2) term 'alien citizen' (Hepworth 2015: 17). Ngai (2004: 2) uses this term to denote those persons 'presumed to be foreign by the mainstream ... and, at times, by the state', despite their legal citizenship.

Scholars have emphasized particularly in relation to unlawful non-citizens that the 'citizenship' constituted by social struggles must be understood as an 'an emergent condition that is both emplaced and embodied' (Hepworth 2015: 37). Despite 'illegal' status and policing practices, political subjectivities such as the 'respectable illegal' can emerge in particular conditions, as it did for some in Milan, Italy, around 2008 and 2009 (Hepworth 2015). Others suggest that the long-term presence of undocumented migrants within the nation (and thus some small measure of social inclusion) may impact on the legal meaning of citizenship (see, e.g., Sassen 2004; Varsanyi 2006). Saskia Sassen (2004) details the potential for legal residence in the United States where documented long-term residence, 'good conduct', and evidence that deportation would be an extreme hardship works to support applications for the legalization of immigration status and thus opens the possibility for an 'effective nationality' to take effect. The social and legal impacts of negotiations over status illustrate that border practices effect racial rule as much through 'differential inclusion' (Mezzadra and Neilson 2013; Sharma 2007) as social exclusion, and produce racial hierarchies across legal categories of citizenship and non-citizenship, lawful and unlawful immigration status.

LIMITED OVERSIGHT OVER RACIALIZED POLICING

Various avenues are available to citizens and non-citizens to challenge the legality of the use of migration policing powers. But these measures are inadequate for addressing racialized migration policing and thus instead prop up the myth of legal racial neutrality. Wrongful arrest and detention can and have been litigated under tort law, although not all cases make it to the court room. The Australian government paid over A$27 million in compensation between 1999 and 2013 for immigration detention related claims of unlawful detention and breach of duty of care (Australian Lawyers Alliance n.d.). A recent racial discrimination case in Australia, which was settled out of court, revealed that young men of African ethnicity were about two-and-a-half times more likely to be stopped and searched by police than suggested by their proportion of the population in the area (Flemington & Kensington Community Legal Centre n.d; Mason et al. 2016: 682). This racial discrimination case also illustrated the extensive resources required to bring such a case as it relied on expert analysis of police data by a statistician, and other expert reports. Litigation involves considerable costs for legal representation, stress, and uncertainty in the lengthy periods until resolution and, at least for criminal trials, requires a criminal standard of proof that can be difficult to achieve (Australian Law Reform Commission 2000; Community Law Australia 2012). The additional barrier of access for non-citizens seeking recognition and redress for officers' wrongdoing is that it does not provide grounds for legal stay in Australia because it is unrelated to a person's eligibility or application for a substantive visa (Migration Regulations 1994 (Cwlth) Schedule 2, Subclass 050, 050.212). This is a significant barrier because continued physical presence in Australia supports non-citizens' ability to self-represent, properly instruct representation, and sometimes access pro bono legal services.

Administrative law poses specific barriers to accountability for the action of officers (Boon-Kuo 2017: 93–8). It does not provide a legal avenue for recognition and redress for officers' wrongdoing that is *integrated* into non-citizen's substantive litigation. In criminal justice, judicial discretion to exclude evidence that is unlawfully or improperly obtained provides a streamlined means for oversight of police conduct with direct consequences for the case before the court. In their review of the rules of evidence prior to the introduction of uniform statutory evidence laws across the nation, the Australian Law Reform Commission (1985) commented on the significance of this discretion, stating that 'on occasion, there are *no real alternative methods* to obtain justice available to an individual citizen whose rights have been infringed' (emphasis added). Yet in migration law, the rules of evidence do not apply (Migration Act, ss 353, 420), and non-citizens have little incentive to bring evidence of officers' wrongdoing into visa-related matters. As a consequence, it is rare for officers' wrongdoing, much less racialized migration policing practices, to make it onto tribunal or court records.

Features of the administrative jurisdiction thus make the immigration decision to 'arrest' and detain paradigmatic of 'low visibility' policing (Boon-Kuo 2017: 72–3). Unlike a criminal arrest, persons are not detained for the purpose of commencing proceedings, nor are they detained for judicial determination of status (*Goldie v. Commonwealth* [2002] FCA 433, [6]). Persons are simply detained under 'administrative fiat' (*Goldie v. Commonwealth* [2002], [6]). The problems facilitated by low visibility policing and limited accountability are not unique to non-citizens. The term 'low visibility policing' was coined to describe police intervention that does not result in charge, and thus does not enable the judicial scrutiny afforded by criminal prosecution and trial (Ericson 1982; Goldstein 1960: 12). But the administrative forum of migration law further diminishes judicial oversight over policing practices, and thus marginalizes the potential for exposure of the racialized practice of migration policing.

CONCLUSION

The introduction of mandatory immigration detention policy in Australia did more than create a web of institutions within which unlawful non-citizens could lawfully be indefinitely detained. It also formally empowered administrative detention by officers from a range of institutions including immigration, customs, and the police on the basis of reasonable suspicion of unlawful status. In establishing the lawfulness of intervention for suspect status, the mandatory detention policy instituted a status-based police power long associated with subjective deployment in street settings. While the criminal law in principle protects the liberty of citizens and non-citizens alike from arbitrary interference and detention by the state, the Migration Act mandates arbitrary detention on the basis of 'reasonably suspected' unlawful status. As a distinction that relies on distinguishing between those who belong as citizens and lawful non-citizens and others, it is not surprising that migration policing practices produce racialized hierarchies.

The practices and ramifications of the empowerment of street-level migration policing discretion have only started to be investigated (see, e.g., Dekkers et al. 2016; Parmar, this volume; Weber 2013). The discussion in this chapter illuminates implications for how the methodological boundaries of research into racialized hierarchies in street or other migration policing settings should be conceptualized. Studies of policing must not be limited to migration law or to criminal law if research seeks to understand how 'race' is formed through policing practices. Both areas of law are implicated in the production of racialized hierarchies, particularly in the initial intervention. In practice (and in contravention to the expectations of law) it is not always possible to identify the precise legal power that prompted initial intervention, and this is particularly true for inter-agency street-based operations. Further, the interrelation between migration and criminal law powers are important in constituting discretionary authority that facilitates a subjective and racialized basis for intervention.

Yet studies of the policing of public order commonly restrict their purview to criminal justice. Empirical research into how people are being policed and who is being policed will help answer such questions as: to what extent are non-citizens being dealt with by administrative rather than criminal law mechanisms; is this increasing given the trend in temporary migration from the Global South to the Global North; and how does the racialized stop affect which justice route public order problems are steered towards. Research into these questions provides a means to evaluate the extent to which non-citizens are governed fundamentally by migration law in order to better understand the relationship between the state and non-citizens. If non-citizens are primarily governed by migration law, then questions of the extent of judicial oversight over the practices of state officials, as discussed in this chapter, become even more acute.

Studies of the experiences and perceptions of migration policing should not restrict their subject by the binary legal categories of unlawful and lawful, non-citizen and citizen status. Migration policing may treat some citizens as unlawful (as the 'alien citizen') and presume some unlawful non-citizens hold lawful status (producing an 'emergent citizenship') (Hepworth 2015: 17, 37; Ngai 2004: 2; Sassen 2004). In street policing practices legal status is decentred as the impetus for initial intervention, and thus the starting point for research that seeks to understand processes of racialization (and its articulation with gender, class, and sexuality) must reject the artificial legal boundary of legal and citizenship status. Both may be affected by racial profiling and migration policing. Further research is particularly needed on the effect of racialized migration policing practices on citizens. The significance of such research in the criminal justice arena is highlighted by Karen Glover's (2009: 80–1, 91–115) finding that respondents in the United States experienced the racialized traffic stop not only as a micro-level moment of discrimination, but as 'an everyday reminder of a much broader system of racial inequality' that amounted, to 'a break from citizenship', which fundamentally altered their relationship to the state.

This chapter has focused on processes of racialization of migrant illegality within the nation. However, it would be wrong to view these processes as in any way complete in the production of the policed subject as unlawful. High-level administrators and politics 'partially scripts' the work of street-level officers (Dekkers et al. 2016: 383). Migration policing is best understood as an assemblage, reflecting heterogeneous elements that may produce an effect in the absence of an overarching or coherent principle (Salter 2013). Prior to arrival in Australia, individual visa applicants are subject to multiple border processes including those designed to assess credibility of the nominated reason for travel and verification of identity. Visa application assessment and review processes are also engaged in racial inscription, translating credibility through risk factors applied to applicants and constructions of bad intent (Boon-Kuo 2017: 142–80). Technologies that map genetic difference onto 'race' through biometric border practices such as facial recognition and iris scanning are also implicated (see, e.g., Vukov 2016). To understand how border practices produce race, practices within the nation must be understood as part of a process of bordering that the Australian immigration department refers to as a complex multi-dimensional 'continuum' (Australian Border Force n.d.) in which race may be inscribed before and after arrival.

Migration law and policing fundamentally encourage consciousness of migration legal status by the state and civil society (see, e.g., Aliverti 2015; Berg 2016). The challenge in researching processes of racialization in migration is to traverse the conventional boundaries of research: to examine criminal law alongside migration law, the experience of citizens alongside non-citizens, the experience of lawful non-citizens alongside unlawful non-citizens, practices within the nation alongside those outside the nation, state practices alongside civil practices, technological processes alongside embodied experiences. This is necessary if we are to understand and challenge the extent and methods through which migration laws and policing embed 'race' in laws that are racially neutral on their face.

REFERENCES

Aliverti A. (2015), Enlisting the Public in the Policing of Immigration, *British Journal of Criminology* 55(2): 215–30.

Australian Border Force (n.d.), 'About the Australian Border Force'. Available at: https://www.border.gov.au/australian-border-force-abf/who-we-are

Australian Bureau of Statistics (2016), *3412.0 – Migration, Australia, 2014–15*, 30 March. Available at: http://www.abs.gov.au/ausstats/abs@.nsf/Previousproducts/3412.0Main%20Features12014-15?opendocument&tabname=Summary&prodno=3412.0&issue=2014-15&num=&view=

Australian Law Reform Commission (1985), *Evidence (Interim) ALRC Report 26*. Canberra: Australian Law Reform Commission.

Australian Law Reform Commission (2000), *Managing Justice: A Review of the Federal Civil Justice System*. Sydney: Australian Law Reform Commission.

Australian Lawyers Alliance (n.d.), *Freedom of Information Request—FOI 13/69*. Available at: http://www.lawyersalliance.com.au/documents/item/13

Berg, L. (2016), *Migrant Rights at Work: Law's Precariousness at the Intersection of Immigration and Labour*. Abingdon: Routledge.

Boon-Kuo, L. (2017), *Policing Undocumented Migrants: Law, Violence and Responsibility*. Abingdon: Routledge.

Collins, J., Noble, G., and Poynting, S. (2000), *Kebabs, Kids, Cops and Crime: Youth Ethnicity and Crime*. Annandale, NSW: Pluto Press.

Commonwealth and Immigration Ombudsman (2006a), *Report into Referred Immigration Cases: Mental Health and Incapacity*. Canberra: Commonwealth Ombudsman.

Commonwealth and Immigration Ombudsman (2006b), *Report into Referred Immigration Cases: Mr T*. Canberra: Commonwealth Ombudsman.

Commonwealth and Immigration Ombudsman (2007), *Report into Referred Immigration Cases: Detention Process Issues*. Canberra: Commonwealth Ombudsman.

Commonwealth of Australia (2006), *Parliamentary Debates: House of Representatives Official Hansard*, 19 June, 130–2.

Commonwealth Ombudsman (2005), *Inquiry into the Circumstances of the Vivian Alvarez Matter: Report under the Ombudsman Act 1976 by the Commonwealth Ombudsman, Prof. John McMillan, of an Inquiry Undertaken by Mr Neil Comrie AO APM*. Canberra: Commonwealth Ombudsman.

Community Law Australia (2012), *Unaffordable and out of Reach: The Problem of Access to the Australian Legal System*.

Community Relations Commission (2007), *Submission to the NSW Ombudsman Law Enforcement Legislation Amendment (Public Safety) Act 2005 Review*, 21 February.

Crenshaw, K., Gotanda, N., Peller, G., and Thomas, K. (1995), 'Introduction', in K. Crenshaw, N. Gotanda, G. Peller, and K. Thomas (eds), *Critical Race Theory: The Key Writings That Formed the Movement*. New York: New Press, xiii–xxxii.

Crock, M. (ed.) (1993), *Protection or Punishment: The Detention of Asylum Seekers in Australia*. Leichhardt: Federation Press.

Cunneen C. (2009), 'Law, Policing and Public Order: The Aftermath of Cronulla', in G. Noble (ed.), *Lines in the Sand: The Cronulla Riots, Multiculturalism and National Belonging.* Sydney: Sydney Institute of Criminology, 220–31.

Dauvergne, C. (2016), *The New Politics of Immigration and the End of Settler Societies.* Cambridge: Cambridge University Press.

De Genova N.P. (2002), 'Migrant "Illegality" and Deportability in Everyday Life', *Annual Review of Anthropology* 31: 419–47.

Dekkers, T. J. M., van der Woude, M. A. H., and van der Leun, J. P. (2016), 'Exercising Discretion in Border Areas: On the Changing Social Surround and Decision Field of Internal Border Control in the Netherlands', *International Journal of Migration and Border Studies* 2(4): 382–402.

Dixon, D., Bottomley, A. K., Coleman, C. A., Gill, M., and Wall, D. (1989), 'Reality and Rules in the Construction and Regulation of Police Suspicion', *International Journal of the Sociology of Law* 17(2): 185–206.

Dubber, M. D. (2005), *The Police Power: Patriarchy and the Foundations of American Government.* New York: Columbia University Press.

Ericson, R. (1982), *Reproducing Order: A Study of Police Patrolwork.* Toronto: University of Toronto Press.

Flemington & Kensington Community Legal Centre (n.d.), *Daniel Haile-Michael & Ors v Nick Konstantinidis & Ors VID 969 of 2010 Summary of Professor Gordon's and Dr Henstridge's First Reports.* Available at: http://www.communitylaw.org.au/flemingtonkensington/cb_pages/files/Summary%20of%20Experts'%20report.pdf

Glover, K. S. (2009), *Racial Profiling: Research, Racism and Resistance.* Lanham, MD: Rowman & Littlefield.

Goggin, G. (2006), 'SMS Riot: Transmitting Race on a Sydney Beach, December 2005', *M/C Journal* 9(1). Available at: http://journal.media-culture.org.au/0603/02-goggin.php

Goldberg, D. T. (2002), *The Racial State.* Malden, MA: Blackwell Publishers.

Goldstein, J. (1960), 'Police Discretion Not to Invoke the Criminal Process: Low-Visibility Decisions in the Administration of Justice', *Yale Law Journal* 69(4): 543–94.

Grewal, K. (2016), *Racialised Gang Rape and the Reinforcement of Dominant Order: Discourses of Gender, Race and Nation.* Surrey: Ashgate.

Grewcock, M. (2009), *Border Crimes: Australia's War on Illicit Migrants.* Sydney: Institute of Criminology Press.

Hazzard, N. (2006), *Strikeforce Neil Cronulla Riots: Review of the Police Response, Vol 1.* Sydney: NSW Police.

Hepworth, K. (2015), *At the Edges of Citizenship: Security and the Constitution of Non-Citizen Subjects.* Farnham: Ashgate.

Mason, G., McCulloch, J., and Maher, J. (2016), 'Policing Hate Crime: Markers for Negotiating Common Ground in Policy Implementation', *Policing and Society* 26(6): 680–97.

Mezzadra, S. and Neilson, B. (2013), *Border as Method, or, the Multiplication of Labor.* Durham, NC: Duke University Press.

Moreton-Robinson, A. (2015), *The White Possessive: Property, Power, and Indigenous Sovereignty.* Minnesota: University of Minnesota Press.

Ngai, M. (2004), *Impossible Subjects: Illegal Aliens and the Making of Modern America.* Princeton, NJ: Princeton University Press.

Noble, G. (ed.) (2009a), *Lines in the Sand: The Cronulla Riots, Multiculturalism and National Belonging*. Sydney: Sydney Institute of Criminology.

Noble, G. (2009b), 'Where the Bloody Hell Are We? Multicultural Manners in a World of Hyperdiversity', in G. Noble (ed.), *Lines in the Sand: The Cronulla Riots, Multiculturalism and National Belonging*. Sydney: Sydney Institute of Criminology, 1–22.

Palmer, M. (2005), *Inquiry into the Circumstances of the Immigration Detention of Cornelia Rau*. Canberra: Commonwealth of Australia.

Parmar, A. (2011), 'Stop and Search in London: Counter-terrorist or Counter-productive?' *Policing and Society* 21(4): 369–82.

Perera, S. (2002), 'A Line in the Sea', *Race & Class* 44(2): 23–39.

Poynting, S. (2006), 'What Caused the Cronulla Riot?' *Race & Class* 48(1): 85–92.

Proust, E. (2008), *Evaluation of the Palmer and Comrie Reform Agenda—Including Related Ombudsman Reports*. Canberra: Department of Immigration and Border Protection.

Salter M. B. (2013), 'To Make Move and Let Stop: Mobility and the Assemblage of Circulation', *Mobilities* 8(1): 7–19.

Sassen S. (2004), 'The Repositioning of Citizenship: Emergent Subjects and Spaces for Politics', in P. A. Passavant and J. Dean (eds), *Empire's New Clothes: Reading Hardt and Negri*. New York: Routledge, 175–98.

Sentas, V. (2014), *Traces of Terror: Counter-terrorism Law, Policing, and Race*. Oxford: Oxford University Press.

Sharma, N. (2007), 'Global Apartheid and Nation-Statehood: Instituting Border Regimes', in J. Goodman and P. James (eds), *Nationalism And Global Solidarities: Alternative Projections To Neoliberal Globalisation*. London: Routledge, 71–89.

Soldatic, K. and Fiske, L. (2009), 'Bodies "locked up": Intersections of Disability and Race in Australian Immigration', *Disability & Society* 24(3): 289–301.

Varsanyi, M. W. (2006), 'Interrogating "Urban Citizenship" vis-à-vis Undocumented Migration', *Citizenship Studies* 10(2): 229–49.

Vukov, T. (2016), 'Target Practice: The Algorithmics and Biopolitics of Race in Emerging Smart Border Practices and Technologies', *Transfers* 6: 80–97.

Weber, L. (2013), *Policing Non-Citizens*. Abingdon: Routledge.

Wolfe, P. (2006), 'Settler Colonialism and the Elimination of the Native', *Journal of Genocide Research* 8(4): 387–409.

Case law

Goldie v. Commonwealth [2002] FCA 433; (2002) 117 FCR 566.

Minister for Immigration and Multicultural and Indigenous Affairs v. VFAD [2002] FCAFC 390; (2002) 125 FCR 249.

SU v. Commonwealth of Australia; BS v. Commonwealth of Australia [2016] NSWSC 8; (2016) 307 FLR 357.

7

Policing Belonging

Race and Nation in the UK

*Alpa Parmar**

> Lorry drop Thursdays ... is what we call it. Our work has increased because of
> the influx of migrants over the last few years ... the [motorway] service station
> staff have become good at identifying people who've been dumped and are
> hanging around ... they recognize who doesn't quite belong ... and they let
> us know. Trouble is that once we pick 'em up and bring them in, they don't
> really belong in custody and immigration aren't exactly quick to pick them up
> or sort them out. They are in limbo, while my twenty four hour custody clock
> is ticking.
>
> (Police custody sergeant)

> Migrants are hyper-visible, socially badged by a mix of non-belonging markers
> like language, dress, and implicitly skin color. They are made nevertheless to
> occupy the hidden corners of the social, more or less invisible in their hyper-
> visibility, at once seen and unseen.
>
> (Goldberg 2015: 148)[1]

Drawing on research I have conducted in police custody suites, in this chapter I
argue that the policing of migration raises questions about the presence of minority
ethnic groups in the UK. In so doing, it illuminates how notions of belonging are
racialized through interactions with the police. More specifically I consider how, and
with what consequences, criminalization, migration, race, gender, and socio-economic status intersect when the police are asked to respond to migration and fears
about migrants. The priority to remove foreign national criminals is clearly affecting
the *nature of policing* and the everyday governance of minority ethnic groups (House
of Commons Report 2015).

* I would like to thank the research participants who took part in this project for their time and cand-
our. I am also grateful to the participants at the Border Criminologies' Seminar on Race, Migration and
Criminal Justice in September 2016 for their useful feedback, and Mary Bosworth, Yolanda Vázquez
and Lucia Zedner in particular who commented on earlier drafts. This publication arises from research
funded by the John Fell Oxford University Press (OUP) Research Fund.
[1] The author wishes to thank and acknowledge Polity for granting permission to publish this extract.

Policing Belonging: Race and Nation in the UK. Alpa Parmar. © Alpa Parmar, 2018. Published 2018 by
Oxford University Press.

The research I describe reveals the widening reach of the police, whose work is increasingly carried out in conjunction with other actors including members of the public who have been enlisted to monitor and report migrants to help enforce migration policy (Aliverti 2015). Conceptually, the chapter brings to light the everyday forms of racism that are renewed through the policing of migrants while exploring how new and familiar modes of policing minority ethnic groups coalesce to racialize and 'other' those who are deemed not to belong, who are risky, criminal, or a threat to social and economic resources. Policing, as will be shown in the following discussion, reinforces the racialization of some migrants and not others (Erel et al. 2016).

A key question raised by the discussion is whether the policing of migration represents continuity or change in the monitoring of groups that are racialized in society. Anti-immigrant sentiment, police brutality, and racially charged comments by public figures all mark a continuation of raciological articulation in current times, albeit through deployment of novel racially coded concepts (e.g. migrant, foreign national offender). I suggest that forms of policing and the expression of attitudes towards migration (and migrants) reflect the post-racial paradox of the present. The popular belief that we are post-racial suggests that we inhabit a society where the key conditions of social life are less predicated on racial preferences, choices, and resources. This idea, however, has been vehemently criticized as illusory and paradoxical. Instead, new expressions of race are present in contemporary times and post-raciality is at once seen to be both an assertion and aspiration (Goldberg 2015; Hollinger 2011).

Notwithstanding scholarship by some, including Aas and Bosworth (2013), Barker (2013), Bhui (2016), and Bowling (2013), few connections are made between the way in which both historically and in current times the immigration system is shaped by a racial order that upholds white privilege and enables the mobility of some, whilst restricting that of others. Colonialism was key to the creation of 'race' and racial categories and whiteness 'at home' was inextricably connected to blackness 'abroad', thus bolstering the creation of whiteness as a national identity (Anderson 2013; Back 2008; Stoler 1995). Yet this process is rarely mapped onto scholarship that examines contemporary patterns of global migration flow and restriction. Although academic analyses have addressed the ways in which immigration and criminalization intersect, less has been written about the racialization that these systems perpetuate through their intersection. Critical race theorists have long argued that immigration controls, laws, bureaucracy, and government technologies are used to reinforce racialized, classed, and gendered hierarchies around citizenship and belonging (Armenta 2016; Goldberg 2001; Sudbury 2005). Furthermore, little research has empirically addressed the crossovers with criminalization in the UK. The racialized politics of citizenship (De Genova and Ramos-Zaya 2003) continues to elude close scrutiny, and instead race and its social construction remain unexplored and written about euphemistically.

POLICING RACE

The intersections of migration, crime, and race have featured in political culture most markedly following the Second World War in 1945, when Britain's empire was receding. From 1948, Commonwealth citizens from the Caribbean and else-where arrived in Britain to respond to the labour shortage. From here onwards, migration was controlled and was particularly racialized following the Notting Hill riots in 1958. At this time, connections were made between the numbers of black people and strains on housing, employment, and crime, and the proposed solu-tion was to limit the migration of black Commonwealth citizens (Layton-Henry 1994; Schuster and Solomos 2004). The focus of immigration politics in the UK has therefore moved from restricting people arriving from the Commonwealth to reducing asylum migration and labour migration flows (Düvell 2008). Although the official purpose of migration policy has shifted to economic status and nation-ality (thus claiming to be race-neutral) the consequences are wholly racializing (Anderson 2013).

The governance and enforcement of immigration has been traditionally per-formed by the police in the UK. Following the 1971 Immigration Act, for instance, the police would conduct passport raids on black and Asian communities and places of work (Gordon 1985; Whitfield 2006). Ordinary police procedures that involved attending to minority ethnic groups as victims of crime would often include offic-ers carrying out impromptu passport checks (Bowling and Phillips 2002). Recent scholarship has described 'policing migration' as policing the boundaries of belong-ing, i.e. the boundaries between citizens and non-citizens (Düvell 2014; Weber 2013). The increased blurring of crime and immigration systems and the crimin-alization of migration—crimmigration (Stumpf 2006)—have expanded the con-nections between policing and immigration. Significant numbers of police officers have been seconded to immigration criminal investigation teams to provide training (Ashworth and Zedner 2014), while they are also expected to work closely and col-laboratively with immigration officers to ensure the removal of those who do not have (or have lost) the right to remain in the UK because of their criminal convic-tions (or other breaches of their visa regulations).

Police involvement in migration control intensified in the UK following 9/11 and the July 2005 attacks in London. Despite the fact that three of the four London attackers were British citizens (belonging to minority ethnic groups), British migration policy became influenced by security concerns about the 'war on terror' (Bosworth 2008; Coleman 2007) and fears about the 'enemy within' intensified (Hudson 2009) alongside the pre-existing perception of threat from external migrants. British Muslims were treated with suspicion and the everyday policing of members of these groups, through practices such as stop and search, increased significantly (Parmar 2011). Alongside these fears of terrorism, more gen-erally fears about 'foreign' offenders had been ratcheting up over the years.[2] The foreign national 'crisis', as it was framed, marks the moment when dealing with for-eign national offenders became a political priority (Bhui 2007; de Noronha 2015; Kaufman 2013). Through years of emergency measures and new policies, various

---

[2] For example, in 2006 information was released about the fact that few foreign national offenders had been removed despite their eligibility for removal because of their criminal conviction (National Audit Office 2014).

attempts have been made to make the removal of offenders convicted of an offence[3] in the UK swifter. One such recent initiative, discussed further below, is Operation Nexus, which formally partners the police with immigration control.

Policing in the UK, as elsewhere, has a long history of being disproportionately applied towards visible minority ethnic groups (Bowling and Phillips 2007; Weber and Bowling 2011). These same minorities have always been most vulnerable to exclusion beyond national borders (Weber and Bowling 2008). Today, the consequences of disproportionate policing of visible minorities is evident in stop and search practices, police brutality, and killings in the UK and USA. In response, public and academic attention has turned to race and intersectionality (Crenshaw 1991; Potter 2015). At the same time, however, similar attention to race within scholarship about border control and border practices has been scarce (Bowling 2013; Garner 2015; Gordon and Lenhardt 2007; Vázquez 2015). How racialization is maintained and reinforced by everyday practices in policing and immigration enforcement, has, quite simply, not received detailed attention in the immigration and policing scholarship (Romero 2008).

This is not to detract from the small number of accounts that have discussed how policing to secure control over immigration has racially discriminatory consequences (Bosworth 2008; Provine and Sanchez 2011; Weber and Bowling 2004; Weber and Bowling 2008). For example, immigration powers are said to enable the police to deploy race in order to stop and search people (Carbado and Harris 2011). Much of this research is based in the United States and recent work has shown that immigration enforcement through policing promotes racial profiling and fear among immigrant communities, eroding the very forms of trust and co-operation that are vital to relations between police and public, particularly for minority ethnic communities (Provine et al. 2016). We also know that victims of police violence are more likely to be migrants and that much of the alleged abuse occurs when the police stop individuals on suspicion of having committed a criminal offence or during identity checks (Amnesty International 1995). The policing of groups on the basis of their race and nationality and their apparent 'lack of belonging' is thus clear, yet policies appear to entrench the practices rather than dislodge them.

The criminalization of race has long structured the criminal justice system and immigration legislation is arguably a key site of racial formation (Provine and Doty 2011; Sanchez 1997). The regulation of immigration has historically been socially and politically driven by stereotypes of immigrant criminality and a fear of immigrants. Social constructions of Roma migrants being predisposed to criminality, vagrancy, and idleness were described by Sigona and Trehan (2011) as being centuries in the making, underscoring the longstanding racialized nature of the migrant–crime linkage (Palidda 2016; Parkin 2013). The criminalization of African migrant women travelling to Europe is gendered and racialized (Sudbury 2005). Racist linkages between criminal behaviours and nationalities are so commonplace that

---

[3] The offence must be one leading to twelve months in prison, as stated in the UK Borders Act 2007, s. 32(2).

representations of prostitution are usually exhibited through black African female bodies (Angel-Ajani 2003).

As this overview demonstrates, policing often targets those who appear not to belong on the basis of their race, nationality, gender, and culture as well as on their perceived criminality. When the police question a person's citizenship status or right to belong, they reinforce practices of racialization that already exist in the criminal justice system. Racialized immigration law enforcement practices therefore permit a person's appearance to serve as 'reasonable suspicion' or 'probable cause' (Romero 2008).

POLICING MIGRATION IN THE UK

Amidst public fears about levels of migration, as well as concerns about criminality and terrorism related to increased mobility, British police have become more involved in border control. Under the terms of Operation Nexus, which was piloted in 2012 to 'identify and remove or deport those who pose a risk to the public or who are not entitled to be in the UK' (Vine 2014: 2), immigration officers are now stationed at police custody suites in London, the Midlands, and selected other areas, in a bid to identify foreign national offenders more swiftly and arrange their detention pending removal from the UK. The programme targets and deports foreign nationals who have broken the law for relatively serious offences, and continues to be rolled out across the UK.[4] The overarching aim of Operation Nexus is to improve the management of foreign nationals and foreign national offenders with a focus on strengthening cross-organizational working between the Home Office and police (Home Office 2017). Under the agreed Nexus process, police in London are required to refer all foreign nationals, or suspected foreign nationals, encountered or arrested to the Home Office's Command and Control Unit (CCU) for a status check. Outside London, practice varies with some forces using the CCU for status checks and others doing so when an immigration officer is not available or stationed in the custody suite (Bolt 2016).

Between October 2015 and June 2016, I conducted observations in six police stations to gain an understanding of how foreign national suspects were identified and treated (this included police stations that were implementing Operation Nexus, as well as those that were not). Over this period, I completed a total of 170 hours of observation and twenty-four interviews with police custody sergeants and custody detention officers. Despite the fact that Operation Nexus was only formally operating in two of the police stations where the research was being conducted, all had foreign national suspects brought into their suites, so I was able to see how the

---

[4] Operation Nexus was initially rolled out by the Metropolitan Police Service and Immigration Enforcement in September 2012. It was officially launched by senior police and Home Office staff on 9 November 2012. West Midlands Police joined in June 2013, followed by Greater Manchester and forces from East Midlands in 2014. Police forces in Hampshire, Avon and Somerset, and Sussex have all begun to engage with Operation Nexus High Harm as the operation continues to roll out across the UK.

policing of foreign nationals operated more generally. I was interested in whether (and how) people's nationality becomes a tool of suspicion and who was targeted for further checks on their offending histories in the UK and in their 'home' countries. Operation Nexus guidance states that 'all foreign nationals (or those whose nationality is unclear) should be referred to the CCU' (Bolt 2016). Where found, identity and other documents may confirm nationality, as will comparison on fingerprints taken in a custody suite with Home Office fingerprint databases.[5] However, little guidance is provided about how 'foreign nationality' should be established in the first place, the implicit message being that police officers should use their discretion in deciding who to check. The discretionary nature of checking nationality became clear in some of my observations and was at times prompted by custody detention officers[6] rather than the police custody sergeant:

he'll need an FNO [foreign national offender] check sarg ... can't get exact nationality from him, but by the sounds of it, he's Eastern European
                    (fieldwork notes, custody detention officer communication, white British)

Officially, the role of custody detention officers is to 'process' detainees brought into the police station on suspicion of an offence, to make regular welfare checks, and to provide food and water. However, during my observations, it soon became clear that custody detention officers held a significant amount of influence, particularly if they had been working at the same police station for a long period of time. These custody detention officers seemed to have developed good relationships with police sergeants and an understanding of the institutional logic within the custody suite. The way in which routines and discretion interacted in certain police stations was important for understanding the 'story' of policing migration and its cultural context within wider policing culture (van Hulst 2013).

   Identification of those suspected to be 'foreign' was largely based on the suspect's appearance—namely skin colour, their unwillingness to disclose their nationality (which heightened suspicion that they were foreign), and language/accent. Although some suspects stated that they were British citizens, if they were not believed, or if the police information system did not verify their citizenship, officers would make a request to the Criminal Records Office (ACRO) to establish nationality and whether they had any previous convictions in their 'home' country. If the suspect had committed prior crimes in the UK, in theory it should have been flagged on the criminal records information system when the suspect's fingerprints were

---

[5] Both police and immigration officers have powers to search for identity documents. Section 18 of the Police and Criminal Evidence Act (PACE) 1984 provides the police with the power to search any premises occupied or controlled by a person under arrest. Section 44 of the Borders Act 2007 provides the police or an immigration officer with the power to enter and search premises for evidence of nationality.

[6] Police custody suites usually have one police custody sergeant on duty and a number of custody detention officers on duty. Custody detention officers are not official police personnel and do not have police powers of arrest. They are contracted by the police and are employed by private security firms such as G4S, SERCO, and TASCOR. For further detail on the organization of police custody suites, see Skinns (2011).

taken. Questioning a person's nationality on the basis that they may be committing an offence (by falsely claiming that they held British citizenship) was regarded as less contentious than asking about ethnic background (see also Bosworth this volume). As one officer explained:

we have to be careful with ethnicity and religious rights ... but with nationality it's a bit more clear ... either you are a citizen or not, or you are in the system as an asylum seeker

(interview with police custody officer, white British)

Nationality was treated as an initial line of inquiry in order to establish other facts, and was closely tied to 'placing' someone within racial hierarchies. A Pakistani national, Irfan,[7] who stated that he was a British citizen, but was then found not to hold British citizenship, was not asked further questions and recorded as Pakistani-Muslim and a likely economic migrant. It was noted that his dietary requirements were halal and when taken to his cell he was informed that the painted arrow on the ceiling pointed to mecca, should he wish to pray. At once, this man was typecast as belonging to a particular nationality, citizen category, and an ethnic and religious group without any thought given to the potentially fluid nature of his actual identity, i.e. whether he was a practising Muslim and what his actual preferences or requirements might be.

The racialization of Muslim identities was palpable in the spaces of police custody, extending arguments about the intensification of surveillance, detention, and the suspension of rights for those who are 'Muslim-looking', demonstrative of the 'new culture of exception, wherein states increasingly exercise the sovereign right to exclude and abandon populations in the interests of governance' (Razack 2008: 175). The way in which Asian and black Muslims were treated (via cultural and religious assumptions made about them) also reiterated the necessity for cultural dimensions of race expressed through anti-Muslim sentiment (Rana 2011) to be better analysed and understood as current examples of racial formation where new types of racialized subjectivities are emerging (see Goldberg 2015 on post-raciality). As Omi and Winant explain, race is increasingly viewed as a cultural phenomenon that is understood fundamentally as an ethnic (i.e. cultural) matter. Race is thus 'conceptualized in terms of attitudes, beliefs, religion, language, "lifestyle" and group identification' and 'reduced to something like a preference, something variable and chosen' (2015: 22).

It was common for a person's darker skin colour to prompt questions about their nationality and to establish their right to belong, despite their insistence that they were British citizens. Imran, a 'British Pakistani'[8] was brought into police custody on suspicion of assault. The police custody sergeant was keen to establish that he did indeed have 'all his papers in order'. Comments such as these were commonplace. Establishing a person's citizenship status therefore clearly acted as a policing

---

[7] Pseudonyms are used throughout the chapter in order to protect the anonymity of those who came into police custody.

[8] Where possible I asked participants to self-identify their ethnicity so I could include this information in the research.

tool, seized upon particularly if the suspect was not white. On one occasion, a man, Ajmal, who had lived in the UK since the age of four was brought in on suspicion of dealing drugs. He was born in Bangladesh, and had been living with his aunt and uncle since 1995. He had a history of previous serious offending and this time, the police custody sergeant decided to treat him as a 'high harm' repeat offender. The immigration officer at the station was informed about Ajmal's case history, and on investigation, found that Ajmal had no right to remain in the UK. Although he had been living in the UK for most of his life, he had never made a citizenship application. Given his history of offending, he could, therefore, have a case made for his removal from the UK. The police custody sergeant liaised with the immigration officer (based in the station) and also informed the criminal investigation detective about the potential to remove him to Bangladesh. Ajmal had not visited Bangladesh since childhood, yet was in line to be deported to a country he knew very little about. The police officer commented that:

I know it's probably harsh … living in Bangladesh is probably as alien as it would be for someone like me. But you know, if he'd behaved and not continued with his lifestyle … you know … offending, he wouldn't be in this position.

(police officer, female, white British)

The moralizing tone exemplified in this comment was something I heard often within the custody spaces. The right to belong was treated as a privilege that, once granted, should be protected and was a reason to abide by the law. Hence any infractions of the law were seen as a vitiation of the right to belong, as demonstrated by the emphasis on culpability in the police officer's comment. As Stumpf (2006) explains in the US context, when non-citizens are classified as criminals, expulsion presents itself as a natural solution. The individual's stake in the community such as family ties, employment, contribution to the community, and whether the non-citizen has spent the majority of his life in the United States becomes secondary to the perceived need to protect the community.

Another suspect, Duwayne ('Black Caribbean'), was brought into police custody as he was seen exiting a house that was of interest to the police for suspected drug dealing. However, on being searched in police custody, no evidence was found. Whilst Duwayne was held in custody, his mobile phones were checked thoroughly, his car searched, his previous offending history scrutinized, and his citizenship checked. Although Duwayne had a British accent, the fact that he was of Jamaican descent meant that there may have been a chink in his profile (i.e. previous offending or interactions with the police) that could have provided the police with a lead to allow them to investigate for further crimes and to build a case for his deportation. Instances such as these demonstrate the way in which citizenship status is used as a way to further interrogate visible minorities as part of the policing toolkit. The 'raceless' or race-neutral claims of immigration and citizenship policy (Anderson 2013) sanction and shroud the racist premise of immigration controls and enable their invocation as part of police investigations for some suspects and not others. In comparison, Eric, a suspect brought in on the same shift as Duwayne, was not asked about his ethnicity, nationality, citizenship status, or religion. Eric was white, spoke with a working-class accent and when asked where he lived, he stated the name of the city and added 'where I've lived all my life'. Instances such as these served to confirm the place of those such as Eric amongst the group that 'belonged', without the need for their nationality to be verified. The type of crime for which the person was brought into police custody also played a part. For example, Eric was arrested on suspicion of sending lewd text messages to his grand-daughter and, given that it was a crime connected to a family member, this was treated differently and aroused less suspicion than if the suspect was a foreign national.

Ambivalence and discretion

During interviews with the police, most expressed some ambivalence about the formalization of the partnership with the Home Office, designed to make identification of foreign national offenders swifter. Similar feelings have been found amongst staff working in carceral environments (Kaufman 2013) and on immigration matters. As Bosworth (2014) has shown, immigration officers often have difficulty in reconciling themselves to the tasks they are supposed to carry out. Within the police station, uncertainty was linked to fears of immigration personnel encroaching on police 'space'. Some police officers suggested that they did not necessarily need a resident immigration officer to carry out checks and serve immigration notices, and instead they felt the system would be better if the police could have all of the immigration powers as part of their own repertoire to use when they deemed necessary (Melossi 2015). The different working cultures were difficult to surmount, one Asian British police officer observed, 'immigration like to do things their way and at their pace, and we have our way'.

Immigration officers disrupted the usual hierarchy that operated within the police stations and brought together two different sets of working practices that employed the use of discretion in competing ways. Police work continues to rely on discretion and the law both constrains and enables it (Bronitt and Stenning 2011). This was confirmed in my research where discretion was employed in exactly these ways—within the constraints of the law and at times because of the interaction of human rights, PACE codes and immigration legislation. As the quote at the beginning of this chapter highlights, those cautioned can be held in police custody for a period of twenty-four hours, after which further permission needs to be sought if a person is suspected of a serious offence such as murder.[9] For the most part, this was strictly adhered to by the police. However, immigration notices were sometimes issued after delays, which led to the twenty-four-hour threshold being surpassed. This was a practice that I only saw with those suspected or established as being foreign nationals, who were most likely to be non-white. Discretion thus operated along decision-making channels, procedures, and assumptions that were racialized from the outset.

---

[9] Those arrested under the Terrorism Act 2000 can be held for up to fourteen days without charge.

Categories of belonging

People who were brought into police custody having been abandoned at service stations by people smugglers, 'found' on the street, reported as homeless, begging, or arrested during workplace or rented accommodation raids were also subject to checks for their histories of offending. While these checks were carried out, the individuals were locked in cells in custody suites. Police officers across the stations commented that these were by far the most 'compliant' group in police custody and that at times it felt inappropriate to have them there at all. As one police custody sergeant commented:

today I've booked in four illegal aliens, one of them is a minor—around 11 years old—and in the next wing I've got a suspect in for armed robbery and another guy who's suspected of sexual offences against a minor. This ain't the place for the foreign nationals and actually makes my life harder. They are just grateful for somewhere warm and us giving them food and checking in on them, it's ironic really. But they've got health issues that need to be looked at often. If those who are detained pass each other in the corridor or something happens when they interact, it could be problematic. I'm on tenterhooks shifts like this . . . we're waiting for immigration to come and pick them up

Officers did recognize that some migrants entering the country without leave to remain needed help and care rather than investigation. These perceptions were gendered and racialized as women were often categorized as 'deserving' or 'undeserving' migrants (Dhaliwal and Forkert 2015) based on their nationality, age, and race. Groups were also spoken about in familiar terms of 'trade-offs' based on their advantages and disadvantages (Anderson and Ruhs 2010). For example, 'Eritreans usually come as families and are quiet, though their English is usually not there'; 'Turkish lads tend to know more English than they'll let on'; 'Vietnamese and Nigerian women tend to have been trafficked and have been caught up in the system' (fieldwork notes). Remarkably, stereotyped perceptions expressed through comments about nationality (and grouping migrants' background and behaviour together) were openly talked about, without apparent concern about being perceived as racist or xenophobic:

You'll get Albanian women who tend to be involved in bag theft and are usually working with a group of men. That's often a mix of here illegally, offending history as long as your arm and so on
   Afghans are often genuinely seeking asylum . . . young boys and men usually . . . but then it's harder to get any previous info on them
      those people who have largely grown up here and that, they are a bit wiser to their rights and that. Usually those who have been dumped are the most compliant . . . no trouble at all
(fieldwork notes)

When police and custody detention officers would mention nationality, the racialized connotations of framing nationalities with certain types of deviant behaviour and physical appearances were overlooked and instead talked about openly. For example, comments imbued with cultural judgement such as 'don't they know how we do things here?' to demarcate accepted forms of Britishness were commonly made and appeared to me to be used as a distancing technique between minority ethnic group detention officers and migrants being held in cells. Officers described groups according to their nationality confidently and without the restraint they demonstrated when talking about race[10] (see also Mary Bosworth's chapter in this volume). One police custody sergeant expressed his frustration at trying to establish nationality when a suspect refused to provide it:

sometimes they'll just not tell you where they are from and if they've got no record or no identity documents on them it's hard to tell ... and it means that if I want to do an ACRO check, I can't because you do need a nationality for that. You can sometimes make a call based on the language they speak, but that's really difficult if they're not saying anything except 'no comment' which is what they've been briefed to say

(police custody sergeant, white British)

The Immigration Act 2016 provides British police with powers to order people who have been arrested to state their nationality and require those believed to be for-eign nationals to produce their nationality documents. Plans for this requirement were generally welcomed by police custody sergeants, even though they believed they would be impractical to enforce. In many respects this new law would sim-ply sanction practices already occurring. If an officer suspects that a person is not a British citizen they can demand a passport or they can send officers to go and search premises. I saw numerous requests for citizenship proof with mostly black, Asian-Indian and Asian-Pakistanis, and Turkish suspects, even though they held British citizenship and clearly said they did. Being asked for proof of citizenship in these cases often aggravated interactions. For example, when Marcus (Black British) was brought into the police station, he was asked if he was a UK citizen and he replied, 'of course I am, man. What do you think ... geez ... how can you even ask me that? You lot, man.'

In response to Marcus's protests, the police custody sergeant became annoyed by the apparent lack of respect that he demonstrated and verbally reprimanded him. The situation continued to escalate, and led to Marcus being handcuffed and placed in a dry cell. Dry cells are usually reserved for those who may be required to give forensic evidence following a rape or murder charge and therefore do not contain an internal lavatory. Marcus had been brought in suspected of domestic abuse and, had the situation not escalated, would have been placed in an ordinary cell whilst awaiting charge or release.

Situations such as the one described above show how racialized assumptions about nationality operated in practice. Whereas an English or London accent spoken by a white person would serve to confirm their British nationality, an English accent spoken by a black man did not serve the same purpose. Instead, the 'rules' on foreign national status checks were deployed to control and coerce visible ethnic minorities. Other non-verbal cues were also noticeable. For example, when the suspect was non-white, custody detention officers and police officers tended to

[10] This may have been because the police staff knew that I was British and born in the UK and there-fore may have felt at ease talking to me about nationality rather than ethnicity or race.

speak at a slower pace and automatically used hand gestures to augment their verbal communication.

WE'RE NOT RACIST ... BUT

Police work around immigration was also reliant upon public reporting, as the quote at the beginning of the chapter illustrates. Police working practices seemed increasingly to involve responding to those who appeared to be 'out of place' or 'didn't belong' often involved responding to complaints made by the public of groups hanging around, or on the street asking for money. When probed about this, it was clear that the police did not frame public reporting as racist or xenophobic and instead regarded it as part of anti-immigration narratives, which commonly erase racist labels. The encouragement of public surveillance and informants in order to harden borders had created a channel of communication between the police and public, in support of extant scholarship, supporting findings of previous scholarship (Aliverti 2015; Walsh 2014).

The role of public assistance provided to the police in their role regarding migration control was a finding that I did not expect to witness or hear about so vividly in the police custody suites. However, the police supported and neatly distanced the reporting of anti-immigration sentiment from racist intent, and instead rationalized public reporting through tandem narratives of crime risk (of terrorism, fraud, abuse) and mounting pressures on public services, and that 'everyday members of the public have legitimate fears about foreign national criminals being allowed to go free in the country' (police officer, fieldwork notes). The public were most visibly enlisted in migration policing in 2013 through the Home Office's aim to create a hostile environment for 'illegal immigrants' (Dhaliwal and Forkert 2015). 'Go Home' vans patrolled around ethnically diverse areas of London, advertising the number to call, should someone want to 'go home'. The fact that the campaign reapplied the racist epithet of 'go home' which many migrants—established and new—have experienced hearing was something that government policy had either neglectfully overlooked or willingly mobilized. The consequences were excoriating for the government and damaged minority ethnic group relations with the government (Wintour 2013).

So how does anti-immigrant sentiment fit with the myth of post-raciality described at the beginning of this chapter? Firstly, any naiveté that we were ever post-racial was powerfully deflated in 2016 when the UK vote to leave the European Union, driven by the stoking of familiar anti-immigrant fears (Versi 2016) and support for the UK Independence Party—a right-wing populist political party which has the politics of British national identity at its core, is anti-Islamic and openly criminalizes migrants. Secondly, the US election of Donald Trump, who utilized and expressed racist and misogynistic views to galvanize support for his campaign has been interpreted as the result of a 'white lash' against the election of the United States' first black president—Barack Obama. All of this serves to underscore complex and contradictory workings of race that require unpacking. For example, it is important to understand that racism and anti-racism do not sit as binaries or in unchanging and absolute ways. As Hannah-Jones (2016) states:

what's missing from the American conversation on race is the fact that you don't have to hate black people, or Latinos or Muslims to be uncomfortable of them, to be suspicious of them, to fear their ascension as an upheaval of the natural order of things. A smart demagogue plays to those fears under the guise of economic anxieties. Things not as good as you'd hoped? These folks are the reason.

Anti-immigrant sentiment and the police's willingness to integrate the public's assistance is arguably an expression of race amidst the myth of post-raciality (Goldberg 2015). It is within this context that the migrants oscillate between being hyper-visible and invisible. This was most clearly exemplified by the fact that many of the custody detention officers in the police custody suites were visible ethnic minorities and from migrant backgrounds, yet their 'foreignness' was conveniently overlooked. The stigma of racialization thus attaches and detaches to some bodies and not others and 'this is the primordial act of racism of our day, denying certain people the possibility of passing unnoticed' (Delgado Ruiz 2003: 221, cited in Calavita 2007).

Timing and context are clearly also key. As Back et al. (2012) remind us, Gilroy in 2004 powerfully argued that 'the figure of the immigrant' provides a key political and intellectual mechanism through which our thinking is held hostage: 'The colonial citizen-migrants who came to Britain after the second world war were transformed from 'citizens' into 'immigrants' on their arrival' (Back et al. 2012: 141). As the research discussed in this chapter has shown, migrants are treated and policed differently according to the colour of their skin and other modes of racialization. Whilst some migrants are invisible (i.e. chiefly white migrants), 'others are marked out for distinction and differentiation' (Back et al. 2012: 141).

CONCLUSION: MAPPING OLD AND
NEW FORMS OF POLICING

Although the policing of migration has clearly made police work more complex and increased its volume, I did not witness police being overburdened by foreign national offenders, as is often suggested by politicians and the media. It was clear that the policing of migration is not monolithic in its application, and that rather there were different types of police responses towards different migrants. At times, for instance, police repudiated their immigration powers. This supports previous research that has highlighted the complexity of police officers' perceptions of their role in policing immigration. For example, Van der Leun (2003) has found that police officers in the Netherlands viewed their role as crime fighters and safety keepers and did not automatically see themselves as assuming the additional role of immigration officers. Rather, migration control continues to act as a background resource for police that may be used at will and if deemed useful (Melossi 2015). This may shed light on why some of the police officers regarded the embedding of immigration officers under Operation Nexus as unnecessary or an ill-considered allocation of resources:

there's just not enough foreign nationals brought in regularly, that mean an immigration officer is needed all the time. When an IS91[11] has to be served they can organize for that quickly and they can push immigration along to come in themselves to collect detainees, but other than that . . .

(interview with police officer)

What is clear, however, is that police institutional racism and immigration laws are intersecting in ways that both recast and perpetuate narratives of (un)belonging in the UK that have existed for many decades and are intimately tied to race. The intersection of policing and immigration practice is not a new phenomenon. An illegal immigration intelligence unit was first set up at New Scotland Yard in London in 1972 and the police have long used evidence of identity as a tool against visible minorities (Gordon 1985). However, the political, conceptual, and operational move to formally conjoin policing with immigration in contemporary times is troubling because police work has long been reputed for using prejudice as a tool through which the ends are thought to justify the means (Fabini 2014). As the findings in this chapter have demonstrated, policing, with its acrimonious history of racialization, its 'real world' alchemy of laws, procedural rules, cultural norms, and discretionary practice, is questionably placed to manage migration. Mapping new and formal police–immigration partnerships onto old practices of policing, as this chapter has shown, is symbolic of the changing, *yet simultaneously unchanging,* nature of police work in contemporary times.

REFERENCES

Aas, K. and Bosworth, M. (2013), *The Borders of Punishment: Migration, Citizenship and Social Exclusion*. Oxford: Oxford University Press.

Aliverti, A. (2015), 'Enlisting the Public in the Policing of Immigration', *British Journal of Criminology* 55(2): 215–30.

Amnesty International (1995), *Italy: Alleged Torture and Ill-treatment by Law Enforcement and Prison Officers*. London: Amnesty International.

Anderson, B. (2013), *Us and Them*. Oxford: Oxford University Press.

Anderson, B. and Ruhs, M. (2010), 'Migrant Workers: Who Needs Them? A Framework for the Analysis of Staff Shortages, Immigration and Public Policy', in M. Ruhs and B. Anderson (eds), *Who Needs Migrant Workers? Labour Shortages, Immigration and Public Policy*. Oxford: Oxford University Press, 15–52.

Angel-Ajani, A. (2003), 'A Question of Dangerous Races?', *Punishment and Society* 5(4): 433–48.

Armenta, A. (2016, 'Racializing Crimmigration: Structural Racism, Colorblindness and the Institutional Production of Immigrant Criminality', *Sociology of Race and Ethnicity* 3(1): 82–95.

Ashworth, A. and Zedner, L. (2014), *Preventive Justice*. Oxford: Oxford University Press.

---

[11] A notice providing authority to detain.

Back, L. (2008), 'The Problem of the Immigration Line: State Racism and Bare Life', in A. Lentin and R. Lentin (eds), *Race and State*. Newcastle Upon Tyne: Cambridge Scholars Publishing, 32–52.

Back, L., Sinha, S., and Bryan, C. (2012), 'New Hierarchies of Belonging', *European Journal of Cultural Studies* 15(2): 139–54.

Barker, V. (2013), 'Democracy and Deportation: Why Membership Matters Most', in K. F. Aas and M. Bosworth (eds), *The Borders of Punishment: Migration, Citizenship and Social Exclusion*. Oxford: Oxford University Press, 237–54.

Bhui, H. S. (2007), 'Alien Experience: Foreign National Prisoners after the Deportation Crisis', *Probation Journal: The Journal of Community and Criminal Justice* 54(4): 368–82.

Bhui, H. S. (2016), 'The Place of "Race" in Understanding Immigration Control and the Detention of Foreign Nationals', *Criminology and Criminal Justice* 16(3): 267–85.

Bolt, D. (2016), *An Inspection into the Extent to which the Police are Identifying and Flagging Arrested Foreign Nationals to the Home Office and Checking their Status*. Independent Chief Inspector of Borders and Immigration Report. London: Crown Copyright.

Bosworth, M. (2008), 'Border Controls and the Limits of the Sovereign State', *Social and Legal Studies* 17(2): 199–215.

Bosworth, M. (2014), *Inside Immigration Detention*. Oxford: Oxford University Press.

Bowling, B. (2013), 'Epilogue. The Borders of Punishment: Towards a Criminology of Mobility', in K. F. Aas and M. Bosworth (eds), *The Borders of Punishment*. Oxford: Oxford University Press, 291–306.

Bowling, B. and Phillips, C. (2002), *Racism, Crime and Justice*. Harlow: Longman.

Bowling, B. and Phillips, C. (2007), 'Disproportionate and Discriminatory? Reviewing the Evidence on Stop and Search', *Modern Law Review* 70(6): 936–61.

Bronitt, S. and Stenning, P. (2011), 'Understanding Discretion in Modern Policing', *Criminal Law Journal* 35(6): 319–32.

Calavita, K. (2007), 'Law, Immigration and Exclusion in Italy and Spain'. *Papers 85*. Available at: http://www.raco.cat/index.php/papers/article/viewFile/74163/94206

Carbado, D. and Harris, C. (2011), 'Undocumented Criminal Procedure', *UCLA Law Review* 58: 1543–616.

Coleman, M. (2007), 'Immigration Geopolitics beyond the Mexico-U.S. Border', *Antipode* 39(1): 54–76.

Crenshaw, K. (1991), 'Mapping the Margins: Intersectionality, Identity Politics, and Violence against Women of Color', *Stanford Law Review* 43(6): 1241–99.

De Genova, N. and Ramos-Zaya, A. (2003), *Latino Crossings: Mexicans, Puerto Ricans, and the Politics of Race and Citizenship*. New York: Taylor & Francis.

De Noronha, L. (2015), 'Unpacking the Figure of the "Foreign Criminal": Race, Gender and the Victim-Villain Binary', *COMPAS Working Paper* 15–121.

Delgado Ruiz, M. (2003), 'Criminalización de los immigrantes?', in M. Delgado Ruiz, R. Bergalli, and Y. El-gharbaoui (eds), *Actas de las Jornadas del Graduat en Criminologia i Política Criminal*. Barcelona: Universitat de Barcelona, 216–50.

Dhaliwal, S. and Forkert, K. (2015), 'Deserving and Undeserving Migrants', *Soundings* 61: 49–61.

Düvell, F. (2008), 'Report from the United Kingdom', in J. Doomernik and M. Jandl (eds), *Modes of Migration Regulation and Control in Europe*. Amsterdam: Amsterdam University Press, 187–202.

Düvell, F. (2014), 'Does Immigration Enforcement Matter? Irregular Immigrants and Control Policies in the UK, Policing, Law Enforcement and Immigration Law Enforcement in the UK: Introduction and Background: Project Report I'. Oxford: Centre of Migration,

Policy and Society (COMPAS). Available at: https://www.compas.ox.ac.uk/media/PR-2014-DIEM_Policing_Background.pdf

Erel, U., Murji, K., and Nahaboo, Z. (2016), 'Understanding the Contemporary Race–Migration Nexus', *Ethnic and Racial Studies* 39(8): 1339–60.

Fabini, G. (2014), 'The Illegal Immigration Law: A Regime of Law, Discourses and Police Practices', *AmeriQuest Online Journal* 11(2): 1–17.

Garner, S. (2015), 'Crimmigration: When Criminology (Nearly) Met the Sociology of Race and Ethnicity', *Sociology of Race and Ethnicity* 1(1): 198–203.

Gilroy, P. (2004), *After Empire: Melancholia or Convivial Culture?* London: Routledge.

Goldberg, D. T. (2001), *The Racial State*. Oxford: Wiley-Blackwell.

Goldberg, D. T. (2015), *Are We All Postracial Yet?* Cambridge: Polity.

Gordon, J. and Lenhardt, R. A. (2007), 'Rethinking Work and Citizenship', *UCLA Law Review* 55: 1161–238.

Gordon, P. (1985), *Policing Immigration. Britain's Internal Controls*. London: Pluto Press.

Hannah-Jones, N. (2016), 'The End of the Postracial Myth.' Available at: http://www.nytimes.com/interactive/2016/11/20/magazine/donald-trumps-america-iowa-race.html?_r=0

Hollinger, D. (2011), 'The Concept of Post-Racial: How its Easy Dismissal Obscures Important Questions', *Daedalus* 140(1): 174–82.

Home Office (2017), *Operation Nexus—High Harm. Version 1.0*. London: Home Office. Available at: https://www.gov.uk/government/uploads/system/uploads/attachment_data/file/599878/Operation-Nexus-High-Harm-v1.pdf

House of Commons Committee of Public Accounts Report (2015), *Managing and Removing Foreign National Offenders, Twenty-ninth Report of Session 2014–15, HC 708*. London: The Stationery Office.

Hudson, B. (2009), 'Justice in a Time of Terror', *British Journal of Criminology* 49(5): 702–17.

Kaufman, E. (2013), 'Hubs and Spokes: The Transformation of the British Prison', in K. F. Aas and M. Bosworth (eds), *The Borders of Punishment: Migration, Citizenship and Social Exclusion*. Oxford: Oxford University Press, 166–82.

Layton-Henry, Z. (1994), 'Britain: The Would-Be Zero Immigration Country', in W. A. Cornelius, T. Tsuda, P. L. Martin, and J. F. Hollifield (eds), *Controlling Immigration: A Global Perspective*. Stanford, CA: Stanford University Press, 273–96.

Melossi, D. (2015), *Crime, Punishment and Migration*. London: Sage.

National Audit Office (2014), *Managing and Removing Foreign National Offenders, HC 441, Session 2014–2015*. Report by the Comptroller and Auditor General.

Omi, M. and Winant, H. (2015), *Racial Formation in the United States* (3rd edn). New York: Routledge.

Palidda, S. (2016), *Racial Criminalization of Migrants in the 21st Century*. London: Routledge.

Parkin, J. (2013), 'The Criminalization of Migration in Europe'. Paper in *Liberty and Security in Europe*. CEPS.

Parmar, A. (2011), 'Stop and Search in London: Counter-terrorist or Counter-productive?' *Policing and Society* 21(4): 369–82.

Potter, H. (2015), *Intersectionality and Criminology: Disrupting and Revolutionizing Studies of Crime*. London: Routledge.

Provine, D. and Doty, R. (2011), 'The Criminalization of Immigrants as a Racial Project', *Journal of Contemporary Criminal Justice* 27(3): 261–77.

Provine, D. and Sanchez, G. (2011), 'Suspecting Immigrants: Exploring Links between Racialized Anxieties and Expanded Police Powers in Arizona', *Policing and Society* 21(4): 468–79.

Provine, D., Varsyni, M., Lewis, P., and Decker, S. (2016), *Policing Immigrants: Local Law Enforcement on the Front Lines*. Chicago, IL: University of Chicago Press.

Rana, J. (2011), *Terrifying Muslims: Race and Labour in the South Asian Diaspora*. Durham, NC: Duke University Press.

Razack, S. (2008), *Casting Out: The Eviction of Muslims from Western Law and Politics*. Toronto: University of Toronto Press.

Romero, M. (2008), 'Crossing the Immigration and Race-Border: A Critical Race Theory Approach to Immigration Studies', *Contemporary Justice Review* 11(1): 23–37.

Sanchez, G. (1997), 'Face the Nation: Race, Immigration and the Rise of Nativism in Late Twentieth Century America', *International Migration Review* 31(4): 1009–30.

Schuster, L. and Solomos, J. (2004), 'Race, Immigration and Asylum: New Labour's Agenda and its Consequences', *Ethnicities* 4(2): 267–300.

Sigona, N. and Trehan, N. (2011), 'The (re)Criminalization of Roma Communities in a Neoliberal Europe', in S. Palidda (ed.), *Racial Criminalization of Migrants in the 21st Century*. London: Ashgate, 119–32.

Skinns, L. (2011), *Police Custody: Governance, Legitimacy and Reform in the Criminal Justice Process*. Abingdon: Willan Publishing.

Stoler, A. (1995), *Race and the Education of Desire*. Durham, NC: Duke University Press.

Stumpf, J. (2006), 'The Crimmigration Crisis: Immigrants, Crime and Sovereign Power', Bepress Legal Series, Working Paper 1635.

Sudbury, J. (2005), *Global Lockdown: Race, Gender and the Prison Industrial Complex*. London: Routledge.

Van Hulst, M. (2013), 'Storytelling at the Police Station: The Canteen Culture Revisited', *British Journal of Criminology* 53(4): 624–42.

Van der Leun, J. (2003), *Looking for Loopholes. Processes of Incorporation of Illegal Immigrants in the Netherlands*. Amsterdam: Amsterdam University Press.

Vázquez, Y. (2015), 'Constructing Crimmigration: Latino Subordination in a "Post-Racial" World', *Ohio State Law Journal* 76(3): 599–657.

Versi, M. (2016), 'Brexit Has Given a Voice to Racism—and Too Many are Complicit', *The Guardian*, 27 June. Available at: https://www.theguardian.com/commentisfree/2016/jun/27/brexit-racism-eu-referendum-racist-incidents-politicians-media

Vine, J. (2014), *An Inspection of Immigration Enforcement Activity in London and the West Midlands ('Operation Nexus') March–June 2014*. Independent Chief Inspector of Borders and Immigration, Crown Copyright.

Walsh, J. (2014), 'Watchful Citizens: Immigration Control, Surveillance and Societal Participation', *Social & Legal Studies* 23(2): 237–59.

Weber, L. (2013), *Policing Non-citizens*. Abingdon: Routledge.

Weber, L. and Bowling, B. (2004), 'Policing Migration: A Framework for Investigating the Regulation of Global Mobility', *Policing and Society* 14(3): 195–212.

Weber, L. and Bowling, B. (2008), 'Valiant Beggars and Global Vagabonds: Select, Eject, Immobilise', *Theoretical Criminology* 12(3): 355–75.

Weber, L. and Bowling, B. (2011), ' "It Sounds Like They Shouldn't Be Here": Immigration Checks on the Streets of Sydney', *Policing and Society* 21(4): 456–67.

Whitfield, J. (2006), 'Policing the Windrush Generation', *History and Policy*, 1 September. Available at: www.historyandpolicy.org/archive/policy-paper-45.html

Wintour, P. (2013), ' "Go Home" Vans to be Scrapped after Experiment Deemed a Failure', *The Guardian*, 22 October. Available at: https://www.theguardian.com/uk-news/2013/oct/22/go-home-vans-scrapped-failure

III

RACE, COURTS, AND THE LAW

8

Strangers in our Midst

The Construction of Difference through Cultural Appeals in Criminal Justice Litigation

*Ana Aliverti**

[T]here is no doubt that the kind of immigrants whom we get from the Asian community in Kenya are the kind who will be much easier to deal with. They are used to living in a British society. They are reasonably educated. Some of them have a considerable amount of money. They are not the kind of unskilled people whom we bring in from India, Pakistan, the West Indies or some other countries

> (David Steel MP, Parliamentary debate on the Commonwealth Immigrants Bill 1968, Hansard, House of Commons, 27 February 1968, col. 1291).

[I]t is not unreasonable for us to wish to have in this country good quality new people from around the world who want to be British citizens, people who speak English and make an economic contribution to our society

> (Stewart Jackson MP, Parliamentary debate on the Immigration Bill 2014, Hansard, House of Commons, 22 October 2013, col. 202).

INTRODUCTION

Historically, policies and debates about immigration in Britain have been preoccupied with identifying the features of the 'good' and the 'bad' migrant –those who deserved to be welcomed, and others who should not be allowed in or should be pushed out. The desirability of individuals and national groups has been predominantly assessed against the perceived, idealized, and racialized qualities of the natives.

* Thanks to my interviewees for their time and to the British Academy for funding the project from which this chapter draws. I am also grateful to Laurène Soubise and Sanjeeb Hossain for excellent research assistance, to the editors of this volume for their inputs, and to the participants of the workshop 'Race, Migration and Criminal Justice' (Oxford, September 2016) for inspiring debates and helpful suggestions on an earlier draft.

'Being like us' in terms of language, ethnicity, and cultural background is considered a virtue in its own right and important for social integration and cohesion. When Home Secretary, R. A. Butler, introduced new restrictions on citizens from the Commonwealth on entering the country in 1961, he sought to appease his critics by arguing that one of the purposes of the new law would be to exempt from controls 'persons who in common parlance belong to the United Kingdom' because of their ancestry (Hansard, HC Deb, 16 November 1961, col. 695). Examining the question of belonging in past and contemporary public debates on migration reveals the central role of colonialism in the British 'imagined community' (Ahmed 2000; Anderson 2016) and the social hierarchies that spring from this imagery. It can also help us understand the production of racial differences, and how they are reflected in the law.

Race is crucial for understanding contemporary border regimes. As a social construct, foreignness implies difference and inferiority; it is deeply constituted by racial categories. In what Sanchez and Romero (2010: 782) have called the 'social construction of racialized citizenship', foreignness unifies citizens and non-citizens in their treatment as racialized minorities. Through the lens of race, we can better grasp who gets designated as 'out of place', perceived as not belonging to the nation and excluded from it (Armenta 2017; Chacón, this volume). 'Citizenship status', Romero (2008: 28) bluntly asserts, 'is inscribed on the body'.

Other scholars draw attention to the ways in which racialized categories and the articulation of racism follow not just bodily traits but also less visible and more subtle markers of difference such as language, accent, national origin, and cultural and religious difference. As they point out, the black/brown–white binary fails to capture the extent of contemporary racisms through which some groups have been stripped of their whiteness and cast as 'others' due to their class, cultural background, and national origin (Fox et al. 2012; Garner, 2009; Webster 2008). These days, Coretta Phillips and Colin Webster (2013: 7) point out, expressions of racialized difference are more 'indirect, subtle and "cultural"'.

Despite an official repudiation of racism, appeals to 'culture' reveal how ideas of racialized difference remain prominent in many social institutions and relationships (Back 1993; Parmar and Bosworth, both in this volume). As such, cultural difference is crucial for understanding what Ahmed (2012: 2) calls the contemporary 'politics of stranger making'. In Britain, as elsewhere, it features prominently in racialized stereotypes of deviance and crime by ethnic minorities within public discourse, particularly in the context of heightened hostilities towards immigrants and anti-Muslim sentiments (Bhui, this volume; Fox et al. 2012; Parmar 2011; 2014). Not unexpectedly, mundane articulations of 'cultural racism' have also seeped into the criminal justice system (Hudson and Bramhall 2005; Millings 2013; Phillips 2008; Weenink 2009).

This chapter explores the legal construction of culture and cultural difference in criminal litigation as they appeared in interviews with court staff[1] and a selection

---

[1] Interviews were conducted in a project investigating the relevance of immigration status and citizenship in criminal justice decision-making entitled 'Foreign Nationals before the Criminal

of Court of Appeal decisions.[2] By taking stock of social stereotypes about particular racialized groups, the courts often automatically ascribe certain traits to individuals based on their categorized membership. Through close reading of cases, this chapter documents the ideas of culture that are used in courts, and their effect on criminal litigation. While cultural norms and values might be relevant for understanding people's reasons for action, the cultural stereotypes often deployed by court litigants and the importance attributed to them for explaining behaviour can have damaging consequences that extend beyond the legal case. Cultural difference is not a neutral marker separating social groups in the courtroom. Rather it is often deployed to explain behaviour in relation to specific groups, and is loaded with prejudices and stereotypical representations of racialized minorities.

As a legal strategy in criminal litigation, the reliance on 'culture' has worrying effects. First, it fixes people into separate and essentialized categories that fail to assess their individual conduct while dehumanizing them and reproducing demeaning stereotypes. Second, ascribing bad behaviour to 'culture' conceals structural social inequalities, racism, and discrimination. It also hides how the law perpetuates the subordination of these groups. Finally, a reliance on culture as an explanation of criminal behaviour marks out undesirable practices, norms, and values from the terrain of the British nation by ascribing them to specific groups. In so doing, it underpins an idealized image of a unified nation governed by democratic, liberal, and civilized values and rules, while reinforcing the boundaries of belonging and legitimizing exclusion.

IDENTIFYING 'STRANGERS' INSIDE THE COURTROOM: CULTURE, IMMIGRATION STATUS, AND POWER

Criminal courts in Britain are confronted daily with the challenge of apportioning punishment to a highly diverse population. In an attempt to render their clientele intelligible, lawyers and court operators rely on various tropes to single out groups within the courtroom. Attesting to the difficulties in sorting out human beings by their citizenship status (Bosworth 2012: 132), 'immigrants' and 'foreign nationals' are often identified by their non-English sounding names, accent, and language (Aliverti 2016: Aliverti and Seoighe 2017). In referring to this rather elastic and vague group, lawyers tend to classify their clients by crime types: 'Romanians' are pick-pockets, 'Poles' tend to be caught in alcohol-related crimes, 'Vietnamese'

Courts: Immigration Status, Deportability and Punishment', funded by the British Academy (SG140235). 'Culture' emerged as an important theme in these interviews and alerted me as to its relevance for understanding court operators' assumptions, categorizations, and ideas of citizenship and national identity.

[2] Reported judgments by the Court of Appeal, Criminal Division, were searched using key terms (such as 'culture', 'cultural defence', 'cultural background'). The search included decisions from 1996 to 2016, and resulted in around fifty matches. Some of these decisions are considered here.

are marihuana growers, 'Asians' are brought in for domestic and sexual violence, and so on.

In aiding this classificatory work, court operators often resort to familiar racial and gender stereotypes about non-western others. In a case reported in the national media that involved a defendant charged with harassment of a woman, the deputy district judge criticized the complainant's failure to attend a hearing by remarking condescendingly that: 'She can't be doing anything important'. When prompted by the prosecutor to explain what he meant, the judge was more explicit still: 'With a name like Patel she can only be working in a corner shop or off licence'. These remarks were rightly condemned and cost Justice Hollingworth his job.[3] Yet, subtler expressions of racism and sexism in court cases are far more common and often go unchallenged. These surfaced in interviews I conducted with judges, lawyers, and court staff at Birmingham's criminal courts.

Alluding to the 'cultural issues' that may have a bearing on the decision of a case involving 'foreign nationals', one crown court judge explained to me:

[P]art of the background to a lot of matrimonial violence and sexual offending can be very different cultural attitudes towards relationships between men and women ... they form part of the background because of expectations that are created, the nature of the relationship which is not what I might describe as love marriages but also may well involve dowries and therefore there is an element of commerciality about marriages. And so those are issues which sometimes need to be explained or explored with the jury during the course of a trial because people may not understand them.

More forthrightly, a magistrate asserted:

[D]omestic violence is increasingly common in the courts and you often get cases where in the Asian culture particularly, on the day of the trial, the lady who's the victim wants to withdraw. A sort of pressure from the family and that kind of community environment that they live in.

In the first example, the judge described features of marriage in 'Asian' culture as characterized by commerciality, rather than 'true' love. In the second, the magistrate suggested that gender subordination, patriarchal rule, and isolation from the wider society were typically prevalent in Asian communities. In both instances violence was presented as a product of the values and norms of Asians and implicitly juxtaposed to those ascribed to the British nation.

These kinds of appeal to culture produce a simple, uncontextualized story that glosses over the complexities of the case and can potentially alter the framing of the facts under consideration and the credibility of the witnesses, while reifying the image of certain national groups as inferior and uncivilized (Chiu 1994; Phillips 2003; Volpp 2000). As Volpp (1996; 2011) noted, explaining behaviour by culture overlooks power and neglects the political dimensions of marginality, racism, and poverty. It implies that violence is circumscribed to certain communities, thereby

---

[3] As reported in *The Mirror*, 'Top Judge Quits after Racist Slur in Court Made Against Asian Harassment Victim', 14 December 2014, available at: http://www.mirror.co.uk/news/uk-news/top-judge-quits-after-racist-4762640.

absolving the wider society and the state from creating the conditions for oppression and violence (Volpp 1994: 94). The assertion that migrant women's isolation and reluctance to denounce domestic maltreatment is the product of an oppressive, patriarchal, and misogynist community environment, while broader conditions of gender and racial subordination which block access to work and create dependence particularly as a result of immigration status are left unexamined.

This narrative has been put forward by litigants in numerous Court of Appeal cases. In *R v. MM*,[4] for instance, the applicant and complainant—a married couple—were Pakistani nationals. When the applicant obtained a highly skilled visa, they settled in the UK. His wife and their two children had no independent immigration status. The complainant filed a claim against her husband for rape and indecent assault. The prosecution justified her late reporting and lack of resistance to her husband's sexual violence because 'it was culturally unacceptable' to ventilate these marital matters and because 'her culture required her to submit'.[5] To attest to this aspect of the prosecution case, a police inspector, named Asrar Ul-Haq, testified about 'Asian culture and practice' and 'Islamic teaching on sexual practices'. Casting doubts over the allegations, the applicant argued that her motivation for pursuing him criminally was to gain immigration status, which she lost when she left the family home. Similarly, in another case of domestic violence, *R v. R*,[6] involving a couple from Bangladesh, the complainant claimed that her husband raped and assaulted her. The trial judge admitted evidence to the effect of proving that '[t]he [Bangladeshi] Muslim community is one that is founded upon a patriarchal system. In that regard women often find that they are subordinate in their position and role ... Members of the community may find it difficult to disclose and/or report [divorce, sexual relations, marital disagreement, and domestic violence] allegations'. This was agreed by both parties.

In much the same way that the defendant's background information is often admitted to inform decision-making, the introduction of cultural evidence in criminal litigation can be relevant and important for understanding why people act in certain ways. It may also assist judges to avoid subjecting disadvantaged minorities to the standards and expectations of privileged and dominant groups (Dundes Renteln 2004: 15; Phillips 2007: 83; Volpp 1994). Yet, as the cases cited above showed, the construction of 'cultural difference' in court can be highly problematic. In these cases, counsel on both sides abused stereotypes in the portrayal of the Pakistani and Bangladeshi cultures and implied that their clients were determined by those assumed cultural norms, while conveniently isolating factors related to the experience of these couples as migrants in the UK in the presentation of evidence. In particular, they did not factor in the way in which migration policies reinforce gender inequality. As scholars (Anderson 2007; Wray 2015) have shown, migration

---

[4] [2011] EWCA Crim 937; see also *R v. Shafqat Ali* [2006] EWCA Crim 2235.
[5] Cultural information can be important for assessing the credibility of the complainant as well as for sentencing purposes. According to sentencing guidelines on domestic violence, an aggravated feature of these cases is the vulnerability of the victim because of 'cultural, religious, language, financial or any other reasons' (Sentencing Council, *Overarching Principles: Domestic Violence*, Guideline ii, 3.7). Available at: https://www.sentencingcouncil.org.uk/wp-content/uploads/web_domestic_violence.pdf.
[6] [2013] EWCA Crim 1271.

policies assume the status of women as dependent and place women in a family role as carers, in contrast to men who are deemed independent and providers. When they are able to access the labour market, migrant women generally occupy positions that extend such domestic roles, are poorly rewarded, and attract less social prestige than those available to men. So, too, for some men, the migration process can entail a change in their social and economic status. Violence stemming from an attempt to reassert their sense of self and masculinity may be a response of some men to their subordinated status (Bosworth and Slade 2014).

In the United States, some legal scholars have objected to the admissibility of cultural information in court proceedings, arguing that it inevitably leads to the condoning of sexual violence and the reproduction of gender and racial stereotypes and injustices (e.g. Chiu 1994; Coleman 1996). Others insist on the importance of attending to cultural and structural factors in criminal adjudication to ensure equal justice and to address the sources behind the socially subordinated status of certain groups (Volpp 1996). For Holly Maguigan (1995: 55), the solution is not to limit the admissibility of this information but rather to subject to stricter scrutiny the definition of culture, the voices who purport to speak for a culture, the characteristics of the culture that merit recognition, and the degree of cultural immersion needed to be covered by any potential defence or sentencing advantage. Courts should not receive this information uncritically, she argues, and prosecutors should be able to contextualize it so that juries and judges do not accept damaging stereotypes and caricaturized versions of some cultures.

Drawing the line between proper and improper use of cultural difference in criminal litigation is difficult, however. References to culture are often a pretext for race and can, therefore, lead to racialization. According to Woodman (2009: 16), English criminal law has been historically reluctant to accommodate cultural diversity and to admit expert witnesses to attest on this aspect of a case. Yet, the adverse attitude towards recognizing cultural difference as a valid consideration in criminal justice decision-making does not mean that the courts remain impermeable to it. Cultural information is often fed into the court process by probation officers and lawyers who reproduce an essentialized, antagonistic, and inferior image of non-western cultures. In other cases, such as in *R v. MM*, pseudo-experts purport to speak on behalf of a particular culture with the same disturbing outcomes. Further, presentence reports may lack the level of contextualization necessary to appreciate how cultural and structural factors may have influenced offending (Hannah-Moffat and Maurutto 2010). As anthropologist Anthony Good observed, '[l]awyers and judges, when making such classifications, are inevitably constituting their own culture in opposition to that of the litigant ... This othering process is almost bound to lead to reification, especially when the lawyers' own culture remains, unexamined, in the background' (Good 2008: 54; see also D'hondt 2010).

Sentencing studies have found that judges are not indifferent to broader social stereotypes about certain groups, and these can heighten their view of the defendant's culpability, thereby leading them to enhance their punishment. Research on sentencing of domestic violence cases involving Indigenous and non-Indigenous offenders in Australia, for example, found that while convictions for domestic violence significantly reduce the likelihood of imprisonment for non-Indigenous offenders this effect is not as marked in cases involving Indigenous offenders. This finding suggests that while domestic violence is generally conceived as a private issue and less blameworthy than other forms of violence, domestic violence among Indigenous men is taken more seriously and considered a public problem that demands a stiffer, more deterrent criminal justice response (Bond and Jeffries 2014; Jeffries and Bond 2015). The difference in treatment of domestic violence offenders goes back to the interaction of gender, sexuality, and race in stereotypical assumptions about wife and children beaters. Risk assessments and sentencing choices may be influenced by the premise that crime and violence for some is 'engrained' in their culture—or as one solicitor I talked to put it, it is 'their way of life'—and thus they are less amenable to change.

In an illustration of how racial categories are actualized through nationality and cultural tropes, court operators create their own judicial typologies of the court clientele and sometimes attach sentencing consequences to them. A lawyer who counted among his clientele 'foreign nationals' commented about the difficulties he encounters when defending Romanian people due to negative perceptions about them among judges, before suggesting that differential treatment of defendant from certain nationalities may be explained by the operation of negative stereotypes:

I have had the "all you Romanians want when you come over here is to nick people's handbags"—it's not put quite as crudely as that but there is an undercurrent, I feel. And sometimes it is quite difficult to counter that argument ... We make a joke about it ... An aggravating factor is: you are Romanian ... But other white east European—Polish, Lithuanian, Latvian defendants—. . . tend to get treated as if they were more British citizens.

The blatant racialization of certain groups was challenged in *Odewale and others*.[7] In that case involving three men convicted of conspiracy to defraud, the crown court judge prefaced his sentencing remarks thus: 'I am not going to shy away from the fact—because it is a fact within the experience of this court—that a significant and, some might say, a disproportionate number of participants in these sorts of crimes, this particular species of crime, are either Nigerians or people who have connections to other Nigerians'. The assumed prevalence of this crime among 'Nigerians' justified in his view the imposition of deterrent sentences against them, to discourage others—presumably, Nigerians—from engaging in similar conducts and neutralize the cultural threat embodied by them: 'the court has a responsibility, in passing sentence, to not only mark the gravity of the offence that it is instantly dealing with, but, where it is appropriate, to seek to deter others that might be tempted to do the same thing from doing it; and I have such a duty in mind when passing sentence now'. In allowing the appeal against sentence, the appeal judges reasoned: 'It is quite simply irrelevant that [one of the appellants] is Nigerian and that the other two appellants, although British citizens, are of Nigerian origin ... We think the judge confused the appellants' racial origin with the question of deterrence in sentencing for identity frauds, which he was legitimately entitled to consider. Excessive sentences may have been passed because of this error.'

---

[7] *R v. Ayodele Odewale, Moses Awofadeju, Kazeem Oshungbure* [2004] EWCA Crim 145.

The impact of racial stereotypes on the outcome of cases is often harder to spot. Yet, the resort to culture in criminal litigation shows how difference is manufactured through criminal justice practices. As I will demonstrate in the next section, this racialization process has consequences that extend beyond the legal case.

RECREATING AN IMAGINED COMMUNITY BY RECOGNIZING 'STRANGERS': NATION, RACE, AND GENDER

In my research, it was clear that appeals to culture did not occur at random. Rather, cultural differences were praised in court in relation to certain individuals and groups. Usually it was considered relevant only to those perceived to be different from the dominant majority; those 'outsiders', who are not 'our people', by dint of their national origin, ethnicity, or ancestry. It was also more frequently pondered in cases involving domestic violence. This selectivity reveals the highly contingent nature of national identity and belonging (Back 1993). Historically, the racialization of Irish people in England relied on stereotypes of them as drunk and uncivilized. Similar labels are now applied to Eastern Europeans. As Waters (1997: 227) noted, many of the attributes of today's racialized groups were once ascribed to the vernacular working class, including primitiveness, violence, and hyper-sexuality.

Cultural theorist Sara Ahmed (2000; 2014) explains how the figure of the stranger is constitutive to the formation of the nation which requires her in order to exist. Colonial histories are deeply implicated in creating the figure of the stranger as that of the colonized. Encounters between the colonizer and the colonized are asymmetric, and inform techniques of differentiation between the familiar and the strange that delineate the boundaries of national identity and belonging. '[T]he nation', she writes, 'is a concrete effect of how some bodies have moved towards and away from other bodies, a movement that works to create boundaries and borders' (Ahmed 2014: 133). In a multicultural society like the UK, the idealized image of the nation is one of tolerance to and celebration of difference. The notion of whiteness, she argues, is confirmed by the capacity of the nation to incorporate the coloured. Yet, '[w]hilst some differences are taken in, other differences get constructed as violating the ideals posited by multicultural[ism]' (Ahmed 2014: 137). Difference is accepted as part of the multicultural nation as long as it supplements or can be contained within the coherent image of the nation (Ahmed 2000: 103). 'Cultural others' represent an existential threat to the nation, to its values and 'way of life'. 'Migrants' are thus required to embrace these values, to become 'British'. Segregation and insularity—and the uncivilized behaviour that comes with it—is a failure to live up to the collective ideal of inclusiveness and tolerance, the imperative to mix and to love difference. In other words, it is a failure to be thankful.

The nation as an imagined and idealized community is produced through everyday discourses of nationhood. Legal discourse is part of this repertoire. By implying that undesirable behaviour is a product of 'strange' cultures, the law recreates the image of the nation as guided by progressive, civilized, and feminist values. This 'extra-territorialization' of bad behaviour and attendant racialization of certain groups as carriers of 'foreign' cultures, is evident in certain references to cultural difference in criminal litigation in English courts. According to the Court of Appeal, 'cultural background' is generally only relevant for apportioning guilt and punishment in relation to new arrivals.[8] This rule lies on the premise (and the prescription) that a long time spent in the country should result in 'acculturation' and assimilation. Long-time residents are unlikely to benefit from any mitigation from raising their 'culture' as a defence either because they are lying about the bearing of their culture on the alleged crime or they are to blame for not mixing up. As Woodman (2009: 33) explained, 'the frequent reference to "English values" [in English criminal law] suggest that there is still a widespread belief in the desirability, and perhaps in the inevitability of the assimilation of minorities into the dominant culture'.

While, as anthropologists remind us, the dichotomy between a uniform dominant culture and a monolithic and opposing 'foreign' one rarely exists (Baumann 1996: 30; Good 2008: 53), it often appears in pre-sentence reports, which weigh heavily on sentencing decisions. They highlight the contraposition of 'western values' to those supposedly held by offenders, and conceive wrongdoing as a reflection of those values. In one of them, reported in a Court of Appeal case involving a man convicted for sexual assault against a woman, the author of the report noted that '[this man's] attitude towards English girls appeared to have resulted in a sense of entitlement to act as he did ... He did not understand English culture, despite having lived here for a number of years', suggesting that there was a 'racial element' to the offence.[9] The Court of Appeal agreed with that assessment, yet substituted a custodial sentence recommended by probation for a community order to address his 'deep seated, anti social attitudes'. In another Court of Appeal decision involving a man convicted of assaulting his wife and daughter, the trial judge based her sentencing decision on the pre-sentence report, which read: '[The appellant's] offending is linked to holding power and control within his family and to inappropriate, unacceptable views developed from his own experience growing up in Sri Lanka'.[10] The Court of Appeal dismissed the appeal against sentence.

As other Court of Appeal cases reveal, crime among racialized groups is often explained by their 'foreign' culture, which is juxtaposed to the norms and values ascribed to the British nation. In *R v. Matloob Ahmed*,[11] for instance, the applicant, a man from Pakistan who entered an arranged marriage in Pakistan with a

---

[8] See for example *R v A(N); Attorney General's Reference No1 of 2011* (2011) Times, 11 April where the Court of Appeal ruled that since the offender had lived in Britain for some years his cultural background to explain his culpability was not relevant as a mitigating circumstance.

[9] *R v. Juned Ahmed* [2011] EWCA Crim 775. Although the judgment made no explicit reference to the ethnicity and/or national origin of the applicant and complainant, it suggested that the man is non-white, Muslim, and presumably non-British, and the woman is white British. See also *R v. Awad* [2007] EWCA Crim 159 and *R v. Fazli* [2009] EWCA Crim 939.

[10] As quoted in *R v. Selvatharai* [2011] EWCA Crim 250 [at para 9].

[11] [2012] EWCA Crim 1646.

British woman and then settled with her in the UK, was convicted of six counts of rape and an assault occasioning actual bodily harm against his wife, and sentenced to imprisonment for public protection with a minimum term of eight years. The defence appealed the sentence imposed arguing that the trial judge ' "could have treated [him] slightly differently from a man who had been brought up in the United Kingdom" ... [which would] reflect that his offending was based on his belief that he had a right to rape his wife, and so his offending was not aggravated by a deliberate disregard of what is culturally acceptable or by the norms in this country'.[12] The Court of Appeal rejected this submission categorically: 'No man, whatever his background, whatever his race, whatever his creed, has the right to rape his wife'. Despite this claim, marital rape was not regarded as a crime in English law until 1991 following the decision of the House of Lords in *R v. R*.[13] Further, sexual violence in the domestic context continued to be vastly under-reported and under-criminalized, for some a sign of social tolerance towards domestic abuse and of gender inequality. As research has found, domestic violence is not circumscribed to specific groups but occurs across all social and economic levels (Menjívar and Salcido 2002).

An analogous hypocrisy is apparent in relation to cases of child maltreatment. In *R v. SM*,[14] for example, a man originally from Zimbabwe was convicted of cruelty against his stepson. He caused several injuries to the child in his attempt to discipline him. Concurring with the trial judge's considerations that the applicant was influenced by his upbringing in Zimbabwe where beating a kid is 'culturally acceptable', the Court of Appeal ruled nonetheless that he 'was old enough and had been in the country long enough to know that what he was doing, at any rate by the standards of 21st century Britain, was very wrong'. Thus it denied any extenuating advantage. In contrast, in *R v. RL*, the sentencing judge regarded the fact that the offender—a mother of three convicted of cruelty against them—was 'brought up in a different culture' along with other aspects which highlighted her attributes as a caring and conscientious mother as mitigating circumstances.[15] The Court of Appeal agreed. Although the cultural background of the carers was weighted differently—in part due to the operation of gender expectations, in both cases it served to underscore the foreignness of their ideas about child chastisement.

A similar distancing approach was adopted in the 1960s case of *R v. Derridiere*,[16] where the Court deemed the 'standards of parental correction [as] different in the West Indies from those which are acceptable in this country' admitting that 'immigrants coming to this country may find initially that our ideas are different from those upon which they have been brought up in regard to the methods and manner in which children are to be disciplined'. In ruling as excessive and outside the remits of reasonable chastisement acceptable in Britain, these decisions portrayed an image of a liberal and egalitarian society where child cruelty is not tolerated. Yet, they conveniently glossed over the fact that the UK has been criticized by human rights

---

[12] As reported in *R v. Matloob Ahmed*.　　　[13] [1992] 1 AC 599.
[14] [2014] EWCA Crim 702.
[15] As quoted in *R v. RL* [2015] EWCA Crim 1215 [at para 23].
[16] (1969) 53 Cr. App. R. 637.

bodies and ruled in breach of the European Convention on Human Rights by the European Court for not providing adequate protection to children against cruel, inhuman, and degrading treatment.[17] The law allowing corporal punishment was only changed in 2004 to limit the use of the defence of reasonable chastisement to offences resulting in minor or no bodily injuries.[18]

The belief that culture explains behaviour is also gendered. As Anne Phillips (2003; 2007: 85) has observed, in identifying the characteristics of the foreign culture that get picked up by court operators, gender stereotypes play an important role. In the case of men, culture works to exacerbate and condone their violent, hyper-masculine, and sexual behaviour. For women, their cultural background is brought up to explain their passivity, lack of agency, and propensity to be manipulated by male relatives. References to 'culture' convey broader stereotypes about certain groups which are in sync with dominant perceptions of appropriate gender roles (Chiu 1994: 1119).

A number of Court of Appeal cases illustrate this point. The appellant in *R v. Mirzabegi*[19] was a middle-aged woman and a single mother of two. She was convicted for assisting her former husband in depositing money obtained through fraud into her bank account and for obtaining services by deception, and sentenced to a two-year custody term. In allowing her appeal against her sentence, the Court of Appeal remarked the fact that she was of previous good character and started to work full-time, and thus at low risk of reoffending. It also noted that 'she was subject to a certain amount of influence from her husband, not only because of the natural influence of a husband (albeit an estranged one), but because he was Iranian, from a traditional family, which gave rise to certain cultural pressures'. In *R v. Asha Khan*,[20] the appellant was described by her lawyer as naive and of limited intelligence, despite holding a law degree and being trained as a solicitor. Coming from a strict Muslim family, she was likely to be influenced by male members of her family. Asha was indicted for lying about the identity of the driver of her car, who was caught speeding. The driver was her father, who held a provisional driving licence and had prior driving convictions. On appeal, she objected to the decision of the trial judge to reject 'cultural evidence' offered to prove that 'she would not have sought to challenge as untrue that which she was told by her father or brother'. In dismissing the appeal against her conviction, the Court of Appeal did not argue against the admissibility of 'cultural evidence' per se; rather it stated that the evidence offered was unnecessary since the 'cultural issues were put before the jury and their potential relevance for both defence and prosecution was explained in clear terms [by the trial judge]'. In both cases, the courts accepted the parties' strategic depiction of the applicants as both submissive and victimized by their own family, which connects to gender and racial stereotypes of Asian communities as controlling, insular, and patriarchal (Hudson and Bramhall 2005: 736; Parmar 2014: 347).

---

[17] See, e.g., UN Committee on the Rights of the Child, Concluding Observations on the UK, October 2002; ECHR, *A v. UK* (1999) 27 EHRR 611.

[18] Children Act 2004, s. 58.   [19] [2009] EWCA Crim 1292.

[20] [2014] EWCA Crim 2440.

These cases show the tendency to attribute undesirable and discreditable conducts and values to certain groups in a manner that contributes to their racialization,
while failing to draw continuities with those prevalent, albeit buried, in the indigenous society. Even apparently neutral assertions based on mistake or ignorance of the
law often contain similar orientalizing undertones. Such matters were articulated
by court operators during interviews. Commenting on his experience of pursuing
Eastern Europeans for wildlife crimes, for example, one crown prosecutor reck-
oned: 'Because of cultural issues, they are used to do this [killing animals to eat] and
they don't know that that's a crime in this country'.[21] A magistrate reflected on the
propensity of foreigners to be brought to court for certain crimes: 'for them to come
to the UK, it's a lack of understanding and appreciation that maybe carrying a knife
for example—quite normal wherever they came from—it's illegal in this country to
carry a weapon'. Not only do they pigeonhole individuals into enduring exaggerated and belittling versions of non-western cultures historically crafted by western
intellectuals and colonial administrators (Said 2003), these assertions partake in the
construction of difference and a unifying image of the nation (Gilroy 1990: 75).
As Volpp (1996: 1601) nicely put it, '[e]xaggerating cultural difference from a supposed mainstream culture allows the notion of race and nation to fuse, so that the
culture of certain groups is considered to fall outside the borders of "our society" '.

CONCLUDING REMARKS

This chapter has illuminated the ways in which the law and its operation are implicated in processes of racialization through recreating old imageries of the 'cultural
other' as they fuse with new markers of difference in the context of mass migration
and globalization. As legal scholars noted in criticizing the standard of the 'reasonable person' in various common law jurisdictions (Dundes Renteln 2004: 32; Lacey
2014; Power 2006; Sing 1999; Woodman 2009), the law constructs difference and
hierarchies. By establishing whose standards should count to assess individual liability, the law upholds the validity of standards of 'normality' and privileges the outlook
of a particular individual—that of a white middle-class man. According to them,
the law is not 'accultured', neutral, and universal but rather deeply embedded in the
dominant culture.

The law and its operation reinforces the link between race and nation, national
identity and belonging, and upholds the image of Britain as a one, white nation
(Gilroy 1990). Attesting to the constitutive and strategic character of national identity, certain traits are identified as alien, while others blend in. As Garner (2009: 794)
notes, white British identity requires the 'performance of values and norms that are
reflexively juxtaposed against competing and inferior ones' and are strongly rooted
in Britain's colonial past. In a multi-ethnic, multicultural society, he concluded,
values serve to delimit the borders of identity. The circulation of images of 'cultural

---

[21] This comment needs to be read in the context of the perception, largely propelled by the British
tabloid media, of Eastern European as 'swan eaters' (Fox et al. 2012: 9).

otherness' ascribed to certain groups in court cases resonates with broader stereo-types and often goes unquestioned. In reifying difference, they work to deny the fluid and hybrid nature of cultural identity in contemporary Britain.

REFERENCES

Ahmed, S. (2000), *Strange Encounters: Embodied Others in Post-Coloniality*. Abingdon: Routledge.

Ahmed, S. (2012), *On Being Included: Racism and Diversity in Institutional Life*. Durham, NC and London: Duke University Press.

Ahmed, S. (2014), *The Cultural Politics of Emotion*. Edinburgh: Edinburgh University Press.

Aliverti, A. (2016), 'Researching the Global Criminal Court', in M. Bosworth, C. Hoyle, and L. Zedner (eds), *Changing Contours of Criminal Justice: Research, Politics and Policy*. Oxford: Oxford University Press, 73–86.

Aliverti, A. and Seoighe, R. (2017), 'Lost in Translation? Examining the Role of Court Interpreters in Cases Involving Foreign National Defendants in England and Wales', *New Criminal Law Review* 20: 130–56.

Anderson, B. (2007), 'A Very Private Business', *European Journal of Women's Studies* 14: 247–64.

Anderson, B. (2016), *Imagined Communities: Reflections on the Origin and Spread of Nationalism*. London: Verso.

Armenta, A. (2017), 'Racializing Crimmigration: Structural Racism, Colorblindness, and the Institutional Production of Immigrant Criminality', *Sociology of Race and Ethnicity* 3: 82–95.

Back, L. (1993), 'Race, Identity and Nation within an Adolescent Community in South London', *Journal of Ethnic and Migration Studies* 19: 217–33.

Baumann, G. (1996), *Contesting Culture: Discourses of Identity in Multi-ethnic London*. Cambridge: Cambridge University Press.

Bond, C. and Jeffries, S. (2014), 'Similar Punishment? Comparing Sentencing Outcomes in Domestic and Non-Domestic Violence Cases', *British Journal of Criminology* 54: 849–72.

Bosworth, M. (2012), 'Subjectivity and Identity in Detention: Punishment and Society in a Global Age', *Theoretical Criminology* 16: 123–40.

Bosworth, M. and Slade, G. (2014), 'In Search of Recognition: Gender and Staff–Detainee Relations in a British Immigration Removal Centre', *Punishment & Society* 16: 169–86.

Chiu, D. (1994), 'The Cultural Defense: Beyond Exclusion, Assimilation, and Guilty Liberalism', *California Law Review* 82: 1053–125.

Coleman, D. (1996), 'Individualizing Justice through Multiculturalism: The Liberal's Dilemma', *Columbia Law Review* 96: 1093–167.

D'hondt, S. (2010), 'The Cultural Defense as Courtroom Drama: The Enactment of Identity, Sameness, and Difference in Criminal Trial Discourse', *Law & Social Inquiry* 35: 67–98.

Dundes Renteln, A. (2004), *The Cultural Defense*. New York: Oxford University Press.

Fox, J., Moroşanu, L., and Szilassy, E. (2012), 'The Racialization of the New European Migration to the UK', *Sociology* 46: 680–95.

Garner, S. (2009), 'Empirical Research into White Racialized Identities in Britain', *Sociology Compass* 3: 789–802.

Gilroy, P. (1990), 'The End of Anti-racism', *Journal of Ethnic and Migration Studies* 17: 71–83.

Good, A. (2008), 'Cultural Evidence in Courts of Law', *Journal of the Royal Anthropological Institute* 14: 47–60.

Hannah-Moffat, K. and Maurutto, P. (2010), 'Re-contextualizing Pre-sentence Reports: Risk and Race', *Punishment & Society* 12: 262–86.

Hudson, B. and Bramhall, G. (2005), 'Assessing the "Other": Constructions of "Asianness" in Risk Assessments by Probation Officers', *British Journal of Criminology* 45: 721–40.

Jeffries, S. and Bond, C. (2015), 'Taking the Problem Seriously? Sentencing Indigenous and Non-Indigenous Domestic Violence Offenders', *Australian & New Zealand Journal of Criminology* 48: 463–82.

Lacey, N. (2014), 'Community, Culture and Criminalization', in W. Kymlicka, C. Lernestedt, and M. Matravers (eds), *Criminal Law and Cultural Diversity*. Oxford: Oxford University Press, 47–66.

Maguigan, H. (1995), 'Cultural Evidence and Male Violence: Are Feminist and Multiculturalist Reformers on a Collision Course in Criminal Courts?' *New York University Law Review* 70: 36–99.

Menjívar, C. and Salcido, O. (2002), 'Immigrant Women and Domestic Violence: Common Experiences in Different Countries', *Gender & Society* 16: 898–920.

Millings, M. (2013), 'Policing British Asian Identities: The Enduring Role of the Police in Young British Asian Men's Situated Negotiation of Identity and Belonging', *British Journal of Criminology* 53(6): 1075–92.

Parmar, A. (2011), 'Stop and Search in London: Counter-terrorist or Counter-productive?' *Policing and Society* 21: 369–82.

Parmar, A. (2014), 'Ethnicities, Racism, and Crime in England and Wales', in S. Bucerius and M. Tonry (eds), *Oxford Handbook of Ethnicity, Crime, and Immigration*. Oxford: Oxford University Press, 321–59.

Phillips, A. (2003), 'When Culture Means Gender: Issues of Cultural Defence in the English Courts', *The Modern Law Review* 66: 510–31.

Phillips, A. (2007), *Multiculturalism without Culture*. Princeton, NJ: Princeton University Press.

Phillips, C. (2008), 'Negotiating Identities: Ethnicity and Social Relations in a Young Offenders' Institution', *Theoretical Criminology* 12: 313–31.

Phillips, C. and Webster, C. (2013), 'Introduction: Bending the Paradigm—New Directions and New Generations', in C. Phillips and C. Webster (eds), *New Directions in Race, Ethnicity and Crime*. Abingdon: Routledge, 1–17.

Power, H. (2006), 'Provocation and Culture', *Criminal Law Review* October: 871–88.

Romero, M. (2008), 'Crossing the Immigration and Race Border: A Critical Race Theory Approach to Immigration Studies', *Contemporary Justice Review* 11: 23–37.

Said, E. (2003), *Orientalism*. London: Penguin.

Sanchez, G. and Romero, M. (2010), 'Critical Race Theory in the US Sociology of Immigration', *Sociology Compass* 4: 779–88.

Sing, J. (1999), 'Culture as Sameness: Towards a Synthetic View of Provocation and Culture in the Criminal Law', *Yale Law Journal* 108: 1844–84.

Volpp, L. (1994), '(Mis)Identifying Culture: Asian Women and the "Cultural Defense"', *Harvard Women's Law Journal* 57: 57–101.

Volpp, L. (1996), 'Talking "Culture": Gender, Race, Nation, and the Politics of Multiculturalism', *Columbia Law Review* 96: 1573–617.

Volpp, L. (2000), 'Blaming Culture for Bad Behavior', *Yale Journal of Law & the Humanities* 12: 89–116.

Volpp, L. (2011), 'Framing Cultural Difference: Immigrant Women and Discourses of Tradition', *differences: A Journal of Feminist Cultural Studies* 22: 90–110.

Waters, C. (1997), '"Dark Strangers" in Our Midst: Discourses of Race and Nation in Britain, 1947–1963', *Journal of British Studies* 36: 207–38.

Webster, C. (2008), 'Marginalized White Ethnicity, Race and Crime', *Theoretical Criminology* 12: 293–312.

Weenink, D. (2009), 'Explaining Ethnic Inequality in the Juvenile Justice System: An Analysis of the Outcomes of Dutch Prosecutorial Decision Making', *British Journal of Criminology* 49: 220–42.

Woodman, G. (2009), 'The Culture Defence in English Common Law: The Potential for Development', in M. Foblets and A. Dundes Renteln (eds), *Multicultural Jurisprudence.* Oxford: Hart, 7–34.

Wray, H. (2015), '"A Thing Apart": Controlling Male Family Migration to the United Kingdom', *Men and Masculinities* 18: 424–47.

9

Enforcing the Politics of Race and Identity in Migration and Crime Control Policies

Yolanda Vázquez[*]

> The law embodies racial categories and inequalities and at the same time, the law makes race meaningful through its articulation and application.
>
> (Van Cleve and Mayes 2015: 409).

INTRODUCTION

This chapter examines how the US figure of the 'criminal alien' over the last thirty years has been racialized as Latino. While a growing number of legal scholars examine the proliferation of migration and crime policies (Eagly 2013; Stumpf 2006), few have explored the role of race and racism in the development of these laws and policies or their influence on racial identity and hierarchy within American society (García Hernández 2013; Vázquez 2015; see also Chacón and Bibler Coutin, this volume). Yet, as criminality is increasingly used as a mechanism of migration control, it has shaped contemporary notions of race and racial identity. At the same time, and despite being purportedly race neutral since the 1960s, the law has been influenced by notions of race and racial identity (Han 2015; Moran and Carbado 2008; Perea et al. 2015).

Individuals brought into the criminal justice system are subjected to exclusion and unequal treatment through the law. Those labelled as 'criminal' can be legally excluded from certain employment, housing, social programmes, freedom of association, and voting. As a result, they are more likely to live in poverty, be unemployed, be less healthy, under-educated, and their children, families, and communities are

[*] I would like to thank everyone who took part in this project, which started with Oxford's Border Criminologies' Seminar on Race, Migration and Criminal Justice in September 2016 and has cumulated into this volume, for their dedication, insight, and support for its success. In particular, I thank Mary Bosworth and Alpa Parmar for creating the vision, space, and support for both this project and my work as well as their hospitality during my visit at Oxford.

more likely to suffer from the same social disadvantages. Such matters are racialized, due to the over-representation of blacks and Latinos in the system in which almost 7 million individuals[1] are under the control of the state (DOJ 2016). For decades, critics have referred to the criminal justice system as the 'most oppressive tool that creates racial inequality' (Van Cleve and Mayes 2015). Racial disparities exist within the criminal justice system at every stage: arrest, prosecution, sentencing, and incarceration (Hartney and Vuong 2009).

Inequality is also legitimized by immigration status. Like offenders, those who are not US citizens, 'aliens' within American immigration law, can be legally excluded from employment, voting, and social welfare programmes, among other things. In addition, they are subject to removal from the United States, something that citizens, even 'criminals', do not face. Currently, immigration law impacts hundreds of thousands of individuals a year, disproportionately affecting people of colour. In 2015, for example, over 450,000 non-citizens were removed or returned to their country of origin from the United States or its borders, of whom over 96 per cent were from Mexico, Guatemala, Honduras, and El Salvador (DHS 2016a).[2]

While the criminal justice and immigration systems have historically been delineated from each other, focusing on the 'criminal' and the 'alien' as distinct populations, a new figure of the 'criminal alien' melds them, creating a 'dynamic process by which both systems converge at points to create a new system of social control that draws from both immigration and criminal justice, but it is purely neither' (Miller 2003: 618). This new system dissolves the lines between the criminal and civil court systems, to the detriment of those in both. Migration and crime policies incorporate criminal norms into the civil system, while at the same time incorporate civil norms into the criminal justice system (Eagly 2010; Legomsky 2007).

In a system, in which all individuals are 'equal in the eye of the law' (dissent Justice Harlan, *Plessy v. Ferguson*), racial disparities are considered cultural and moral flaws with no correlation to race and racism. The law is 'color-blind' (Harlan, *Plessy v. Ferguson*). Such a view obscures the impact of migration and crime policies on racial identities, racial perception, and how they give racialized meaning to legal categories. It also makes it hard to discern how the expansion of migration and crime policies have exacerbated racial disparities within both systems in the 'hunt' for the 'criminal alien'.

In this chapter, I will demonstrate how the legal concept of the 'criminal alien' creates and reinforces US understanding about race. I will argue that this figure has been racialized as Latino, specifically as someone from Mexico or Central America. The chapter proceeds in two parts. The first will discuss the rise of migration and crime control policies and the 'criminal alien'. The second will discuss the laws and political framing through which race-neutral migration and crime policies have shaped the identity of Latinos as dangerous and foreign. Together I will conclude, these developments have reinforced racial inequality.

---

[1] In 2015, approximately 2.2 million individuals were incarcerated with 4.7 million on supervision or parole.

[2] The other countries on the top ten list in order by highest percentage are: The Dominican Republic, Ecuador, Colombia, Nicaragua, Brazil, and Jamaica.

THE RISE AND IMPACT OF MIGRATION AND CRIME CONTROL POLICIES

The United States currently incarcerates, detains, and deports more individuals than any other country in the world. While the United States removed 22,314 individuals in 1986 (with only 4 per cent for criminal offence), over 400,000 were removed in 2012 (55 per cent 'criminal aliens') (DOJ 2000; DHS 2012). Currently, the overall number of removals remains high and removal of those classified as 'criminal aliens' remains near 55 per cent close to the border, rising to 92 per cent of those removed in the interior (DOJ 2000; DHS 2016a). These days, more than half of all federal cases prosecuted are for immigration violations. From 2003 to 2012, federal prison inmates sentenced for immigration violations increased by 83 per cent (Raphael and Stoll 2013: 62, 64, 66). Non-citizens are now the largest group within the Federal Bureau of Prisons, comprising over 40 per cent of this population over the most recent years (US Sentencing Commission 2016). Immigration detention has also increased dramatically, with approximately 400,000 detained per year, twice as many as those detained in the Bureau of Federal Prisons (DHS 2016a; DOJ 2017a).

While harsh crime and migration policies have largely been associated with conservative politics, much like the War on Crime, both political parties have contributed to policies that have negatively impacted migrants. Indeed, at the time of writing, the largest increase of removals occurred during the Obama administration, 2009–2017. During Obama's eight years in office, US Immigration and Customs Enforcement (ICE) removed approximately 3 million people, not including those who were returned at the border or not handed over to ICE (DHS 2015a; 2016b). If we include the number of border apprehensions by the Customs and Bureau Patrol, this figure would rise by approximately 3.4 million (DHS 2015a; 2016b).

Decades of increasingly restrictive policies and enforcement have led to the current era of mass prosecution, detention, and removal, much of which targets those labelled as 'criminal aliens'. In the words of the ICE agency: 'ICE has prioritized its limited resources on the identification and removal of threats to national security, border security, and public safety' (DHS 2016a). While this statement is broad, ICE purports that emphasis is placed on migrants convicted of crimes and focuses government resources on those convicted of felonies and unauthorized migration (DHS 2015a, 2015b).

Consequences for Latinos

The massive rise in the numbers of migrants within the criminal justice system as well as in the sum of those subject to removal proceedings are not the only consequences of current migration and crime policies. Additionally, each stage of the process is marked by stark racial disparities. As stated above, over 97 per cent of those removed from the United States are from predominately Latin and Caribbean countries with over 96 per cent from Mexico, Guatemala, Honduras, and El Salvador. Latinos similarly account for over 90 per cent of those detained for immigration violations in civil detention facilities, and 94 per cent of those removed under the label of 'criminal alien'.

These trends have detrimentally impacted citizens and non-citizen Latinos alike. Since 1988, the number of Latinos incarcerated has nearly quintupled (Currie 2013), rendering them the fastest growing prison population of any minority group. They are particularly over-represented in the federal system.[3] The increasing criminal prosecution of immigration violations in the federal criminal court has largely been responsible for the disproportionate number of Latinos in the federal system (US Sentencing Commission 2016). Of the migrants in custody for immigration violations, Latinos comprise over 92 per cent, with the majority being men (US Sentencing Commission 2016). As Light has expressed, 'Latinos are now the most disadvantaged group in the [criminal] courts' (Light et al. 2014: 831, citing Doerner and Demuth 2010).

The removal of individuals also impacts their families, communities, and nations of origin. High numbers of families have been broken apart (Hagan et al. 2010; see also Golash-Boza, this volume). Many of those removed come from families that have both citizen and non-citizen members. Children are increasingly taken away from their families due to removal (Maddali 2014). Children and spouses who remain are more likely to be poor and suffer mental and physical health problems (Capps et al. 2007; Delva et al. 2013). Children are likely to enter foster care as well as drop out of school, become pregnant, and live in poverty (Vázquez 2011). All these factors will contribute to situational poverty for individual families and generational poverty and subordination of Latinos more broadly.

Migrants and the Mythology of their Criminality

The high percentage of migrants, particularly Latinos, brought into the criminal justice and immigration system over the years is often used to justify increasingly harsh migration and crime policies. Their criminalization legitimates policy directed at the Mexican–US border and at Latinos more generally (Pérez-Peña 2017; Trump 2016). It also bolsters beliefs that current migrants cause more crime, especially Latinos. However, as this section will demonstrate, these assumptions do not hold up under scrutiny.

Contrary to political rhetoric, for instance, research has largely found that migrants are less likely than their US citizen counterparts to commit crimes (Ewing et al. 2015; Rumbaut and Ewing 2007; Salas-Wright 2016). In fact, evidence exists that migrants may have contributed to declining crime rates since 1991 (Sampson 2008). Studies have found that residential neighbourhoods with larger numbers of migrants have decreasing rates of crime, especially violent crimes, such as robbery and murder (Stowell et al. 2009; Wadsworth 2010; Williams Reid et al. 2005). So, too, have overall crime rates been declining since the early 1980s, over the same period that unauthorized immigration and the 'criminal alien' threat has been on

---

[3] In 2015, Latinos made up 52.7 per cent of the federal prison population, compared to 23.5 per cent of those incarcerated who were white (US Sentencing Commission 2016: 2).

the rise (Weaver 2007). Rates of firearms crimes have been declining since the early 1990s, most rapidly between 1994 and 1999, at the same time that two of the harshest immigration bills against 'criminal aliens' and unauthorized migration were enacted. In fact, during that time, violent crime rates were dropping as well (Truman and Morgan 2016).

It is not just in the area of crime control that statistics about the dangers posed by migrants do no hold up. Similar points can be made about the scale of the problem. In contrast to the heat of political rhetoric about this issue, unauthorized migrants comprise only 3.5 per cent of the total population of the United States and this proportion has been declining since 2007 (Passel and Cohn 2010). In 2015, apprehensions at the US–Mexico border hit an all-time low and are currently what they were in 2005 (Gonzalez-Barrera 2016). Indeed, the rate of unauthorized Mexican migration into the United States has been declining since 2005. By 2008, the number of Mexican migrants entering the United States had decreased by 40 per cent (Gonzalez-Barrera 2016). While Mexican migration has been declining, other groups of unauthorized migrants from Asia, Central America, and Sub-Saharan Africa have been increasing. Today, out of the approximately 11 million unauthorized migrants in the United States, almost half of them are from somewhere other than Mexico (Passel and Cohn 2016).

Finally, in contrast to populist claims of dangerousness, the majority of migrants defined within the framework of the 'criminal alien' have been convicted of non-violent and regulatory offences. Although the Department of Homeland Security (DHS) claims that the immigrants removed from the United States are the 'most serious public safety and national security threat', DHS annual reports and growing research prove otherwise (DHS 2014; DHS 2016a; 2016b). Prior to 2014, for example, most migrants were removed as 'criminal aliens' for immigration, drug offences, and traffic offences (Simanski 2014). More recently, statistics show that over 92 per cent of those removed in the most serious Priority 1 category were for immigration violations (DHS 2016a). According to DHS, 'Aliens described in this priority represent the highest priority to which enforcement resources should be directed.' Those in the group are described as being the highest 'threats to national security, border security, and public safety'.

In short, current migration and crime policies do not correlate to rising levels of crime, violence, national security risks, or migration rates. The current implementation of migration and crime policies do little to address national security and public safety but cost billions of dollars (DHS 2013; Meissner 2013; National Immigration Forum 2013). Yet, politicians and the media continue to rely on and promote a view of migrants as violent offenders (Perez-Peña 2017; see Sanchez, this volume). If little correlation exists between migrants and crime and dangerousness then underlying explanations should be explored as to the reasons that migration and crime policies are growing and impacting groups, particularly Latinos, at an exponentially higher rate than all other groups.[4] As the next section will discuss,

---

[4] This chapter does not address the high rate of black immigrants who are lawful, permanent residents who are caught by migration and crime policies at a disproportionate rate as well. More research

while the laws may purport to be race neutral, their creation, implementation, and enforcement are not. Race and racism continue to impact laws and the identity of Latinos in the United States.

THE SHAPING OF LATINO IDENTITY THROUGH MIGRATION AND CRIME POLICIES

The relationship between the United States and Latin American countries has been shaped by a history of racism and racial ideology based on the superiority of white Anglo-Saxons (Horsman 1981; see Gutiérrez-Rivera, this volume). Western Europeans considered Latinos with Native American, European, and African ancestry to be inferior (Horsman 1981: Gómez 2008). Those identified as Latino were seen as an abomination of racial purity and those who were visually more 'mixed', or held darker colours, or more Afro or indigenous features were treated more harshly still (Negrón-Muntaner and Grosfoguel 1997). Early Americans identified Latinos as lazy, sexually inappropriate, and dishonest. They were considered to be less than fully human; 'mongrels', who, like animals, were vicious, dirty, stupid, and unable to control their sexual behaviour (Grosfoguel and Georas 1996; Horsman 1981, citing Thompson 1846 and Weber 1973).

While many Anglo-Saxon Americans regarded Latinos as too inferior for citizenship, they needed them for work along with other racial minorities, such as Asians and blacks (Calavita 1992). Through immigration and constitutional laws as well as informal policies, early migrant groups were rendered temporary workers within the nation's borders. Latinos who came into the United States were discriminated against based on their ascribed identity (Vázquez 2015). Entry into the United States was determined through discretionary decisions by border officers and work contracts that reinforced their temporary nature for menial labour (Ngai 2004). When Latinos were no longer needed for their labour, immigration laws were put into place to terminate their entry and deport them en masse in response to the growing anti-Latino sentiment framed in 'illegal' migration. Couched as a response to unauthorized migration and its threat to the national economy and US citizen jobs, immigration law programmes such as Mexican Repatriation and Operation Wetback[5] led to the removal of approximately one million Mexicans, including US citizens, from the United States (García Hernández 2013; Gyory 2000; Hadley; 1956; Johnson 2005; Vázquez 2011).

Since the 1960s, civil rights laws have legally prohibited racially discriminatory legislation. As a result, programmes such as the Chinese Exclusion Act, Operation Wetback and Mexican Repatriation are no longer viable government responses.

---

should be conducted on the relationship between race and immigration status as it pertains to black, lawful, permanent residents as their introduction into the criminal system as black criminals or foreignness or both.

[5] Wetback is a derogatory name for Mexicans. The word was derived from their identity as 'illegal' migrants who would wade through the Rio Grande to cross into the United States and, therefore, arrived with wet backs.

However, perceptions of Latinos as inferior, foreign, and a threat to national identity, security, and economic well-being remain within large parts of American society, both implicitly and explicitly (Kteily et al. 2015). These feelings have become
more pronounced as the population of Latinos has steadily grown over the last few
decades (Morin 2016).[6]

Latinos are now the largest minority group in the country, surpassing the US black
population in 2000. While approximately 65 per cent of Latinos are US citizens,
they are also the largest immigrant population (US Census 2010). The majority of
Latinos, both citizen and non-citizen, are from Mexico.[7] While only comprising
approximately 17 per cent of the national population, their majority minority status
has caused many to argue that Latinos are a serious threat to America's traditional
national identity (Brimelow 1995; Huntington 2004). While not all Americans
are willing to be so blunt about their racial animus, research suggests that Latinos,
Mexicans in particular, along with blacks, are not only negatively viewed, but are
one of the most despised groups within American society (Lee and Fiske 2006;
Massey 2007).

As Michelle Alexander (2010) has made clear, after the civil rights movement
ended racially discriminatory laws, the criminal justice system became the primary
institution for controlling blacks. Because Latinos could originally be controlled
primarily through immigration laws, they were not the traditional focus of the criminal justice system. Today, however, reflecting their various subject positions, as citizen, lawful migrant, and unauthorized migrant, Latinos fall under the control of
both systems.

While the immigration and criminal justice systems have been successful institutions for racial subordination, they were historically so by delineating between the
'alien' and the 'criminal'—brown and black. A new system needed to be framed
to combat the Latino demographics in the United States. As such, the creation of
migration and crime policies through the merger of the immigration and criminal
justice system could reinforce racial subordination, for citizens and non-citizens,
with the use of race-neutral laws, and maintain beliefs in a racial ideology that promotes American society as 'colour-blind.'

Latinos as the 'criminal alien'

The current perception of migrants as a potential threat to national security dates
to the Reagan administration of the 1980s (Massey 2007) and, in particular to the
1986 Immigration Reform and Control Act (IRCA). As the US Department of
Justice's 1998 Immigration Report states, 'The passage of the Immigration Reform
and Control Act in 1986 helped the INS focus on the removal of those aliens

---

[6] Although Asians comprise only 3 per cent of the total population, they are now the fastest growing
racial group in the United States.

[7] Approximately 64 per cent are Mexicans, 9.5 per cent are Puerto Rican, 3.8 per cent Salvadoran,
3.2 per cent Dominican, 2.4 per cent Guatemalan, and the remainder are from other Latin American
countries.

determined to be the greatest threat to society [criminal aliens]' (DOJ 2000: 203). While many know IRCA as a legislative act that gave 'amnesty' to some who were already present in the United States, IRCA was the beginning of the militarization of the US–Mexican border and solidification of the Latino as foreign and 'illegal'.

IRCA was framed as the necessary legislation to combat the rise of the 'illegal' immigrant within the United States and the threat of more people arriving from Latin America. Specifically, Reagan tied the threat of communism to the 'hordes' of 'Latin people' he said would be fleeing from the Southern border into the United States if funding was not increased and borders were not enforced (Reagan March 16, 1986). Reagan's framing bears a striking resemblance to the Court's holding in the Chinese Exclusion cases, which were the first immigration laws to restrict entry explicitly based on race. In *Chae Chan Ping*, the Court, in supporting the government's racially discriminatory law, stated, 'It matters not in what form such aggression and encroachment come, whether from the foreign nation acting in its national character or from *vast hordes* of its people crowding in upon us' (*Chae Chan Ping v. United States* 1889, p. 606, emphasis added). Playing off the Court's opinion, Reagan linked 'dangerous to the peace and security', [8] with the need to exclude 'illegal aliens'. Shifting from racially explicit terms, this law adversely affected Latinos from the South through the race-neutral category of the 'illegal alien'.

This legislation, and the debate surrounding it, presented 'illegal' immigrants as productive labourers on the one hand, although mostly referring to non-Latinos when referencing this group, yet on the other as illegitimate law breakers, who were largely connected to Mexicans and other Latinos south of the border (Menjívar and Kanstroom 2014). In this view, not only did 'illegal aliens' become synonymous with Mexicans and other Latinos (Reagan 1981), but their threat to national security and identity defined them. IRCA marked the beginning of two decades of concentrated US–Mexico border enforcement expansion through increasing border patrol officers as well as the use of military technology (Menjívar and Kanstroom 2014).

What Reagan and other politicians failed to make transparent was the way in which immigration laws were being created and abolished at the expense of Mexican migration. While immigration laws abolished national origins quotas and other discriminatory provisions, they also decreased the means for legal migration from Mexico and other Latin American countries.[9] Yet, the need for their menial labour continued (Johnson and Trujillo 2011; Vázquez 2015). IRCA and Reagan's rhetoric ensured that Latinos would be forever temporary by their 'illegal' status. As they became a large majority of unauthorized migrants entering the United States,

---

[8] The Chinese Exclusion cases allowed the federal government to enact immigration laws against certain groups, even racial categories, if it 'considers the presence of foreigners of a different race in this country, who will not assimilate with us, to be dangerous to its peace and security, their exclusion is not to be stayed because at the time there are no actual hostilities with the nation of which the foreigners are subjects' (*Chae Chan Ping v. United States*, 1889, p. 606).

[9] For example, President Ford stated his concerns that the reduction of legal immigration from Mexico into the United States would come as a result of the 1976 amendments to the Immigration and Nationality Act.

they were also cast as perpetually 'dangerous to the peace and security' of the nation (Menjívar and Kanstroom 2014).

In addition to the increasing number of unauthorized migrants cast as a dangerous security threat, the character of migrants entering the United States, including those authorized to enter, came into question. In the 1980s and 1990s, state and federal politicians began to link migrants to criminality and their apparent dangerousness to public safety as well as national security. At first, migrants from the South, including the Caribbean, were mainly linked to drug trafficking and the associated violence (Dunn 1996). As a result, a litany of bills was proposed and many of them enacted, such as the Anti-Drug Abuse Acts of 1986 and 1988. But while these bills were race neutral, congressional intent gave away their racial bias. Drug trafficking was seen as coming from the South and the Caribbean and resources were focused on those areas, disproportionately impacting Latinos and reinforcing the rhetoric of Latino 'criminality' and 'illegality' (Dunn 1996). As the years passed, however, growing concern over migrants and their propensity towards all categories of crime began to take hold. Migrants were seen not only as drug traffickers and murderers, but as responsible for much of the crime and social collapse that was perceived to exist (Brimelow 1995; Simes and Waters 2014).

Democrats as well as Republicans have contributed to the construction of Latinos as both 'illegal' and 'criminal' over the last several decades. President Clinton, taking lessons from the Republicans, continued to frame migrants from the South, both unauthorized and authorized, in the same age-old rhetoric: abusing immigration laws, taking jobs that belonged to US citizens, and removed high numbers of immigrants convicted of crimes (Clinton 1995; Nevins 2010).[10] Programmes such as Operation Hold the Line (1993), Operation Gatekeeper (1994), and Operation Safeguard (1994 and 1997), were all created as anti-crime measures that sought to deter unauthorized migration through the rhetoric of 'dangerousness' (Luna 2008; Nevins 2010). Yet, the programmes remained at the US–Mexico border, and one year later, Clinton signed two of the harshest immigration bills in history, the Antiterrorism and Effective Death Penalty Act of 1996 and the Illegal Immigration Reform and Immigrant Responsibility Act of 1996.

Both were created to combat the perceived tide of migrants who were purportedly entering the United States to commit crimes against the nation state and its citizens. These Acts did several things that have contributed to the rise of 'criminal aliens' over the last two decades. First, they expanded the number of crimes that were removable offences. Second, they reduced the ability for relief in the immigration court in general, but especially for those convicted of crimes. They also increased enforcement through continued budget increases to immigration enforcement as well as provisions that allowed for state and local law enforcement to enforce immigration laws

---

[10] Clinton took the same hardline approach as Republicans to the criminal justice system and the poor. The 'Tough on Crime' movement remained strong during Clinton's administration as harsh crime bills as well as decreased assistance from social welfare programmes for the poor were enacted (the Violent Crime Control and Law Enforcement Act of 1994 and the Personal Responsibility and Work Opportunity Reconciliation Act of 1996), detrimentally impacting both citizens and non-citizens.

and receive compensation for it (Violent Crime Control and Law Enforcement Act of 1994; Illegal Immigration Reform and Immigrant Responsibility Act of 1996).

It was the enactment of Operation Streamline, however, that solidified the unauthorized Latino migrant as 'criminal'. Introduced in 2005, at a time when border apprehensions were actually declining, Operation Streamline was a zero-tolerance programme that brought apprehended migrants into the federal criminal court to be prosecuted and criminally convicted for unlawful entry, instead of being transferred immediately into civil immigration proceedings for removal (Transactional Records Access Clearinghouse 2013). While Operation Streamline was implemented as a deterrence policy against unlawful migration, it was only implemented at six sectors of the US–Mexico border.[11]

Since its implementation, Operation Streamline has shifted the way the federal court system operates, prosecuting hundreds of migrants per day for their unauthorized entry or reentry at the Southwest border (DHS 2015c). In 2015, almost 70,000 individuals were prosecuted through Operation Streamline. Estimates state that over 700,000 individuals, the majority Latinos, have been prosecuted through Operation Streamline since its inception. Currently, almost half of the entire federal court docket is made up of immigration violations, contributing to the percentage of those charged in the federal court who are of Latino origin (DOJ 2016; 2017b). And since the vast majority receive a prison sentence, Latino migrants are the largest inmate population (DOJ 2017b). As a result, no longer are unauthorized migrants viewed only in discourse as 'criminal' and 'dangerous', but their prosecution within the federal criminal system for their unauthorized entry or re-entry has formally transformed a civil immigration violation into a federal criminal conviction and labelled them as 'criminal aliens' (DHS 2014; Raphael and Stoll 2013).

The federal laws enacted and policies put into place over these short years not only created the 'criminal alien' but developed mechanisms for federal, state, and local courts and law enforcement to assist in the location, arrest, and transfer of non-citizens into ICE custody (8 U.S.C. § 1357(g), 2012). The DHS, with the cooperation of local law enforcement, appears on a regular basis in local and state jails in an attempt to identify potential non-citizens that may be subject to removal. Programmes such as ACCESS, 287(g), the Criminal Alien Program, National Fugitive Operations Program, Secure Communities, and the Priority Enforcement Program were all put into place so that law enforcement and corrections could assist DHS in locating non-citizens suspected of being removable under immigration law. And while all of these policies and practices are on the face of it neutral, location, implementation, and enforcement are not (Golash-Boza, this volume; Provine and Doty 2011).

Furthermore, the increased use and national implementation of Secure Communities during the Obama administration typifies how race-neutral policies

---

[11] Operation Streamline operates in sectors of Del Rio, Laredo, and El Paso, Texas, and Yuma and Tucson, Arizona. In Tucson, Arizona, one magistrate handled 25,000 cases during a 12-month period with 70–100 per day under Operation Streamline (*United States v. Roblero-Solis*, 588 F.3d 692 (2009)).

serve to obscure racial disparities. Responding to complaints that law enforcement was engaging in racial profiling, Secure Communities emerged to take 'race' out of the enforcement because everyone who was arrested and booked by law enforcement under Secure Communities would be fingerprinted and their prints would be sent to DHS. However, race remained a significant factor in its implementation. The Obama administration 'rolled out' the programme, not in jurisdictions with high crime rates or even high rates of unauthorized migrants, but in areas that had high Latino populations, both citizens and non-citizens alike (Cox 2013). As a result, Secure Communities disproportionately impacted Latinos and continued to legitimize their criminality through its racially skewed implementation and the increasing numbers of Latinos caught in the system and labelled 'criminal aliens'.

Police discretion has been widely criticized for its racially discriminatory enforcement. While every person may be fingerprinted once brought into the station, law enforcement still has the ability to determine who is arrested, booked, and fingerprinted. In fact, in 2014, Attorney General Holder announced a programme to curb racial profiling in the federal system and certain state and local law enforcement offices (DOJ 2014).[12] Obama, while criticizing the criminal justice system for its racial disparities, touted the immigration system as one that was focused on 'Felons, not families. Criminals, not children. Gang members, not a mom who's working hard to provide for her kids. *We'll prioritize, just like law enforcement does every day.*' (Obama 2014; emphasis added). Statements such as these clearly dismissed the problems of racially discriminatory policing that already existed within the criminal justice system.

On 20 January 2017, Donald Trump formally became the US President. His presidency was already marked by an explicit connection between not only migration and crime but Mexican migration and crime during his run for office: 'When Mexico sends its people, they are not sending their best . . . They are bringing drugs. They are bringing crime. They are rapists' (Trump 2016). Rather than the sentiment of just one man, this kind of statement represents attitudes reinforced by migration and crime policies during the last thirty years: the identity of Mexicans as dangerous to the nation and its citizens. Migration and crime policies have been able to solidify the identity of Latinos into the most despised group through migration and crime policies by incorporating the categories of 'criminal', 'drug dealer', and 'illegal alien' into the contemporary 'criminal alien' (Lee and Fiske 2006; Massey 2007).

The connection between migration and crime continues to be heard in the Trump administration. On 11 April 2017, Attorney General Jeff Sessions in a speech made at the US–Mexico border announced that unauthorized migrants would be targeted and criminally prosecuted as felons in federal court. Sessions stated, 'Under the president's [Trump] leadership and through his executive orders, we will secure this border and bring the full weight of both the immigration courts and federal criminal enforcement to combat this attack on our national security and

---

[12] Although the guidance does not pertain to interdiction activities at the border.

sovereignty.' Much like the implementation of prior programmes, Attorney General Sessions cast unauthorized migration as criminal and a threat to national security. His speech at the Southwest border made it explicit that Latinos would be targeted, despite his race-neutral language. Despite the lack of evidence between migrants and dangerous crime, the decrease in Mexican migration, and the removal of mostly non-violent migration violators, Trump continues to target the Latino 'criminal alien' stating, 'In these dangerous times, our increased attention to public safety and national security sends a clear message to the world. It follows through on my promise to focus on keeping Americans safe, keeping terrorists out of our nation, and putting violent offenders behind bars' (Hirschfeld Davis and Nixon 2017).

CONCLUSION

As Omi and Winant stated, 'Racial ideology and social structure, mutually shape the nature of racism in a complex, dialectical, and overdetermined way' (Omi and Winant 1994: 74). During the last several decades, migration and crime policies have reinforced the racial subordination of Latinos by casting them as 'criminal aliens' in 'post-racial' contemporary America. Race-neutral laws legitimate racial disparities as a consequence of a 'defect' in the particular group, denying their connection to laws or policies. However, laws and policies, regardless of their race neutrality, are instrumental in shaping and organizing society while at the same time defining the way in which individuals are represented within the social structures that exist, and often in a racially distinctive way (Omi and Winant 1994).

Current migration and crime policies are examples of this as their creation and implementation have been instrumental in shaping the nation's current understanding of race and identity as well as continuing the historical legacy of racial subordination. By substituting threats to national security and public safety for race, the illusion of a post-racial ideology can continue. The threat to national security, dangerousness, and criminality has long been used to create racial categories, to give them identity, and to shape the way both 'human bodies and social structures are represented and organized' (Omi and Winant 1994). It organizes the world and the people in it. Unfortunately, migration and crime policies continue to shape the identity of Latinos as 'dangerous', 'threatening', and 'criminal'.

There is little indication that the enactment of migration and crime policies will decline. In fact, based on the current climate, the number will probably continue to rise despite increasing evidence that migrants are less likely to cause crime and may even be responsible for decreasing crime rates. In addition, it seems that increasing focus will remain on Latinos, specifically Mexicans and along the Southwest border, despite the fact that unauthorized migration from Mexico is at an all-time low and almost 50 per cent of the current unauthorized population are from elsewhere (Ewing et al. 2015; Passel and Cohn 2017; Rumbaut and Ewing 2007). Despite post-racial ideology, race and racism impact the identity of 'criminal aliens'. Advocates, researchers, and scholars must study these policies within a racial framework so that migration and crime policies can be fully unpacked to gain an understanding of the ulterior motives behind the policies and to combat the growing use of these policies to reinforce racial hierarchies and inequality across the globe.

REFERENCES

Alexander, M. (2010), *The New Jim Crow: Mass Incarceration in the Age of Colorblindness*. New York: The New Press.

Brimelow, P. (1995), *Alien Nation: Common Sense About America*. New York: Random House Publishing.

Calavita, K. (1992), *Inside the State: The Bracero Program, Immigration, and the I.N.S.* New York: Routledge.

Capps, R., Castaneda, R. M., Chaudry, A., and Santos, R. (2007), *Paying the Price: The Impact of Immigration Raids on America's Children*. Washington, DC: Urban Institute.

Clinton, W. (1995), *State of the Union Address*. Available at: https://www.c-span.org/video/?c4631739/bill-clinton-illegal-immigration

Cox. A. (2013), 'Policing Immigration', *The University of Chicago Law Review* 80: 87–136.

Currie, E. (2013), *Crime and Punishment in America*. New York: Picador.

Delva, J., Horner, P., Martinez, R., Sanders L., Lopez, W. D., and Doering-White, J. (2013), 'Mental Health Problems of Children of Undocumented Parents in the United States: A Hidden Crisis', *Journal of Community Positive Practices* 13(3): 25–35.

DHS (2012), *Yearbook of Immigration Statistics*. Available at: https://www.dhs.gov/sites/default/files/publications/Yearbook_Immigration_Statistics_2012.pdf and archived at: https://perma.cc/MWG8-A9CE

DHS (2013), *FY2013 Budget in Brief*. Available at: http://www.dhs.gov/xlibrary/assets/mgmt/dhs-budget-in-brief-fy2013.pdf> and archived at: <http://perma.cc/97KN-SG9A

DHS (2014), *ICE Enforcement and Removal Operations Report Fiscal Year 2014*. Available at: https://www.ice.gov/doclib/about/offices/ero/pdf/2014-ice-immigration-removals.pdf and archived at http://perma.cc/GJU4-V8HM

DHS (2015a), *ICE Enforcement and Removal Operations Report: FY 2015*. Available at: https://www.ice.gov/sites/default/files/documents/Report/2016/fy2015removalStats.pdf

DHS (2015b), *FY 2015 ICE Immigration Removals*. Available at: https://www.ice.gov/removal-statistics

DHS (2015c), *Streamline: Measuring its Effect on Illegal Border Crossing*. Available at: https://www.oig.dhs.gov/assets/Mgmt/2015/OIG_15-95_May15.pdf

DHS (2016a), *Fiscal Year 2016 ICE Enforcement and Removal Operations Report*. Available at: https://www.ice.gov/sites/default/files/documents/Report/2016/removal-stats-2016.pdf and archived at: https://perma.cc/D4VH-BPS4

DHS (2016b), *2015 Yearbook of Immigration Statistics, Table 39: Aliens Removed or Returned: Fiscal Years 1892–2015*. Available at: https://www.dhs.gov/immigration-statistics/yearbook/2015/table39 and archived at: https://perma.cc/MWG8-A9CE

Doerner, J. K. and Demuth, S. (2010), 'The Independent and Joint Effects of Race/Ethnicity, Gender, and Age on Sentencing Outcomes in U.S. Federal Courts', *Justice Quarterly* 27(1): 1–27.

DOJ (2000), *1998 Statistical Yearbook of the Immigration and Naturalization Service*. Available at: http://dhs.gov/xlibrary/assets/statistics/yearbook/1998/1998yb.pdf, archived at perma.cc/VA8W-JQZ5

DOJ (2014), *Guidance for Federal Law Enforcement Agencies Regarding the Use for Race, Ethnicity, Gender, National Origin, Religion, Sexual Orientation or Gender Identity*.

Available at: https://www.justice.gov/sites/default/files/ag/pages/attachments/2014/12/08/use-of-race-policy.pdf

DOJ (2016), *Correctional Populations in the United States: 2015*. Available at: https://www.bjs.gov/index.cfm?ty=pbdetail&iid=5870

DOJ (2017a), *Population Statistics*, 24 August. Available at: https://www.bop.gov/about/statistics/population_statistics.jsp, archived at https://perma.cc/MM9M-6V8k

DOJ (2017b), *Federal Justice Statistics: 2013–2014*. Available at: https://www.bjs.gov/content/pub/pdf/fjs1314.pdf

Dunn, T. (1996), *The Militarization of the U.S.–Mexico Border 1978–1992*. Austin, TX: CMAS Book.

Eagly, I. V. (2010), 'Prosecuting Immigration', *Northwestern Law Review* 104(4): 1281–361.

Eagly, I. V. (2013), 'Criminal Justice for Noncitizens: An Analysis of Variation in Local Enforcement', *New York University Law Review* 88: 1126–223.

Ewing, W., Martínez, D., and Rumbaut, R. (2015), *American Immigration Council, The Criminalization of Immigration in the United States: A Special Report*. Available at: https://www.americanimmigrationcouncil.org/sites/default/files/research/the_criminalization_of_immigration_in_the_united_states.pdf

García Hernández, C. C. (2013), 'Creating Crimmigration', *Brigham Young University Law Review* 2013(6): 1457–516.

Gomez, L. (2008), *Manifest Destinies: The Making of the Mexican American Race*. New York: NYU Press.

Gonzalez-Barrera, A. (2016), 'Apprehensions of Mexican Migrants at U.S. Borders Reach Near-historic Low', *Pew Research Center*. Available at: http://www.pewresearch.org/fact-tank/2016/04/14/mexico-us-border-apprehensions/

Grosfoguel, R. and Georas, C. S. (1996), 'The Racialization of Latino Caribbean Migrants in the New York Metropolitian Area', *CENTRO Journal of the Center for Puerto Rican Studies* 8(1–2):191–201.

Gyory, A. (2000), *Closing the Gate: Race, Politics, and the Chinese Exclusion Act*. Chapel Hill, NC: University of North Carolina Press.

Hadley, E. M. (1956), 'A Critical Analysis of the Wetback Problem', *Law and Contemporary Problems* 21: 334–57.

Hagan, J., Castro, B., and Rodriguez, N. (2010), 'The Effects of US Deportation Policies on Immigrant Families and Communities: Cross-border Perspectives', *North Carolina Law Review* 88: 1799–824.

Han, S. (2015), *Letters of the Law: Race and the Fantasy of Colorblindness in American Law*. Stanford, CA: Stanford University Press.

Hartney, C. and Vuong, L. (2009), 'Created Equal: Racial and Ethnic Disparities in the US Criminal Justice System', National Council on Crime & Delinquency.

Hirschfeld Davis, J. and Nixon, R. (2017), 'Trump Takes Broad Aim at Undocumented Immigrants', *The New York Times*, 25 May. Available at: https://www.nytimes.com/2017/05/25/us/politics/undocumented-immigrants-trump-budget-wall.html?_r=0

Horsman, R. (1981), *Manifest Destiny: The Origins of American Racial Anglo-Saxonism*. Boston, MA: Harvard University Press.

Huntington, S. (2004), *Who are We? The Challenges to America's National Identity*. New York: Simon & Schuster.

Johnson, K. (2005), 'The Forgotten "Repatriation" of Persons of Mexican Ancestry and Lessons for the "War on Terror"', *Pace Law Review* 26(1): 1–26.

Johnson, K. and Trujillo, B. (2011), *Immigration Law and the U.S.-Mexico Border*. Tucson, AZ: University of Arizona Press.

Kteily, N., Bruneau, E., Waytz, A., and Cotterill, S. (2015), 'The Ascent of Man: Theoretical and Empirical Evidence for Blatant Dehumanization', *Journal of Personality and Social Psychology* 109(5): 901–31.

Lee, T. L. and Fiske, S. T. (2006), 'Not an Outgroup, not yet an Ingroup: Immigrants in the Sterotype Content Model', *International Journal of Intercultural Relations* 30: 751–68.

Legomsky, S. (2007), 'The New Path of Immigration Law: Asymmetric Incorporation of Criminal Justice Norms', *Washington & Lee Law Review* 64: 469–528.

Light, M., Massoglia, M., and King, R. D. (2014), 'Ctiizenship and Punishment: The Salience of National Membership in U.S. Criminal Courts', *American Sociological Review* 79: 825–47.

Luna, B. S. (2008), 'Race, Immigration and the U.S.-Mexico Border: A History of the Border Patrol and the Mexican-origin Population in the Southwest', MA thesis, University of California, San Diego. Available at: http://escholarship.org/uc/item/2qc669rb

Maddali, A. (2014), 'The Immigrant "Other": Racialized Identity and the Devaluation of Immigrant Family Relations', *Indiana Law Journal* 89: 643–702.

Massey, D. (2007), *Categorically Unequal: The American Stratification System.* New York: Russell Sage Foundation.

Meissner, D. (2013), 'Border Budget Is Already Enormous', *The New York Times*, 31 January. Archived at: http://perma.cc/Q7ZS-8UQ8

Menjívar, C. and Kanstroom, D. (eds) (2014), *Constructing Immigrant "Illegality".* Cambridge: Cambridge University Press.

Miller, T. (2003), 'Citzenship and Severity: Recent Immigration Reforms and the New Penalogy', *Georgetown Immigration Law Journal* 17: 611–66.

Moran, R. and Carbado, D. (eds) (2008), *Race Law Stories.* New York: Foundation Press.

Morín, J. (ed.) (2016), *Latinos and Criminal Justice: An Encyclopedia.* Santa Barbara, CA: Greenwood.

National Immigration Forum (2013), *The Math of Immigration Detention: Runaway Costs for Immigration Detention Do Not Add Up to Sensible Policies.* Available at: http://www.immigrationforum.org/images/uploads/mathofimmigrationdetention.pdf

Negrón-Muntaner, F. and Grosfoguel, R. (1997), *Puerto Rican Jam: Rethinking Colonialism and Nationalism.* Minneapolis, MN: University of Minnesota Press.

Nevins, J. (2010), *Operation Gatekeeper and Beyond: The War on 'Illegals' and the Remaking of the U.S.–Mexico Boundary.* New York: Routledge.

Ngai, M. (2004), *Impossible Subjects: Illegal Aliens and the Making of Modern America.* Princeton, NJ: Princeton University Press.

Obama, B. (2014), 'Remarks by the President in Address to the Nation on Immigration', *The White House, Office of the Press Secretary.* Available at: https://obamawhitehouse.archives.gov/the-press-office/2014/11/20/remarks-president-address-nation-immigration

Omi, M. and Winant, H. (1994), *Racial Formation in the United States* (2nd edn). New York: Routledge.

Passel, J. and Cohn, D. (2010), *U.S. Unauthorized Immigration Flows are Down Sharply Since Mid-Decade.* Pew Hispanic Center. Available at: http://www.pewhispanic.org/files/reports/126.pdf and archived at: http://perma.cc/968G- WXDA

Passel, J. and Cohn, D. (2016), *Overall Number of U.S. Unauthorized Immigrants Holds Steady Since 2009: Decline in Share of Mexico Mostly Offset by Growth from Asia, Central America and Sub-Saharan Africa.* Pew Hispanic Center. Available at: http://www.pewhispanic.org/2016/09/20/overall-number-of-u-s-unauthorized-immigrants-holds-steady-since-2009/

Passel, J. and Cohn, D. (2017), *As Mexican Share Declined, U.S. Unauthorized Immigration Population Fell in 2015 Below Recession Level,* Pew Hispanic Center. Available at: http://

www.pewresearch.org/fact-tank/2017/04/25/as-mexican-share-declined-u-s-unauthorized-immigrant-population-fell-in-2015-below-recession-level/

Perea, J., Delgado, R., Harris, A., Stefancic, J., and Wildman, S. (eds) (2015), *Race and Races: Cases and Resources for a Diverse America* (3rd edn). St. Paul, MN: West Academic Press.

Pérez-Peña, R. (2017), 'Contrary to Trump's Claims, Immigrants Are Less Likely to Commit Crimes', *The New York Times*, 26 January.

Provine, D. M. and Doty, R. L. (2011), 'The Criminalization of Immigrants as a Racial Project', *Journal of Contemporary Criminal Justice* 27(3): 261–77.

Raphael, S. and Stoll, M. (2013), *Why Are So Many Americans in Prison?* New York: Russell Sage Foundation.

Reagan, R. (1981), 'Statement on United States Immigration and Refugee Policy', *The American Presidency Project*. Available at: http://www.presidency.ucsb.edu/ws/?pid=44128

Reagan, R. (1986), 'Address to the Nation on the Situation in Nicaragua', *The American Presidency Project*. Available at: http://www.presidency.ucsb.edu/ws/?pid=36999

Rumbaut, R. and Ewing, W. (2007), *The Myth of Immigrant Criminality and the Paradox of Assimilation: Incarceration Rates Among Native and Foreign Born Men*. Immigration Policy Center.

Salas-Wright, C. (2016), 'The "Immigrant Paradox" for Adolescent Externalizing Behavior? Evidence from a National Sample', *Social Psychiatry and Psychiatric Epidemiology* 51: 27–37.

Sampson, R. (2008), 'Rethinking Crime and Immigration', *Contexts,* 7: 28–33.

Simanski, J. (2014), *Annual Report: Immigration Enforcement Action: 2013*. Available at: https://www.dhs.gov/sites/default/files/publications/ois_enforcement_ar_2013.pdf

Simes, J. and Waters, M. (2014), 'The Politics of Immigration and Crime', in S. Bucerius and M. Tonry (eds), *The Oxford Handbook of Ethnicity, Crime and Immigration*. Oxford: Oxford University Press, 457–81.

Stowell, J. I., Messner, S. F., McGeever, K. F., and Raffalovich, L. E. (2009), 'Immigration and the Recent Crime Drop in the U.S.: A Pooled, Cross-sectional Time-Series Analysis of Metropolitan Areas', *Criminology* 47: 889–928.

Stumpf, J. (2006), 'The Crimmigraiton Crisis: Immigrants, Crime, and Sovereign Power', *American University Law Review* 56(2): 367–419.

Thompson, W. (1846), *Recollecions of Mexico*. New York: Wiley and Putnam.

Transactional Records Access Clearinghouse (2013), *Spike in Criminal Prosecutions Caused by Jump in Immigration Referrals*. Available at: http://trac.syr.edu/immigration/reports/312/

Truman, J. and Morgan, R. (2016), *U.S. Department of Justice, Bureau of Justice Statistics, Criminal Victimization: 2015*. Available at: https://www.bjs.gov/content/pub/pdf/cv15.pdf

Trump, D. (2016), 'Presidential Campaign Announcement' *CSPAN3*. Available at: http://www.realclearpolitics.com/video/2015/06/16/trump_mexico_not_sending_us_their_best_criminals_drug_dealers_and_rapists_are_crossing_border.html

U.S. Census 2010 (2010). Available at: https://www.census.gov/2010census/

U.S. Sentencing Commission (2016), *Overview of Federal Criminal Cases Fiscal Year 2015*. Available at: http://www.ussc.gov/sites/default/files/pdf/research-and-publications/research-publications/2016/FY15_Overview_Federal_Criminal_Cases.pdf

Van Cleve, N. and Mayes, L. (2015), 'Criminal Justice Through "Colorbind" Lenses: A Call to Examine the Mutual Constitution of Race and Criminal Justice', *Law & Social Inquiry* 40(2): 406–32.

Vázquez, Y. (2011), 'Perpetuating the Marginalization of Latinos: A Collateral Consequence of the Incorporation of Immigration Law into the Criminal Justice System', *Howard Law Journal* 54: 639–73.

Vázquez, Y. (2015), 'Constructing Crimmigration: Latino Subordination in a "Post-Racial" World', *Ohio State Law Journal* 76(3): 599–657.

Vázquez, Y. (2017), 'Crimmigration: The Missing Piece of Criminal Justice Reform', *University of Richmond Law Review* 51: 1093–147.

Wadsworth, T. (2010), 'Is Immigration Responsbile for the Crime Drop? An Assessment of the Influence of Immigration on Changes in Violent Crime Between 1990 and 2000', *Social Science Quarterly* 91(2): 531–53.

Weaver, V. M. (2007), 'Frontlash: Race and the Development of Punitive Crime Policy', *Studies in American Political Development* 21: 230–65.

Weber, D. J. (1973), *Foreigners in their Native Land: Historical Roots of the Mexican American*. Albuquerque, NM: University of New Mexico Press.

Williams Reid, L., Weiss, H. E., Aldeman, R. M., and Jaret, C. (2005), 'The Immigration–Crime Relationship: Evidence across US Metropolitian Areas', *Social Science Research* 34: 77–80.

Legislation

Illegal Immigration Reform and Immigrant Responsibility Act of 1996, Pub. L..No. 104-208, § 133, 110 Stat. 3009-546, 3009-563 to -564 (codified at 8 U.S.C. § 1357 (2013)) (regarding section 287(g) programs).

Illegal Immigration Reform and Immigrant Responsibility Act of 1996, Pub. L. No. 104-208, § 112, 110 Stat. at 3009-559 (codified at 8 U.S.C.§ 1221) (concerning the computerized database system known as IDENT).

Immigration Reform and Control Act, Pub. L. 99-603, 100 Stat. 3445 (1986).

Personal Responsibility and Work Opportunity Reconciliation Act of 1996. 1996. Pub. L. 104-193, 110 Stat 2105.

The Antiterrorism and Effective Death Penalty Act of 1996, Pub. L. No. 104-132, 110 Stat. 1214 (1996).

Violent Crime Control and Law Enforcement Act of 1994, Pub. L. No. 103-322, § 130007, 108 Stat. 1796, 2029 (codified at 8 U.S.C. § 1252 note (2013)).

Case law

Chae Chan Ping v. United States, 130 U.S. 581 (1889).

Plessy v. Ferguson, 163 U.S. 537 (1896).

United States v. Roblero-Solis, 588 F.3d 692 (2009).

10

Racialization through Enforcement

Jennifer M. Chacón and Susan Bibler Coutin

Immigration law and enforcement practices are important forces in the construction of race in the United States. This has long been true, and an existing body of literature discusses the historical role of immigration law and immigration enforcement on racial formation (Haney-Lopez 2006; Ngai 2004). This chapter examines contemporary manifestations of this phenomenon at the level of legal doctrine and of everyday practices to help illuminate how Latino racial identity in the United States is understood by and produced through immigration law and responses to it. This brief chapter focuses on the Latino case, but it is important to note that the strong conflation of Latino identity and unauthorized immigration status in the United States not only operates to the detriment of Latinos, but also renders socially invisible unauthorized migrants belonging to other white, black, and Asian racial groups and sub-groups. This impedes the development of social and legal policies needed to address the sometimes unique needs of the members of these groups. It also generates false oppositional narratives about Asian immigrant groups as legal and economically desirable (in moderation), and Latino immigrant groups as 'illegal' and economically undesirable. And it reifies white racial privilege by obscuring the existence of unauthorized migrants who are socially constructed as white. The topic of how these group identity constructions interact in a complex, constitutive way is the theme of ongoing research (Ashar et al. 2016), and will be discussed more fully in a later project. This chapter focuses on Latino racial identity, which has particular salience in the US context because unauthorized migrants are frequently stereotyped as Latino, and conversely, Latinos are frequently stereotyped as unauthorized migrants.

The first part of this chapter focuses on the doctrinal exceptions that allow for consideration of race in immigration policing, with attention to how this has both been taken for granted and come to define Latino racial identity. Over time, US courts have developed a unique line of reasoning to justify racially discriminatory practices in immigration enforcement. The resulting doctrinal exceptionalism authorizes race-based practices that impact individuals regardless of citizenship (Chacón 2010). Immigration enforcement exceptions to constitutional protections against racial profiling also have a way of migrating into mainstream criminal procedure, reducing legal protections against racial profiling in cases involving other marginalized racial groups outside the immigration context (Carbado and Harris 2011).

Racialization through Enforcement. Jennifer M. Chacón and Susan Bibler Coutin. © Jennifer M. Chacón and Susan Bibler Coutin, 2018. Published 2018 by Oxford University Press.

These well-documented legal trends are also accompanied by less well-examined legal reasoning that isolates immigration enforcement practices from mainstream constitutional protections through a studied judicial and administrative refusal to acknowledge the workings of racial animus in immigration enforcement. By characterizing immigration enforcement practices as rooted in distinctions of national origin, and treating these distinctions both as proper and as distinct from racial discrimination, administrative agencies and judges incorrectly remove concerns of racial discrimination from consideration in evaluating immigration laws and legal practices. In fact, immigration law concerns itself with nationality, not national origin. National origin is used as a proxy for nationality in the street policing of immigration, but national origin and nationality are not the same thing. At the same time, racial discrimination and national origin discrimination are not hermetically sealed categories but overlap in complex and significant ways and are co-constitutive. Over-reliance on national origin profiling and a concomitant failure to acknowledge the racial dimensions of alleged 'national origin' discrimination in immigration enforcement ensure that racially discriminatory enforcement practices flourish within and outside the context of immigration. Racial profiling is naturalized by law. The first part of the chapter explores this naturalization of racial profiling in the context of immigration enforcement.

The second part of this chapter then shifts from law and legal doctrine to practice, exploring some of the ways in which Latino racial identity is produced on the ground in the United States through the enforcement of immigration law, and through political resistance to the violence engendered by immigration law. This section draws in part on interview data gathered over a period of three years with immigrants and immigrant justice organizations in Los Angeles and Orange Counties in Southern California (Ashar et al. 2016). These interviews illustrate how racial tropes are mobilized not just by politicians seeking substantial new restrictions on immigration and vigorous enforcement of existing immigration bars ('restrictionists'), but also by immigrants themselves. In the case of restrictionists, racial tropes are used to channel the political power of white nationalism. For immigrants and the organizations they work for and with, racial tropes generally are used to fuel political mobilization and to resist oppressive laws and practices, although some individuals express notions of racial identity that reflect their absorption of or alignment with restrictionist racial constructions. Taken as a whole, this chapter reveals the ways in which immigration law is operating as a central node for the production of Latino racial identity and the perpetuation of racial hierarchy in the United States.

IMMIGRATION EXCEPTIONALISM AND THE PRODUCTION OF RACIAL IDENTITY

A deeply complicated, often volatile, relationship exists between racism directed toward citizens and that aimed at noncitizens.

Johnson (1998: 1112)

Kevin Johnson, one of the leading commentators on the role of race in US immigration law and its enforcement, has argued that 'the differential treatment of citizens and noncitizens serves as a "magic mirror" revealing how dominant society might treat domestic minorities if legal constraints were abrogated'. He argues that 'the harsh treatment of noncitizens of color reveals terrifying lessons about how society views citizens of color' (Johnson 1998: 1114). In his 1998 article, Johnson points out that, even at that time, scholars like Dinesh D'Souza were already claiming that racism was a diminishing force in American life, and that Peter Schuck and others were proclaiming race to be largely irrelevant in shaping immigration policy. Johnson himself took a different view. He argued that the historical and continuing practice of *de jure* national origin discrimination that was contained in immigration law provided a window into the continued salience of race in American politics.

In Johnson's view,

[b]y barring admission of the outsider group that is subordinated domestically, society rationalizes the disparate treatment of the domestic racial minority group in question and reinforces that group's inferiority. Exclusion in the immigration laws must be viewed as an integral part of a larger mosaic of racial discrimination in American society. (Johnson 1998: 1153)

The events of the intervening twenty years and, most recently, the successful presidential campaign of Donald Trump have provided additional evidence in support of this view. President Trump launched his candidacy with a speech that involved a grotesque caricature of Mexican immigrants in the United States and used this express appeal to racial animus as the central justification for his campaign.[1]

But immigration law functions as more than just a site of displaced animus enacted into and justified by exclusionary policies. It also generates a host of *practices* that redound to the disadvantage of those citizens who share characteristics with immigrant communities. Citizens who are perceived to look and speak like foreign nationals and who live in immigrant communities are, in fact, subjected to the very same practices of enforcement that are aimed at their foreign national counterparts (Chacón 2010; Elias 2008; Gardner and Kohli 2009). They are racially profiled in ways that produce heightened law enforcement surveillance of their lives, they are questioned about their citizenship and required to prove their belonging in ways that individuals who are identified as 'white' are not, and they are sometimes erroneously detained and deported (Stevens 2011). Moreover, the relaxed legal standards that apply to enforcement practices in this context migrate over time into the legal doctrines governing the policing of other racially subordinated groups (Carbado and Harris 2011; Chacón 2010).

In the post-Civil Rights era in the United States, immigration law is one of the few exceptional areas of law where express and overt reliance on race is constitutionally

---

[1] In his announcement speech, Trump stated: 'When Mexico sends its people, they are not sending their best. They are not sending you. They are sending people that have lots of problems, and they are bringing those problems to us. They are bringing drugs and they are bringing crime, and they're rapists. Some, I assume, are good people.' *Time*, 16 June 2015. Available at: http://time.com/3923128/donald-trump-announcement-speech/.

permissible and frequently upheld. In a pair of cases from the late 1970s, a period of growing and hyper-inflated concerns over Mexican immigration (Chavez 2001), the Supreme Court blessed reliance on race as a factor to establish 'reasonable suspicion' for an investigative stop in immigration enforcement in the context of both roving patrols (*United States v. Brignoni-Ponce* (1975)) and checkpoint stops (*United States v. Martinez-Fuerte* (1976)). The racial characteristic in question in these cases was 'Mexican appearance'—a descriptor that is as legally nebulous as it is socially meaningful in a world rife with stereotypes of Mexicans (Johnson 2010). Mexicans are as varied in appearance as the people of the globe, but judicial conceptions of Mexican appearance sweep in only poor people of small stature and darker skin tone and hair colour, particularly those speaking Spanish, or speaking heavily accented English, regardless of their actual nationality (Ortiz and Telles 2012). According to the court, such 'Mexican appearance', taken in conjunction with other characteristics, including geographic location, haircut, and mode of dress, can provide a basis for 'reasonable suspicion' that an individual lacks lawful immigration status (*U.S. v. Brignoni-Ponce* (1975)).[2] In fact, such markers speak to little beyond class and geography. They may provide weak evidence of national origin in the sense that they can provide imperfect clues to an individual's ancestral roots. But in a multi-racial, multi-ethnic, multilingual society like the United States, these indicators offer no meaningful information about nationality, and nationality (coupled with immigration status) is the only fact that actually matters for immigration law purposes.

The cases that validate racial profiling in immigration enforcement are old, but they remain good law and are still cited in government briefs in support of the legitimacy of immigration enforcement practices that rely on racial profiling. Even as the demography of the United States has changed to include a substantial number of citizens of Mexican descent,[3] profiling largely on the basis of apparent Mexican ancestry for immigration violations remains permissible. One lower federal appellate court, the Ninth Circuit Court of Appeals, has repudiated reliance on Mexican ancestry as a factor in immigration stops in Southern California, where the population of lawful residents of Mexican ancestry—and therefore, under the court's thin reasoning, bearing 'Mexican appearance'—is high (*U.S. v. Montero-Camargo* (2000)). But the same court upheld racial profiling in Montana, where the number of Mexican-Americans (and, again, presumably of individuals with what the court calls 'Mexican appearance') is low (*U.S. v. Manzo-Jurado* (2006)). Most other jurisdictions continue to treat Mexican appearance as a legitimate factor in developing suspicion of unlawful immigration status. And in recent decisions, the Supreme

---

[2] The Court in *Brignoni-Ponce* did reject reliance on Mexican appearance alone, but then undercut any potential protection against racial profiling by adding that appearance taken in conjunction with factors such as haircut could serve as the basis for reasonable suspicion of immigration violations.

[3] The US Census Bureau reports that Hispanics make up 17.6 per cent of the US population and that 63.4 per cent of these individuals are of Mexican ancestry. United States Census Bureau, Hispanic Heritage Month 2016, 12 October 2016. Available at: http://www.census.gov/newsroom/facts-for-features/2016/cb16-ff16.html. Los Angeles County has the largest population of Hispanics in the country.

Court has also implicitly extended this permission to engage in extraordinary race-based policing practices to state and local law enforcement agents who have no formal role or training in immigration enforcement (*U.S. v. Arizona* (2012); Chacón 2012a).

The Supreme Court and the lower federal courts continue to uphold empirically unmoored reliance on racial profiling in immigration policing on the grounds that the government's extraordinary national security interests demand this. Courts treat reliance on Mexican appearance in immigration enforcement as something that is physically and genetically real, rather than as a racialized composite deeply connected to the long history of racial discrimination in the southwestern United States against individuals perceived to be of Mexican origin. Developing those historical connections would have elucidated why these particular enforcement strategies were and are so problematic. In *Brignoni-Ponce*, the Supreme Court concludes (without any supporting statistical evidence) that '[t]he likelihood that any given person of Mexican ancestry is an alien is high enough to make Mexican appearance a relevant factor', although not the sole factor, in a 'reasonable' investigative stop. Reliance on Mexican appearance therefore can be part of a 'reasonable ... seizure' under the Fourth Amendment of the US Constitution. The court never attempts to explain what is meant by Mexican appearance—but it does not need to because the notion draws from stereotypical assumptions about Mexican appearance that pervade the dominant culture. By endorsing reliance on characteristics descriptively defined only as 'Mexican' as a means of policing immigration status, the Court does not just endorse racial profiling; it also racializes Mexicans.

This approach to race and policing stands in contrast to the Supreme Court's approach to race and national origin in cases outside the Fourth Amendment immigration enforcement cases. For example, the Fifth and Fourteenth Amendments of the US Constitution require equal protection under the law. When the government (federal or state) draws legal distinctions on the basis of race, the court applies its highest level of scrutiny to determine whether the legal distinctions are sufficiently justified to withstand constitutional challenge. In *Korematsu v. United States*—the infamous 1944 constitutional case upholding the internment of individuals of Japanese descent during the Second World War—the Supreme Court easily understood the challenged practices in that case to be *racially* discriminatory (although they shamefully found the discrimination to be justified). The court applied strict scrutiny to the federal order in question, with the explanation that 'all legal restrictions which curtail the civil rights of *a single racial group* are immediately suspect'. The court did not reason that this could not be racial discrimination because other individuals of Asian ancestry who spoke different languages were situated differently within the national community and were not targeted for internment. The court accepted that individuals of Japanese descent had been effectively racialized in this context, and that their targeting constituted invidious racial discrimination, even as it allowed the relevant racially discriminatory policy to persist because of the purported exigencies of national security.

That this appropriately contextual understanding of the legal category of 'race' persists in the equal protection jurisprudence was demonstrated as recently as March

2017, when the Supreme Court decided the case of *Peña-Rodriguez v. Colorado*. Peña-Rodriguez, a US citizen of Mexican descent, had been a defendant in a criminal trial where a jury convicted him of one misdemeanour count of unlawful sexual contact and two misdemeanour counts of harassment. After the trial, his counsel learned that one of the jurors had made statements expressing anti-Mexican animus during deliberations. Two jurors swore out affidavits indicating that another juror (a former police officer) had stated that Peña-Rodriguez must be guilty of the sexual assault charges at issue 'because he's Mexican, and Mexican men take whatever they want', and that 'Mexican men had a bravado that caused them to believe they could "do whatever they want" with women'. The question in the case was whether the Sixth Amendment's requirement of an impartial jury trumped Colorado's no-impeachment rule that prohibited the reconsideration of a criminal conviction based on post-conviction evidence concerning jury deliberations.

The government argued that reopening proceedings in the *Peña-Rodriguez* case based on such post-conviction evidence would be problematic and impracticable and was not constitutionally required. But both the government lawyers and counsel for Peña-Rodriguez—as well as all of the members of the various courts to review the question—were unified in treating this case as involving a question of racial discrimination. Despite the fact that the juror's comments were about 'Mexicans', everyone's proper working assumption was that Peña-Rodriguez was a case about impermissible racial discrimination. The Supreme Court took the same approach. It had no difficulty concluding that the anti-Mexican bias at issue in the case was racial bias. Justice Kennedy, writing for the majority, opined:

Juror H. C.'s bias was based on petitioner's Hispanic identity, which the Court in prior cases has referred to as ethnicity, and that may be an instructive term here. Yet we have also used the language of race when discussing the relevant constitutional principles in cases involving Hispanic persons. Petitioner and respondent both refer to race, or to race and ethnicity, in this more expansive sense in their briefs to the Court. This opinion refers to the nature of the bias as racial in keeping with the primary terminology employed by the parties and used in our precedents.[4]

As Peña-Rodriguez's racist juror's comments suggest, individuals use national origin descriptors not as the basis for describing legal categorical realities, but as the basis for groundless and sweeping generalizations about a particular 'race' of people. Individuals who deploy racist rhetoric about someone who is 'Mexican' or 'Japanese' are not particularly concerned about the niceties of whether they are using accurate national origin descriptors, and might use those labels to describe someone who is actually Guatemalan or Peruvian. They are using national origin descriptors to suggest that the individual in question is a social outsider, and they are doing so in a context that further expresses the sentiment that the outsider is inassimilable and inferior in ways that justify their exclusion. This sort of exclusion is certainly not about nationality, it is not really even about national origin; this is racism.

---

[4] 137 S.Ct. 855, 863 (2017).

Equal protection jurisprudence in the United States, unlike Fourth Amendment jurisprudence, rests upon an understanding of the intertwined nature of racial and national origin discrimination, as do US statutory anti-discrimination schemes. Title VII, for example, acknowledges the possibility of both racial and national origin discrimination, but treats them as the same evil. Title VII prohibits discrimination on the basis of 'sex, race, color, national origin, and religion'. All are equally impermissible because, among other things, to exclude 'color', 'national origin', and 'religion' from this list runs the risk of granting cover to particular manifestations of racism.

Some might argue that racial discrimination is distinct—that it can speak only to categories of race recognized by the US census: 'black', 'white', 'American Indian or Alaska Native', 'Asian', and 'Native Hawaiian or other Pacific Islander'. But a mere look at this list reveals the constructed nature of the racial categories themselves (Haney-Lopez 2006). Transplanted to other countries (and even within the United States), these racial categories would be nonsensical: overbroad in some categories, hyper-specific in others. Race only has meaning within a context because it is constructed by the social and political realities of that context (Omi and Winant 1994). The same can be said about national origin discrimination as it is challenged in the case law and regulated in statute.

Recent immigration enforcement highlights the ways that Fourth Amendment protections continue to be subverted in the context of immigration enforcement through judicially imagined distinctions between illegitimate race discrimination and purportedly legitimate national origin discrimination. One of the clearest examples is the Second Circuit's 2014 decision in the case *Maldonado v. Holder*. By refusing to see racism in certain discriminatory practices, the reasoning deployed by courts in cases like these opens up troubling new paths towards the legal legitimation of racial discrimination.

Maldonado involved a law enforcement action undertaken by the city police department of Danbury, Connecticut. Officers of the Danbury Police Department (DPD) disguised themselves in plain clothes and drove up to a park where a group of day labourers, the vast majority of whom were Spanish-speaking immigrants from Latin America (in this case, primarily Ecuador), were awaiting possible work. Plain-clothed DPD policemen 'hired' a group of these day labourers and asked them to get into the back of their vehicle, purportedly to drive them to work. The DPD officers then drove the vehicle full of workers to Immigration and Customs Enforcement officials who interrogated them about their immigration status and initiated deportation proceedings against them. The petitioners in the case sought to suppress evidence about their immigration status. They argued that they had been impermissibly profiled by the DPD on the basis of race and that DPD's unconstitutional reliance on race required the suppression of the evidence that was gathered as the fruits of their initial unconstitutional behaviour.

Because they were in an immigration court and not a criminal court, obtaining the remedy of suppression required not only that the petitioners establish a Fourth Amendment violation—that is, that their seizure was 'unreasonable' as a legal matter—but also that the violation was 'egregious' (*INS v. Lopez-Mendoza* (1984)).

In the past, various courts have held that profiling on the basis of race constitutes an egregious violation of the Fourth Amendment that could warrant the suppression of illegally seized evidence in immigration proceedings. In this case, however, the Second Circuit declined to suppress the evidence.

The court in *Maldonado* made a number of interpretive moves that encapsulate the elision of race that is occurring in immigration enforcement cases. First, the court ignored the role of race in DPD's selection of the enforcement site. As dissenting Judge Lynch noted, the geographic area that the DPD selected for its sting operation was chosen precisely because it was the place where Ecuadoran day labourers congregated. Other sites were not targeted. Still, the majority blithely reasoned that it was the petitioners who had selected themselves into the enforcement action by volunteering to work. By ignoring the deliberate consideration of race in site selection, the court erased DPD's racial profiling.

Second, and even more troublingly, the court acknowledged that profiling on the basis of race could constitute an 'egregious violation' of the US constitution's Fourth Amendment protections against unreasonable searches and seizures, but then faulted the petitioners for conflating race and national origin. The court stressed—quoting page six of the petitioners' brief—that:

"DPD never targeted the city's better-assimilated Brazilian immigrant population, whose day laborers congregated at a different local site." This alleged disparity would seem to refute rather than suggest race-based animus.[5]

In other words, the court incorrectly suggested that because not all individuals with ancestral origins in Latin America had been targeted, there could be no finding of racial discrimination against a new and less 'assimilated' immigrant group from a distinct country in Latin America. This understanding of racial discrimination seems not only intentionally naive, but also flatly inconsistent with the contextual and grounded legal understanding of race that is reflected over decades of constitutional case law in cases involving equal protection claims.

Third, after constructing a fictive, bright line distinction between 'race' and 'national origin' in a case where one was clearly interchangeable with the other from the perspective of the DPD officers, the court in *Maldonado* reasoned that, far from being *prohibited* in immigration enforcement, national origin discrimination is *essential* to immigration enforcement. The court wrote that rules prohibiting such discrimination:

would in effect require ICE to stop only the specific individuals it already knows are here illegally, and render egregious (and therefore forbidden) ICE raids on sweatshops, forced brothels, and other settings in which illegal aliens are exploited and threatened—and much worse ... No system of immigration enforcement can run under these constraints.[6]

It is difficult to understate the mirror-world quality of this statement. The court suggests that it actually would be *wrong* to require individualized suspicion in immigration enforcement efforts, and that the ability to profile groups on the basis of their

---

[5] 763 F.3d. at 162.   [6] 763 F.3d. at 162.

presumed national origin is essential to protecting immigrants. Given that individualized suspicion is a touchstone of reasonableness in most Fourth Amendment analyses, the court's express endorsement of group-based profiling as the key to enforcement is a stunning inversion of the dictates of equal protection.

The reasoning in *Maldonado* encapsulates a larger legal reality in which at the same moment that law enforcement agencies at all levels of government overtly repudiate race-based policing practices, they continue to champion 'national origin' profiling in the immigration context. The reasoning behind this paradox is neatly illustrated by the US Department of Justice's guidelines on racial profiling.

Broadly stated, the Department of Justice guidelines prohibit federal law enforcement officers from making investigative stops that rely on 'race, ethnicity, gender, national origin, religion, sexual orientation, or gender identity to any degree, except that officers may rely on the listed characteristics in a specific suspect description'. Footnote one of the document distinguishes nationality—which is an individual's country of nationality and which can obviously be a legal basis for enforcement distinctions in certain contexts—and national origin, which the memo defines as 'an individual's, or his or her ancestor's, country of birth or origin, or an individual's possession of the physical, cultural or linguistic characteristics commonly associated with a particular country'. National origin, like race, is purportedly off limits as the basis for investigative and enforcement activities, even while nationality may be legally relevant in certain enforcement contexts. The *Maldonado* case illustrates a common, sloppy conflation of the concepts of nationality and national origin—a conflation that allows law enforcement to rely on stereotyping as an investigative and enforcement technique.

The Supreme Court's immigration enforcement jurisprudence and the distillation of those cases in the federal government's own guidelines on racial profiling exacerbate the problems that flow from such deficient reasoning. Footnote two of the federal guidelines on racial profiling explains that its restrictions on racial profiling do not apply at all 'to interdiction activities in the vicinity of the border, or to protective, inspection, or screening activities', thereby inscribing practices of race and national origin discrimination into immigration enforcement in the border region, notwithstanding the fact that the border region in the United States is increasingly populated by lawfully present residents and citizens of Latin American descent. While it is not at all obvious that constitutional tolerance for racial profiling can and should extend as far as the memo's exemptions suggest, at present, immigration policing and interdiction efforts in the border region are in fact regulated differently; racial profiling is tolerated. *Maldonado* and cases like it then extend this questionable tolerance for racial profiling far beyond the 'vicinity of the border'. Although colour-blind racism is certainly at work in the practices of immigration policing (Bonilla-Silva 2009; Douglas et al. 2015), it is important to acknowledge the full extent to which the law tolerates overt reliance on race in this realm.

Unsurprisingly, the behaviour of law enforcement agents on the ground reflects this judicial and administrative tolerance of profiling. The combination of policies that explicitly tolerate racial profiling in immigration enforcement and judicial decision-making that remains wilfully oblivious to the impermissible profiling that exceeds even the already over-generous legal limits produces an immigration enforcement system comfortably reliant on racial stereotypes in its functioning. The operative stereotypes reinforce images of those perceived to be Mexicans as outsiders. Mexican-ness itself is policed based on appearance, language, and geographies of residence and workplace, broadly sweeping in all Latinos who fit the stereotype. That is to say, while immigration law and policy choices in the period from 1924 to 1965 helped to transform Mexicans into the 'iconic illegal alien' (Ngai 2004), in the decades since, enforcement practices have ensured that Latinos who fit stereotyped notions of Mexican-ness have been subsumed under the umbrella of 'illegals'. As immigration enforcement efforts have proliferated and become more widespread (Chacón 2012b), these interactions play an ever-expanding role in shaping racial identity in the United States.

THE PRODUCTION AND RESISTANCE OF RACIAL HIERARCHY

The construction of Latinos as a racial group has not sprung only from choices made by courts and lawmakers. It relies more broadly on state actors making discretionary enforcement decisions, and is reflected in and reinforced by individuals' own characterizations and understandings of their treatment by state actors. This section briefly explores some of the ways that racial identity is constructed within immigrant communities as manifestations of and in response to repressive state practices (Romero 2008; Sanchez and Romero 2010). The discussion is necessarily cursory, but seeks to illustrate a set of themes that will be further developed in later work.[7]

Defining and being defined by enforcement

Research suggests that individual law enforcement agents rely more heavily on Latino racial identity in targeting individuals for enforcement in jurisdictions where restrictive immigration policies are in place (Gardner and Kohli 2009; Weissman et al. 2009). Some studies have demonstrated that in states and localities with more restrictive immigration laws and policies, Latinos are more likely to be targeted for law enforcement investigation and enforcement measures (Armenta 2016; Gardner and Kohli 2009; Southern Poverty Law Center 2009; US Department of Justice 2012; Weissman 2009). The effects are so palpable that scholars have traced out the negative health effects such policies have on Latinos in these jurisdictions (Almeida

[7] Among other sources, this section draws on over a hundred interviews that I and other members of a research team have done in the period 2014–2017 with grants from the Russell Sage Foundation (Award Number: 88-14-06) and the National Science Foundation Law and Social Sciences program (Award Number: SES-1535501). We spoke with the representatives of immigrant-serving organizations in the Southern California area and immigrants who are in some way affiliated with these organizations. Our research team will be publishing more detailed accounts of its findings in later publications. Because of her extensive role in spearheading the collection of the interview data relied upon in this chapter, the Principal Investigator on the project, Susan Bibler Coutin, is a credited co-author.

et al. 2016; Flores et al. 2008). As previously explained, existing legal doctrines are not designed to deter racial profiling in cases where criminal prosecutions are not an important goal. Much of the immigration enforcement-related profiling occurs precisely because federal, state, and local law enforcement agents presume that Latino identity is synonymous with non-citizen status and seek to channel individuals into immigration proceedings where illegally secured evidence will often be admissible (Chacón 2010). At the systemic level, these individual enforcement choices can signal a message of non-belonging to most Latino residents.

Developments in California help to illustrate how laws that purport to disfavour individuals on the basis of immigration status can be experienced on the ground as a form of racial profiling, even in jurisdictions that adopt some immigrant-friendly policies and practices. In 2013, California enacted legislation enabling unauthorized migrants to obtain state driver's licences. But for almost two decades prior to that, unauthorized migrants had been barred by state law from receiving California driver's licences. Beginning in 1994, with the passage of Proposition 187, the state stopped issuing driver's licences to individuals who were present in the United States without authorization (Grad 2014). Many unauthorized immigrants who were long-time residents of the state were therefore driving without a licence.

When individuals are driving without a licence, the police can impound their vehicles and make the vehicle owners pay a fine to reclaim the vehicles. Among other things, this practice is a source of revenue for the department. Because police in California were aware that unauthorized migrants were unlikely to have a licence, they could (and apparently did) target them for licence checks. This practice is a quintessential example of how immigration enforcement measures combine with ordinary street policing of criminal laws to create distinctive negative effects for foreign nationals in the criminal justice system. This can occur even in jurisdictions such as Los Angeles—a county that limits its enforcement cooperation with federal immigration enforcement agencies and that has long purported to police in a way that is blind to immigration status (Gates 1979).

Interviews with a number of residents of Los Angeles County suggest that the pre-2013 driver's licence policy encouraged police to target unauthorized migrants for enforcement. This targeting was achieved not through probable cause concerning immigration status, but through broad racial profiling. For example, Erasmo,[8] a middle-aged Mexican national living in Los Angeles, indicated that police relied on race to make stops. He explained:

One is detained because one is seen as Latino. [When the police stop you] they don't know your status yet; whether you're an immigrant or not. I've seen people who are Latino, who have their license. They're not immigrants and they've been pulled over. The first thing [the police] ask for is the license. When [the police] see that you have a license, they just give you a pretext or a random fee. They'll say, 'I pulled you over because you don't make a complete stop, because you didn't turn correctly. Try to do it right.' And that's it. They don't even fine you after that. When one is Latino, they'll pull you over just to investigate whether one is licensed or not. Sometimes even though you don't do anything, they'll pull you over.

---

[8] The names of individuals identified in this chapter have been changed.

Erasmo's description of the sequence of events is resonant of the plaintiffs' arguments in *U.S. v. Arizona* that S.B. 1070—a law that encouraged state and local police to engage in investigations of immigration status—would promote racial profiling (Johnson 2012). By creating incentives for stopping unauthorized immigrants, the law promotes a police practice of stopping anyone perceived as an unauthorized immigrant. As Erasmo observed, because Latinos are stereotyped as unauthorized migrants, they are targeted for these stops.

Erasmo is not alone in his assessment of how police rely on Latino racial identity to shape their enforcement decisions. Many other respondents described their perception of a policy of racial profiling around auto stops, and all of these individuals described the targeting as based on 'Latino' identity, sometimes in combination with markers of class (like the kind of car driven). This suggests that foreign nationals are thinking about Latino identity as something more salient than national origin and as something that drives law enforcement practices in everyday street policing. They do not describe the practices as aimed at particular nationalities but, rather, as aimed at 'Latinos'.[9]

Interview data as well as publically available information from the websites of immigrant-serving organizations suggest that this understanding is shared by many of the organizers, attorneys, and activists at immigrant-serving organizations working in Southern California and throughout the country. Immigrant-serving organizations and their clients and constituents have a shared narrative of the work done by racial identity in this context. That shared narrative is shaped by exposure to law enforcement practices, but it also generates a lens for understanding those practices, and an organizing tool for responding to them. By highlighting the ways that immigration enforcement efforts contribute to racialized law enforcement practices that affect Latinos, immigrants and immigrant-serving organizations are able to stregthen their political alliances with the broader Latino community.

Resisting/reinforcing categories

Unsurprisingly, in reaction to a homogenizing and often negative racial rhetoric, some individuals of Latin American origin attempt to insulate themselves from harsh state practices or to gain the benefits of assimilation by distancing themselves from other Latinos. Alondra, a middle-aged woman from Peru, entered the United States over fifteen years ago when her husband was granted a temporary work visa. That visa has long since expired, but Alondra has remained. In conversations, she acknowledges the deep racism experienced by Latinos in the United States even as she simultaneously distances herself in some ways from that group. In an interview in November 2014, for example, she stated that the neighbourhood where she lives:

---

[9] Indeed, Beth Baker-Cristales (2004) has noted that Salvadoran immigrants who previously identified themselves in class terms come to adopt such racial and ethnic designations after living in the United States for a substantial period of time.

is a middle class community. Here you don't find many immigrants. It is not a *barrio* of immigrants. There are few Latinos. The Latinos are in the restaurants, cooking. It is a calm *barrio*. The people we know here are very agreeable . . . But for Hispanic people, they probably prefer to be in Van Nuys or in Canoga Park [more predominantly Latino neighbourhoods].

Alondra has many features, including her phenotype and language preference, that mark her as 'Latina' in the United States, and she identifies as part of that group. At the same time, however, she implicitly connects the 'calmness' of her neighbourhood with the scarcity of Latinos, who are only present to do menial work, not to live. Alondra herself has chosen not to live in what she calls an 'immigrant city'. In characterizing her neighbourhood and choices as she does, Alondra unconsciously echoes conservative commentators and immigration restrictionists (Chacón 2007), and reinforces the negative narratives of Latino identity that justify the very exclusionary immigration laws and discriminatory law enforcement practices that have had such a negative effect on her own life. She raises no questions as to whether Latinos (or '*Hispanos*') are an identifiable group or whether she is part of it—but she persistently raises the issue of the intra-group distinctions among Latinos in the United States and often distinguishes herself from Latinos of lower socio-economic status. In this way, she offers a class-based narrative that allows her to distinguish herself from other Latinos who she views as less desirable residents. In so doing, she constructs an understanding of Latino identity that is easier to square with her own self-perception, but that also inadvertently reinforces the negative racial narratives that ensnare her. Interviews reveal that even Latinos who eschew such distancing strategies sometimes practise them, sometimes apparently unconsciously. This, in turn, contributes to negative constructions of Latino racial identity in the United States.

Citizenship and (relative) political power are additional wedges that individuals use to resist the negative ascriptions of Latino identity. Like class-based distinctions, these resistance strategies also shore up the negative stereotypes of the Latino identity that the individual seeks to resist.

Latinos in law enforcement provide a case study of this process in action. Many Latino immigrants interviewed in Southern California in the 2014–2016 period express surprise and dismay that Latinos in law enforcement and other positions of power fail to demonstrate solidarity with them. They often viewed Latino police officers as imposing on them harsher treatment than law enforcement officials of other races. For example, Fatima, an unauthorized immigrant from Mexico described a car accident in which the other driver was at fault. She recounted:

[F]our police, patrollers, showed up. They were Latinos. They spoke Spanish, like me. Shouldn't they have come to talk to me? It was me who got hit. They should have been asking me if I was ok. But no, because he [the driver of the vehicle that struck her] was an American, they went to him, talked to him.

The race of the officers might be seen as irrelevant to her underlying complaint: as the victim in the accident, perhaps she should have been addressed first. She might have attributed the sequence of events to gender or random luck. But Fatima was particularly aggrieved because the acts were perpetrated by Latinos, and she quickly makes clear her concern that the Latino officer in question treated her worse because of her race:

I said, 'What do you think? Because you see the color of my skin and that I don't speak English, you think that I am less significant? I'm not less significant. I am not doing anything wrong by asking for insurance.'

After a protracted discussion in which the officer refuses to help Fatima, she recounts:

Then in English he [the police officer] says to the American [driver], 'I don't believe *these people*.' (Emphasis in original)

She later recounts a series of more positive experiences with white officers. She mentions a time when her husband was stopped with expired licence tags. The interviewer asked whether the officer was 'a gringo' (common slang for white Americans), and Fatima answered, '[y]es, *American* American', using the term American twice to specify whiteness, or true American-ness, as opposed to the Latino officers she previously tangled with. She recounts her conversation with the officer:

'Ok, look: this is a warning. But look, you need to go to the DMV and pay for new tags.' Ok. That was it. So you come to realize that the majority of the police officers that are Hispanic are always going to be more racist with their race.

Fatima ultimately gave three examples of positive interactions with white officers in contrast to her negative interaction with Latino officers. Her experience is echoed in other interviews. The notion that Latinos in positions of (relative) authority are particularly harsh in their treatment of their co-ethnic immigrants also carries over to other contexts such as work and school.

Fatima's words highlight how Latino citizens with relatively greater power than similarly situated foreign nationals are sometimes perceived by unauthorized migrants as particularly unlikely to help them. These anecdotes may reflect actual practice; perhaps their own efforts to escape the negative consequences of Latino identity drive some Latinos to distance themselves from more marginalized Latinos (Heyman 2002). Alternatively, Latinos with relatively greater power may simply be failing to meet higher expectations for fair treatment that their co-ethnics impose upon them. Latinos may be more attentive to injustices wrought by people from whom they expect greater sympathy. It may be a combination of these factors, or something else entirely. What is clear is that individuals who are perceived as and identify as Latino can engage in conduct that signals their own internalization of the negative stereotypes associated with Latino identity.

Taken collectively, these moments reflect the complexity of Latino racial identity in the United States, which is driven by differences in skin colour, class, occupational strata, English language ability, and immigration status (López 2013). They also help to illustrate the ways that profiling practices 'bind and reif[y] the concepts of race and criminality, fixing them into the subconscious of the profiled, the profiler, and society at large' (Gardner 2014). Finally, they demonstrate the degree to which immigrants' own racial understandings often implicitly reinforce the notion that American identity tracks 'white' racial identity.

Fatima's words provide a fairly typical example of how immigrants' own perceptions of Latino identity reinforce notions of true American identity as 'white'. Fatima and other immigrants often used terminology that identified whiteness as the racial norm of US citizenship. They used the term 'American' (*Americano*) to refer only to white Americans. When interviewees talk about members of other racial groups, they use descriptors: black, African-American, Asian, *Chino* (used broadly to describe all individuals of perceived East Asian descent), and Latino. So, for example, when Erasmo recounts one of his experiences with a police officer in Los Angeles, he notes that '[t]he police officer was Asian and he was generous. He gave me an opportunity.' Only whites are identified by interviewees as 'Americans' unmodified. Even in the heart of 'progressive' California, the language of interviewees reflects a vision of the work race is still doing in the United States to sort insiders from outsiders, and Americans from *American* Americans.

CONCLUSION

Latino racial identity is real and tangible to those living in the United States today. Immigration law and law enforcement choices have enhanced the salience of this racial category not only in immigration enforcement but in every aspect of law enforcement, and, indeed, in a whole host of interactions between government actors and individual residents. Immigrants understand this to be true. They mobilize against racialized enforcement in expressly racial terms. They also sometimes engage in distancing strategies that can inadvertently fuel the negative stereotypes associated with Latino identity and feed the discriminatory practices driven by those stereotypes.

Yet, to date, courts and administrative agencies have proven remarkably inept at confronting head on the role of race in immigration enforcement practices. Courts improperly conflate legal nationality and 'national origin' and maintain the primacy of purported security concerns over the equal protection concerns raised by racial profiling in run-of-the-mill immigration enforcement activities. Sometimes, as in *Maldonado*, judges go so far as to suggest that such discriminatory enforcement efforts are essential to protecting immigrants in 'brothels' and 'sweatshops'. In fact, there is nothing protective about discrimination, and discriminatory enforcement creates the very conditions in which immigrant exploitation flourishes (Chacón 2006).

President Donald Trump, who stereotyped 'Mexicans' as 'rapists' and 'murderers' in announcing his campaign and who has vowed to deport two to three million people in his first term, took office in January 2017. The aggressive immigration enforcement practices that such a policy will require will impact not just unauthorized migrants, but many long-term residents and citizens. This includes the tens of thousands of Latinos who voted for Donald Trump, most likely with the hope and belief that their own citizenship status and assimilation would protect them from the racial intolerance that Trump's campaign rhetoric has legitimated. Since the US legal system so often allows impermissible racial profiling in immigration enforcement to go unacknowledged and without remedy, those voters will have very little recourse if events prove them wrong.

REFERENCES

Almeida, J., Biello, K. B., Pedraza, F., Wintner, S., and Viruell-Fuentes, E. (2016), 'The Association Between Anti-immigrant Policies and Perceived Discrimination among Latinos in the US: A Multilevel Analysis', *Population Health* 2: 897–903.

Armenta, A. (2016), 'Racializing Crimmigration: Structural Racism, Colorblindness, and the Institutional Production of Immigrant Criminality', *Sociology of Race and Ethnicity* online first: 1–14.

Ashar, S., Burciaga, E. M., Chacón, J., Bibler Coutin, S., Garza, A., and Lee, S. (2016), *Navigating Liminal Legalities Along Pathways to Citizenship: Immigrant Vulnerability and the Role of Mediating Institutions*, UC Irvine School of Law Research Paper Series.

Baker-Cristales, B. (2004), 'Salvadoran Transformations: Class Consciousness and Ethnic Identity in a Transnational Milieu', *Latin American Perspectives* 31(5): 15–33.

Bonilla-Silva, E. (2009), *Racism Without Racists: Color-blind Racism and the Persistence of Racial Inequality in America*. Lanham, MD: Rowman & Littlefield Publishers.

Carbado, D. and Harris, C. (2011), 'Undocumented Criminal Procedure', *U.C.L.A. Law Review* 58: 1543–616.

Chacón, J. (2006), 'Misery and Myopia: Understanding the Failures of U.S. Efforts to Stop Human Trafficking', *Fordham Law Review* 74: 2977–3040.

Chacón, J. (2007), 'Unsecured Borders: Immigration Restriction, National Security and Crime Control', *Connecticut Law Review* 39(5): 1827–91.

Chacón, J. (2010), 'A Diversion of Attention? Immigration Courts and the Adjudication of Fourth and Fifth Amendment Rights', *Duke Law Journal* 59(8): 1564–633.

Chacón, J. (2012a), 'The Transformation of Immigration Federalism', *William and Mary Bill of Rights Journal* 21(2): 577–618.

Chacón, J. (2012b), 'Overcriminalizing Immigration', *Journal of Criminal Law & Criminology* 102(3): 613–52.

Chavez, L. (2001), *Covering Immigration: Popular Images and the Politics of the Nation*. Berkeley, CA and London: University of California Press.

Douglas, K. M., Sáenz, R., and Murga, A. L. (2015), 'Immigration in the Era of Color-blind Racism', *American Behavioral Scientist* 59(1)1: 1429–51.

Elias, S. B. (2008), ' "Good Reason to Believe": Widespread Constitutional Violations in the Course of Immigration Enforcement and the Case for Revisiting Lopez-Mendoza', *Wisconsin Law Review* 1109–59.

Flores, E., Tschann, J. M., Dimas J. M., Bachen, E. A., Pasch, L. A., and de Groat, C. L. (2008), 'Perceived Discrimination, Perceived Stress and Mental and Physical Health among Mexican-origin Adults', *Hispanic Journal of Behavioral Sciences* 30(4): 401–24.

Gardner, T. (2014), 'Racial Profiling as Collective Definition', *Social Inclusion* 2(3): 52–9.

Gardner, T. and Kohli, A. (2009), 'The C.A.P. Effect: Racial Profiling in the ICE Criminal Alien Program', September. The Warren Institute on Race, Ethnicity and Diversity. Available at: http://www.motherjones.com/files/policybrief_irving_FINAL.pdf

Gates, D. (1979), Special Order 40, 27 November. Office of the Chief of Police: Los Angeles Police Department.

Grad, S. (2014), 'Immigrants Can Soon Get Driver's Licenses, but it's Been a Long Road', *Los Angeles Times*, 28 December.

Haney-Lopez, I. (2006), *White by Law: The Legal Construction of Race*. New York: New York University Press.

Heyman, J. (2002), 'U.S. Immigration Officers of Mexican Ancestry as Mexican Americans, Citizens, and Immigration Police', *Current Anthropology* 43(3): 479–507.

Johnson, K. (1998), 'Race, Immigration Laws and Domestic Race Relations: A Magic Mirror into the Heart of Darkness', *Indiana Law Review* 73: 1111–58.

Johnson, K. (2010), 'How Racial Profiling Became the Law of the Land: *United States v. Brignoni-Ponce* and *Whren v. United States* and the Need for Truly Rebellious Lawyering', *Georgetown Law Journal* 98: 1005–77.

Johnson, K. (2012), 'A Case Study of Color-Blindness: The Racially Disparate Impacts of Arizona's S.B. 1070 and the Failures of Immigration Reform', *U.C. Irvine Law Review* 2: 313–58.

López, N. (2013), 'Contextualizing Lived-race Gender and the Racialized-gendered Social Determinants of Health', in L. Gómez and N. López (eds), *Mapping 'Race': Critical Approaches to Health Disparities Research*. New Brunswick, NJ: Rutgers University Press, 256–304.

Ngai, M. (2004), *Impossible Subjects: Illegal Aliens and the Making of Modern America*. Princeton, NJ: Princeton University Press.

Omi, M. and Winant, H. (1994), *Racial Formation in the United States: From the 1960s to the 1990s*. New York and London: Routledge.

Ortiz, V. and Telles, E. (2012), 'Racial Identity and Racial Treatment of Mexican Americans', *Race and Social Problems* 4(1), 10.1007/s12552-012-9064-8. http://doi.org/10.1007/s12552-012-9064-8

Romero, M. (2008), 'Crossing the Immigration and Race Border: A Critical Race Theory Approach to Immigration Studies', *Contemporary Justice Review* 11: 23–37.

Sáenz, R. and Douglas, K. M. (2015), 'A Call for the Racialization of Immigration Studies on the Transition of Ethnic Immigrants to Racialized Immigrants', *Sociology of Race and Ethnicity* 1(1): 166–80.

Sanchez, G. and Romero, M. (2010), 'Critical Race Theory in the US Sociology of Immigration', *Sociology Compass* 4: 779–88.

Southern Poverty Law Center (2009), *Under Siege: Life for Low-Income Latinos in the South*. Montgomery, AL.

Stevens, J. (2011), 'Detaining and Deporting U.S. Citizens as Aliens', *Virginia Journal of Social Policy & the Law* 18: 606–720.

U.S. Department of Justice, Office of Public Affairs (2012), 'Justice Department Releases Investigative Findings on the Alamance County, N.C., Sheriff's Office: Findings Show Pattern or Practice of Discriminatory Policing Against Latinos', press release, 18 September.

Weissman, D. M., Headen, R. C., and Lewis Parker, K. (2009), 'The Policies and Politics of Local Immigration Enforcement Laws'. Available at: http://www.law.unc.edu/documents/clinicalprograms/287gpolicyreview.pdf

Case Law

Arizona v. United States, 567 U.S. (2012).

I.N.S. v. Lopez-Mendoza, 468 U.S. 1032 (1984).

Korematsu v. United States, 323 U.S. 214 (1944).

Maldonado v. Holder, 763 F.3d 155 (2d Cir. 2014).

Peña-Rodriguez v. Colorado, Case No. 15-606 (11 October, 2016).

United States v. Brignoni-Ponce, 422 U.S. 873 (1975).

United States. v. Manzo-Jurado, 457 F.3d 928 (9th Cir. 2006).

United States v. Martinez-Fuerte, 428 U.S. 543 (1976).

United States v. Montero-Camargo, 208 F.3d 1122 (9th Cir. 2000).

11

Refugee Law in Crisis

Decolonizing the Architecture of Violence

Eddie Bruce-Jones*

On the morning of 14 June 2017, all of London and much of the UK awoke to news alerts of a tower block that had caught fire at around midnight and burned through the night. Sure enough, as I stepped onto the third-storey walkway of our building, above the trees I saw a tall plume of smoke, still rising. The video footage was devastating, the sides of the building had ignited, helping the flames along and around, floor after floor. The heart-rending accounts by tenants and neighbours, and prior written complaints by the tenants' authority, painted a damning picture of negligence concerning the condition of the building, its fire-regulation compliance, proper wiring, and austerity-driven housing policies more broadly (Gapper 2017). Still other news reports made clear that the tower block housed overwhelmingly minorities, migrants, asylum applicants, and white working-class people (Malik 2017). MP David Lammy has likened this disaster to Dickens' *A Tale of Two Cities* (Roberts 2017), where the disparity between the richest and poorest residents is staggering (Gapper 2017). In terms of scholarly literature, one might also think of Franz Fanon's 'zones of being and non-being' or Balibar's 'death zones' to describe the extreme precarity and proximity to the ever-present potential for violence and death experienced by the people living in that tower, even in the midst of such luxurious safety and wealth (Balibar 2001; Fanon 1967; see also Gordon 2007).

What might it mean for us, as scholars and legal practitioners, to attempt to decolonize refugee law? Does identifying colonial logics within structures of border control or humanitarian protection leave no other choice than to swiftly and decisively abandon those structures in search of something new? Or can an ongoing process of critically reconsidering the theory and practice of refugee law inspire and guide other forms of engagement? According to Walter Mignolo, '[d]ecolonial thinking and doing starts from the analytic of the levels and spheres in which it can be effective in the process of decolonization and liberation from the colonial matrix'

* I would like to thank the editors of this volume for their insightful feedback, and Devin Carbado, for encouragement in pursuing this line of inquiry. I would also like to thank my colleagues, Nadine El-Enany and Thanos Zartaloudis, with whom I have taught courses on migration law over the years.

(Mignolo 2011: 17). At stake in a project of decolonial thinking is the investment in potentially liberating modes of being in the world. In this context, one might understand decolonization to refer to liberation from forms of thought as well as the structures and material conditions that remain, comprising contemporary coloniality, implicitly rejecting the notion that colonial logics and arrangements of power have been remedied by the formal independence of former colonial states and territories. It is the possibility of liberation from the known harm of colonial relations that drives the decolonial project; as with any project of transformative change, it is meant to be visionary and provide theoretical foundations for radically reimagining our world.

For those of us interested in a decolonial approach to refugee law, which involves interrogating colonial logics, investigating the interconnectedness of historical configurations that continue to shape our present, and examining global power structures not only in terms of geography or capital but also in terms of epistemology (Mignolo 2011: 17–19), we might first consider the difficult position that refugee law occupies, as a field of legal practice and as a discipline of study. When we practice and teach refugee law, we are generally guided by doctrine and case law, as is conventional. This is to say, it is commonly regarded as good practice in teaching law, generally, to place legal rationales, particularly statutory interpretation and judicial reasoning, at the centre of the analysis; from a practice-based perspective, when litigating or legislating on refugee law, it goes without saying that a failure to stick closely to accepted modes of legal analysis may impede the success of a certain outcome for a client or constituency. However, in framing refugee law closely along the rationales of legal decisions, we risk giving licence to refugee law's impoverished notions of violence, particularly when we fail to examine the continuities between persecution as defined by the 1951 Geneva Convention Relating to the Status of Refugees and its 1967 Protocol (hereinafter: Refugee Convention) and broader forms of harm faced by people on the move. Predictably, the innovations that we might make through decolonial critiques of refugee law doctrine will not necessarily be immediately helpful to those in need of refugee protection in the current system, which is a crucial consideration.

This chapter sketches two critiques of refugee law's structures and assumptions. First, it argues that a crisis model frames our notions of the violence experienced by refugees, which entrenches the problematic idea that their legal claims reflect an exceptional and generally individualized form of violence, and that systemic violence is bound by political borders. Second, it highlights recent social imaginings of the refugee in Europe, and in particular in the UK, as both a racialized criminal subject and a racialized subject in need of humanitarian intervention—a dual characterization that serves both to legitimize state logics of security and further stabilize state-building discourses of human rights. This latter point is not a particularly new one, but it serves to underscore how receiving states produce the systemic marginality of refugees.

The chapter then argues for the radical inclusion of a broader conception of systemic, transnational, and historically situated violence, particularly against people coming from the Global South to Europe and North America, when we teach refugee law, rather than only that violence narrowly defined as persecution originating in a foreign state. With regard to this proposal for shifting our conceptions of violence in refugee law teaching, it is important to acknowledge the pragmatism inherent in Mignolo's assertion that decolonial praxis should begin in the spheres in which it can be most effective. I focus, therefore, more on legal teaching than refugee law practice, as the type of deep structural critique possible in academia may, in a legal setting, be considered irrelevant to the given legal issues and it could, in direct advocacy settings, put claimants at unnecessary risk of harm.

REFUGEE LAW IN CRISIS

> The ongoing crisis of capital in the form of migrants fleeing lives made unliveable is becoming more and more visible, or, perhaps, less and less able to be ignored. Think of the thousands of migrants rescued and those who have been allowed to die at sea over the course of the year 2015. The crisis is often framed as one of refugees fleeing internal economic stress and internal conflicts, but subtending this crisis is the crisis of capital and the wreckage from the continuation of military and other colonial projects of US/European wealth extraction and immiseration.
>
> (Sharpe 2016: 59)

> If either the 'crisis' or its 'perpetuity' are removed from the frame, those in need of refugee protection will suffer. Underlying this conclusion is the awkward fit of refugees with international human rights law. An entitlement to human rights protection ought to be based simply on being human. That this is not, and never has been, enough, is the reason for refugee law ... Without the crisis element, the now-all-too-evident perpetuity of refugees will lapse back into 'ordinary' human rights. This would be a significant loss indeed, as international human rights law has been much less successful *as law* than international refugee law.
>
> (Dauvergne 2013: 30)

As Hilary Charlesworth eloquently argued fifteen years ago, international law is a 'discipline of crisis'. The crisis model, which generally emphasizes only the most extreme articulations of violence, human suffering, and environmental degradation (Charlesworth 2002), allows for what may seem a robust justification for the presence of international law—to intervene in situations, the magnitude of which is so great and the victims of which enjoy such empathy, that inaction invokes a sense of moral unconscionability. Yet, the language of crisis, Charlesworth points out, can obscure the systems and structures that undergird violence and suffering, focusing perhaps too exclusively on extremes rather than the quotidian suffering that refugees experience during their journeys and in their reception in host countries. It authorizes action with the moral force of last-chance reasoning—evoking a duty to mitigate these extreme forms of suffering. This is not to say that Charlesworth argues that international law is a solution to all forms of violence; she does not. However, as Charlesworth and others suggest, just as we attempt to use international law to manage global crises, we use the discourse of crisis to manage our notions of which suffering counts, what type of international action has legitimacy, and what aspects of the human rights system should be rigorously enforced.[1]

Sharpe (2016) and Dauvergne (2013) add layers to Charlesworth's analysis on crisis—layers that are central to conceptualizing international refugee law as well as the violence that refugees face. Neither Sharpe nor Dauvergne is unaware of the use of 'crisis' discourse as a tool for managing and administering violence—on the contrary. However, they choose to focus on different aspects of this discourse in their critiques of dominant framings of contemporary refugee law.

Christina Sharpe, in *In the Wake: On Blackness and Being* (2016), gives us direction as black researchers and researchers on race, law, and history more broadly. She draws out the connections between the trans-Atlantic trade of human beings, the systemic violence and precarity that people racialized as black endure on an ongoing basis, and the relevance of material conditions and logics of racial capital, bodies, and minds in our abilities to conceive of slavery and colonial relations as having a presence in our present. In brief, she suggests that the wake, with its multiple dimensions (e.g. the wake left behind a moving ship (p. 3), a funeral wake (p. 21), the wake in the line of recoil of a gun (p. 8), and to be awake or conscious (p. 21)) may help us frame the challenges we have in actively confronting the trauma and structures left from slavery; it is a dimension of life that encompasses the work that is left to be done. This work includes theoretical contributions towards understanding the often fatal circumstance of 'blackness and being'.

In the quote that began this section, Sharpe adds two points to the concept of crisis I have outlined. She argues that crisis is 'ongoing', and given her articulation of the concept of 'the wake', she is not merely referring to a contemporary 'crisis', but an ever-present state of affairs that relates to the arc of US and European exploits since the colonization of Africa and the Americas. She critiques, then, the temporality and singularity of the 'crisis'. Supporting the idea that this is really a question of colonial domination, she then explicitly describes this not as a crisis of humans fleeing the violence or destitution of their particular places, but as a crisis of capital that flows and demarcates the 'wreckage' left from colonial endeavours. These two interventions suggest that if we are to call anything a crisis, it should be the trans-historical system of military and economic conquest that has long underpinned the intense, urgent, and often forced movement of people across borders, and in particular, across perilous waters. Sharpe inverts the idea of crisis through a radical connectedness across the histories and geographies of racial capital and the devastation of empire.

Dauvergne approaches the same set of issues from a legal realist perspective. She is centrally concerned with the ability of law to offer protection. Her argument, that the crisis model provides a sense of urgency and separate status indispensable for maintaining the reliability and strength of international refugee law, is about the effectiveness of legal protection and is contextualized within contemporary debates

---

[1] This proposition, of course, does not address the question of who the actors of international law are and what countervailing political, economic, and social interests are at play in deciding on the content and enforcement of human rights.

as to whether international refugee law belongs in the field of immigration law or in human rights. Ultimately, Dauvergne becomes a reluctant advocate for instrumentalizing the crisis model as a *modus operandi*, and with it, acknowledges that, in the broader context of structural violence, human rights law does not have the capacity to effectively protect vulnerable populations (2013: 30). Conversely, refugee law is available to only a privileged few who have the resources and good fortune to be able to cross borders. It is slightly more effective precisely due to a narrow set of exceptional circumstances (i.e. crisis as opposed to quotidian precarity) in which refugees are imagined to exist, and highlights only one part of what Sharpe might identify as a geopolitical, trans-historical crisis. In short, the use of crisis as an analytical lens, without Sharpe's radical inversion, keeps the position of the refugee, and the status of refugee law, in the realm of the exceptional (and thus, Dauvergne would argue, enforceable).

Of course, individual asylum claims are critically important for claimants, often meaning the difference between life and death. However, other claims that do not qualify as refugee claims, or even claims for humanitarian leave to remain or similar forms of residency allowance,[2] may be similarly urgent, and the situations underlying them related to global political and economic structures that span various times and places (Mezzadra and Neilson 2013). People are forced to move for many reasons, including the coupling of poor infrastructure and environmental disaster, consistent economic need, and social alienation, as, for example, in the context of British colonial laws on same-sex sexual relations (Kirby 2011). While legal pedagogy allows for these aspects to be considered within broader refugee law analysis, legal advocacy considerations of refugee law and, in particular, arguments related to refugee status determination leave little room for attempts to feature the colonial logics that undergird the need for protection (Bruce-Jones 2015).

There is a presumption that refugee law teachers ought to begin with the concept of persecution and work outwards. That is to say, they should begin like much legal teaching does: with the relevant source of law, or the legal instrument. Effectively, then, if there is an indictment here, it is not of refugee law teachers in particular, but of legal pedagogy more generally. In this way, the Refugee Convention tends to occupy the central gravitational force in the teaching about refugee law. A typical refugee law syllabus commences with a discussion of how the Refugee Convention frames and defines the refugee, and it then examines the case law on refugee status determination and perhaps on other regulatory frameworks (e.g. reception conditions, human rights, to freedom from torture, and to family and private life). This structure is not without good reason. Taught courses can only ever be of limited scope, and lawyers and students aiming to be legal practitioners expect to (and need to) fully understand how the law works, in its own terms and within its own fora. However, it is worth troubling this conventional teaching structure, which allows the Refugee Convention to set the terms of conversations about violence faced by

---

[2] For example, subsidiary protection under Article 15(c), European Union Qualifications Directive. See McAdam (2007).

people on the move, particularly in the current state of the world, and more particularly in Europe.

A CURRICULUM BEYOND PERSECUTION: WHY NOW?

The way legal academics typically teach refugee law is to focus on what makes a good claim, as reflected in the jurisprudence of a particular jurisdiction or with a view towards regional or international trends. In a purely legal sense, this is simply the way law works—protection is defined around rule-based parameters. However, in a wider sense of understanding violence, subjectivity, and broader relations of power, this approach to teaching misses the forest through the trees.[3]

The core of the teaching of refugee law is on the status determination aspect of the journey of the refugee—this includes the questions of who will be granted asylum and why, who will be refused, what constitutes the test for a successful claim in the relevant jurisdiction, and so forth. Given that focusing on the rules and doctrines governing status determination provides a relative wealth of case law material, this approach to teaching seems sensible if the goal is to teach how refugee laws are operationalized. However, if we fail to discuss the treatment of refugees in receiving states, including the interplay between criminal law, immigration law, and public law in the context of the broader social well-being of refugees, we may fail to see the ways in which their claims are instrumentalized and their stories are understood, legally and socially. Put another way, if Sharpe's analysis of the trans-historical structures of anti-Blackness are to be taken seriously, how might we interpret refugee law vis-à-vis 'the wake' (Sharpe 2016)? This is a question that even the most nuanced and hopeful readings of the protections offered by the Refugee Convention will not help answer. In addition, if we fail to teach about the context of the masses of people who might cross borders if they gain the opportunity, security, or energy to do so, including the global and historical circumstances which may have catalysed such want or need for movement, we risk failing to understand the core of the violence that people on the move face and in which we, as a global community, are complicit.

Migration experts predict that even larger number of refugees will be crossing borders in the future due to environmental catastrophes and social instability caused by global disparities and economic downturn (Betts 2013; Juss 2006). While groups that migrate for these reasons are not currently entitled to refugee status as per contemporary interpretations of persecution under the Refugee Convention, the question of whether this will or should remain the case will become increasingly urgent. There are already debates about whether the project of refugee law is irredeemably flawed, given its compromised position between human rights and immigration law

---

[3] In this chapter, when I refer to violence, I do not mean persecution but, rather, broader forms of physical and epistemic harm that are inflicted on individuals and groups. As the decolonial approach I am using is most interested in harms attributed to the state and historical geopolitical and economic power relations, which can be described as structural, I am less interested in interpersonal violence.

(El-Enany 2017), and whether it will be even less fit for purpose in the near future (Juss 2006).

In the context of teaching and in determining border policies, we should be seriously considering a great deal more about other aspects of the refugee's journey, some of which would have been set in motion years or even generations before the personal stories of the respective applicants recognized their own need to flee.[4] Taking a wider view would not only offer a fuller sense of the applicant's circumstances, but it also might help explain how contemporary geopolitical arrangements, power relations, colonial legacies, regional economic stability, social attitudes, and legal fixtures are part of an historical trajectory of international developments.

This context is, for an immigration judge determining the status of an asylum applicant, just that: merely context. However, the continuities between underlying power relations and of the resultant conditions that prompt people to flee their homes and regions should not be taught with the same degree of erasure with which they are practised if the teaching of refugee law is to take advantage of its ability to contest the deadening strictures of refugee law's narrowness. Considering Mignolo's assertions that one should begin thinking about decolonial approaches in spheres where there is a possibility to be effective and that epistemological change is an important element of decoloniality (Mignolo 2011: 17–19), the impact of this wider view is to create openings for decolonial analysis to play a greater role in educating future lawyers and academics. Law practitioners might, at least, become aware of the underpinning logics of refugee law and integrate ever-sharper systemic critiques into their praxis.

In order to trouble refugee law's narrowness in our curriculum, we could perhaps begin by locating refugee law within three broader, overlapping frames of analysis. First, we should think of the problems that arise in refugee law not only as stemming from a restrictive rather than expansive conception of the refugee, but as direct extensions of the problems of borders more generally. It is important, in the context of going beyond persecution, to understand refugee law not merely as a process by which the state grants humanitarian protection (only) to those in (particular) need—which can be regarded as a narrative of benevolence. Rather, we may conceive of it as a form of border regulation. In this view, the law acts as a way for states to release the pressure at the margins by helping those who manage to cross borders to evade extreme forms of violence, much like a pressure cooker releases small amounts of steam in order to keep the vast majority of the steam inside the pot while avoiding an explosion. It is important to reject the benevolent narrative of refugee law because it positions the receiving states, and Western states in particular, as acting towards a net benefit of refugees without acknowledging the violence they cause refugees nor the instrumentalizing function of refugees in securing the human rights authority of the state. It is worth thinking, instead, along quite a different axis—one

---

[4] Here, I do not mean to suggest that we should engage in a broader conception of the refugee journey simply as a way to liberalize border policies, but I do acknowledge that, short of oversimplifying or ignoring the relationship between reform and transformative change, it may be that border policy can be reformed *en route* to a more structural rethinking of borders in the future.

that positions the receiving state as complicit in maintaining the pressure-cooker of border control and the use of borders as a global system of regulating movement and the global conditions of violence.

Second, we should present refugee law, and immigration law more generally, within the broader context of global power relations in order to properly identify its limits, if we are indeed concerned with the transformative potential that decolonial thinking promises. We should do this in a way that takes historical developments into account, including and indeed especially racialized colonial relations. We should be able to confront the use of nationality as a proxy for racial and other types of difference in the regulation of borders, demonstrated for example in the negotiations of the 1962 and 1968 Commonwealth Immigration Acts in the UK.[5] The promulgation of fears of 'cultural swamping' (Ricci 2016; Sky News 2014) and a loss of national identity, common mantras of the proponents of strict immigration regulation, are racial as much as they are cultural. More broadly, global power relations, including the UK's role in exploitative economic relations with countries in the Global South, are part of the engine of economically and politically motivated migration to the north. Frances Webber, an immigration barrister with over two decades of experience in the field, writes:

Justice Collins recognised that 'the so-called economic migrants are frequently trying to escape conditions which no one in this country would regard as tolerable'. What does this have to do with us? Sivanandan memorably said, 'We are here because you are there.' One way or another most of those who come to these shores without official permission are refugees from globalisation, from a poor world getting poorer as it is shaped to serve the interests, appetites and whims of the rich world, a world where our astonishing standard of living, our freedoms, the absurd array of consumer novelties, fashions and foods available to us, and thrown away by us, are bought at the cost of health, freedoms and lives of others. This cost is felt in the terms of trade and intellectual property agreements, in the imposition on poor countries by global economic police of policies that remove food self-sufficiency and drive small producers off the land, in the substitution by agribusiness of biofuels for food production in the vast tracts of Africa and Asia bought up by corporations for profit, in the soaring food prices in the poor world which sparked riots in Egypt and Tunisia. (Webber 2012: 4)

Here, Webber points to the inability to separate the specific conditions that force refugees and other migrants to emigrate from the larger global economic and political relations that create these conditions. An example of this is LGBTI refugees, who are questioned on whether they are 'really' gay and sometimes made to feel as though they must expose their physiognomy, desires, and sexual practices, as distinguished from economic factors that might also compel their movement, as though the legal regulation of sexuality and gender norms or the economic plight of many

---

[5] The 1962 and 1968 Commonwealth Immigration Acts served to restrict immigration of British colonial subjects largely along colour lines. The effects of these Acts were admonished in a 1973 report adopted by the European Commission, in response to applications brought on behalf of East African Asians against the UK, where it declared the UK immigration laws to be in violation of Article 14 of the European Convention on Human Rights (ECHR) (on the grounds of racial discrimination) in conjunction with Articles 3, 5, and 8. See European Commission (14 December 1973), *East African Asians v. United Kingdom*.

migrants are completely unrelated to colonialism or global inequality (Bruce-Jones 2015). Popular discussions, like legal ones, tend to portray the persecution of refugees as a function of local or regional circumstances, rather than embedded within global historical structures—of course, this is by design, as refugee law was never meant to address the root causes of global material inequality, war, and devastation represented by those who cross borders in search of peace, health, and safety.

This brings us to a third frame—the location of violence. To understand the complex engine behind the movement of people across borders, we must resist oversimplifying how and where violence impacts the lives of refugees. Just as we discuss violence in the states of origin in an effort to establish the legal efficacy of asylum status claims, we should teach about and understand state violence in the receiving state as central to the stories of refugees. Rather than reinforce the notion that violence is located only in refugees' respective countries of origin, it is important to recognize the material deprivation, social marginalization, and precarity that refugees face in the countries that receive them (United for Intercultural Action 2015). It surfaces in religious animosities and fears (Burnett 2016a; Wike et al. 2016) and it reveals itself, for example, in a disbelief in refugees' stories (Webber 2012). It is evidenced in the systemic ways in which refugees may be forced to navigate physical spaces of potential danger, such as that described with the Grenfell Tower disaster in the introduction. So, while many refugees flee from dire situations, they do not find themselves, by and large, free from precarity when they enter the receiving state. However, the idea that refugees do not have an easy road in the UK, for example, does little to undermine the legitimizing function of the refugee category for the UK in the international arena, so far as its human rights record is concerned, as other states in Europe have been considered worse in one way or another.[6] Furthermore, it is generally taken for granted that the often harsh and isolating conditions in Europe are, with some minor exceptions, acceptable because they are assumed better than persecution.

This third frame, then, suggests that we should be teaching refugee law from a perspective that critically examines the violence imparted by the receiving state. Rather than set the bar low and focus solely on minimum standards of protection legally permissible under regional and national human rights laws, this perspective asks whether we can imagine treating refugees as human-rights-bearing citizens, bearing in mind, of course, that their precarity as non-citizens exacerbates those aspects of state violence they face that already imperil citizens and other residents who face racial, sexual, and religious discrimination and violence (Dembour and Kelly 2011). To extend this decolonial thinking into the realms of practice and policy, it may prove useful to consider the exacerbation of the violence against refugees to be an inexcusable extension of colonial conditions. Is it imaginable that we treat refugees as citizens with the full rights of citizenship as soon as they apply for status as a matter

---

[6] See e.g. *M.S.S. v. Belgium and Greece* (no. 30696/09), where it was held that returning an asylum applicant from Belgium to Greece under the EU Dublin Regulation II was a violation of Article 3 ECHR, given the deficiencies in asylum procedures in Greece as well as the poor living conditions to which asylum applicants were subjected.

of (decolonial) principle? Furthermore, can such a principle really be considered decolonial if the machinery and logics of refugee law are left largely intact?

IMAGINING VIOLENCE, CREATING REFUGEES

Violence and persecution are legally different in the context of refugee law. While violence is a generalized concept of harm, persecution is a very specific type of harm in refugee law. Persecution generally amounts to extreme forms of violence or social exclusion, including, for example, torture or the withdrawal of fundamental rights protection (Goodwin-Gill and McAdam 2007). Persecution does not enjoy a precise definition under the Refugee Convention and can be considered to lack determinacy for this reason (Maiani 2011); however, member states tend to interpret the bar on the level of violence or social exclusion to be quite high (Goodwin-Gill and McAdam 2007). Other forms of violence, which do not meet the threshold that states understand as constitutive of persecution, are not considered when refugee status is being determined.[7]

In addition to the high bar on the violence constitutive of persecution, there must also be specific reasons for such persecution for a claim of refugee status. Under the Refugee Convention, a refugee is defined as a person who,

owing to well founded fear of being persecuted for reasons of race, religion, nationality, membership of a particular social group or political opinion, is outside the country of his nationality and is unable or, owing to such fear, is unwilling to avail himself of the protection of that country; or who, not having a nationality and being outside the country of his former habitual residence as a result of such events, is unable or, owing to such fear, is unwilling to return to it. (Refugee Convention, Article 1(2))

The grounds enumerated in the Refugee Convention specify the reasons for persecution recognized in advancing individual asylum claims. However, there are other groups of migrants that cross borders for other reasons, including to escape physical and psychological harm, economic despair, and environmental catastrophe.

In the UK, public discussions of the 'refugee crisis' have taken on a specific tone, scrutinizing refugees as a class. Mainstream UK newspapers have been the most polarized across Europe, with the politically right-of-centre press (which occupies a prominent media platform in the UK) having regularly featured interviews with 'citizen voices who were overwhelmingly hostile to asylum and immigration' (Berry et al. 2016: 32). A comparative report on media coverage of the refugee situation in 2015 mentioned that, in the context of the *Sun* and the *Daily Mail*, 'although some refugee voices in the right-wing press sometimes did feature accounts of suffering they were more likely to merely state that they were determined to get to the UK because they would be safe, or provided for by the British state' (Berry et al. 2016: 32). This fits with the rhetoric of the 'bogus' asylum seeker discussed by Francis

---

[7] It may be considered in other contexts, such as determining other forms of humanitarian protection or residency permission.

Webber (2012) in *Borderline Justice*, a retrospective account of British asylum law since the late 1980s. Prakash Shah illustrates, in his account of refugees and racism in public reactions to refugee populations in the UK at the turn of the century, that there was public backlash, in particular, against African and Asian refugees (Shah 2000) and Monish Bhatia suggests that the racialization and criminalization of asylum seekers continues (Bhatia 2014; 2015).

The current social and political climate in the UK has produced an ever more restrictive environment for migrants, generally. The UK's Institute of Race Relations has examined how the new immigration and housing laws will functionally increase poverty, homelessness, and destitution among migrant and black and minority communities in Britain (Burnett 2016a). There has been a tightening of state control on the lives of migrants in the domestic sphere which, in the lead-up to the 2014 Immigration Bill, was described by the then Home Secretary Theresa May as an attempt to create a hostile environment for illegal migrants (Burnett 2016a; Travis 2013). Under Part 3, Chapter 1 of the Immigration Act 2014, tenancy agreements are restricted to those with leave to remain, and landlords are fined if they fail to carry out proper checks or knowingly rent to someone without leave to remain. There have also been drastic cuts to legal aid for immigration matters (Peck 2016). The proliferation of laws and policies that police the daily lives of immigrants is not limited to the contemporary political moment, and indeed some scholars acknowledge that there is a systemic alienation of migrants from human rights protection (Dembour and Kelly 2011: 9–11; Webber 2012: 119–31). However, the current moment in Europe, marked by a shift to right-wing populism and increased social restrictions for migrants in countries such as the UK, underscores the need to urgently look beyond the question of status determination and towards the violence meted out by the receiving state when analysing the situation of refugees.

The criminalization of refugees

In the UK, immigration detention is used more prevalently than in other EU countries to house asylum applicants (Silverman 2016) including those whose claims have been rejected (Bosworth 2014). Despite the 2015 decision by the High Court of Appeal to stop the use of the detention fast track appeals process that disadvantaged refugees by detaining them for the duration of an expedited asylum application process (*Detention Action v. First Tier Tribunal, Second Tier Tribunal and Lord Chancellor* [2015]), detention is still used in the UK in some circumstances.

It is well established that detention has significant deleterious effects on the health and well-being of refugees and asylum seekers (Bosworth 2016). Such matters are compounded for those who have experienced torture and other types of trauma, as detention frustrates their recovery and even exacerbates people's conditions (Robant et al. 2009; Shaw 2016). The continued use of detention in the UK as standard practice, then, indicates a number of things. It demonstrates that we systemically prolong the experience of violence that refugees encounter during their journey, by keeping them in a state of sometimes extreme physical and mental precarity. It also serves to normalize the carceral logic of linking criminal justice issues with migration policy. The fact that immigration detention resembles prison, and immigration removal centres such as the Verne in Dorset are actually repurposed prisons, sends a particular message to the general population about the position that migrants, and refugees in particular, occupy in society. According to a briefing of the Migration Observatory at Oxford, which analyses UK Home Office statistics, in 2015 45 per cent of all people admitted into immigration detention in the UK had at some point made an asylum application (Silverman 2016).

The discursive criminalization of refugees was echoed in the 2013 'Go Home' Home Office campaign. The Home Office commissioned vans to circulate around six boroughs of London with a message, meant for particular migrant communities.[8] Each of the vans carried a large billboard that read 'In the UK illegally?'. The secondary caption below this read: 'Go home or face arrest. Text home to 78070'. Slightly askew, stamp-like, in its own corner of the poster was the statement '106 arrests last week in your area'. These texts were laid over the image of an officer's dark jacket, bearing the Home Office emblem, his light-coloured hand holding out a metal handcuff. Offering it? Promising it? Threatening with its application?

These messages were directed at those living in the UK without proper documentation, including those who had overstayed their visas. This includes refugees whose applications have been denied.[9] However, the messages also spoke to the majority society, underlining the public service of effective policing, by enumerating the numbers of people arrested in the local area for violating immigration laws. This campaign, and its construction of who makes up *the public*, or the community, was not a singular misjudgement of Home Office campaigning, but rather a coordinated set of policies that work to saturate domestic life with aspects of border control. Through messaging, material restrictions, and systems co-ordination, non-citizens have been made to confront derivative border policies in their everyday lives. These policies reinstantiate the border everywhere—in our daily interactions and within the fabric of the domestic (Balibar 2001). As Mezzadra and Neilson (2013: 7) argue, there has been a proliferation of borders and, with it, 'mutations of labour, space, time, law, power and citizenship' that is about constant regulation rather than mere exclusion. In their work, *Border as Method*, Mezzadra and Neilson argue that borders are a way of thinking, a way of framing social life, and that the distinguishing between physical borders and border thinking is becoming a difficult and perhaps even misguided endeavour (Mezzadra and Neilson 2013: 8–9).

---

[8] In its response to complaints about the discriminatory and misleading nature of the van campaign, the Home Office stated that the vans 'covered specific, targeted areas and were designed to improve awareness of local immigration enforcement activity so that those with no legal right to be in UK were made aware that there was a real and present risk of being arrested'. See Advertising Standards Association Adjudication of the Home Office (2013).

[9] I still refer to people on the move as refugees because they are fleeing from some circumstance, even if their claims may not meet the standard of 'refugee' defined under the Refugee Convention. See discussion of 'de facto refugees' in Tuitt (1996).

Brexit and counterterrorism

In the UK, for some time leading up to the 23 June 2016 referendum on membership of the European Union, there was a resurgence of popular nationalist discourse in mainstream politics in the form of the rise of the UK Independence Party, or UKIP (Berry et al. 2015: 34–40). Its leadership argued in favour of drastically reducing immigration and withdrawing the UK from the European Union in an effort to establish independent self-governance, to 'take back control' of Britain (Stewart and Mason 2016). The campaign for leaving the European Union capitalized on fears that were already present in British society about immigration and the supposed inability of the UK to absorb large numbers of refugees. Nigel Farage, the former leader of UKIP, in the last days before the referendum, stood in front of a large campaign billboard that showed a queue of refugees crossing the border from Croatia into Slovenia in 2015, with a large text overlay that read 'Breaking Point' and a small caption reading 'We must break free of the EU and take back control.' The use of this poster in the campaign was lambasted in the press as 'a blatant attempt to incite racial hatred' and was likened to Nazi propaganda (Stewart and Mason 2016). Indeed, instances of racial violence increased dramatically leading up to and following the Brexit referendum (Burnett 2016b).

The Brexit (or Leave) campaign was run with a clear mandate to reduce immigration from Europe.[10] This anti-immigration stance was reinforced by right-wing media outlets through harsh rhetoric and suggestive images (Public Radio International 2016), benefiting also from the pre-existing discursive loop between governmental counterterrorism initiatives, racial stereotypes, and discourse on immigration. For instance, the Prevent Duty set out in the Counter-Terrorism and Security Act 2015 requires public service providers and educational institutions to refer people to the police in an effort to counter 'radicalisation', but problematically relies on social ideas about how to recognize signs of radicalization (Bowcott and Adams 2016).

When I arrived home a few weeks before the Brexit Referendum, I found a leaflet on the kitchen table. Its author: the Vote Leave campaign. The leaflet, 'The European Union and Your Family: The Facts', had a map on its back cover with the title 'Countries set to join the EU'. Aside from the five countries listed by name on the map that were presented by the campaign as set to join the EU, namely Turkey, Serbia, Montenegro, Macedonia, and Albania, the only countries labelled on the map were the UK, Syria, and Iraq. The populations of each of the five countries were listed, suggesting the magnitude of potential for migration to other EU countries. Syria and Iraq were in colour while the EU itself (with the exception of the UK) was depicted as a backdrop, in tones of light grey. The message is ostensibly that the EU, as a region, offers a geographical and relatively borderless bridge between the UK and zones of danger and political instability. The map has been sharply criticized as scare-mongering and 'fanning the flames of division'. It is more than that. It capitalizes

---

[10] It has also been argued that immigration issues were more important to voters than economic issues. See Khan (2016).

on fear, Islamophobia, and racism and promotes a thorough misunderstanding of EU politics, in the middle of a humanitarian catastrophe for Syrian people. Turkey is not close to joining the EU at present, but that possibility is portrayed as a future threat—a bridge between the EU and places (and people) that instil fear.

The fact that the EU was faded into the background of the map was also revealing. These particular scare tactics were not about the EU at all, really. Rather, they relied on nativist, xenophobic, and highly racialized ideas about the position of the UK in the world, including who gets to come to the UK. They advance a logic that would sooner see the moat get bigger than smaller, see the UK as a sovereign fortress floating in the sky, out of reach. This map was meant to indulge the nativism of the mind, and if the success of the campaign in winning a majority vote in the referendum and the rise in violence against non-white people and continental Europeans are any indication (Burnett 2016b), this and other such media messages, such as Farage's billboard campaign, are effective.

The criminalization of refugees in the UK and the discursive connections with counterterrorism, racism, and anti-immigration logics demonstrate how government policies meant to address social problems (resource scarcity, terrorism, and criminality) focus on refugees in various ways. This includes aspects of the UK Immigration Act 2016, which includes the categorization of undocumented work as a criminal offence and 'extension of "deport first, appeal later" provisions' (Burnett 2016b). This foregrounds the welfare of refugees with security rationales, displacing refugees from their positions of vulnerability and forcing them to inhabit a position of the ever-possible threat. Given the well-rehearsed social anxieties about the growing numbers of refugees arriving in Europe from Syria (Chan and Bluth 2017) and the racist stereotypes about Muslims and people from the Middle East and Muslim countries being terrorists, migrants of colour in particular have been assigned an added dimension of stigma. As a result, migration across borders, even when the purpose is to escape hardship, is met with fears that refugees are masquerading under the guise of vulnerability—faking it (Webber 2012).

The figure of the refugee, then, is rendered as both in need of assistance and as a potential threat, an indecipherable figure of both victim and perpetrator who is viewed, by default, as suspect. This is contextualized within a very narrow idea of what constitutes violence—so that the violence in the receiving state of the UK is not as an object of scrutiny, and it is justified or at least calibrated against the horrors in the state of origin and the potential for violence attributed to the refugee herself.

TOWARDS A DECOLONIAL SET OF COMMITMENTS

On May 18, 2015, the European Union (EU) voted to replace humanitarian patrols of the Mediterranean with military ones. Under this new plan, and with Libyan cooperation that is 'complicated by the fact that there is not just one government in Libya, the boats of the smugglers will be intercepted and then destroyed.' The EU says that their 'aim is to disrupt the business model that makes people-smuggling across the Mediterranean such a lucrative trade.' But

> the EU has no intention of disrupting the other business models, profitable to multinational corporations, that set those people flowing. (Sharpe 2016: 59)

The questions produced in this chapter are: can we be concerned with status determination without being concerned about the totality of violence faced by refugees? Can we ask about the legal, technical aspects of refugee law without also being deeply concerned with the project itself, including the global historical conditions that still prompt movement, such as the ones Sharpe discusses? The way we teach refugee law demonstrates that we try to isolate these issues from one another, but perhaps we should teach towards their entanglement instead.

There is a conventional view of refugee law that the processes of determining persecution, and thus relief, are fit for purpose. In this view, the function of refugee law is not to reckon with history, but rather to assist those people who are most in need.[11] However, in teaching refugee law, in context, we must reconfigure the margins and the centre of the discourse on violence. While active state violence and failure to prevent third-party violence from persecuting individuals for convention reasons is at the heart of the Refugee Convention's scrutiny, forms of state inaction or callousness outside this evaluative framework and the resulting human suffering are not addressed as a core feature of refugee law teaching. This is no surprise, as the purpose of the Refugee Convention was never to mitigate *all* types of violence, even if extreme. However, our mission as educators, particularly if we are to grapple with colonial structures of racism, must go beyond the Refugee Convention's formal protections and examine the place of refugee law more holistically in our social world. This means, at the very least, examining the complicity of refugee law's provisions and assumptions in extending such colonial structures.

The way we conceptualize refugee law in our teaching, research, and, to some extent, our practice of it must go beyond the highly specific focus on persecution in order to grasp the reality of global inequality and properly capture the co-ordination of state processes, borders, and overlapping forms of exclusion (see also Chacón and Bibler Coutin, this volume). The teaching of asylum and refugee law must confront not only the violence of persecution as defined by the Refugee Convention and interpreted by state parties but it must reckon with the forms of violence faced by refugees and asylum seekers that do not formally constitute persecution, but are nevertheless pervasive aspects of the experiences of these people in their countries of origin, on the journey to new lands, and in receiving states. This is important if decolonial modes of analysis are to allow us the space to be visionary about anti-racism and the politics of borders, and there is no time like the present to focus this needed attention on the way we teach refugee law.

---

[11] This is a controversial point, as asylum seekers, as opposed to refugees being resettled, must have crossed a border physically into the place where they wish to apply for asylum, which suggests that only those with the means or ability to make a physical journey of this kind will have access to the protection of the Geneva Convention. In other words, there is a question as to whether refugee law does, in fact, help those in most need, or whether it is primarily a way to balance humanitarian protection and immigration regulation in the receiving states.

REFERENCES

Advertising Standards Authority (2013), *Adjudication of the Home Office*, 9 October. Available at: https://www.asa.org.uk/rulings/home-office-a13-237331.html

Balibar, E. (2001), 'Outlines of a Topography of Cruelty: Citizenship and Civility in the Era of Global Violence', *Constellations* 8(1): 15–29.

Berry, M. (2016), 'Understanding the Role of the Mass Media in the EU Referendum', in D. Jackson, E. Thorsen, and D. Wring (eds), *EU Referendum Analysis 2016: Media, Voters and the Campaign*. Bournemouth: Centre for the Study of Journalism, Culture and Community, Bournemouth University, 14. Available at: http://eprints.bournemouth.ac.uk/24337/1/EU%20Referendum%20Analysis%202016%20-%20Jackson%20Thorsen%20and%20Wring%20v1.pdf

Betts, A. (2013), *Survival Migration: Failed Governance and the Crisis of Displacement*. Ithaca, NY: Cornell University Press.

Bhatia, M. (2014), 'Creating and Managing "Mad", "Bad" and "Dangerous": The Role of the Immigration System', in V. Canning (ed.), *Sites of Confinement*. Liverpool: The Centre for the Study of Crime, Criminalization and Social Exclusion/The European Group of the Study of Deviance and Social Control, 29–42.

Bhatia, M. (2015), 'Turning Asylum Seekers into "Dangerous Criminals": Experiences of the Criminal Justice System of those Seeking Sanctuary', *International Journal for Crime, Justice and Social Democracy* 4(3): 97–111.

Bosworth, M. (2014), *Inside Immigration Detention*. Oxford: Oxford University Press.

Bosworth, M. (2016), *Mental Health in Immigration Detention: A Literature Review*. Review into the Welfare in Detention of Vulnerable Persons, Cm 9186. London: HSMO. Criminal Justice, Borders and Citizenship Research Paper No. 2732892. Available at SSRN: https://ssrn.com/abstract=2732892

Bowcott, O. and Adams, R. (2016), 'Human Rights Group Condemns Prevent Anti-radicalisation Strategy', *The Guardian*, 13 July. Available at: https://www.theguardian.com/politics/2016/jul/13/human-rights-group-condemns-prevent-anti-radicalisation-strategy

Bruce-Jones, E. (2015), 'Death Zones, Comfort Zones: Queering the Refugee Question', *International Journal of Minority and Group Rights* 22(1): 101–27.

Burnett, J. (2016a), *Entitlement and Belonging: Social Restructuring and Multicultural Britain*. London: Institute of Race Relations.

Burnett, J. (2016b), *Racial Violence and the Brexit State*. London: Institute of Race Relations.

Chan, M. and Bluth, N. (2017), 'Map Room: Fear thy neighbour: Crime and Xenophobia in Europe', *World Policy Journal* 34(2): 36–7.

Charlesworth, H. (2002), 'International Law: A Discipline of Crisis', *Modern Law Review* 65(3): 377–92.

Dauvergne, C. (2013), 'Refugee Law as Perpetual Crisis', in S. S. Juss and C. Harvey (eds), *Contemporary Issues in Refugee Law*. Cheltenham: Edward Elgar, 13–30.

Dembour, M. B. and Kelly, T. (2011), *Are Human Rights for Migrants? Critical Reflections on the Status of Irregular Migrants in Europe and the United States*. Abingdon: Routledge.

El-Enany, N. (2017), 'Asylum in the Context of Immigration Control: Exclusion by Default or Design', in M. O'Sullivan and D. Stevens (eds), *States, the Law and Access to Refugee Protection*. Oxford: Hart, 29–44.

Fanon, F. (1967). *Black Skin, White Masks*. New York: Grove Press.

Gapper, J. (2017), 'Grenfell: The Anatomy of a Housing Disaster', *Financial Times*, 29 June. Available at: https://www.ft.com/content/5381b5d2-5c1c-11e7-9bc8-8055f264aa8b?mhq5j=e1

Goodwin-Gill, G. S. and McAdam, J. (2007), *The Refugee in International Law* (3rd edn). Oxford: Oxford University Press.

Gordon, L. (2007), 'Through the Hellish Zone of Nonbeing: Thinking Through Fanon, Disaster and the Damned of the Earth', *Human Architecture* Summer, 5–12.

Juss, S. S. (2006), *International Migration and Global Justice*. Aldershot: Ashgate.

Khan, A. (2016), 'Four Ways the Anti-immigration Vote Won the Referendum for Brexit', *The New Statesman*, 7 July. Available at: http://www.newstatesman.com/politics/staggers/2016/07/four-ways-anti-immigration-vote-won-referendum-brexit

Kirby, M. (2011), 'The Sodomy Offence: England's Least Lovely Criminal Export?' *Journal of Commonwealth Criminal Law* 1: 22–43.

Maiani, F. (2011), 'The Concept of "Persecution" in Refugee Law: Indeterminacy, Context-sensitivity, and the Quest for a Principled Approach', *Les Dossiers du Grihl, Les dossiers de Jean-Pierre Cavaillé, De la persécution*, 28 February. Available at: http://dossiersgrihl.revues.org/3896

Malik, N. (2017), 'Grenfell Shows Just how Britain Fails Migrants', *The Guardian*, 16 June. Available at: https://www.theguardian.com/commentisfree/2017/jun/16/grenfell-britain-fails-migrants-north-kensington-london-refugee

McAdam, J. (2007), *Complimentary Protection in International Refugee Law*. Oxford: Oxford University Press.

Mezzadra, S. and Neilson, B. (2013), *Border as Method, or the Multiplication of Labor*. London: Duke University Press.

Mignolo, W. (2011), *The Darker Side of Western Modernity: Global Futures, Decolonial Options*. Durham, NC: Duke University Press.

Peck, T. (2016), 'Half of Immigration Detainees in UK Have no Representation because of Legal Aid Cuts, Report Finds', *The Independent*, 9 December. Available at: http://www.independent.co.uk/news/uk/politics/legal-aid-cuts-migrants-immigrants-detention-centre-half-no-representation-help-report-survey-a7464301.html

Public Radio International (2016), 'How the Brexit Campaign Used Refugees to Scare Voters', 24 June. Available at: https://www.pri.org/stories/2016-06-24/how-brexit-campaign-used-refugees-scare-voters

Ricci, C. (2016), ' "They Might Feel Rather Swamped": Understanding the Roots of Cultural Arguments in Anti-immigration Rhetoric in 1950s–1980s Britain', *Global Histories* 2(1): 33–49.

Robant, K., Hassan, R., and Katona, C. (2009), 'Mental Health Implications of Detaining Asylum Seekers: Systematic Review', *The British Journal of Psychiatry* 194(4): 306–12.

Roberts, R. (2017), 'Grenfell Fire: David Lammy MP Breaks Down in Tears Speaking about his Friend who Died', *The Independent*, 16 June. Available at: http://www.independent.co.uk/news/uk/home-news/david-lammy-mp-breaks-down-friend-died-grenfell-tower-fire-khadija-saye-a7794396.html

Shah, P. (2000), *Refugees, Race and the Legal Concept of Asylum in Britain*. London: Routledge-Cavendish.

Sharpe, C. (2016), *In the Wake: On Blackness and Being*. London: Duke University Press.

Shaw, S. (2016), *Review into the Welfare in Detention of Vulnerable Persons*. London: Her Majesty's Stationery Office.

Silverman, S. (2016), *Briefing: Immigration Detention in the UK*. Oxford: Migration Observatory. Available at: http://www.migrationobservatory.ox.ac.uk

Sky News (2014), 'Senior Tory: Some Towns "Swamped" by Migrants', 26 October. Available at: http://news.sky.com/story/senior-tory-some-towns-swamped-by-migrants-10384980

Stewart, H. and Mason, R. (2016), 'Nigel Farage's Anti-immigrant Poster Reported to Police', *The Guardian*, 16 June. Available at: https://www.theguardian.com/politics/2016/jun/16/nigel-farage-defends-ukip-breaking-point-poster-queue-of-migrants

Travis, A. (2013), 'Immigration Bill: Theresa May Defends Plans to Create "Hostile Environment"', *The Guardian*, 10 October. Available at: https://www.theguardian.com/politics/2013/oct/10/immigration-bill-theresa-may-hostile-environment

Tuitt, P. (1996), *False Images: The Law's Construction of the Refugee*. London: Pluto Press.

United for Intercultural Action (2015), *List of 22.394 Documented Deaths of Asylum Seekers, Refugees and Migrants due to the Restrictive Policies of Fortress Europe*, 19 May. Available at: http://www.unitedagainstracism.org/campaigns/refugee-campaign/fortress-europe/

Webber, F. (2012), *Borderline Justice: The Fight for Refugee and Migrant Rights*. London: Pluto Press.

Wike, R., Stokes, B., and Simmons, K. (2016), 'Europeans Fear Wave of Refugees Will Mean More Terrorism, Fewer Jobs', 11 July. Pew Research Center.

Legislation

1951 Convention Relating to the Status of Refugees
Counter-terrorism and Security Act 2016 (UK)
European Union Directive 2013/55/EU (Qualifications Directive)
Immigration Act 2014 (UK)
Immigration Act 2016 (UK)

Case Law

Detention Action v. First Tier Tribunal, Second Tier Tribunal and Lord Chancellor [2015] EWHC 1689 (Admin).

European Commission (14 December 1973), *East African Asians v. United Kingdom*.

M.S.S. v. Belgium and Greece (no. 30696/09), Grand Chamber (European Court of Human Rights) (11 January 2011).

IV

RACE, DETENTION, AND DEPORTATION

12

Understanding Muslim Prisoners through a Global Lens

Hindpal Singh Bhui*

INTRODUCTION

This chapter discusses how the development of narratives about security, extremism, and migration may be influenced by racist stereotyping, and how this undermines positive engagement between prison staff and Muslim prisoners in England and Wales. I argue that wider discourses about Muslim prisoners are dominated by a narrative of cumulative and composite threat that draws strongly on anti-migrant feelings and racism, encouraged by growing scepticism about British multicultural-ism and essentialist conceptualizations of minority groups. I suggest that the dam-aging impact of this narrative can be challenged through better incorporation of the insights of research on foreign prisoners, as well as empirical studies on Muslim prisoners. To illustrate this point, in the following piece I draw on a range of empir-ical research, including a major review of the experiences of Muslim prisoners by Her Majesty's Inspectorate of Prisons (HMIP 2010).[1]

This study provided detailed evidence of how legitimate efforts to address the threat of violent extremism were affecting Muslim prisoners in general, a group that comprises around 11 per cent of the prison population in England and Wales. The key concern emerging from the report was that a failure to see Muslim prisoners as individuals with diverse identities and beliefs risked entrenching or even creating the alienation and disaffection that can fuel extremism. As I will demonstrate, the lessons of this work remain highly relevant today given that renewed efforts are being made to confront the dangers of prison radicalization in England and Wales (BBC News 2017; see also Acheson 2016), and Muslims are increasingly over-represented in prisons and detention centres across the world. Before turning to the study, I will discuss the theoretical context which will help in understanding the report's find-ings, and then discuss how it links to research on migration and foreign prisoners.

* I would like to thank the editors and Martin Kettle for their very helpful comments on earlier drafts. This chapter is written in a personal capacity and does not necessarily represent the views of HM Inspectorate of Prisons.

[1] I led and drafted this review, and will draw on it in this chapter.

THE 'MIGRANT THREAT' AND FOREIGN NATIONAL PRISONERS

A number of themes have emerged from the literature on migration and foreign prisoners, which have corollaries in accounts of Muslim prisoners and migrants. They include a 'migrant as threat' discourse that has served as a justification for criminalization (e.g. Oberoi 2009); an assumed but weakly evidenced link between immigration and crime (e.g. McDonald 2009); a link between criminalization and imprisonment of foreigners and analyses of social control, sovereignty, and migration (Bhui 2014; Bosworth and Guild 2008; Garland 2001); and the expansion of criminal law, resulting in disproportionality and punitive victimization (Aliverti 2013).

A number of authors argue that current approaches to immigration have created a notion of 'enemy immigrants' in the popular imagination, which helps to justify the mass incarceration of foreign nationals (e.g. Cohen 2002; Oberoi 2009; Palidda 2009; 2011; Wacquant 1999; 2010). Oberoi (2009: 22) highlights the pressure on states to set removal targets, which not only send deterrent messages to incoming migrants, but 'also calm the domestic audience's anxieties about "the enemy within"'. In this context, the threatening figure of the illegal migrant legitimates actions that would be considered disproportionate in other circumstances. Mass migration is leading to a position where citizens are finding it harder to differentiate 'us' from 'them'. Differences that help to develop national cohesion on the basis of oppositional identity are eroded, creating pressure towards a more dramatic representation of differences (see Bosworth 2007; Griffiths 2012; 2013). This helps to explain the popularity of restrictive immigration policies and practices such as detention, and their utility to national social cohesion and the assertion of national sovereignty.

Anti-immigration rhetoric is often accompanied by reference to the criminality of immigrants and the greater security and order that is to be achieved if they are removed from the country. A striking example of an immigration policy based on this premise was evident in both the 2012 and 2016 US presidential elections. The Republican candidates on both occasions announced a mass deportation policy as a way of restoring the rule of law and making the country safer (Pilkington 2012; Wang 2016). New US President Donald Trump went a stage further by proposing a wall on the Mexican border to keep migrants out, temporary restrictions on refugees, and even a travel ban on people from some predominantly Muslim countries. The latter has often been justified with reference to terrorist attacks in Europe, thus neatly conflating migrants, Muslims, and terrorism (Blake 2016; Criss 2017). The desire to exclude people who are considered to be undesirable recurs throughout history (Garland 2001) and has often focused on offenders. Now, it finds a more convenient, weaker, and more vulnerable figure in the form of migrants and foreign nationals, and a highly legitimate one in Islamist terrorists who are poorly distinguished from Muslims and 'normal' offenders.

In England and Wales, foreign national prisoners were considered a relatively compliant and easy to manage group until the deportation crisis of 2006, when about 1000 foreign prisoners were released before they had been considered for deportation by the Home Office (Bhui 2007). Most were not eventually deported and there was no evidence of their increased danger to the community compared to British nationals who were released at the end of their sentences (Bhui 2007). I led a major thematic review of foreign prisoners for HMIP at the time of these events, which found that Muslim foreign nationals reported particular difficulties as a result of what they perceived to be racist stereotyping by staff (Bhui 2007; HMIP 2006; 2007). Many of the findings of this research were echoed in the study on Muslim prisoners that took place three years later (HMIP 2010) discussed later in this chapter, including the persistent insinuation that Muslims as a whole pose a threat and that all Muslims should answer for the actions of Islamist terrorists:

Some joke that Muslims are terrorists. I was asked why suicide bombings are right; I don't think it is right. This happened in education. (HMIP 2006: 10)

People talk of Muslims as terrorists. I find it hard which is why I keep myself to myself and keep away from these people. You hear things like 'you have a beard, you're a terrorist'. (HMIP 2006: 12)

Many foreign nationals of all religions felt they had become targets of discriminatory treatment. Consequently, a key conclusion of this research was that foreign national prisoner strategies should be closely linked to wider diversity strategies that seek to understand and address prejudice and discrimination as a whole. The 2006 deportation crisis appears to show how fear of migrants as a group—the symbolic 'enemy immigrant'—legitimated what in many cases were found to be disproportionate measures (HMIP 2006; 2007). When 'enemy immigrants' are also Muslim, the cultural and terrorist threat assumes greater importance. Anti-Muslim feelings may be particularly 'accessible' in this scenario because of the legitimate fear of terrorist attack or violence, which can then become a conduit for broader cultural prejudices.

SECURITY AND MIGRANTS AS MUSLIM EXTREMISTS

While public debate about free movement within Europe routinely focuses on matters of economic security, debate about migration *to* Europe is usually dominated by concerns about cultural and/or physical insecurity. Cultural insecurity focuses largely on the threatening 'other', characterized by a wariness, fear, and perhaps rejection of difference. To this end, religious and cultural differences of Muslims from majority Christian Europeans are emphasized and exploited. The often gendered nature of the narrative is evident in the opposition to women wearing the face veil (niqab), full body covering (burqa) and even beachwear ('burkhini') (Bilefsky 2016). For its opponents, who exist on both sides of the political spectrum, the burqa is a symbol of oppression and gender inequality. For its supporters, who include fundamentalist religious voices, it is a symbol of a woman's dignity and her devotion to family values (Cesari 2013). In such debates, women's bodies have become a battleground for essentialized discourses; their clothing a symbolic rejection of western democratic values and an ill-defined threat to security (Cesari 2013).

Physical insecurity can also be gendered. In 2016, a number of sexual attacks by male refugees in Cologne generated considerable alarm in Germany,[2] while the claims of a similar threat during the EU referendum campaign in the UK were found to be spurious.[3] The prominence of male sexual threat in migration discourse is familiar, and there is substantial evidence that black and minority ethnic migrants have often been viewed as sexual predators (see, e.g., Smith and Marmo 2011). Physical insecurity related to migration is more often related specifically to a fear of terrorist attack; this was demonstrated by commentary following the 2016 attacks in France about the origins of some of the attackers and rising concerns in Germany about the consequences of a welcoming stance towards migrants fleeing upheaval in the Middle East. The gendered nature of terrorism itself is illustrated by Kimmel's work. Kimmel (2003) explores the similarities between white supremacists and Islamist terrorists: both groups deploy 'masculinity' as a means of understanding their own disaffection in a globalizing world and as a way of generating support. Kimmel argues that these movements look back nostalgically to a pre-global time when white men and Muslim men were able to assume the places in society to which they believed themselves entitled; they seek in a perverse fashion to restore that unquestioned entitlement (Kimmel 2003: 615; see also Schraut and Weinhauer 2014).

Although the idea of a common Muslim identity is over-stated (Phillips 2014: 88), there is evidence that Muslim prisoners are attracted by the sense of solidarity, identity, and to some extent psychological and physical protection that adherence to Islam is seen to bring (HMIP 2010; Marranci 2009; Phillips 2012). More generally, the Islamic concept of the 'ummah'[4] emphasizes the international solidarity of Muslims regardless of their physical location. Muslim extremists, from the 7/7 London bombers to the 2013 Woolwich murderers, have integrated this concept into their justifications for violence, citing the occupation of 'Muslim lands' as a reason for their behaviours, simultaneously evoking crusader imagery (Casciani 2013; HMSO 2006). In this world-view, allegiance becomes a zero-sum concept, suggesting that Muslims are not able to be citizens who identify with their national communities. Such reductionist distortions can be amplified by the response to extremism.

In his discussion of how the response to the London bombings by Muslim extremists on 7 July 2005 was dominated by discourses of fear and threat, sociologist Chris Allen (2010a: 223) notes that the idea that Muslims and Islam present a direct threat to 'our' culture, values, institutions, and way of life, 'has found expression across all shades of the political spectrum'. The resonances of this analysis with the discourse around the threat from immigration are striking. One particular element of Allen's (2010a) discussion helps to explain why this is so. Drawing on several projects that

---

[2] BBC News (2016a). Reports of similar attacks by migrants in Frankfurt the following year were shown to be false; see, e.g., Eddy (2017).

[3] No evidence was offered of sexual attacks by refugees in the UK. See, e.g., Asthana and Mason (2016).

[4] 'Ummah' is an Arabic word meaning 'community' or 'nation' and refers to the Muslim world.

included strong elements of discourse and documentary content analysis, he notes the stress put on the *internal* nature of the threat:

As well as focusing on the Muslim heritage of the four young men, more was made of the fact that they were British born. Or, as this has become more widely referred to in both social and political parlance, 'home-grown'. Unlike 9/11, the perpetrators—and by consequence others like them—had emerged from within British society. As some put it in the media, the 'enemy' was now within. (Allen 2010a: 222)

The very fact that politicians, media, and other commentators found it so hard to accept the Britishness of the 7 July bombers is revealing. It is more comfortable to see threats as external and easier to think of the solution—'close the borders' and challenge Islamist ideology. The distinction between 'us' and 'them' should have been disrupted by British terrorists who could not have been stopped at any border. However, their nationality did not dent the hostility towards immigration. Instead, the response showed how compelling the urge is to expel threats—the bombers could not technically be described as a foreign threat that could have been repelled at the border and their Britishness was an inconvenience. The prospect today of people returning from the war in Syria or Iraq reinforces the urge to exclude people who have, in the eyes of some, relinquished any claim to Britishness by identifying themselves with a foreign entity such as the 'Islamic State' group, either by depriving them of legal citizenship or 'banishing' them. Both measures are procedurally and ethically highly problematic (Gibney 2014; Macklin 2014; Zedner 2016).

It now appears virtually impossible to create a practical or conceptual division between the perceived threat from migration and from Islamist terrorism.[5] Following the attacks on Paris in November 2015, it was discovered that the known attackers were nearly all EU citizens. However, media and politicians called for tougher controls on migration into Europe as a way of responding to such threats (BBC News 2016b; Taylor 2015). Greek and Italian politicians have similarly used threats of migration and terrorism together, with talk of 'flooding' Europe with migrants including 'jihadists of the Islamic State' (Bove and Böhmelt 2016: 573), and some politicians have been quick to suggest a need for cultural defence. For example, in Hungary, the prime minister argued that he was defending European Christianity against a Muslim influx that threatened the continent's identity (Noack 2015).

This narrative has been strengthened by further terrorist attacks in 2016, this time perpetrated by non-EU nationals, including former asylum seekers and refugees. After a Tunisian man awaiting deportation was identified as the perpetrator of the attack in Germany in December 2016, the far right political party quickly ascribed

---

[5] The difficulty of making this distinction is clear from popular discourse on immigration. Inspired by the debate on the impact of Romanian and Bulgarian EU immigrants, English television's Channel 5 aired a programme entitled 'The Big British Immigration Row' (17 February 2014), including a number of politicians, social commentators, and community activists. It included a lengthy interview with the radical Muslim Anjum Choudhary, followed by a discussion about the dramatically brutal murder of a soldier, Lee Rigby, in Woolwich by two Muslim British citizens. This had no obvious link with immigration and enraged some panel and audience members, but was nevertheless defended by the presenters as being a legitimate part of the programme.

the problem of terrorism to migration (BBC News 2016c). While the facts may now appear to fit the anti-immigrant critique more neatly, this appears no more than a coincidental alignment. While some studies suggest that many transnational terrorists are migrants to their host country, there is no direct evidence that immigration actually induces terrorism (Bove and Bohmelt 2016). Rather, many of those arriving in Europe from Muslim countries are themselves fleeing the consequences of a fundamentalist interpretation of Islam (see, e.g., Shankland 2016). Bove and Böhmelt's (2016) considerable study analysed migrant inflows and terrorist attacks in 145 countries between 1970 and 2000. It found that a minority of migrants from terrorism-prone states were indeed associated with increases in terrorism, but not necessarily in a direct way, and that migration in general (i.e. that is not linked to terrorism in the migrant's home country) was associated with *lower* levels of terrorism (Bove and Bohmelt 2016: 573).

ANTI-MUSLIM AND ANTI-MIGRANT RACISM

How does racism contribute to the prevalence and power of anti-Muslim and anti-migrant imagery? Western Europe's long colonial legacy has generated strong post-colonial, socio-economic, and cultural ties with former colonies with large Muslim populations (Abbas 2007). This has contributed to high numbers of Muslims migrating to Europe, both as asylum seekers and economic migrants (Abbas 2007; Allen 2010a; Home Affairs Committee 2016).[6] Fekete's (2001; 2009) concept of 'xeno-racism' describes discrimination against people not just because of the colour of their skin or their countries of origin, but also because of a range of other identities, including poverty, asylum-seeking status, and religion. Xeno-racism thus seems to better articulate the contemporary nature of racism, which is often driven by the belief that excluding certain categories of people from the western world will preserve or reinforce national identity and economic prosperity (Fekete 2001; 2009).[7] By eschewing a narrow focus on religion (as in, for example, 'Islamophobia'), xeno-racism helps to locate debates about anti Muslim discrimination firmly in the realm of racism, and avoids identifying religions or followers of religion as problematic in themselves (Earle and Phillips 2013).

Said's (1978) notion of 'Orientalism' is also useful for understanding the deep-rooted nature of anti-Muslim racism. His work suggests that reductionist depictions of Islam and the West can be seen as neo-imperialist echoes of the debate about empire and the psychology that sustained it. Said (1978) argues that the West's fantasy of the Islamic world relied on colonizers producing knowledge about the

---

[6] Majority Muslim countries account for most asylum applications and refugees: the top three countries of citizenship of asylum applicants in the EU in 2015 were Syria, Afghanistan, and Iraq, who together comprised more than half of all applications (Home Affairs Committee 2016: 4). In 2014, more than half of all refugees came from Syria (3.9 million), Afghanistan (2.6 million), and Somalia (1.1 million) (Home Affairs Committee 2016).

[7] Xeno-racism is also a more active phenomenon than xenophobia, which suggests a purely psychological condition. See Harewood (2006).

colonized that sought to justify oppression, imposing a degenerate identity on colonial peoples that stresses their inferiority, dangerousness, and need to be controlled (see also Fanon 1967a; 1967b). This makes it easier to perceive Muslims today as part of an alien 'other', to be feared and opposed. For example, the dehumanization of Algerian Arabs in colonial France that was arguably required to legitimate their oppression (Said 1993; Fanon 1967a; 1967b) has perhaps been renewed today through the identification of Arabs not only as somehow inferior or foreign or black or Muslim, but also as the source of terrorism. The label of terrorism draws in and binds those other identities with a particular stress on the negative imagery associated with them; this in turn helps to justify powerful mechanisms of state control.

The process of negative labelling is illustrated by a major UK research study on representations of Muslims in the print media (Moore et al. 2008), which found that more than one third of the stories related to terrorism of which a large number exaggerated or distorted information, with an emphasis on newsworthy angles at the expense of balance and context. The authors noted a recent shift towards stories about the religious and cultural differences between Islam and 'British' culture, reinforcing the 'otherness' of Muslims and implying an incompatibility between Britain and Islam. By 2008 such stories had overtaken terrorism-related stories for the first time. Portrayals of Islam as 'dangerous, backward or irrational' and as being 'in opposition to dominant British values' (Moore et al. 2008: 15) were very common, and at the same time, coverage of attacks on, or problems facing, Muslims had steadily declined. Such findings are supported by studies of public perceptions of Muslims across western countries (Dunn et al. 2007; Spruyt and Elchardus 2012; see also Allen 2010b). In two separate studies, Spruyt and Elchardus (2012) examined both anti-Muslim and anti-foreign feelings in Europe, concluding that the former were more pronounced across a range of themes:

criticism of Islam and of Muslims is formulated as a defence of important, consensual values, particularly liberal and/or Enlightenment ones. The discourse of Islam scepticism legitimates itself as a defence of tolerance ... democratic citizenship, individual rights and free speech (Spruyt and Elchardus 2012: 817).

In the UK, Allen (2010a) discusses how Barker's (1981) original discussion of 'new racism' referred to the shift away from biological markers as the basis for discriminatory processes; he notes the disproportionate focus in this discourse on issues such as immigration 'and the allegation that this would somehow eventually destroy the cultural homogeneity of the British nation and ultimately, its indigenous population's identity ... More simply, immigrants were seen to be threatening to the very existence of 'British-ness' (Allen 2010a: 230–1).

This move towards culturally based discrimination and the normalization of anti-Muslim sentiment (Allen 2010a; Runnymede Trust 1997) parallels the acceptance of anti-immigration and anti-asylum-seeker rhetoric today. The mainstreaming of such prejudice is more troubling, Allen (2010a: 233) argues, than the British National Party's extreme agenda: the climate is such that 'challenges and problems will continue to be transformed into issues of survival ... against Muslims and Islam whether they be ordinary Muslims or the Jihadis and preachers of hate preferred by some'. The debate referred to earlier in the chapter about whether women should be able to wear a 'burkhini' in a secular French Republic still reeling from numerous terrorist attacks is a case in point. It resonates with a resurgent British debate on multiculturalism, a concept that emerged in the 1980s as an alternative to hitherto assimilationist policies but has been blamed for increased segregation of communities and for giving too much support to cultural differences that are considered incompatible with 'Britishness' (Smith 2009). Multiculturalism developed because of the desire to value and respect the different cultures of migrants to the UK. It has become a more legitimate subject for attack in recent years, partly because that very respect for difference is seen as undermining national identity, western democratic values, and membership of a wider society (Smith 2009). There are undoubtedly parts of the UK where there is very limited integration between Muslim and non-Muslim communities (Casey 2016); this is often blamed on multiculturalism, while Islamophobia, racism, and economic disadvantage are under-recognized as reasons for that lack of integration (Equality and Human Rights Commission 2010; Marranci 2009; Penal Reform International 2016). A similar risk-based narrative dominates discourse on migrants and Muslims, leaving much less space for discussion of the victimization of those fleeing war zones or the cultural and post-colonial ties that often encourage migration to Europe (Harding 2012). I will now consider how these theoretical insights can help to understand the situation in prisons.

MUSLIM PRISONERS IN A GLOBAL CONTEXT

Muslims, whether European nationals or from majority Muslim countries, are often in contact with the prison system in England and Wales. Prisons currently hold around 12,500 Muslims, with the proportion of Muslim prisoners increasing from 8 per cent in 2002 to 15 per cent in 2016, significantly exceeding their proportion (around 5 per cent) in the general population (Allen and Dempsey 2016). There is a considerable intersection between Muslim, foreign national, and minority ethnic identities in prison (HMIP 2010) as many Muslim prisoners, especially those from African or Caribbean backgrounds, are either converts (see HMIP 2010; Liebling et al. 2011; Mulcahy et al. 2013)[8] or foreign national prisoners (Allen and Dempsey 2016).[9] While there is a body of research on foreign nationals in prisons (see Bhui

[8] In HMIP's 2010 sample of 164 Muslim prisoner interviewees, 30 per cent (n=49) were converts and 65 per cent (n=32) of this group identified themselves as 'black' and 16 per cent (n=8) as 'mixed heritage'. No clear reasons emerged from the research on the reasons for such high numbers of converts from black and minority ethnic backgrounds.

[9] Hansard (31 December 2013), Column 700W, Table 3: Prison population by nationality and religion, England and Wales: http://www.publications.parliament.uk/pa/cm201314/cmhansrd/cm140514/text/140514w0005.htm. UK Home Office detention statistics show that the five largest nationalities leaving immigration detention in March 2016 were from Pakistan, India, Albania, Bangladesh, and Nigeria, all countries that are mainly Muslim or have very large Muslim populations. Snapshot statistics collected over the last three years show that about half (49 per cent) of those detained in male UK immigration removal centres (IRCs) are Muslim, with percentages in individual centres ranging from 61 per cent in Dover IRC down to 37 per cent in The Verne IRC. These figures are taken from the data provided at the last inspection of each immigration removal

2009a; 2009b; 2014), evidence about the experiences of Muslim prisoners and the impact of higher numbers of Muslims on social relations in prison communities remains limited (HMIP 2010; Marranci 2009; Phillips 2012). These institutions hold people who have intersecting identities including 'Muslim', 'migrant', 'foreigner', 'Sunni', 'Shia', and 'asylum seeker'.

In 2010, HMIP published a major thematic review of the experiences of Muslim prisoners across ten establishments and this research remains relevant.[10] It found that prisons tended to use two separate, and sometimes conflicting, approaches to a complex and multi-dimensional Muslim population. The first, in which prisoners were managed through a 'diversity lens', focused on ensuring appropriate religious observance and identifying and preventing discrimination on grounds of religion—prisons had become reasonably proficient at this. The second approach, which emphasized security, tended to focus on Muslims as potential or actual extremists, and was 'better resourced, better understood and more prevalent' (HMIP 2010: 5). This prisoner represented many who felt they were singled out and watched:

Officers line up around the mosque and it feels uncomfortable when you're praying. It's like a concentration camp and it feels like you're being forced there when you're choosing to go and being watched ... are [they] watching us or the Imam or is their presence there for another reason? Are there that many staff in church? Radicalisation won't happen in the mosque. In [previous prison] they would take notes of what the Imam was saying.

Muslim prisoners were not only critical of a simple staff knowledge gap, but rather believed that the void was filled with stereotypes of violent extremism encouraged by an unsophisticated view of diverse human identity and motivation. Some felt they had to hide their Muslim identity in case they were labelled as radicals (HMIP 2010: 22). Even when Muslim prisoners were positive about staff—and many were—they felt that staff were more distant and uncomfortable than with other prisoners:

Hard to explain [views on staff], staff are ... cautious around you. Feel embarrassed for them. They tip toe around you, would prefer it if they were upfront. (HMIP 2010: 21)

Sometimes you get on well with people [staff] until they find out you are a Muslim ... Then they are not as friendly, more cautious. (HMIP 2010: 21)

Staff appreciated that their lack of knowledge was creating problems. They confirmed that they lacked the confidence to engage with Muslim prisoners and many said they needed training to help them understand and respond more effectively to Muslim prisoners' needs (HMIP 2010: 18). Muslims were much more likely to report feeling unsafe than others and it became clear that it was not just physical safety that concerned them, but feelings of psychological insecurity, often driven by the way they felt they were perceived. The single most prominent theme to emerge

centre in the UK between 2013 and 2016. For all individual figures, see the population statistics section of the reports listed at: http://www.justiceinspectorates.gov.uk/hmiprisons/inspections/?post_type=inspection&s&prison-inspection-type=immigration-removal-centre-inspections.

[10] More recent HMIP survey findings (HMIP 2014; 2015) show that the perceptions of Muslim prisoners remain worse than those of non-Muslims across a range of indicators.

from interviews with prisoners was their frustration at media portrayals of Muslims and Islam as posing a global and local threat, and the consequences of this for their experiences in prison. As one prisoner put it, 'for many non-Muslims the media is their only education into Islam' (HMIP 2010: 21). Insufficient distinction between terrorists who happened to be Muslim and Muslims in general was another cause of discontent:

Fanatics are always identified as Muslims, not as 'Egyptians' or 'Bangladeshis'. Identify by religion rather than nationality. (HMIP 2010: 21)

In common with academic research in criminal justice settings the HMIP study uncovered a fluidity of ethnic identities and the importance of recognizing the dynamics of group and individual identity formation (Earle and Phillips 2013; Parmar 2013). It found intra-ethnic diversity among Muslim prisoners that is often missing from policy discussions. Muslim prisoners were much more likely to be from a minority ethnic group and to be foreign national; and Muslims in each ethnic group reported less positively than non-Muslims in the same ethnic/national group. For example, black Muslim prisoners responded more negatively than black non-Muslims to 101 out of 184 survey questions they were asked and more positively to only 10. Asian and white Muslims tended to report the most positive experiences of prison life, and black and mixed-heritage Muslims the worst. There was less difference in the views of Asian Muslims and non-Muslims than for other ethnic groups. There was some evidence that this was because all Asians were assumed by staff and other prisoners to be Muslims. This meant that they were all treated with particular suspicion or, ironically, with more deference as they were considered by staff and prisoners alike to be what one prisoner said were 'proper' Muslims.

The HMIP (2010) study concluded that coordinated strategic work to help understand and meet the specific needs of Muslim prisoners was therefore as important as a strategy on tackling extremism, a recommendation that was never implemented by the National Offender Management Service, the agency that managed prisons in England and Wales.[11] The key findings of the HMIP review have been echoed in other, more recent studies and in different countries (Liebling et al. 2011; Penal Reform International 2016). Notably, in research on relationships between prisoners and staff at an English high security prison, Liebling et al. (2011, v) found that staff 'over-estimated extremism' among Muslim prisoners and 'viewed any outward appearance of Islam as evidence of radicalisation, rather than a manifestation of faith'. Liebling and colleagues and HMIP (2010) both concluded that the perceived threat of Islamic extremism in prisons had led to insufficient attention to the diversity or heterogeneity of Muslim prisoners.

Both studies also stress the importance of prisons needing to continue what has been long established as effective in the running of good prisons, namely keeping prisons 'relational', and balancing concern about radicalization with an understanding of how to engage positively with prisoners. This is said to promote both staff

[11] NOMS was replaced in February 2017 by 'HM Prison and Probation Service'. See https://www.gov.uk/government/news/justice-secretary-launches-new-prison-and-probation-service-to-reform-offenders.

safety and allows prisoners to achieve personal development and ensure 'psychological survival' (Liebling et al. 2011: v; see also Marranci 2009; Phillips 2012).

RADICALIZATION IN PRISONS

While research on prison radicalization is still limited, it is widely accepted that prisons can provide fertile ground for the recruitment of violent extremists (Home Affairs Committee 2012; ICSR 2016; Mulcahy et al. 2013; Silke 2014). They provide 'places of vulnerability' where extremists can find plenty of unhappy young men with weak social ties and limited opportunities for reintegration, living in an environment that provides opportunities for networking and criminal/terrorist skills transfer (ICSR 2016: 4). The reasons why some men become radicalized while others do not are less clear, but the Home Affairs Committee's (2012) inquiry into the 'Roots of Radicalisation' (Home Affairs Committee 2012: para 22) stated that:

One of the few clear conclusions we were able to draw about the drivers of radicalisation is that a sense of grievance is key to the process. Addressing perceptions of Islamophobia, and demonstrating that the British state is not antithetical to Islam, should constitute a main focus ... [of strategy] designed to counter the ideology feeding violent radicalisation.

'Prevent' (HM Government 2011) is one part of the UK government's counterterrorism strategy, 'CONTEST' (HM Government 2016).[12] It aims to stop people becoming terrorists or supporting terrorism and has three key objectives: to confront the ideology of extremism, to support those vulnerable to radicalization and to work with key sectors, which include prisons (HM Government 2011). I will not comment on the strategy in any detail here but suffice to say that while it has received some criticism for its implementation (e.g. from Commissioner for Human Rights 2016),[13] the Prevent strategy acknowledges much of the disquiet that has been expressed about the potential for discrimination against Muslims. It makes an unequivocal commitment to challenging extremism as opposed to religion as such, and also directly references HMIP's concerns about the dangers of seeing Muslim prisoners primarily as security threats and encouraging alienation: 'We know that extremists can play on a sense of grievance to reinforce their messages' (HMG 2011: 87).

Recently there has been a renewed focus on tackling extremism in prisons. A report commissioned by the Ministry of Justice (Acheson 2016)[14] concludes that despite the existence of Prevent, the prison system has failed to take a coordinated,

---

[12] The others are 'pursue', 'protect', and 'prepare'.

[13] The Council of Europe's Commissioner for Human Rights (Council of Europe 2016: 9) argues that 'Certain groups of persons, namely Arabs, Jews, Muslims, certain asylum seekers, refugees and immigrants, certain visible minorities and persons perceived as belonging to those groups have become particularly vulnerable to racism and/or racial discrimination across many fields of public life as a result of the fight against terrorism.'

[14] See also the Ministry of Justice response: 'Government Response to the Review of Islamist Extremism in Prisons, Probation and Youth Justice' (August 2016). Available at: https://www.gov.uk/government/publications/islamist-extremism-in-prisons-probation-and-youth-justice/government-response-to-the-review-of-islamist-extremism-in-prisons-probation-and-youth-justice.

consistent, and evolving approach to the identified threats of Islamic extremism. The full Acheson review (2016: 1) was classified on the grounds of public safety and security. It is not therefore possible to consider the evidence on which it is based. In one respect, the summary report represents a noteworthy departure from the judicious approach of the Prevent strategy (HMG 2011). It does not consider the potentially adverse consequences of narrow security-focused policies that may encourage the alienation that anti-extremism strategies seek to address. Indeed, the report expresses concern that 'cultural sensitivity among NOMS staff towards Muslim prisoners has extended beyond the basic requirements of faith observance and could inhibit the effective confrontation of extremist views ... swift and clear direction [should be] provided for all staff on this matter' (Acheson 2016: 4).[15]

It is not difficult to discern the danger of mainstreaming prejudice (Allen 2010a) in its warning about cultural sensitivity. It is self-evident that a fear of being seen to be culturally insensitive might inhibit a clear-minded confrontation of extremism. However, cultural sensitivity cannot be discharged simply through allowing observance of faith, as the summary appears to suggest. Understanding cultures requires more than a knowledge of religious rituals and, as noted above, running an effective prison requires, above all, strong relationships between staff and prisoners, and efforts to understand individuals, their motivations, and concerns. The announcement of a Muslim prisoner engagement grant[16] recognized this and is a welcome step. Considerable research also suggests that factors such as overcrowding, lack of safety in prisons, mental health issues, and poor rehabilitation opportunities (see, e.g., ICSR 2016; Silke 2014) are drivers of radicalization, and the importance of these should not be minimized. The tenor of the Acheson report largely supports a tendency towards essentialist views of Muslim prisoners, contrary to the warnings of these and other empirical studies (HMIP 2010; Liebling et al. 2011; Marranci 2009; National Offender Management Service 2008), as well as the Home Affairs Select Committee's (2012) inquiry.

The vast majority of Muslim prisoners in the HMIP study (2010: 23) felt their religion was more important in defining them than ethnicity, nationality, age, or gender. The idea that suspicion and hostility towards a person's religious identity is anything other than suspicion of his or her entire identity is therefore arguably meaningless to most Muslims (see also Marranci 2009). It would seem both sensible and pragmatic therefore to build on the work already done in prisons to develop an *appreciative* approach to how religion can help to achieve the aims of promoting a safer community (Marranci 2009; Pickering 2014). While prison staff have quickly become attuned to messages about vigilance and security, they have historically found it more difficult to work effectively with diverse groups, and nuanced messages about proportionality are harder to absorb (HMIP 2010). Most importantly,

---

[15] It also proposes placing some Muslim extremists in small separate units, playing out the logic of exclusion that has become familiar in discourse on migration (p. 4).

[16] In Spring 2017 HM Prison and Probation Service invited applications for a £100,000 grant for initiatives to help understand and increase engagement with Muslim prisoners. See: https://www.contractsfinder.service.gov.uk/Notice/982950b4-f23a-4f06-b351-fa38f80ef9b6.

prison staff should be enabled to form constructive relationships with prisoners that can help to run safe prisons and best prepare them for release.

CONCLUSION

This chapter has explored intersections between debates about migration, Muslim identity, criminal justice and security. It has also considered, tentatively, how this intersecting discourse may have influenced thinking about radicalization in prisons. Prejudice and discrimination towards Muslims has become more 'mainstreamed' through racism that focuses primarily on cultural attributes rather than/as well as on skin colour. The diversity of Muslims' experiences and identities is largely lost as they are represented as having internal homogeneity. Anti-Muslim racism also seems inseparable from current debates about migration, globalization, and state responses to these pressures. Suspicion of migrants and of Muslims are mutually reinforcing, and negative depictions of migrants, asylum-seekers, and refugees are amplified if they have a Muslim identity.

The prison system in England and Wales is currently undergoing a period of disruption, instability, and increased violence (HMIP 2016). At such moments, the need for immediate stability can override all other priorities. The research discussed above suggests that conditions of unrest can increase the potential for radicalization. A policy that fails to balance a security approach with positive engagement seems unlikely to be effective in combating extremism. Indeed, it risks embedding the desire among Muslims vulnerable to radicalization to reject other perspectives, thereby encouraging alienation. Anti-radicalization strategies could usefully refocus on an ethos of safeguarding those vulnerable to radicalization and building strong relationships between staff and Muslim prisoners that could help to protect the vulnerable.

It remains to be seen how prison policy will evolve as a considerable programme of reform is underway in England and Wales (Ministry of Justice 2016). The evidence points to the the value of a policy approach that combines a clear appreciation and response to the dangers of radicalization, alongside an explicit focus on promoting equality and good communication between staff and Muslim prisoners, including anti-discrimination policies designed to encourage social inclusion. There seems no empirical basis for devaluing the importance of the latter. The wider 'zeitgeist' however appears to be promoting a tendency to do just that, as racist intolerance, essentialism, and divisive politics are in ascendancy in many western countries. It is therefore important to assert the value of a balanced, research-informed approach to Muslim prisoners, and a critical appreciation of the common threads in debates about Islamist terrorism, Muslims, prisoners, and migration.

REFERENCES

Abbas, T. (2007), 'Muslim Minorities in Britain: Integration, Multiculturalism and Radicalism in the Post-7/7 Period', *Journal of Intercultural Studies* 28(3): 287–300.

Acheson, I. (2016), *Summary of the Main Findings of the Review of Islamist Extremism in Prisons, Probation and Youth Justice*. London: Ministry of Justice.

Aliverti, A. (2013), *Crimes of Mobility: Criminal Law and the Regulation of Immigration*. Abingdon: Routledge.

Allen, C. (2010a), 'Fear and Loathing: The Political Discourse in Relation to Muslims and Islam in the British Contemporary Setting', *Politics and Religion* 2(4): 221–36.

Allen, C. (2010b), *Islamophobia*. Farnham: Ashgate.

Allen, G. and Dempsey, N. (2016), *Prison Population Statistics*. London: House of Commons Library. Available at: www.parliament.uk/briefing-papers/sn04334.pdf

Asthana, A. and Mason, R. (2016), 'Nigel Farage Accused of "Age-Old Racist" Claim in Linking Migrants to Sexual Assault', *The Guardian*, 7 June. Available at: http://www.theguardian.com/politics/2016/jun/06/nigel-farage-accused-of-age-old-racist-claim-in-linking-migrants-to-sexual-assault

Barker, M. (1981), *The New Racism: Conservatives and the Ideology of the Tribe*. London: Junction Books.

BBC News (2016a), 'Cologne sex attacks: Women Describe "Terrible" Assaults', 7 January. Available at: http://www.bbc.co.uk/news/world-europe-35250903

BBC News (2016b), 'Paris Attacks: Who Were the Attackers?' 19 January. Available at: http://www.bbc.co.uk/news/world-europe-34832512

BBC News (2016c), 'Merkel: Islamist Terror is "Greatest Threat" to Germany', 31 December. Available at: http://www.bbc.co.uk/news/world-latin-america-38473936

BBC News (2017), 'Extremism in Prisons to be Tackled by a Specialist Taskforce', 2 April. Available at: http://www.bbc.co.uk/news/uk-39470210

Bhui, H. S. (2007), 'Alien Experience: Foreign National Prisoners after the Deportation Crisis', *Probation Journal* 54(4): 368–82.

Bhui, H. S. (2009a), 'Foreign National Prisoners: Diversity, Disadvantage and Public Censure', *Contemporary Issues in Law* 9(2): 65–80.

Bhui, H. S. (2009b), 'Prisons and Race Equality', in H. S. Bhui (ed.), *Race and Criminal Justice*. London: Sage.

Bhui, H. S. (2014), 'Understanding the Experiences of Foreign Prisoners and Immigration Detainees: Issues of Coherence and Legitimacy'. Unpublished Ph.D thesis, Lancaster University.

Bilefsky, D. (2016), 'France's Burkini Debate Reverberates Around the World', *The New York Times*, 31 August. Available at: http://www.nytimes.com/2016/09/01/world/europe/burkini-france-us-germany-africa.html?_r=0

Blake, A. (2016), 'Trump Says We've Known his Muslim Ban and database plans "all along." But we still don't — not really', *The Washington Post*, 21 December. Available at: https://www.washingtonpost.com/news/the-fix/wp/2016/11/17/the-evolution-of-donald-trump-and-the-muslim-database/?utm_term=.2da78b5eb7c8

Bosworth, M. (2007), 'Immigration Detention in the UK', in M. Lee (ed.), *Human Trafficking*. Collumpton: Willan Publishing, 159–77.

Bosworth, M. and Guild, M. (2008), 'Governing through Migration Control: Security and Citizenship in Britain', *British Journal of Criminology* 48(6): 703–19.

Bove, V. and Böhmelt, T. (2016), 'Does Immigration Induce Terrorism?', *The Journal of Politics* 78(2): 572–88.

Casciani, D. (2013), 'Woolwich: How did Michael Adebolajo Become a Killer?' BBC News, 19 December. Available at: http://www.bbc.co.uk/news/magazine-25424290

Casey, L. (2016), *The Casey Review: A Review into Opportunity and Integration*. London: Department for Communities and Local Government.

Cesari, J. (2013), *Why the West Fears Islam: An Exploration of Muslims in Liberal Democracies*. New York: Palgrave Macmillan.

Cohen, S. (2002), *Folk Devils and Moral Panics: The Creation of Mods and Rockers* (3rd edn). Abingdon: Routledge.

Commissioner for Human Rights (2016), 'Memorandum on Surveillance and Oversight Mechanisms in the United Kingdom. Strasbourg: Council of Europe'. Available at: https://wcd.coe.int/com.instranet.InstraServlet?command=com.instranet.CmdBlobGet&Instra netImage=2919538&SecMode=1&DocId=2375752&Usage=2

Criss, D. (2017), 'Trump Travel Ban: Here's What you Need to Know', CNN, 31 December. Available at: http://edition.cnn.com/2017/01/30/politics/trump-travel-ban-q-and-a/

Dunn, K. M., Klocker, N., and Salabay, T. (2007), 'Contemporary Racism and Islamaphobia in Australia: Racializing Religion', *Ethnicities* 7(4): 564–89.

Earle, R. and Phillips, C. (2013), '"Muslim is the New Black": New Ethnicities and New Essentialisms in the Prison', *Race and Justice* 3(4): 114–29.

Eddy, M. (2017), 'Bild Apologizes for False Article on Sexual Assaults in Frankfurt by Migrants', *The New York Times*, 16 February. Available at: https://www.nytimes.com/2017/02/16/world/europe/bild-fake-story.html?_r=0

Equality and Human Rights Commission (2010), *Triennial Review: How Fair is Britain?* London: EHRC.

Fanon, F. (1967a), *The Wretched of the Earth*. Trans. C. Farrington. First published in French in 1961. London: Penguin.

Fanon, F. (1967b), *Black Skins, White Masks*. Trans. C. L. Markmann. First published in French in 1952. New York: Grove Press.

Fekete, L. (2001), 'The Emergence of Xeno-racism', *Race and Class* 43(2): 23–40.

Fekete, L. (2009), *A Suitable Enemy: Racism, Migration and Islamophobia in Europe*. London: Pluto Press.

Garland, D. (2001), *Culture of Control: Crime and Social Order in Contemporary Society*. Oxford: Oxford University Press.

Gibney, M. J. (2014), 'Beware States Piercing Holes into Citizenship', *Eudo Observatory on Citizenship*, pp. 11–16. Available at: http://eudo-citizenship.eu/commentaries/citizenship-forum/1268-the-return-of-banishment-do-the-new-denationalisation-policies-weaken-citizenship

Griffiths, M. (2012), 'Anonymous Aliens: Questions of Identification in the Detention and Deportation of Failed Asylum Seekers', *Population, Space and Place* 18(6): 715–27.

Griffiths, M. (2013), 'Living with Uncertainty: Indefinite Immigration Detention', *Journal of Legal Anthropology* 1(3): 263–86.

Harding, J. (2012), *Border Vigils: Keeping Migrants out of the Rich World*. London: Verso.

Harewood, A. (2006), 'An Interview with Liz Fekete of the Institute of Race Relations' (2006), *Canadian Dimension*, 27 February. Available at: http://canadiandimension.com/articles/1865

HM Government (2011), *Prevent Strategy, CM8092*. London: HMSO.

HM Government (2016), *CONTEST, The United Kingdom's Strategy for Countering Terrorism: Annual Report for 2015, CM9310*. London: HMSO.

HMIP (2006), *Foreign National Prisoners: A Thematic Review*. London: HMIP.

HMIP (2007), *Foreign National Prisoners: A Follow-up Report*. London: HMIP.

HMIP (2010), *Muslim Prisoners' Experiences: A Thematic Review*. London: HMIP.

HMIP (2014), *Annual Report*. London: HMIP.

HMIP (2015), *Annual Report*. London: HMIP.

HMIP (2016), *Annual Report*. London: HMIP.

HMSO (2006), *Report of the Official Account of the Bombings in London on 7th July 2005.* London: HMSO.

Home Affairs Committee (2012), *Roots of violent radicalisation. Nineteenth Report of Session 2010–12.* London: House of Commons.

Home Affairs Committee (2016), *Migration Crisis. Seventh Report of Session 2016–17.* London: House of Commons.

ICSR (The International Centre for the Study of Radicalisation and Political Violence) (2016), *Criminal Pasts, Terrorist Futures: European Jihadists and the New Crime-Terror Nexus.* London: ICSR.

Kimmel, M. S. (2003), 'Globalization and its Mal(e)contents. The Gendered Moral and Political Economy of Terrorism', *International Sociology* 18(3): 603–20.

Liebling, A., Arnold, A., and Straub, C. (2011), *An Exploration of Staff–Prisoner Relationships at HMP Whitemoor: 12 Years on, Revised Final Report.* London: Ministry of Justice. Available at: http://www.prc.crim.cam.ac.uk/publications/whitemoor-report

Macklin, A. (2014), 'The Return of Banishment: Do the New Denationalisation Policies Weaken Citizenship?' *Eudo Observatory on Citizenship*, pp 11–16. Available at: http://eudo-citizenship.eu/commentaries/citizenship-forum/citizenship-forum-cat/1268-the-return-of-banishment-do-the-new-denationalisation-policies-weaken-citizenship?showall=&limitstart=

Marranci, G. (2009), *Understanding Muslim Identity: Rethinking Fundamentalism.* New York: Palgrave Macmillan.

McDonald, W. F. (ed.) (2009), *Immigration, Crime and Justice.* Vol. 13, *Sociology of Crime, Law and Deviance Series.* Bingley: Emerald Group Publishing Limited.

Ministry of Justice (2016), *Prison Safety and Reform CM9350.* London: Ministry of Justice.

Moore, K., Mason, P., and Lewis, J. (2008), 'Images of Islam in the UK: The Representations of British Muslims in the National Print News Media 2000–08', *Cardiff School of Journalism, Media and Cultural Studies.* Available at: http://www.cardiff.ac.uk/jomec/resources/08channel4dispatches.pdf

Mulcahy, E., Merrington, S., and Bell, P. (2013), 'The Radicalisation of Prison Inmates: Exploring Recruitment, Religion and Prisoner Vulnerability', *Journal of Human Security* 9(1): 4–14.

National Offender Management Service (2008), *Race Review: Implementing Race Equality in Prisons – Five Years On.* London: NOMS.

Noack, R. (2015), 'Muslims Threaten Europe's Christian Identity, Hungary's Leader Says', *Washington Post*, 3 September. Available at: https://www.washingtonpost.com/news/worldviews/wp/2015/09/03/muslims-threaten-europes-christian-identity-hungarys-leader-says/?utm_term=.20e150810aa8

Oberoi, P. (2009), *The Enemy at the Gates and the Enemy Within: Migrants, Social Control and Human Rights.* Geneva: The International Council on Human Rights Policy Research Paper.

Palidda, S. (2009), 'The Criminalization and Victimization of Immigrants: A Critical Perspective', in W. F. McDonald (ed.), *Immigration, Crime and Justice*, Vol. 13, *Sociology of Crime Law and Deviance Series.* Bingley: Emerald Group Publishing Limited, 313–26.

Palidda, S. (ed.) (2011), *Racial Criminalization of Migrants in the 21st Century.* Farnham: Ashgate.

Parmar, A. (2013), 'Configuring Ethnic Identities: Resistance as a Response to Counter-terrorist Policy', in C. Phillips and C. Webster (eds), *New Directions in Race, Ethnicity and Crime.* Abingdon: Routledge, 118–35.

Penal Reform International (2016), *Preventing Radicalisation in Prisons—Developing a Coordinated and Effective Approach*. PRI Briefing Paper. Available at: https://www.penal-reform.org/resource/10282/

Phillips, C. (2012), *The Multicultural Prison: Ethnicity, Masculinity, and Social Relations among Prisoners*. Oxford: Oxford University Press.

Pickering, R. (2014), 'Terrorism, Extremism, Radicalisation and the Offender Management System in England and Wales', in A. Silke (ed.), *Prisons, Terrorism and Extremism: Critical Issues in Management, Radicalisation and Reform*. Abingdon: Routledge, 159–68.

Pilkington, E. (2012), 'Mitt Romney in Talks over Nationwide Version of Tough State Immigration Laws', *The Guardian Online*, 24 February. Available at: http://www.the-guardian.com/world/2012/feb/24/kris-kobach-immigration-law-mastermind

Runnymede Trust (1997), *Islamophobia: A Challenge for Us All*. London: Runnymede Trust.

Said, E. W. (1978), *Orientalism*. New York: Pantheon Books.

Said, E. W. (1993), *Culture and Imperialism*. London: Vintage.

Schraut, S. and Weinhauer, K. (2014), 'Terrorism, Gender, and History—Introduction', *Historical Social Research* 39(3): 7–45.

Shankland, S. (2016), 'Stranded in France: Two Refugees Tell their Stories', CNET News, 14 August. Available at: http://www.cnet.com/news/stranded-in-france-two-refugees-tell-stories-crisis/#ftag=CAD590a51e

Silke, A. (ed.) (2014), *Prisons, Terrorism and Extremism: Critical Issues in Management, Radicalisation and Reform*. Abingdon: Routledge.

Smith, D. (2009), 'Criminology, Contemporary Society and Race Issues', in H. S. Bhui (ed.), *Race and Criminal Justice*. London: Sage, 30–48.

Smith, E. and Marmo, M. (2011), 'Uncovering the "Virginity Testing" Controversy in the National Archives: The Intersectionality of Discrimination in British Immigration History', *Gender and History* 23(1): 147–65.

Spruyt, B. and Elchardus, M. (2012), 'Are Anti-Muslim Feelings more Widespread than Anti-foreigner Feelings? Evidence from Two Split-sample Experiments', *Ethnicities* 12(6): 800–20.

Taylor, P. (2015), 'Europe's Populist Right Targets Migration after Paris Attacks', *Reuters*, 14 November. Available at: http://uk.reuters.com/article/uk-france-shooting-europe-migrants-idUKKCN0T30YI20151114

Wacquant, L. (1999), ' "Suitable Enemies": Foreigners and Immigrants in the Prisons of Europe', *Punishment and Society* 1(2): 215–22.

Wang, A. B. (2016), 'Donald Trump Plans to Immediately Deport 2 Million to 3 Million Undocumented Migrants', *The Washington Post*, 14 November. Available at: https://www.washingtonpost.com/news/the-fix/wp/2016/11/13/donald-trump-plans-to-immediately-deport-2-to-3-million-undocumented-immigrants/

Zedner, L. (2016), 'Citizenship Deprivation, Security and Human Rights', *European Journal of Migration and Law* 18(2): 222–42.

13

'Working in this Place Turns You Racist'

Staff, Race, and Power in Detention

Mary Bosworth[*]

INTRODUCTION

In this chapter, drawing on observations and interviews with staff[1] in the two adjacent facilities that make up Heathrow Immigration Removal Centre (IRC),[2] I will describe how officers deploy racialized notions of national identity as a means of making sense of their job, the detainees, their colleagues, and themselves. This racialized form of nationalism is shaped by and frames officers' experiences and interpretation of their job and the work culture in which they operate. While some believe that they bring their views with them to their job, others describe how the institution itself influences their opinions. In both cases, their views do not remain sequestered within the IRC, but become part of how these people perceive foreigners and ethnic minorities in their communities outside the walls of the establishment. In so doing, they reveal the importance of examining life within these hidden sites for understanding their wider effect.

Nearly all detainees, in any IRC, are not white, while most of those who guard them are. Yet, race in detention, as elsewhere, is rarely a simple binary matter. Not only are some of the staff members in these sites first-generation minority ethnic British citizens, or more recent migrants, but the sheer cultural and linguistic diversity of those who are confined prevents a simple articulation of race or racism. Rather, IRCs are sites where race and ethnicity are primarily decoded and understood through

[*] I would like to thank Dominic Aitken for his assistance in conducting some of the fieldwork for this project, as well as the staff who gave up their time to talk to us. I would also like to thank the participants at the Border Criminologies' Seminar on Race, Migration and Criminal Justice in September 2016 for their useful feedback, and Hindpal Bhui, Emma Kaufman, Alpa Parmar and Yolanda Vázquez in particular who commented on earlier drafts. The research was funded by my 2012–2017 European Research Council Starter Grant, 313362, 'Subjectivity, Identity and Penal Power'.

[1] Over a period of four months, from September to December 2015, the research team conducted a mixed-method study of staff culture. Using a combination of observation, formal and informal interviews, and a survey administered once the fieldwork was over, we gathered a significant amount of data. Material includes testimonies from ninety staff members of all ranks and eighty-eight surveys.

[2] Until 2014, the two centres—IRC Colnbrook and IRC Harmondsworth—were run separately by two different companies. At the time of writing, they are managed by one Senior Management Team (SMT), under a contract awarded to Mitie.

national stereotypes. In them, contemporary concerns about religion, ethnicity, and culture mix with enduring, colour-coded matters of race (Bhui 2016; Bosworth and Kellezi 2015; Cole 2009; Sáenz and Douglas 2015). Accounts are not fully consistent, nor do they go unchallenged. Stereotypes, nonetheless, act as important strategies through which officers transform and domesticate 'difference' into a form of 'expertise'; their ideas about race, ethnicity, and national identity, in other words, are central to how they do their job. They also generate moral and affective distance between staff and detainees. In so doing, symbolically and in quite practical ways, race and ethnicity are used to justify these institutions and their role in casting out specific individuals and groups who live among us (Bosworth 2014; 2016).

In the following sections I offer an overview of the detention system before turning to the research. As I shall demonstrate, officers rely on racialized stereotypes in everyday and more symbolic ways to make sense of their job, the detainees, and themselves. By concentrating on staff testimonies, this chapter offers a small-scale, textured account of the 'racial project' of immigration enforcement practices, in which, 'immigration controls, laws, bureaucracy, and government technologies ... promote racial hierarchies around citizenship and belonging' (Armenta 2017: 83; see also Goldberg 2001; Hernández 2012; Provine and Doty 2011). In so doing, it reminds us that the manner in which ideas of race take root is as much a topic for empirical investigation as it is for conceptual analysis and political action. Detail is crucial for understanding.

CONTEXT: STAFF AND IMMIGRATION DETENTION IN BRITAIN

On any given day the UK has around 3,500 women and men incarcerated across nine IRCs, most of which are located in the South East of the country.[3] A further sum are placed in prison, post-sentence under Immigration Act powers, while another 100 are detained in Short Term Holding Facilities (STHFs) in ports and airports, where they may be held for short periods of time.[4] Over the course of a year, nearly 35,000 people pass through IRCs, of whom half are removed or deported. The rest either remain in detention or are released on bail or temporarily admitted into the UK.

Although there is a national detention system, there is no single provider. Instead, the centres are all contracted out by the Home Office either to HM Prison Service or to private custodial companies, which, at the time of writing, include GEO, G4S, Mitie, and Serco.[5] All but Mitie also run prisons.[6]

[3] While officially the UK stopped detaining children in 2010, small numbers remain in the system, either as 'age contested minors', or in family groups held in 'pre-departure accommodation'.

[4] The three residential facilities allow up to seven days if removal is imminent, five days if not. Under current draft rules, other STHFs would allow for 48 hours, although, at the time of writing, this period has yet to be fully fixed.

[5] Due to difficulties in gaining research to IRCs (Bosworth and Kellezi 2017), little has been written about the implications of privatization for the lived experience of detention, although some work exists on the impact of the involvement of the private sector in expanding the government's capacity to hold foreign nationals in custody (Bacon 2005; Flynn and Cannon 2009).

[6] Much has been made of the overlaps between these two systems (Bosworth 2013; 2014). An exploration of race relations contributes new material to this comparison, as prisons everywhere incarcerate a

Some of those who are placed in detention have been living in Britain for some time. They may have been reporting regularly to a police station or immigration office. Others have been surviving without regular(ized) immigration status. They may have been unknown to the authorities and caught unexpectedly in a workplace raid or found by chance during some other investigation. Still others will have come from prison, held awaiting mandatory deportation due to their criminal offence. A handful of people are detained straight from the border. For most, IRCs are meant to be the final destination before the airport. Yet, only half of those detained are, in fact, removed or deported.

Although one of the first ethnographic studies of immigration detention by Alexandra Hall (2010; 2012) concentrated on staff experiences, nearly all subsequent accounts have focused on detainees. As a result, we know very little about the practicalities of staffing, the number of officers, their race and gender, or their educational attainment, their salary,[7] or training.[8] We also have little evidence about how these employees perceive IRCs, the detainees they guard, or the legitimacy, nature, or purpose of border control practices in general (although see Hall 2010; 2012; Bosworth 2016; Bosworth and Slade 2014). On a more banal note, there is very little information about what they do each day.

Some of these gaps need to be filled if we are to understand how issues of race and ethnicity operate in detention. It is relevant, for instance, to know that the majority of staff members in most centres are white and British-born. At the time of writing, all centre managers are white. Nearly all members of the senior management team (SMT) in all IRCs are white as well. Similarly, reflecting the intersectional nature of identity, most centre managers and other senior staff are men. Although women can be found at all levels of seniority, they are in the minority.

As with other custodial institutions, staff are organized in a steep hierarchy. Starting at the bottom and moving upwards their positions include: Operational Support Officer (OSO), Detainee Custody Officer (DCO), Detainee Custody Manager (DCM), and the SMT.[9] Only SMT members do not wear uniforms. Within these categories people have particular duties, although all staff may be deployed wherever the operational head requires. OSOs usually staff the gate and do not have contact with detainees. DCOs, who spend the most time with those who are confined, may

---

disproportionate number of ethnic minorities, and thus reflect the racialization of crime and its control (Alexander 2010; Earle and Philips 2013; Philips 2012).

[7] A review of recent advertisements suggests that pay is in the mid-£20,000s, although one senior civil servant reported that salaries at IRC Yarl's Wood commenced at £17,700 (personal communication). Long-term officers there, I was told, earn between £22,000 and £24,000. Wherever they work, officers may supplement their basic pay through overtime, and by taking on additional immigration control work, such as overseas escorting.

[8] All that the companies will divulge is that their courses usually include some information about detention centre rules, interpersonal skills, suicide and self-harm, and 'control and restraint' (C&R). Some attention is also paid to matters of 'diversity', where staff receive information about world religions, food, and other cultural practices. Much training occurs 'on the job' with annual refresher courses in C&R. Other aspects related to the safety and care of detainees are also updated from time to time.

[9] All centres also rely on a range of volunteers and other staff, who hold contracts with the Home Office. These employees include healthcare professionals, and organizations such as Hibiscus, which offer guidance about return.

be activities based, or work on welfare. In a number of centres, those employed in activities wear tracksuits. The SMT, whose offices are typically located outside the main institution, are usually divided into heads of regimes, security, units, health-care, and so on. At the top of the hierarchy is the Centre Manager.

Although officers, other than those in the SMT, are permitted to unionize, their capacity for collective bargaining is weak. The contracts protect basic labour rights. As part of cost-cutting measures, most companies are reducing the number of employees as they move towards what senior staff in Serco refer to as a 'hotel model' (personal communication).[10] It is therefore not surprising to find a high staff turn-over in most institutions. Due to corporate confidentiality, however, once again the precise number of staff who resign each year is unknown. Yet, when conducting research in these institutions, it is common to witness groups of new recruits under-going initial onsite training. The companies, it seem, consistently replenish staff numbers even as they seek to keep them at a minimum.

These stratifying issues, and in particular, the precarious nature of working in an IRC, are shaped by the contested nature of this form of custody and its uncertain status or purpose. As a result, few admit to actively pursuing a career in immigration detention. Most have either had lengthy careers in other fields, or have only recently left school.

In this research project, as in previous ones, many officers told me that their attraction to the post was primarily one of convenience; IRCs hire locally. Some had applied out of curiosity, others from economic necessity after being made redundant elsewhere. While some had been persuaded to join by friends and family mem-bers who were already employed in Heathrow IRC, a handful claimed they had responded to a generic post in the company, and were somewhat surprised to find themselves working in custody. 'I had no idea what the job was about', Garima[11] asserted, 'I thought it was actually just transporting detainees around. I didn't actu-ally realize, it wasn't explained to me in the interview that I'll be working in the detention centre. Halfway through my training is when I realized' (DCO, Asian). Even when they knew they would be working in an IRC, few believed they had understood the nature of the job. 'I thought working for immigration, I thought it'd be what, what's on telly, when they're stamping passports', Peter sheepishly admitted (DCM, white).

As in prisons, a certain proportion of officers had previously worked in the mili-tary or in the police (see also Hall 2012). Some had tried out retirement and dis-liked it, or had been forced back to work by economic factors. Other, younger, men aspired to work for the police, and were biding their time in a detention centre while they waited for their local force to open a new recruitment drive.

---

[10] In the sole women's establishment, IRC Yarl's Wood, as part of this bid to reduce the need for officers, Serco has taken the natural next step, introducing computerized terminals to answer detainees' basic questions and demands. At present, these terminals allow the women to order food and sign up for classes as well as to lodge concerns and complaints.

[11] This is not her real name. All participants in this article have been given a pseudonym. The 'racial' or ethnic categories listed by their name are those they gave themselves.

Opinions about working in an IRC were neither uniform nor always self-evident. 'I didn't ever plan on being involved in law enforcement or probation or anything to do with that,' Peter noted defensively. Some of his schoolfriends had 'done time at her Majesty's Pleasure,' he explained, and he feared they would judge him if they knew he worked in a custodial institution. To those old companions, he claimed to be working 'for the Home Office'. His anti-prison credentials were not really compromised, he insisted, since, 'although you prevent them from escaping, and you lock them up, and for all intents, purposes you look like a screw, it's, it's kind of a step up from that.' Matthew, Peter's colleague agreed, asserting evocatively, if rather obscurely, that he thought his job was 'below a policeman but above a milkman' (DCO, white). As with colleagues elsewhere, most officers expressed considerable uncertainty and ambivalence about these sites of confinement and border control more generally (Bosworth 2014; 2016; Bosworth and Slade 2014).

Notwithstanding the enthusiasm of sections of the public and many politicians for these sites of confinement, IRCs have an unclear mission. Designed to facilitate deportation, only about half of their residents are ever expelled. Built like prisons, they are not places of legal punishment. Filled with foreigners, they are based on British soil. All these paradoxical features of the carceral environment create substantial uncertainty for staff and detainees, causing them to search for a vocabulary and framework of explanation. Under these circumstances, stereotypes about race and ethnicity offer an obvious set of tools to identify and make sense of one another. When cast in national stereotypes, these same ideas are presented by officers as evidence of their professionalism and expertise. They become, in effect, a crucial element of staff corporate identity and the legitimacy of these contested institutions.

STAFF, RACE, AND POWER

Race and ethnicity helped officers at Heathrow IRC manage the diverse population in a variety of ways. By drawing on stereotypes, staff were able to arrange the unfamiliar into some semblance of order. Essentialized, albeit inconsistent, accounts of nationality and diversity also allowed them to carve out emotional and moral distance from detainees. At other times, however, particularly for black, Asian, and minority ethnic (BAME) officers, race and ethnicity were themselves a source of confusion and anxiety. Even as stereotypes offered an informal system of classification, staff in all centres struggled to understand or work with people of different skin colour, nationality, and religion. They found those who did not speak English well to be particularly challenging to manage or assist.

As in other removal centres, nearly all the detainees in Heathrow IRC were from the Global South, or from the edges of Europe. In 2015, the year the original research was conducted, the Independent Monitoring Board reported that the 'ten nationalities most highly and consistently represented in the detainee population each month' who accounted for around two-thirds of the total population were 'Indian, Pakistani, Bangladeshi, Sri Lankan, Afghan, Vietnamese, Chinese, Nigerian, Albanian and Polish' (IMB 2016: 8).

As might be expected, few officers openly expressed racist views in front of a university researcher. Instead, for the most part, they drew on the terminology of national stereotypes. It was not just that they were being polite, however, but rather that, in these institutions of border control, nationality is racialized. Like Aliverti's court officials and Parmar's police officers, (see their respective chapters in this volume), staff accounts animated, intersected with, relied on, and amplified other familiar fears about crime and gender (see also Sáenz and Douglas 2015). In staff relations, class and education also played a role, shaping friendship groups and often acting as a barrier to trust among them.

Hugh, who had worked at Heathrow IRC for over a decade, outlasting a number of private contractors, shared his understanding of the men in his care. 'Algeria, North Africa and the Middle East are self-harmers', he asserted confidently. 'Unlike the Africans, who love their bodies too much—they're in the gym all the time. Instead, they do dirty protests.[12] The Chinese can put up a fight, though you wouldn't always know it,' he went on. 'They speak very little English' (DCM, white).

His colleague, Garima, a British Asian officer, used a similarly fine-grained framework that drew heavily on racialized national stereotypes. In her opinion, for instance, unlike other groups, Jamaicans do not really suffer in detention. 'They'll quite happily buy their own ticket and go back', she announced insouciantly. '[Because] they'll just get a new passport and come back again ... we've seen the same faces with different names coming through the system 'cause they get picked up again for doing drugs or what have you' (DCO, Asian). For Maria, Iraqis were particularly difficult to manage because 'guys from Iraq don't respect women in their culture; women are nothing' (DCO, white). Her colleague, Gertrude, took matters even further, pronouncing categorically that detainees 'really are like children: you just need to set them to a task' (DCO, white).

Such accounts, however purportedly 'race neutral' in their reliance on nationality or other 'common sense' generalizations, cleave to traditional racist views, in which all non-whites are inherently childlike and stupid, blacks are aggressive and criminal, Chinese are devious, Asians compliant, and all Muslims misogynist (Fekete 2009; Hall et al. 1978; Kundnani 2007; Lewis 2013; Solomos 2003). All officers spoke about the population in these terms. Yet, only Gertrude was explicitly racist and even then, she was not talking about the detainees, but about her white husband's birthplace. 'South Africa was ruined', she told me casually over chicken Kiev in the staff lunchroom, 'when they handed it back to the natives, who've run it into the ground. The same thing is happening in the UK ... ' (DCO, white).

It may be that everyone agreed with Gertrude, but were simply better at hiding their opinions.[13] A survey I conducted at the end of the fieldwork certainly revealed

---

[12] This terminology refers to the use of urine and faeces by the confined.
[13] As the undercover reporting of officers' 'banter' in Yarl's Wood, caught on camera by Channel 4 in 2014, and the explicit text messages shared among the G4S officers who forcibly restrained and killed Jimmy Mubenga demonstrate, racism in other parts of the detention estate is never far away (http://www.channel4.com/news/yarls-wood-immigration-removal-detention-centre-investigation; Monaghan 2013).

a considerable amount of anti-immigrant sentiment and anti-multiculturalism (Bosworth et al. 2016). When officers were asked to respond to the following statement 'There are too many migrants in the UK', nearly 60 per cent (58.8 per cent) agreed. If we overlook the 20.6 per cent who remained neutral, only 20.6 per cent disagreed. On the following statement, 'The government needs to be tough on migration to avoid the country being overrun', more than two-thirds (69.1 per cent) agreed, while only 17.7 per cent disagreed (Bosworth et al. 2016).

While such results suggest substantial levels of resentment among the staff towards the kinds of people in their care, in interviews and casual conversation, many officers across all grades, referred to the diversity of the population as one of the best aspects of their jobs. 'It is just a big mixing pot of different ages and races', Peter asserted enthusiastically,

and I think that's fantastic. I love it … I think that's partially the reason I stayed in this job for as long as I have, is it's … it isn't what they're going through; it's all of their, their history. I find that fascinating, the fact that you've got guys in here from East Africa and South America and the Far East, and how their life experiences and trauma and this and that has all led them to end up in here, on some little island in Europe. I just find it really interesting how they've all been through various different ways, but they've all ended up here. So yeah. (DCM, white)

That Peter evidently found it stimulating to work with such a global population needs some explanation. The point is not that Peter was not racist whereas Gertrude was. Both relied on race, ethnicity, and nationality to help them to make sense of their role and the detainees without probing any further into difficult questions about the place in which they worked. Emphasizing the diversity of the detainees allowed Peter to differentiate between his job and that of a prison officer and reconcile himself to working in a custodial environment. Being a DCO, he believed, was far more challenging than working in a prison. 'You have to resolve a hell of a lot more problems', he claimed, '[and] you have to do all of that without any real punishment' (DCM, white). While Gertrude referred to detainees as children, Peter found them fascinating, just so long as, as he put it, they did not tell him too much about 'what they're going through'. In an unwitting articulation of 'colonial amnesia' (Bosworth 2016; Gilroy 2002; 2006; S. Hall 2001; Kaufman 2012), Peter evinced interest in the 'history' of detainees, wondering naively how all the men before him had somehow 'ended up' on this 'little island in Europe'.

Denied the penal powers of their colleagues in prison by the administrative nature of detention, officers searched for an explanation of the mission of the institution where they worked and their own professional identity. In reflecting on their job and its complex nature, many claimed that DCOs needed specific skills. In addition to such inexact matters as 'life experience' and 'inter-personal skills', staff often identified race and ethnicity as crucial forms of expertise. According to Paul, for example, matters were simple: a good officer has 'got to have quite a high technical knowledge of culture, of race, religion, [and] to a certain degree of the legal aspect' (DCO, white). This knowledge could be learned and drawn upon as a management skill.

While the six-week training package for DCOs does include some training in 'diversity issues', most officers felt their understanding of foreigners had been transformed by their experience of working in an IRC. Roy, an older man who had been employed in Heathrow IRC for just three years after a long career in the building trade, explained haltingly, 'I was never a racist, but ... I just didn't really know anything. I used to see someone and think, "He's a Pakistani" but now I know, "actually he's an Indian, he's a Sikh" and so on' (DCO, white). Peter described a similar experience: 'I grew up in a predominantly white area', he said, 'and coming here was the first time I'd probably spoken to anybody from Pakistan, or spoken with anybody from West Africa ... this was all in the first week ... and it was a real eye opener' (DCO, white).

Having grown up in a mixed-race family Astrid was more familiar with people from a number of different backgrounds. Yet, she, too, found that working in an IRC had altered her opinions about race and ethnicity. 'I believe the centre has made me put people in boxes, in terms of stereotyping, definitely', she asserted. 'Absolutely. Definitely' (DCO, mixed race). While reluctant to acknowledge the inevitable consequences of such stereotypes, claiming categorically that 'I never have been and I never will be racist', Astrid went on to describe the nationality of detainees in xenophobic terms, stating breezily that, 'I believe that, if you get a guy from Vietnam ... he's been growing cannabis. You get a guy from Jamaica—he's brought drugs into the country. You get a guy from Poland—petty theft, shoplifting, drunk and disorderly. Don't even have to look.'[14]

Like Gertrude and Peter, Astrid did not consider her description of the detainees to be controversial. Her opinions did not spring from prejudice, she thought, but were rather evidence of her professional expertise, garnered after many years on the job. Having worked in detention for over a decade, she 'knew' what to expect of detainees without even having 'to look' at them. No interaction was necessary: she always knew how to make sense of the men she would encounter at work.

Such testimonies suggest that the development of a professionalized bureaucracy and work culture in IRCs hinges on racialized stereotypes. These same categories and this way of viewing detainees normalizes immigration detention, stripping out some of its moral ambiguity that officers might otherwise struggle to absorb when facilitating deportation (Bosworth 2016). By assigning detainees to an essentialized (and subordinate) subject position, officers like Peter, Roy, Gertrude, and Astrid were able to maintain emotional distance from them. As a result, and in contrast to literature about other carceral institutions, face-to-face encounters in detention failed to generate the moral proximity that scholars such as Zygmunt Bauman suggest are necessary for mutual recognition (Eriksson 2016). Rather, individuals were interpolated through universalizing rhetoric, grounded in familiar racial tropes—cast as expert knowledge—that amplified and intersected with criminalizing discourses. Seen in this light, staff expertise about diversity, whether celebratory like Peter's

---

[14] And, indeed, I have found this stereotyping throughout my research in IRCs. In an earlier study, for example, a senior female officer took this view to an extreme point, informing me that she could 'tell someone's nationality by the shape of their head' (Bosworth 2014).

or more condemnatory like Astrid's, has the same effect: it assists in the process of estrangement that permits and justifies detention as well as the politics and practices of expulsion that these institutions enable (Bosworth 2014; Ahmed 2000).

MANAGING DIVERSITY IN THE WORKFORCE

It is not just detainees who have to navigate essentialized notions of race and ethnicity. IRCs hire locally. Therefore, a significant proportion of officers at Heathrow IRC are Asian because the surrounding areas of Hounslow and Southall contain high numbers of Asian and mostly Sikh residents. There are also officers who have more recently arrived from Eastern Europe and Africa.[15] In these institutions whose legitimacy and professionalization hinge on othering and the development of racialized stereotypes, BAME officers as well as those whose first language is not English face particular conflict.

Most staff members at Heathrow IRC believed the diversity of the workforce made a better detention centre. 'We have a massively ethnic-diverse pool of staff in the DCOs, [and] they are beginning to be represented in the DCO manager grades', Jasper stated proudly. Speaking on behalf of the senior management team, he believed the key to a decent establishment lay in representation: 'We need ... to be more representative of our own workforce, [and] the detainees we look after. You know, and a bunch of men managing a place misses a trick. You know, it's classic. Essentially, you know, it just needs to represent the people we care for' (SMT, white).

Others took a more limited stance, arguing only that a linguistically and ethnically diverse workforce made the IRC more efficient because officers could communicate more easily with those the government was seeking to expel. 'I think anyone who can understand the specific culturalisms—let's just put it like that—and can channel that to resolve things, is spot on', Peter said. 'You get an officer who speaks Urdu or Arabic, and they, "Brrababababa" ... That just ... calms it or resolves. In an ideal world', he went on, 'your staff group would be a bit like Noah's ark. So you have a male and a female officer from every country—I think that'd be fantastic. So you don't have cultural barriers, you don't have the language barriers. That would, I think that would resolve probably half of everything' (DCM, white).

Some officers queried whether the racial and ethnic diversity among the staff changed anything substantial about the institution at all. On the one hand, one white officer asserted, BAME colleagues were not necessarily sympathetic to detainees. 'You'll often find staff who are anti-immigration, who themselves are actually immigrants, let alone not white, you know', Marvin claimed, a little indignantly (DCO, white). On the other hand, BAME officers expressed some concerns about staff racism. 'You should have seen it, last shift that I'd done', Garima stated angrily, 'it was hilarious 'cause I went to the dining hall and, and we, and we did say amongst

---

[15] This diversity contrasts strikingly with the staff complement at IRC Dungavel, Scotland's sole detention centre, where, not only are all the staff white, but most hail from the same nearby village.

ourselves, we go, "Could there be a bigger division?" There's two tables, one is full of whites and one is full of Indians and blacks. How's that and that's staff I'm talking about not detainees, staff, right!' (DCO, Asian).

Officers raised a number of concerns, from the burden of being called upon by their white, monolingual, colleagues to interpret to complaints about pay inequalities and status. As others have found in prison, some minority ethnic officers felt under pressure to differentiate themselves from detainees to avoid being stigmatized by the same racialized stereotypes.[16] In particular, many were loath to use their language skills.

'I don't speak to them in Punjabi', Garima announced emphatically. 'I only speak to them in English. Unless I genuinely know that somebody cannot speak English because, if an Indian detainee can speak Punjabi and Hindi, I will answer them back in English 'cause I've heard them speaking English. Why should I then speak to them in Punjabi when they can speak English?'

It was not just that she did not want the extra work, but also that Garima was concerned about how she might be interpreted by her colleagues if she spoke in a language they did not understand. 'I don't want the third person standing there might think that I might be divulging information that I shouldn't or [that] I might be favouritizing them or whatever', she said defensively. 'So, I answer them in English, unless it's a genuine person who really cannot speak English. Only then will I speak to them in Punjabi' (DCO, Asian).

Azima took a similarly strict line. 'Well, yes, you know, I speak languages, and I can speak Punjabi', she admitted. 'So, you know, lots of detainees come to me. But', she went on, 'I treat everybody the same. I just apply the rules.' Evidently worried, like Garima, about charges of potential corruption or favouritism, she went even further, noting that, 'In fact, you know, the guys always say to me, "Miss, you're so strict. Why are you so strict?" And I just say to them, "I'm treating you like I treat everybody else. I'm just doing my job"' (DCM, Asian).

In their interviews, Azima and Garima took different strategies in marking themselves out from detainees. Azima, who was climbing the corporate ladder, sought to emphasize her structural (economic, educational, gendered) difference from the detainees. Rather than her university degree, however, Azima, spoke of her distinction in cultural and nationalist terms. 'I'm British-born Asian', she asserted, 'and we have a particular status. It's very clear to the men that I'm British-born. They can tell by my accent. I don't have an accent' (DCM, Asian).

---

[16] In their study, Bhui and Fossi (2008: 56–7) reported that 'Sixty-two per cent of visible minority staff said they dealt differently with black and Asian prisoners, usually citing the fact that BME prisoners were more likely to approach them because they felt they could better empathize with them than with a white member of staff. Although this was seen as a strength in some establishments, it was perceived as something that could increase the vulnerability of BME staff to suspicion and malicious allegations. Some expressed concern over possibly alienating white colleagues whose support they needed to progress professionally. A number of BME prisoners also suggested that BME staff took an exaggeratedly firm approach towards them for this reason, and some BME staff did suggest that they were under pressure to distance themselves from BME prisoners. One BME officer commented that 'staff see me talking to black inmates and they see it as a problem.' See also Philips (2005).

Garima, in contrast, who had few educational qualifications, emphasized her religious identity. She was Hindu, whereas most of the men in Heathrow IRC, as they are in other detention centres in Britain, are Muslim. Echoing anti-Muslim sentiment that characterizes populist politics around Europe at present (see Bhui, this volume), Garima aggregated them, complaining that:

They are always given priority. There used to be one mosque, one Gurdwara, one temple, one church. That still is the case, apart from now, there being the sports hall, every Friday converted for everybody from all over the centre going there. As if that's not enough, then on each level, they go to the central spine to do it and do their prayers but each level, they have now taken out an association room for the detainees, which is for everybody, but made it for Muslims to do their prayers. So, how many mosques have they got? About fifteen to the ratio of one. Sorry, is it just Muslims that we have in the detention centre? How's that fair? How is that on?

To make matters worse, she continued, the previous custodial contractor 'would never serve any pork because it offended the Muslims but yet they've served beef that offends the Hindus and, and the Sikhs and everybody else.' Recast as a matter of equality, this recognition of religious difference is seen as simply unfair. 'Sorry, you either serve it or you don't, or don't offend anybody. Why is it okay to offend one lot or, and try to protect another lot, it's, it's, it's not on' (DCO, Asian).

By criticizing the institutional emphasis placed on Muslim detainees, Garima reproduced common rhetoric about the 'tight knit' and closed nature of this religious group and more generalized prejudice against them (Bhui 2016; Philips 2012). In so doing, like her colleagues, she effectively created distance between herself and those in her care.

Minority ethnic officers and those who spoke languages other than English such as Garima and Azima were not imagining matters. It was apparent in the research that, despite the official view, they did occupy a complicated and contingent position in these sites of confinement. They were marked out by their colleagues and by the detainees, by their apparent similarities with the detained population. Despite her avowed stance against racial prejudice, for example, Astrid quite openly resented her colleagues if they did not speak in English. 'Sometimes where I work it's quiet, and there's me and a couple of others, and say they are Asian, and they're talking in Urdu or Punjabi or whatever—that irritates me', she reported. 'It does my head in. Because I don't know if they're talking about me. And maybe that's a paranoia thing on my part, but I think anybody in that situation would be like, "Well, why aren't they speaking English?"' (DCO, mixed race).

Even though officers clearly value aspects of the diversity of their colleagues, as they sometimes do about the detained population, they often placed their colleagues into fixed categories based on purported 'difference'. Under these circumstances, and notwithstanding the efforts officers like Garima and Azima made to differentiate themselves out from detainees, BAME staff members were unable to bridge completely the distance from their colleagues. In an institution based on exclusion, it proves hard to eradicate suspicion of others.

CONCLUSION

As states around the world turn to immigration detention as a means of managing populations from the Global South, even while pursuing neoliberal and globalized economic policies that make such immigration inevitable, it is clear that these institutions are playing a crucial role in the construction and legitimation of race relations (Bhui 2016). Yet, as in most state institutions, racialization occurs obliquely. Immigration policies, like all official rules, are 'race neutral', even as they always seem to position the same people in the same place in the same hierarchy (Bonilla-Silva 2010; Goldberg 2015).

Empirically these matters pose a challenge. How can we discuss race and ethnicity when they are officially disavowed as anything other than demographic categories? Officers know better, or at least enough, to mind their language in front of researchers. They may not even perceive their perspective as racist. And yet, as I have argued in this chapter, race and ethnicity, recast through the lens of immigration status and national origin, are key ways in which they make sense of their job, the detainees, and one another.

In seeking to control responses and language on ethnic and racial issues, the officers are and can only ever be partly successful. They are rarely consistent. While there are some commonalities in staff testimonies, the accounts by Azima and Garima remind us that BAME officers face particular challenges in these environments the logic of which draws their very presence into question. What are they doing on this 'small island', to use Peter's terms?

An optimistic interpretation of the inconsistencies of people's views might suggest that IRCs could offer some kind of unexpected lessons about the limits of racism, or the potential for multiculturalism to unite communities and individuals. Yet, erratic accounts of difference do little to ameliorate conditions in detention, or to challenge the logic of border control. So, too, the absence of explicit racism does not mean the institution and its staff are not racist.[17] Instead, it is clear that these institutions are saturated with judgements about difference, not only because of their goal of expulsion, but also because racialized stereotypes help officers understand the complex institutions where they work, their own role, and the population for whom they have responsibility.

In keeping with sociological traditions that tend to present prisons and detention centres as reflections of society shaped by importation and deprivation within

---

[17] Research conducted in other IRCs has found examples of more explicit racist views from staff. For example, in IRC Morton Hall, when asked about changes to security that had occurred when the institution changed from a women's prison that primarily held foreign nationals to an IRC for men, one officer said laughingly: 'we increased security, built another fence as we had two escapes when we first opened as an IRC. When it was a women's prison it was boring. Nothing happened. I mean we had a lot of foreigners even then—big black women, but we were joking: can you imagine the size of the hole in the fence they'd have to cut to try and escape?!' (DCO, white, IRC Morton Hall).

(Crewe 2009; Philips 2012; Sykes 1958; Warr 2016), a member of the SMT down-played the impact of working in an IRC on his employees' views, whereas others disagreed. 'Our staff would probably fit into two boxes', Jasper asserted, '*The Sun* reader' and 'Send them home and bollocks to them', kind of camp; and the more thoughtful, 'Actually, we need to care for people' (SMT, white). His own thoughts, he claimed, had been unaffected by his lengthy custodial career. 'The work doesn't impact my views on immigration at all. I still have my views, really.'

In a lengthy rumination, Peter offered a different view. 'I'd like to say working here hasn't affected my views of immigration', he began,

but I think it has. I think there are stories I read, and you're either swayed one way or another. And I think a lot of it depends on what kind of week you've had. For instance, if you've had a week that's been heavily influenced by the kind of Arabic nations, and you've had a fairly stressful week, and they've been fairly problematic, then you might sway heavily on the, 'I don't want any more guys from that area coming in.' But then if you've had a week where you've helped out three or four guys from that area, and they've been respectful and polite, then you sway the other way. So I think I haven't got any cut and fast opinions on any of them. I think I am heavily swayed by who I've interacted with. (DCM, white)

Astrid was more succinct. Working at IRC Heathrow had affected her interpretation of 'people on the street' (DCO, mixed race). Her views, which she felt were influenced by those she encountered at Heathrow IRC, did not stay within its walls, but rather affected how she interacted and viewed others in her community.

In this final set of examples, the productive role of IRCs in the racial state is made visible. Sites of 'exportation' as well as 'importation' and 'deprivation', they affect us all. These are not the total institutions that their architecture suggests. Rather, as officers generate and adjust their views of race, ethnicity, citizenship, and belonging in response to their experiences at work, they bring their 'expertise' with them into their daily lives outside. When considered in this light, it is clear that IRCs are fundamentally at odds with liberal aspirations for a tolerant and diverse society (Lewis 2005). Like the stereotypes they engender and rely upon, they need careful, robust, and systematic critique. Only then may we hope to challenge some of the racialized inequalities they engender and uphold.

REFERENCES

Ahmed, S. (2000), *Strange Encounters: Embodied Others in Post-Coloniality*. London: Routledge.

Alexander, M. (2010), *The New Jim Crow: Mass Incarceration in the Age of Colorblindness*. New York: The New Press.

Armenta, A. (2017), 'Racializing Crimmigration: Structural Racism, Colorblindness, and the Institutional Production of Immigrant Criminality', *Sociology of Race and Ethnicity* 3(1): 82–95.

Bacon, C. (2005), 'The Evolution of Immigration Detention in the UK: The Involvement of Private Prison Companies'. RSC Working Paper No. 27. Oxford: Refugee Studies Centre. Available at: https://www.rsc.ox.ac.uk/files/publications/working-paper-series/wp27-evolution-immigration-detention-uk-2005.pdf

Bhui, H. S. (2016), 'The Place of "Race" in Understanding Immigration Control and the Detention of Foreign Nationals', *Criminology and Criminal Justice* 16(3): 267–85.

Bhui, H. S. and Fossi, J. (2008), 'The Experiences of Black and Minority Ethnic Prison Staff', in J. Bennett, B. Crewe, and A. Wahidin (eds), *Understanding Prison Staff*. Collumpton: Willan, 49–64.

Bonilla-Silva, E. (2010), *Racism without Racists: Color-blind Racism and the Persistence of Racial Inequality in the United States*. Lanham, MD: Rowman & Littlefield.

Bosworth, M. (2013), 'Can Immigration Detention be Legitimate?', in K. F. Aas and M. Bosworth (eds), *Migration and Punishment: Citizenship, Crime Control, and Social Exclusion*. Oxford: Oxford University Press, 149–64.

Bosworth, M. (2014), *Inside Immigration Detention*. Oxford: Oxford University Press.

Bosworth, M. (2016), 'Immigration Detention, Ambivalence and the Colonial Other', in A. Eriksson (ed.), *Punishing the Other*. Abingdon: Routledge, 145–64.

Bosworth, M., Gerlach, A., and Aitken, D. (2016), *Understanding Staff Culture at IRC Heathrow*. Oxford: Centre for Criminology.

Bosworth, M. and Kellezi, B. (2015), 'Citizenship and Belonging in a Women's Immigration Detention Centre', in C. Phillips and C. Webster (eds), *New Directions in Race, Ethnicity and Crime*. Abingdon: Routledge, pp. 80–96.

Bosworth, M. and Kellezi, B. (2017), 'Getting in, Getting out and Getting back: Access Ethics and Emotions in Immigration Detention Research', in S. Armstrong, J. Blaustein, and A. Henry (eds), *Reflexivity and Criminal Justice: Intersections of Policy, Practice and Research*. London: Palgrave Macmillan, 237–62.

Bosworth, M. and Slade, G. (2014), 'In Search of Recognition: Gender and Staff–Detainee Relations in a British Immigration Detention Centre', *Punishment & Society* 16(2): 169–86.

Bowling, B. (2013), 'Epilogue. The Borders of Punishment: Towards a Criminology of Mobility', in K. F. Aas and M. Bosworth (eds), *The Borders of Punishment: Migration, Citizenship and Social Exclusion*. Oxford: Oxford University Press, 291–306.

Cole, M. (2009), 'A Plethora of 'Suitable Enemies': British Racism at the Dawn of the Twenty-first Century', *Ethnic and Racial Studies* 32(9): 1671–85.

Crewe, B. (2009), *The Prisoner Society: Power, Adaptation and Social Life in an English Prison*. Clarendon Studies in Criminology. Oxford: Oxford University Press.

Earle, R. and Philips, C. (2013), ' "Muslim is the New Black": New Ethnicities and New Essentialisms in the Prison', *Race and Justice* 3(2): 114–29.

Eriksson, A. (ed.) (2016), *Punishing the Other: The Social Production of Immorality Revisited*. Abingdon: Routledge.

Fekete, L. (2009), *A Suitable Enemy: Racism, Migration and Islamophobia in Europe*. London: Pluto Press.

Flynn, M. and Cannon, C. (2009), 'The Privatisation of Immigration Detention: Towards a Global View'. Global Detention Working Papers. Available at: https://www.globalde-tentionproject.org/wp-content/uploads/2016/06/GDP_PrivatizationPaper_Final5.pdf

Gilroy, P. (2002), *There Ain't No Black in the Union Jack: The Cultural Politics of Race and Nation*. Abingdon: Routledge.

Gilroy, P. (2006), *After Empire or Postcolonial Melancholia*. New York: Columbia University Press.

Goldberg. D. T. (2001), *The Racial State*. London: Wiley-Blackwell.

Goldberg, D. T. (2015), *Are we all Postracial Yet?* Cambridge: Polity Press.

Hall, A. (2010), ' "These People Could Be Anyone": Fear, Contempt (and Empathy) in a British Immigration Removal Centre', *Journal of Ethnic and Migration Studies* 36(6): 881–98.

Hall, A. (2012), *Border Watch: Cultures of Immigration, Detention and Control*. London: Pluto Press.

Hall, S. (2001), 'Conclusion: The Multicultural Question', in B. Hesse (ed.), *Un/settled Multiculturalisms: Diasporas, Entanglements, 'Transruptions'*. London: Zed, 209–41.

Hall, S., Critcher, C., Jefferson, T., and Roberts, B. (1978), *Policing the Crisis: Mugging, the State and Law and Order*. London: Macmillan.

Hernández, C. (2012), 'The Perverse Logic of Immigration Detention: Unraveling the Rationality of Imprisoning Immigrants Based on Markers of Race and Class Otherness', *Columbia Journal of Race & Law* 1(3): 353–64.

IMB (2016), *Annual Report 2015, Independent Monitoring Board Heathrow Immigration Removal Centres*. London: IMB. Available at: https://s3-eu-west-2.amazonaws.com/imb-prod-storage-1ocod6bqky0vo/uploads/2016/05/Heathrow-IRC-2015.pdf

Kaufman, E. (2012), 'Finding Foreigners: Race and the Politics of Memory in British Prisons', *Population, Space and Place* 18(6): 710–14.

Kundnani, A. (2007), *The End of Tolerance: Racism in Twenty-First Century Britain*. London: Pluto Press.

Lewis, G. (2005), 'Welcome to the Margins: Diversity, Tolerance, and Policies of Exclusion', *Ethnic and Racial Studies* 28(3): 536–58.

Lewis, G. (2013), 'Unsafe Travel: Experiencing Intersectionality and Feminist Displacements', *Signs: Journal of Women in Culture and Society* 38(4): 869–92.

Monaghan, K. (2013), *Inquest into the Death of Jimmy Kelenda Mubenga. Report by the Assistant Deputy Coroner, Karon Monaghan QC under the Coroner's Rules 1984, Rule 43*. Available at: http://iapdeathsincustody.independent.gov.uk/wp-content/uploads/2013/12/Rule-43-Report-Jimmy-Mubenga.pdf

Philips, C. (2005), 'Facing Inwards and Outwards? Institutional Racism, Race Equality and the Role of Black and Asian Professional Associations', *Criminology & Criminal Justice* 5(4): 357–77.

Philips, C. (2012), *The Multicultural Prison: Ethnicity, Masculinity, and Social Relations among Prisoners*. Oxford: Oxford University Press.

Provine, D. and Doty, R. (2011), 'The Criminalization of Immigrants as a Racial Project', *Journal of Contemporary Criminal Justice* 27(3): 261–77.

Sáenz, R. and Douglas, K. M. (2015), 'A Call for the Racialization of Immigration Studies on the Transition of Ethnic Immigrants to Racialized Immigrants', *Sociology of Race and Ethnicity* 1(1): 166–80.

Solomos, J. (2003), *Race & Racism in Britain* (3rd edn). London: Palgrave Macmillan.

Sykes, G. (1958), *The Society of Captives: A Study of a Maximum Security Prison*. Princeton, NJ: Princeton University Press.

Warr, J. (2016), 'The Deprivation of Certitude, Legitimacy and Hope: Foreign National Prisoners and the Pains of Imprisonment', *Criminology & Criminal Justice* 61(3): 301–18.

14

Raced and Gendered Logics of Immigration Law Enforcement in the United States

Tanya Golash-Boza

On an Autumn day in 2005, Peter was walking down the street in Nashville, Tennessee when a police officer stopped him to question him about a nearby robbery. The officer said Peter fit the description of a suspect. He searched Peter and took him to a nearby police station so the victim could identify him. The victim said Peter was not the assailant. The officer, however, was intent on investigating Peter. Having noticed his 'foreign' accent, the officer asked Peter where he was from. When Peter told him he was from Jamaica, the officer asked if Peter minded if he called immigration authorities. Since he was a legal permanent resident of the United States and believed he had nothing to hide, Peter agreed. The officer contacted immigration authorities, who in turn asked the police officer to detain Peter, as it turned out he had missed an immigration hearing related to a 1997 charge of possession of stolen property.

The police officers detained Peter until immigration agents came to take him to a Corrections Corporation of America private immigration detention centre in Memphis, Tennessee, where he stayed for six weeks, and then to another detention centre in Louisiana, where he spent three months. Subsequently, he was deported to Jamaica, a country he had not even visited in nearly twenty years.

This case of mistaken identity provides a glimpse into how biased policing practices, combined with institutional cooperation between immigration and criminal law enforcement agents, can influence broader trends in deportation. In Peter's case, we know the police officer stopped him because he was a black man. The officer was looking for a black male suspect and Peter fit the description. This seems like a reasonable act of policing. However, it is part of a broader pattern of gendered racial profiling whereby police officers are more likely to stop and arrest black people than white people, and are more likely to arrest men than women (Gelman et al. 2007; Lamberth 1994). It is also evident that the officer engaged in linguistic profiling as he suspected Peter may not be in the United States legally once he heard him speak. Put simply, the series of events that led to Peter's deportation are much less likely to have happened to a white female immigrant from Canada. Whereas Jamaican men have high rates of deportation, Canadian women have very low rates (Golash-Boza 2012).

Raced and Gendered Logics of Immigration Law Enforcement in the United States. Tanya Golash-Boza. © Tanya Golash-Boza, 2018. Published 2018 by Oxford University Press.

Deportation laws in the United States, as written, are race- and gender-blind, but their implementation is decidedly not, as black and Latino immigrant men are the primary targets of these laws. An analysis of how deportations happen that puts together on-the-ground practices of policing with immigration law enforcement cooperation helps us to understand the gendered and racialized patterns of deportation. As we consider which people are deported, and what happens to them after deportation, it also becomes clear that deportations have much broader gendered and racialized implications that extend beyond the territorial boundaries of the United States. This analysis of the policing of immigrants by local and immigration law enforcement as well as criminal law enforcement agents reveals the raced and gendered assumptions about immigrants and their families that undergird immigration laws. The chapter draws from interviews I conducted with deportees in the Dominican Republic, Jamaica, and Guatemala in 2009 and 2010, as part of a larger project that involved interviews with 147 deportees in Jamaica, Guatemala, the Dominican Republic, and Brazil (see Golash-Boza 2015).

DEPORTATION LAWS ARE RACE- AND GENDER-BLIND BUT POLICING IS NOT

Immigration laws in the United States have no explicit race or gender provisions. Whereas people once could be barred from legal entry and citizenship based on their national origin (effectively racial bans), those laws have been struck down and replaced with racially neutral laws. Whereas immigration laws at one time had provisions that favoured men and marginalized women, those provisions no longer exist. The latest revision to immigration laws in the United States—the Immigration and Nationality Act of 1965—does not include any provisions that explicitly discriminate based on gender or race. Nevertheless, its most draconian provisions tend to be applied more frequently to non-whites and to men. In the United States, 97 per cent of deportees are sent to Latin America or the Caribbean and 90 per cent of deportees are men (Golash-Boza and Hondagneu-Sotelo 2013).

These gendered and raced patterns cannot be traced to explicit racial or gendered provisions in the law. They can, however, be attributed to the ways immigration laws are enforced. Immigration law enforcement in the United States is the responsibility of the Department of Homeland Security (DHS) and its two enforcement arms: Customs and Border Patrol (CBP) and Immigration and Customs Enforcement (ICE). In this chapter, I will not examine deportations carried out by CBP, which usually involve apprehending would-be migrants along the border and preventing them from entering the country. Instead, I will focus on deportations from the interior of the United States—those that involve settled migrants, both legally and illegally present, who live in the United States, and who often work and have families in this country. These deportations are called interior removals and are most often carried out by ICE. The patterns for this group are similar to broader deportation patterns: 94 per cent of interior removals involve men, even though women account for 47 per cent of unauthorized immigrants in the United States. And, 88 per cent of interior removals involve people from just four countries: Mexico, Guatemala, Honduras, and El Salvador, even though nationals from these countries make up only 66.3 per cent of unauthorized migrants (Passel and Cohn 2014; Rosenblum and McCabe 2014).

To understand these broad trends, we must think about how deportations happen. Interior removals are rarely provoked by a direct encounter with an ICE agent, as these federal agents do not have licence to patrol the streets of US cities and demand proof of immigration status from people. This federal agency has just 20,000 employees overall, only a fraction of whom are engaged in raiding homes and worksites to arrest undocumented immigrants, and they must seek out warrants prior to these raids. Simply put, ICE does not have the staff, resources, or licence to patrol the country looking for undocumented migrants. Instead, they work closely with criminal law enforcement agencies to apprehend immigrants.

This cooperation between ICE and local law enforcement is a critical component of racial and gendered disparities in deportation trends. Police officers have a fair amount of discretion over whom they choose to stop for investigative stops (Epp et al. 2014), suspected crimes, or traffic violations (Alexander 2011). For a wide variety of reasons, police officers are more likely to stop and arrest black and Latino men, which in turn leads to higher deportation rates for these groups. As Kevin Johnson (2016: 1025) explains, 'the racially disparate consequences of the modern criminal justice system contribute to the racially disparate incidence of contemporary immigration removals'.

The racial disparities in the criminal justice system in the United States are stark. In 2008, less than one-third of the population of the United States was black or Latino. In that same year, however, blacks and Latinos made up 58 per cent of the nation's prison population (Sabol et al. 2009). In 2009, the imprisonment rate of white males was 487 per every 100,000 in the population, as compared to 1,193 per 100,000 Latino males, and 3,110 per 100,000 black males. Black males were six times as likely to be incarcerated as white males in 2009 (West and Sabol 2010).

These disparities are due, in part, to racial profiling by police officers. The propensity of police officers to pull over African Americans more often than whites is so prevalent that the moniker 'driving while black' has emerged to describe this phenomenon. A study carried out by the American Civil Liberties Union (ACLU) found that 73 per cent of the drivers along the I-95 that Maryland state police searched were black, even though 75 per cent of the drivers were white (Harris 1999). In recent years, the moniker 'driving while brown' has also emerged to refer to the disproportionate stops of Latino drivers. A study in Volusia County, Florida found that both black and Hispanic drivers are more likely to be stopped and searched than whites (Mauer 1999). This profiling extends to pedestrians: a study of police officers in New York City found that they were twice as likely to stop black pedestrians as they were white (Gelman et al. 2007).

Racial and gendered disparities in local policing practices become magnified when police cooperate with immigration law enforcement, due to the possibility of deportation. Although police officers are responsible for *criminal* law enforcement, they often have the ability to contact *immigration* law enforcement authorities to inquire about the status of a person whom they have arrested. For this reason, the most common way a person is deported from the interior of the country is subsequent to an arrest by a police officer. The merging of immigration and criminal law enforcement tactics has meant that police officers are often the first step in the deportation pipeline.

POLICE AND IMMIGRATION COOPERATION IN THE UNITED STATES

Formal cooperation between local law enforcement and immigration law enforcement agents dates to the first jail status check programmes, which were created in 1988. The Institutional Removal Program and the Alien Criminal Apprehension Program were designed to screen individuals in federal, state, or local prisons and jails to see if they were eligible for deportation. These programmes were melded together between 2005 and 2007 to create the Criminal Alien Program, which today is active in all state and federal prisons, as well as in more than 300 local jails. The Criminal Alien Program ensures that most prisoners have their immigration status checked prior to being released from jail or prison (Ewing 2014).

Whereas the Criminal Alien Program generally focuses on people who have been convicted of crimes, there is another set of information-sharing programmes that allows local police and sheriffs to check the immigration status of people prior to them being convicted (or even charged) of any crime. The DHS piloted this programme in 2008 and called it 'Secure Communities'. Under this programme, when a person is arrested, their fingerprints are run through an immigration database to see if they have an immigration record. If they do, ICE can request that a 'detainer' be issued to hold the person until ICE comes to pick them up. By 2013, this programme existed in every jail in the country (Ewing 2014). Secure Communities was replaced by the Priority Enforcement Program in November 2014, which has the same information-sharing guidelines. In early 2017, President Trump ordered the revival of Secure Communities.

Some jurisdictions go a step further and deputize their police officers to enforce immigration laws directly through a programme called 287(g), named after its subsection in the Immigration and Nationality Act, which was revised in 1996. In some jurisdictions, 287(g)-deputized police officers are authorized to enforce immigration laws on the streets, meaning people can be detained for immigration offences after being stopped for traffic violations or other minor offences. As of 2016, ICE had 287(g) agreements with 32 law enforcement agencies in 16 states. With 287(g), deputized officers have direct access to federal immigration databases (Ewing 2014). Using the criminal justice system to enforce immigration laws exacerbates racial disparities already present in the criminal justice system (Tonry 2011) insofar as there is now an additional consequence for foreign nationals who are stopped for driving (or walking) while black or brown: they could be placed into the deportation pipeline.

Most removal proceedings are initiated subsequent to a person being arrested and taken to a police station. It may seem that the only people who are treated in this way are those who commit crimes. However, the process is not that straightforward—you do not have to commit a crime to be arrested and you can commit a crime and never be arrested. For example, a group of college students may consume illegal drugs in their shared home and avoid detection by law enforcement because the local police has chosen not to patrol that neighbourhood. In contrast, many people violate the law in the presence of a police officer and are not arrested because the police officer has discretion over whom they choose to arrest (Pratt and Sossin 2009).

For example, it is illegal in the United States to fish in certain bodies of water without a licence. If an officer sees a person fishing, they may or may not choose to ask that person if they have a licence to fish. If the police officer asks and finds that the person does not have a fishing licence, the officer makes a decision either to issue a citation (ticket) or to arrest the person. For most minor offences, police officers are supposed to issue a citation rather than make an arrest. However, the officer may arrest a person if they are unable to produce acceptable identification or if the officer believes the suspect will not appear in court. Most people found to be fishing without a licence will be issued a citation or even just a verbal warning. In those cases, if the person is in the country illegally, this police encounter will not lead to deportation. If, however, the police officer decides to arrest the person, that encounter could lead to deportation. When a police officer brings an arrestee to the police station, the judicial commissioner has the power to dismiss an arrest if it is found that a citation should have been issued instead of an arrest. For example, the commissioner could verify with the arresting officer what sort of identification the suspect produced and whether or not an arrest was warranted. However, a study in Nashville, Tennessee found that a judicial commissioner who is unsympathetic to immigrants may be unlikely to dismiss the arrests of undocumented migrants (ACLU 2012). Thus, even though judicial commissioners are supposed to be a safeguard against unwarranted arrests, they are often not.

In sum, depending on the jurisdiction, people can be placed into the deportation pipeline subsequent to either a stop, an arrest, being charged, or being sentenced. Immigrants who live in jurisdictions where police officers can hand them over to immigration authorities subsequent to a stop are at most risk of deportation, whereas those who live in jurisdictions where authorities only hand over immigrants to immigration authorities subsequent to people having completed a jail or prison sentence are at least risk. In all jurisdictions, nevertheless, there is some form of a police-to-deportation pipeline, which means that across the United States the racial disparities present in policing have a spillover effect on deportations.

THE RACIAL IMPLICATIONS OF DEPORTATION TRENDS

Racism is both an ideology and a set of practices (Golash-Boza 2016a). In the case of deportations, there are racial *ideologies* that justify mass deportation and policing *practices* that ensure certain groups are targeted by deportation policies. The racial ideologies that justify deportation are based on racialized logics and discourses about black and Latino criminality and illegality. The racial ideology that black men have criminal tendencies leads to the deportation of a disproportionate number of Dominicans and Jamaicans. The racial ideology that Mexicans, and those who look 'Mexican', are 'illegals' leads to the targeting of Mexicans and Central Americans in immigration enforcement efforts.

The practices that lead to racial disparities in mass deportation include racially discriminatory laws and policing practices. The copious literature on racial disparities in policing practices (Gottschalk 2016; Tonry 2011) can directly inform our understanding of racial disparities in deportations. In the United States, blacks and Latinos are more likely to be arrested than whites, and these disparities are particularly pronounced for drug-related crimes. African Americans are sent to prison on drug charges at nearly twelve times the rate of whites, even though blacks and whites use and sell drugs at about the same rates (Alexander 2011). One of the main reasons for this disparity is that police officers target open-air drug markets in black neighbourhoods yet often ignore the widespread use of narcotics in primarily white suburban areas and on college campuses. Because whites are less likely to be arrested for drug offences, they are less likely to be charged, convicted, or sentenced to prison for drug offences. This means that harsh penalties for drug offences have had a disproportionate impact on people of colour. When immigrants are caught up in this dragnet, the consequence for them is often deportation, due in part to aggravated felony provisions of US immigration laws.

One of the more draconian provisions of the current version of the Immigration and Nationality Act is related to deportations after aggravated felony convictions, which is the kind of deportation that Peter experienced. Any person convicted of an aggravated felony in the United States faces automatic deportation. An aggravated felony is a specific class of criminal conviction and includes a crime of violence, theft, or burglary for which the term of imprisonment is at least one year. Drug offences count as aggravated felonies for immigration purposes if they either contain a trafficking element or would be punishable as a felony under federal drug laws. When a non-citizen is convicted of this category of offence, they face automatic deportation, which means an immigration judge does not have the opportunity to weigh equities in the case. A Jamaican, for example, could have come to the United States at age two. If, in his early twenties, he is caught riding in a stolen car and pleads guilty to a suspended sentence of one year, he could face automatic deportation to Jamaica even though he has a US citizen wife and two children and no family or friends in Jamaica.

Peter moved to the United States when he was a teenager, in 1989. He was a legal permanent resident and worked in several jobs, including landscaping, the restaurant business, a steel factory, and house painting. In 1997, he ran into problems. He got into an argument with his girlfriend. She was angry, and called the police and said he stole money and jewellery from her apartment. Peter says she had lent him some money and had asked him to clean her gold jewellery. The total value of the items was $1800. When his court date came up, she did not show up, but the state pressed charges anyway. Peter was sentenced to one year in jail. He served part of his sentence, and was let out on parole. Once released, he thought he could put his past behind him and move forward. It took a while for him to get back on his feet, but, eventually, he was painting houses again and making ends meet until he was arrested and the police decided to check on his immigration case.

When the police officer made the call to immigration authorities, he discovered Peter had a Notice to Appear in immigration court. Peter had never received the notice and thus had missed his court date. When he did not show up, the immigration judge ruled in absentia that Peter was deportable. This ruling, however, was not sufficient to ensure Peter's deportation—that would happen only if he were actually apprehended by law enforcement agents.

Due to the way immigration law enforcement works in the United States, there are millions of deportable people who will never actually be forced to leave. Just as there are 35 million illegal drug users, the vast majority of whom will never go to prison (Alexander 2011), there are at least 11 million undocumented immigrants and an unknown additional number of people who have violated the terms of their visa and are thus deportable. Immigration laws are not designed to remove all unauthorized immigrants. Nicholas De Genova (2002: 438) made this clear many years ago when he explained:

It is deportability, and not deportation per se, that has historically rendered undocumented migrant labor a distinctly disposable commodity. There has never been sufficient funding for the INS to evacuate the United States of undocumented migrants by means of deportations, nor even for the Border Patrol to 'hold the line.' The INS is neither equipped nor intended to actually keep the undocumented out.

Since De Genova wrote those lines the Immigration and Naturalization Service (INS) has been replaced by the DHS. Even though the DHS has a much bigger budget than the INS, and deportations have increased five-fold since 2002 (Golash-Boza 2012), De Genova's words continue to ring true—the intention of this agency is not to remove all deportable migrants, but to deport enough to ensure the continued marginalization of those who remain. More recent work has highlighted how the merging of criminal and immigration law enforcement in the United States has enhanced the marginalization of Latinos (Vázquez 2011) and immigrants of colour more broadly (Johnson 2016).

Back in Jamaica, Peter had nowhere to go. His whole family is in the United States. He had not kept in contact with school friends. When he left, his friends did not own telephones, so he could not call them. People in his Kingston neighbourhood scorn him for never sending anything back when he lived in America. They look down on him because he was in America for so long and came back empty handed. When Peter arrived in Jamaica, he had ten dollars in his pocket. He changed it into Jamaican dollars, and took a taxi to the Kingston neighbourhood he grew up in. He found a school friend, who let him spend the night on the porch. He set out to look for work the next day so he could eat, but found it difficult to find employment—a common problem among deportees in Jamaica and beyond (Anderson 2015; Golash-Boza 2016b; Olvera and Muela 2016).

When we spoke, Peter had been back in Kingston for three years and things had become a bit easier for him. A friend had let him stay at his home and he had found a temporary construction job. However, he continued to experience harassment by young men in his neighbourhood and his place had been broken into several times.

Peter was deported to his country of birth and despite considerable difficulties has been able to rekindle old ties to help him in a very difficult situation. Some people, however, are deported to countries they have never visited before. Natalia, for example, was born in the Bahamas to a Haitian woman, which made her a citizen of Haiti, even though she had never been to Haiti. When Natalia was two days old, her mother brought her to the United States. Twenty years later, when Natalia, herself the mother of a newborn, was caught shoplifting. Her attorney advised her to plead guilty to receive a lesser sentence. She did. Based on that plea, she now faces deportation to Haiti, a country she has never set foot in, whose language she does not speak, and that is still recovering from a massive earthquake, political unrest, and a cholera outbreak (Golash-Boza 2011).

If deported to Haiti, Natalia would face extreme difficulties, both because of her unfamiliarity with her country of citizenship, and because of her strong attachments to the United States, including a US citizen child and husband. Because of her status as a legal permanent resident, Natalia could have applied for US citizenship five years after her arrival in the United States. She never applied and thus remained vulnerable to deportation as legal permanent residents can be deported if convicted of aggravated felonies. Between 1992 and 2006, about 300,000 people were deported from the United States under aggravated felony provisions. It is unclear how many of these people were legal permanent residents, yet we do know that all had entered legally, as there is a different set of provisions in the Illegal Immigration Reform and Immigrant Responsibility Act of 1996 for people who entered the country illegally. The top three countries to which these people were deported were: Mexico (43 per cent); the Dominican Republic (8.2 per cent), and Jamaica (5.5 per cent). Nationals of these three countries were thus over-represented among this group of deportees. Mexicans account for 25 per cent of all legal permanent residents, Dominicans for 3.7 per cent, and Jamaicans 1.8 per cent, meaning people from these three countries are over-represented among deported legal permanent residents. In contrast, less than 1 per cent of people deported under aggravated felony provisions were from Canada or the UK, and even fewer from other European countries, even though people from the UK make up 2.2 per cent of the legal permanent resident population and Canadians make up 2.4 per cent.[1]

The aggravated felony provisions are colour-blind in principle, yet rarely applied to white immigrants. Likewise, white people are much less likely to be arrested than the non-white population, particularly black and Latino people. For similar reasons, men are much more likely to be ensnared in the deportation dragnet than women.

When I interviewed deported Jamaicans in 2009 and 2010, many of them recounted stories of discriminatory policing practices that led to their deportations. Their stories, like Peter's, were often sagas of family separation and despair. When I interviewed deportees in the Dominican Republic, also in 2009 and 2010, I heard

---

[1] Figures available at: http://trac.syr.edu/immigration/reports/158/include/rep158table2_a.html and https://www.dhs.gov/sites/default/files/publications/ois_lpr_pe_2012.pdf.

similar accounts. Emanuel's story is one. Emanuel moved to the United States as a legal permanent resident in the late 1970s, when he was a teenager. Upon finishing high school, he served two years in the army. He then completed a technical degree that allowed him to secure a job repairing security cameras for supermarkets.

When Emanuel was in the army, he purchased a gun for his personal use. When he left the army, he moved to North Carolina, where it was legal to own guns. However, he took the gun with him to New Jersey, where he did not have a valid permit for it. One day, in early 1996, a New Jersey police officer pulled Emanuel over for speeding and asked to search his car. Emanuel agreed. Michelle Alexander (2011: 66) explains that these 'pretext stops' are 'favorite tools of law enforcement in the War on Drugs. A classic pretext stop is a traffic stop motivated not by any desire to enforce traffic laws, but instead motivated by a desire to hunt for drugs in the absence of any evidence of illegal drug activity.' In Emanuel's case, the officer found not drugs but an unlicensed firearm.

Emanuel was sentenced to one year in prison for illegal possession of a firearm. He served nine months and was released. Emanuel began working again, but had to report to the parole officer each month. On one occasion, he showed up for his meeting with the parole officer, and, to his surprise, the parole officer turned Emanuel over to immigration. He was then sent to detention and deported to the Dominican Republic in 1998.

The deportation of Emanuel, a college graduate, legal permanent resident, and US army veteran, for illegal possession of a firearm, is considered by the DHS to be the deportation of one more dangerous criminal alien. Emanuel, like many deportees with whom I spoke, qualified for US citizenship, based on being a legal permanent resident for two decades and having served in the US army. However, he chose never to apply. He thus remained a US denizen rather than citizen, and deportable, no matter his ties to the United States.

GENDERED DEPORTATION TRENDS

Less than 10 percent of deportees are women, even though they constitute about half of the non-citizen population (Golash-Boza and Hondagneu-Sotelo 2013). The laws governing deportation do not have any provisions that explicitly prevent the deportation of female non-citizens. Why, then, are mostly men deported? We do not have systematic data on how deportations happen, from the point of arrest to detention, and then deportation. Nevertheless, it is possible to piece together an explanation for these gendered deportation trends based on what we know from interviews with deportees as well as an understanding of how public and private spaces are gendered.

A gendered lens can help us to understand the disparities in deportations and their gendered effects. One of the main reasons men are more likely to be deported is that men are more susceptible to arrest, both because of gendered policing practices and gendered divisions of labour, that is, men are more likely to work outside the home and to drive to work than women. Although the reasons immigrant women are more likely than their male counterparts to have primary responsibilities in the home are related to gendered inequalities, these gendered roles can work as a protective factor against deportation for women. At the same time, these inequalities create a situation where deportation can have severe consequences for women. When men are deported, women are often left behind to support the household on their own. Because of gendered divisions of labour and unequal pay, immigrant women often earn far less than their husbands (Hondagneu-Sotelo 1994; Menjívar 1999; Menjívar et al. 2016), and thus find themselves unable to make ends meet when their husbands are deported.

Of course, some deportees are not in heteronormative relationships, do not have partners, or live alone and unattached. Men and women can be deported without leaving children, wives, girlfriends, or co-parents behind. However, when a man who is the primary provider for a household is deported, his treatment usually has considerable effects on his partner and children, as we can see in the case of Walter, who was sent back to Guatemala.

Dolores, Walter, and their two children lived in a five-bedroom home in a suburb of Washington, DC, had two cars, and took regular vacations with their significant disposable income. With Walter's successful flooring business, they were solidly upper middle class. In 2008, however, immigration agents raided their home, arrested Walter in front of his wife and children, and deported him to Guatemala.[2] Dolores and her children followed him to his home country. However, they quickly depleted the $250,000 they had from their savings combined with the sale of their home and cars. Moreover, the sudden changes put stress on their marriage, and Dolores and the children returned empty-handed to the United States two years after Walter's deportation. Dolores moved in with her parents and secured a job at a gas station, where she earns minimum wage.

Despite their US citizenship, Dolores and their two children are experiencing the full brunt of the collateral consequences of deportation. As Ruth Gomberg-Muñoz (2016: 350) argues, immigration laws 'disproportionately destroy the lives of racial minorities, women, and the working poor'. Importantly, these practices reveal the limited privileges of US citizenship for people with non-citizen family members and show how middle-class immigrant families can be transformed into working poor families with a deportation of a family member. Dolores and her children's US citizenship did not protect them from the dissolution of their nuclear family and middle-class lifestyle.

When women are deported, they often face even more obstacles than their male counterparts. Betty came to the United States as a toddler. She was deported to Guatemala when she was thirty-two, after being arrested in a domestic violence dispute. Betty's mother was Salvadoran, but Betty was born in Guatemala to a Guatemalan father. She had relatively little extended family in Guatemala, yet although she had not seen her father since she was a toddler, he welcomed

---

[2] Walter's arrest is likely to have happened through the National Fugitive Operations Program, in which ICE agents targeted people with criminal convictions as well as those designated as 'fugitive aliens'.

her into his home in Guatemala City when she was deported. However, her step-mother disapproved of Betty and eventually kicked her out. As a homeless woman in Guatemala, Betty fears for her safety, particularly the very real possibility of sexual assault. In addition to the challenges she faces to survival on the streets of Guatemala, Betty has lost all five of her children to foster and adoptive homes in the United States. When men are deported, as when they are sent to prison, the mother of their children usually takes custody of the children even at great personal and financial cost. Men, however, are less likely to take responsibility for their children when the mother is deported. This often means that the children end up in foster care and eventually are adopted into another family.

Betty's experiences in the United States included sexual abuse and domestic vio-lence. Her experiences in Guatemala include living in fear for her safety, unemploy-ment, and a disapproving stepmother. These experiences are all related to the fact that women are viewed as less valuable in both US and Guatemalan society. Betty's stepmother accused her of being promiscuous and that was enough to convince her father to ask her to leave. In contrast, many Guatemalan male deportees were welcomed into their father's homes and none of the thirty-three Guatemalan men I interviewed told me that their father's partner had asked them to leave.

FAMILY SEPARATION AND NATIVISM

Deportation laws are often represented as a means of protecting the interests of US citizens. However, in some cases deportations are counter to the interests of particu-lar US citizens, especially when they are family members of the person deported. It is useful for us to consider how the government deals with parental deportation, as these processes also reveal the racialized and gendered logics of deportation policy.

In the United States, when a parent is arrested, Child Protective Services (CPS) steps in and takes measures designed to ensure that the child's best interests are served. Unlike police officers, CPS workers are not law enforcement agents. Nevertheless, their actions, like those of police officers, can exacerbate inequalities. CPS workers can place the children of parents who have been arrested either in temporary foster care or with relatives. It is often easier for children to deal with the arrest of their parents when they are placed with people familiar to them. However, according to an Applied Research Center (2011) report, when a parent is arrested and the only available relatives are undocumented, CPS workers often opt to place the chil-dren in foster care with strangers. This is due to a belief among CPS workers that a home environment with undocumented caregivers is inadequate. The logic behind this practice is that undocumented caregivers may be at risk of deportation them-selves. However, the likelihood that an undocumented caregiver would actually face deportation proceedings is often less than 1 per cent, particularly if the caregiver is a woman.

If an undocumented parent is arrested, local law enforcement agencies may choose to contact immigration authorities, who may then decide to place the parent in immigration detention. If a parent is in immigration detention and their child is in foster care, the detained immigrant is often unable to attend any hearings related to their parental rights. If the detained immigrant is then deported, CPS may move to terminate parental rights. The deported immigrant can contact the child welfare caseworker and attempt to regain custody of the children. At this point, in some cases, CPS may terminate parental rights anyway. In other cases, they may ask the parent to complete parenting classes, a home study, and secure employment in the country to which they have been deported. In one case described in the Applied Research Center report, a parent did all of these things, working with Mexican child welfare workers, who produced a 'glowing home study'. In addition, the father had a house, a car, and a job that paid a living wage. Nevertheless, the children's attorney objected because at least one of the children was asthmatic. The attorney said: 'It's dusty there and we don't know what kind of care they'd get.' Because of this opinion about Mexico, the parental rights were terminated and the children were adopted.

The facility with which the state renders these (primarily) Latino children orphans is related not only to a system of racist patriarchy but also to a global order in which Mexican and Central American families are deemed unworthy of raising US citizen children, and Mexico and Central America are deemed unsuitable places to raise these children. When Mexican, Central American, and Caribbean parents are deported, caseworkers often decide that living with a stranger in the United States is preferable to a *de facto* deportation for the US citizen child. The facility with which orphaning happens is evident in the story of a Central American woman, one of thousands of women whose children have ended up as wards of the state. This woman was detained due to an immigration violation. As a result, her children were placed in foster care. The caseworker in North Carolina told a reporter:

Reunification has been taken off the table on this one in part because of the deportation that's coming. We would have been working toward reunification had it not been for the fact that she'll be deported. So we made no case plan at all. It would be totally different if she were a citizen ... If she were not going to be deported, we could work toward reunification while she was in jail and then see what happened when she was released. (Applied Research Center 2011: 53).

In this case, the caseworker would not even consider the possibility that the mother may be able to care for the children in her home country. In Florida, another caseworker said:

As long as they are not deported, we give them a case plan, even in detention, but as soon as [they're] deported, a lot of times it goes straight to termination of parental rights ... Once they're gone, it's usually over for them. (Applied Research Center 2011: 53–4).

United States child protection laws operate similarly to other laws in the country insofar as they apply to children who are physically present in the United States, regardless of citizenship. The job of CPS workers is to put the children's best interests first. Of course, it certainly is sometimes the case that biological parents are not ideal parents for their children. However, these interview excerpts make it clear that the caseworker is not making a decision based on the fitness of the parents, but instead the caseworkers have decided that it is in the best interest of children that they be raised in the United States, where they will presumably have access to schools, hospitals, and a safe home environment. Caseworkers often also presume that children will not have access to these basic human rights in their parents' country of birth. These assumptions are not always true.

Caseworkers are cognizant of the pervasive problems associated with the foster care system in the United States. It is also clear that millions of children thrive in homes when they are raised by their Mexican parents in Mexico. Mexico is not in fact a poor country.[3] It is a middle-income country and many Mexican children have more than adequate access to healthcare, schooling, and nutrition. But caseworkers, judges, and many others involved in the child welfare system in the United States presume, based on nativist notions, that these basic amenities are simply not available in Mexico or anywhere south of the US–Mexico border.

That said, it is most likely in the best interest of the child for their parent not to be deported in the first place. When children's parents are deported, the fragility of the children's citizenship rights is revealed, whether they end up in foster care, adopted, or *de facto* deported due to their parents' deportation. Their citizenship does not protect them 'from the destructive effects of state intrusion' (Gomberg-Muñoz 2016: 350).

Deportees often experience a complete loss of parental rights due to CPS practices. In other cases, they do not officially lose their parental rights, but have no way to access them. When a parent of a minor child is deported, and the child stays with the other parent, it is often up to the non-deported parent to ensure they can stay in touch with their children. Sometimes, the parent in the United States chooses to break off contact with the person who has been deported. And there is often nothing a deported person can do to regain contact with their children in the United States. Several men told me that the mothers of their children had chosen not to maintain contact with them.

Harold, a Jamaican deportee, told me that he has lost contact with his thirteen-year-old daughter. The mother chose not to maintain contact, and he has no way to contact his daughter. Another Jamaican deportee, Roy, lived with his four children prior to his deportation, and his ex-wife changed her phone number, and he has no way of contacting his children. Federica, a Dominican woman who had been deported, told me that her ex-husband had cut off ties with her, and refuses to bring the children to the Dominican Republic to visit her. The effective loss of parental rights is of course very painful.

Others remained in contact with their children, but feared that the carer in the United States could lose custody. For example, Diallo, a Guatemalan deportee, had raised his child since she was an infant. When he was deported, he left his daughter with his mother. He fears that his daughter's biological mother could find out and demand custody, even though she abandoned the child years before. For this

---

[3] In 2015, Mexico ranked ninety-first in terms of GDP per capita, placing it right in the middle of all countries. See: https://www.cia.gov/library/publications/the-world-factbook/rankorder/2004rank.html.

reason, his mother has not applied for social services for the child, even though she needs them.

These deportees have not officially lost parental rights, but they have no control over access to their children. They may technically have legal rights, but those rights are only exercisable in the United States, and, insofar as they do not have access to the United States, they have no access to their rights. Deportees who leave children behind in the United States must remain in the good graces of their children's carer, who has complete discretion over whether or not the children should remain in contact with their deported parent.

CONCLUSION

These cases of deportations and family separations allow us to think through how US immigration laws further aggravate inequalities based on race, gender, and citizenship. Deportation exacerbates racial inequalities in criminal law enforcement; it also exacerbates gendered inequalities in caregiving by placing additional financial and emotional burdens on women when their partners are deported. Finally, deportation not only removes non-citizens from the United States, it also often separates them from their children, thereby further deepening the disadvantages non-citizens experience compared to citizens.

Deportation thus not only denies people access to the territorial boundaries of the United States; it can also deprive them of their right to cultivate a relationship with their children and other family members. In US law, deportation is an administrative procedure that denies a non-citizen territorial access to the United States. However, US immigration laws are out of sync with reality insofar as there are millions of undocumented migrants who have settled in the United States and millions of legal permanent residents who are susceptible to deportation. The deportation of all undocumented migrants and all legal permanent residents who have criminal convictions would have devastating effects on a broad swathe of people. For these and other reasons, only a small portion of these populations are deported each year.

Nevertheless, draconian deportation laws have three critical racialized consequences. Firstly, deportations nearly always happen as a consequence of local law enforcement practices, meaning that police–immigration cooperation further exacerbates existing racial disparities within the criminal justice system. Secondly, the vast majority of people who are deported are Latino or black, meaning deportation law exacerbates racial inequality in the United States. When deportees have partners and children, they are usually also black or Latino. Deportations thus further exacerbate racial inequality by removing breadwinners from these families. Thirdly, the spectre of enforcement hangs over the lives of millions of people who are at risk of deportation, thereby further subordinating an already marginalized group.

The United States is exceptional among Western countries both in the harshness of its deportation provisions and in the punitive nature of its criminal laws. The fact that deportation and criminal laws primarily target racialized minority groups is part of the explanation for why the United States is so punitive. The targets of these laws are dehumanized as criminals and criminal aliens and this dehumanization is all the more seamless due to the racialization of these labels in the American imaginary.

REFERENCES

ACLU (2012), *Consequences & Costs: Lessons Learned from Davidson County, Tennessee's Jail Model 287(g) Program*. Available at: http://www.aclu-tn.org/wp-content/uploads/2015/01/287gF.pdf

Alexander, M. (2011), *The New Jim Crow: Mass Incarceration in the Age of Colorblindness*. New York: The New Press.

Anderson, J. (2015), ' "Tagged as a Criminal": Narratives of Deportation and Return Migration in a Mexico City Call Center', *Latino Studies* 13(1): 8–27.

Applied Research Center (2011), *Shattered Families: The Perilous Intersection of Immigration Enforcement and the Child Welfare System*. Available at: https://www.raceforward.org/research/reports/shattered-families?arc=1

De Genova, N. P. (2002), 'Migrant "Illegality" and Deportability in Everyday Life', *Annual Review of Anthropology* 31(1): 419–47.

Epp, C. R., Maynard-Moody, S., and Haider-Markel, D. P. (2014), *Pulled over: How Police Stops Define Race and Citizenship*. Chicago, IL: University of Chicago Press.

Ewing, W. (2014), *The Growth of the U.S. Deportation Machine*. Washington, DC: Immigration Policy Center.

Gelman, A., Fagan, J., and Kiss, A. (2007), 'An Analysis of the New York City Police Department's 'Stop-and-Frisk' Policy in the Context of Claims of Racial Bias', *Journal of the American Statistical Association* 102(479): 813–23.

Golash-Boza, T. (2011), 'Born in the Bahamas, Raised in the US, Deported to … Haiti?' *Counterpunch*, 27 April. Available at: http://www.counterpunch.org/2011/04/27/born-in-the-bahamas-raised-in-the-us-deported-to-haiti/

Golash-Boza, T. (2012), *Immigration Nation: Raids, Detentions, and Deportations in the United States*. Boulder, CO: Paradigm.

Golash-Boza, T. (2015), *Deported: Immigrant Policing, Disposable Labor, and Global Capitalism*. New York: New York University Press.

Golash-Boza, T. (2016a), 'A Critical and Comprehensive Sociological Theory of Race And Racism', *Sociology of Race and Ethnicity* 2(2): 129–41.

Golash-Boza, T. (2016b), ' "Negative Credentials," "Foreign-Earned" Capital, and Call Centers: Guatemalan Deportees' Precarious Reintegration', *Citizenship Studies* 20(3–4): 326–41.

Golash-Boza, T. and Hondagneu-Sotelo, P. (2013), 'Latino Immigrant Men and the Deportation Crisis: A Gendered Racial Removal Program', *Latino Studies* 11(3): 271–92.

Gomberg-Muñoz, R. (2016), 'The Juarez Wives Club: Gendered Citizenship and US Immigration Law', *American Ethnologist* 43(2): 339–52.

Gottschalk, M. (2016), *Caught: The Prison State and the Lockdown of American Politics*. Princeton, NJ: Princeton University Press.

Harris, David A. (1999), *Driving While Black: Racial Profiling on Our Nation's Highways*. American Civil Liberties Union Special Report. Washington, DC: American Civil Liberties Union. Available at: https://www.aclu.org/racial-justice/driving-while-black-racial-profiling-our-nations-highways

Hondagneu-Sotelo, P. (1994), *Gendered Transitions: Mexican Experiences of Immigration*. Berkeley, CA: University of California Press.

Johnson, K. R. (2016), 'Doubling Down on Racial Discrimination: The Racially Disparate Impacts of Crime-Based Removals', *Case Western Reserve Law Review* 66(4): 993–1037.

Lamberth, J. (1994), 'Revised Statistical Analysis of the Incidence of Police Stops and Arrests of Black Drivers: Travelers on the New Jersey Turnpike Between Exits or Interchanges 1 and 3 from the Years 1988 Through 1991'. Unpublished.

Mauer, M. (1999), *The Crisis of the Young African American Male and the Criminal Justice System*. Sentencing Project. Available at: http://www.sentencingproject.org/doc/publications/rd_crisisoftheyoung.pdf

Menjívar, C. (1999), 'The Intersection of Work and Gender: Central American Immigrant Women and Employment in California', *American Behavioral Scientist* 42(4): 601–27.

Menjívar, C., Abrego, L. J., and Schmalzbauer, L. C. (2016), *Immigrant Families*. Hoboken, NJ: John Wiley & Sons.

Olvera, J. J. and Muela, C. (2016), 'Sin familia en México', *Mexican Studies/Estudios Mexicanos* 32(2): 302–27.

Passel, J. S. and Cohn, D. (2014), *Unauthorized Immigrant Totals Rise in 7 States, Fall in 14: Decline in Those From Mexico Fuels Most State Decreases*, November. Washington, DC: Pew Research Center's Hispanic Trends Project.

Pratt, A. and Sossin, L. (2009), 'A Brief Introduction of the Puzzle of Discretion', *Canadian Journal of Law and Society* 24(3): 301–12.

Rosenblum, M. R. and McCabe, K. (2014), *Deportation and Discretion: Reviewing the Record and Options for Change*. Washington, DC: Migration Policy Institute.

Sabol, W., West, H., and Cooper, M. (2009), *Prisoners in 2008*. Bureau of Justice Statistics Bulletin. Available at: http://www.bjs.gov/content/pub/pdf/p08.pdf

Tonry, M. (2011), *Punishing Race: A Continuing American Dilemma*. New York: Oxford University Press.

Vázquez, Y. (2011), 'Perpetuating the Marginalization of Latinos: A Collateral Consequence of the Incorporation of Immigration Law into the Criminal Justice System', *Howard Law Journal* 54: 639–74.

West, H. and Sabol, W. (2010), *Prisoners in 2009*. Bureau of Justice Statistics. Available at: http://www.bjs.gov/content/pub/pdf/p09.pdf

Epilogue
When Citizenship Means Race

Emma Kaufman

The chapters in this collection join a growing body of work on the relationship between criminal justice and migration control (see, e.g., Aas and Bosworth 2013; Chacón 2009; McLeod 2012; Sklansky 2012). Together they reinforce a lesson that has come to define the field: the convergence of criminal law and immigration enforcement has expanded—and distorted—the reach of both. When police act as immigration agents (Bowling and Westenra, this volume; Eagly 2010), prisons house immigration courts (Eagly 2015), and detention centres are built to look like jails (Bosworth 2014), it becomes difficult to distinguish punishing crime from policing mobility.

These developments are not new. Criminologists and legal scholars have been documenting the criminalization of immigration, the rise of nationalism, and the expansion of immigration detention since the 1990s (see, e.g., Kanstroom 2000; Simon 1998). This volume differs from other studies of 'crimmigration' (Stumpf 2006), however, because it places race at the centre of the inquiry. Two insights emerge from this approach.

First, these chapters demonstrate the degree to which immigration regulation enables racism. Take Jennifer Chacón and Susan Bibler Coutin's account of immigration law in the United States. As she points out, immigration is 'one of the few, exceptional areas' in American law where courts permit 'overt reliance on race' (Chacón and Bibler Coutin, this volume). While police and juries in the United States cannot rely on race expressly, she argues, immigration regulators can. The expansion of immigration policing and the effort to incorporate migration control into the daily work of criminal justice enforcement thus allows racial profiling to flourish.

A parallel dynamic plays out when governments use technologies of criminal justice, such as police and prisons, to enforce immigration laws. Cooperative programmes like Britain's Operation Nexus (Parmar, this volume) and the United States Criminal Alien Program (American Immigration Council 2013) turn the criminal justice system, with all its defects, into the front end of the state's migration control apparatus. In many countries, police now enforce immigration laws and enjoy a broad range of immigration powers, including the authority to order people to produce identity documents and to detain them if they cannot (Chacón 2009; Parmar, this volume; Wishnie 2004). As a result, racialized trends in the enforcement of criminal laws are replicated in immigration policy. In the United States, for example, because 'police officers are more likely to stop and arrest black and Latino men', those men end up being deported at disproportionately high rates (Golash-Boza, this volume; see also Johnson 2016). Louise Boon-Kuo's chapter in this book suggests a similar pattern in Australia. Here again, the convergence of criminal justice and immigration enforcement makes race more relevant to the exercise of state power.

If the regulation of mobility enables racism, however, it also changes the meaning of race. This is the second and most promising lesson from this volume. In vivid detail, these chapters describe how unsettled the term 'race' becomes when placed alongside ideas like national origin, citizenship status, and foreignness. Consider Mary Bosworth's account of immigration detention in Britain; in her telling, racialized stereotypes abound in Heathrow Immigration Removal Centre, but at the same time are confused and upended by conceptions of foreignness that conflate race with nationality, ethnicity, and religion (Bosworth, this volume). Jennifer Chacón and Susan Bibler Coutin's chapter describes an analogous phenomenon in the United States, where immigration enforcement is characterized by the 'sloppy conflation' of race, nationality, and national origin.

Perhaps it is odd to call this trend promising. Slippage between race, citizenship status, and national origin certainly facilitates discrimination. Because these terms have no set meaning and shift in the context of particular enforcement regimes, they often become interchangeable in practice. Thus, Ben Bowling and Sophie Westenra report that border agents use 'racial and ethnic differences' to determine which migrants to stop at the British border (Bowling and Westenra, this volume). In their account, immigration officers 'employ markers such as skin colour in forming suspicion' about entering migrants, a strategy the UK Home Office refers to as 'on-arrival visual selection'. I observed the same pattern in my ethnographic study of British prisons, where prison staff employed racial and ethnic stereotypes, which one prison officer called 'obvious evidence', to identify which prisoners were likely to be non-citizens (Kaufman 2015: 155). In these and other instances, the flexibility of race perpetuates racist assumptions about national belonging.

But the conflation of race, citizenship status, and national origin also demonstrates how precarious the term 'race' is—which is one way to challenge the role that race plays in regulating crime and mobility. As criminal and immigration enforcement grow increasingly codependent, criminologists and legal scholars should be tracking when governments treat citizenship status as coextensive with race, ethnicity, religion, and national origin, and when they insist that these concepts are distinct. Migration control 'becomes a racial project' (Bosworth, this volume) not just through the blurring of race and citizenship status, but through the *selective* conflation of these terms. Scholars concerned with the uneven enforcement of immigration laws need to map when citizenship is a legal status, when it is a cultural identity, and when it simply means race.

The corollary question is *where* the conflation of race and citizenship takes place. Chapter by chapter, this volume debunks the idea that border control occurs only at legal boundaries between nation states. Immigration law is, of course, enforced at physical borders such as ports of entry. But the regulation of mobility is a much more diffuse enterprise than the term 'border control' suggests: it happens in police stations, courts, airports, hospitals, universities, and workplaces; and it implicates landlords, lawyers, teachers, doctors, and military officers (see, e.g., Aliverti, this volume; Bowling and Westenra, this volume). The racialization of migration control takes root in all of these enforcement sites, each of which is a border unto itself. Studying this process expands the universe of institutions that criminologists typically explore.

Focusing on the relationship between race and citizenship also generates more nuanced accounts of the criminal justice institutions. Criminologists and legal scholars have argued persuasively that immigration enforcement has become a form of punishment, in practice if not in law (see, e.g., Bosworth 2013; García Hernández 2014). The converse observation is that traditional institutions of criminal justice, such as prisons and police forces, are more involved than ever in regulating migration (Bowling and Westenra, this volume; Vázquez 2017). This development complicates the claim that the criminal justice system is structured by race.

My research, for instance, examines the rise of 'all-foreign' penal institutions— that is, prisons classified by citizenship status, which have emerged in the United States and Britain in the last twenty years (Kaufman 2015; Office of the Inspector General 2015; see also Ugelvik 2012 describing a similar trend in Norway). Although neither government has offered an explicit rationale for these facilities, both have published documents indicating that all-foreign prisons are meant to make it easier to find and deport non-citizens in the prison population. The Bureau of Prisons, which operates federal prisons in the United States, has described its 'criminal alien requirement' prisons as an effort to support the agency tasked with implementing immigration laws (Bureau of Prisons 1999). The Ministry of Justice has offered a similar explanation for the segregation of non-citizens imprisoned in England and Wales (Kaufman 2015; MOJ 2017). All-foreign prisons, in other words, are built to effectuate migration control.

There is no question that race shapes these institutions: like the larger prison system, all-foreign prisons are the result of 'over-policing' in minority communities (Bowling and Westenra, this volume) and racial identity plays a central role in the construction of internal prison hierarchies (Kaufman 2015: 143–53). Unlike other prisons, however, all-foreign penal institutions are dedicated to distinguishing foreigners from citizens, a project that often crosses and scrambles racial lines. In Britain, for example, the effort to concentrate non-citizens in certain prisons separates Eastern European, Australian, American, South Asian, and African non-citizens from British citizens of all races and ethnicities (Bhui 2007; Kaufman 2015; Vine 2012). The relationship between punishment and race is less direct (and less binary) in these facilities than it is in many critiques of the carceral state. In this respect, prisons devoted to border control upset basic assumptions in critical criminology and legal theory.

Rethinking these assumptions requires comparative, empirical work. As the chapters in this volume show, the interaction between race, criminal justice, and immigration regulation is different in Australia and England than in Hong Kong, Honduras, Saudi Arabia, and the United States. Indeed, terms like 'black', 'brown', and 'foreign' have distinct connotations, and distinct relationships to each other, in each of these jurisdictions. It is impossible to understand how race comes to matter—and when it is ignored—without an account of enforcement in practice. Ethnographic studies of race give meaning to the claim that border control is racialized. In the process, they remind us just how local and unstable racism is.

REFERENCES

Aas, K. F. and Bosworth, M. (eds) (2013), *The Borders of Punishment: Migration Control, Citizenship, and Social Exclusion*. Oxford: Oxford University Press.

American Immigration Council (2013), *The Criminal Alien Program (CAP): Immigration Enforcement in Prisons and Jails*.

Bhui, H. (2007), 'Alien Experience: Foreign National Prisoners after the Deportation Crisis', *Probation Journal* 54: 368–82.

Bosworth, M. (2013), 'Can Immigration Detention Be Legitimate? Understanding Confinement in a Global World', in K. F. Aas and M. Bosworth (eds), *The Borders of Punishment: Migration Control, Citizenship, and Social Exclusion*. Oxford: Oxford University Press.

Bosworth, M. (2014), *Inside Immigration Detention: Foreigners in a Carceral Age*. Oxford: Oxford University Press.

Bureau of Prisons, United States Department of Justice (1999), Notice of Intent to Prepare a Draft Environmental Impact Statement for Housing Criminal Alien Population in Non-Federal Low-Security Correctional Facilities, 64 *Federal Register* 20021-02, 1999 WL 234340 (23 April).

Chacón, J. M. (2009), 'Managing Migration through Crime', *Columbia Law Review* 109: 135.

Eagly, I. (2015), 'Remote Adjudication in Immigration', *Northwestern University Law Review* 109(4): 1–87.

Eagly, I. V. (2010), 'Prosecuting Immigration', *Northwestern University Law Review* 104(4): 1281–359.

García Hernández, C. C. (2014), 'Immigration Detention as Punishment', *UCLA Law Review* 61: 1346–414.

Johnson, K. (2016), 'Doubling Down on Racial Discrimination: The Racially Disparate Impacts of Crime-Based Removals', *Case Western Law Review* 66(4): 993–1037.

Kanstroom, D. (2000), 'Deportation, Social Control, and Punishment: Some Thoughts about Why Hard Laws Make Bad Cases', *Harvard Law Review* 11: 190–935.

Kaufman, E. (2015), *Punish and Expel: Border Control, Nationalism, and the New Purpose of the Prison*. Oxford: Oxford University Press.

McLeod, A. (2012), 'The U.S. Criminal-Immigration Convergence and its Possible Undoing', *American Criminal Law Review* 49: 105–78.

MOJ (2017), 'Huntercombe Prison', updated 29 August. Available at: http://www.justice. gov.uk/contacts/prison-finder/huntercombe

Office of the Inspector General, United States Department of Justice (2015), Audit of the Federal Bureau of Prisons Contract No. DJB1PC007 Awarded to Reeves County, Texas to Operate the Reeves County Detention Center I-II Pecos, Texas.

Simon, J. (1998), 'Refugees in a Carceral Age: The Rebirth of Immigration Prisons in the United States', *Public Culture* 10: 577–607.

Sklansky, D. A. (2012), 'Crime, Immigration, and Ad Hoc Instrumentalism', *New Criminal Law Review* 15: 157–223.

Stumpf, J. (2006), 'The Crimmigration Crisis: Immigrants, Crime, and Sovereign Power', *American University Law Review* 56: 367–419.

Ugelvik, T. (2012), 'Imprisoned at the Border: Subjects and Objects of the State in Two Norwegian Prisons', in S. Ugelvik and B. Hudson (eds), *Justice and Security in the 21st Century: Risks, Rights, and the Rule of Law*. London: Routledge, 64–82.

Vázquez, Y. (2017), 'Crimmigration: The Missing Piece of Criminal Justice Reform', *University of Richmond Law Review* 51: 1093–147.

Vine, J. (2012), *Thematic Inspection of How the U.K. Border Agency Manages Foreign National Prisoners, February to May 2011*. London: Independent Chief Inspector of the UK Border Agency.

Wishnie, M. (2004), 'State and Local Police Enforcement of Immigration Laws', *University of Pennsylvania Journal of Constitutional Law* 4: 1084–115.

Index